9-18-70

THE EVOLUTION
OF CHRISTIAN
THOUGHT

THE EVOLUTION

by T. A. BURKILL

OF CHRISTIAN THOUGHT

Cornell University Press

ITHACA
AND
LONDON

International Standard Book Number 0-8014-0581-5
Library of Congress Catalog Card Number 76-127601

PRINTED IN THE UNITED STATES OF AMERICA
BY VAIL-BALLOU PRESS, INC.

1586703

for Jack and Betty Shearmur
and Nell Kerry
in gratitude

⁘ *Preface*

This book surveys and analyzes the major trends in the evolution of Christian thought over the centuries. I have tried to present briefly and comprehensibly, while avoiding unduly technical language so far as possible, the doctrines of representative thinkers in the light of their respective historical situations. It is my hope that the book will prove useful not only in academic circles, as a supplement to more specialized studies, but also to general readers who may wish to enlarge their knowledge of Western culture and of Christianity.

My aim is to be descriptive and objective rather than critical and constructive. For the most part, I have not raised evaluatory questions and have sought to let the facts speak for themselves. Since religious thought must be considered in relation to its setting in life, my treatment to some extent blends intellectual and institutional history with analytical description. In a number of instances, of course, there is room for differences of interpretation even on basic issues, and I have done my best to avoid dogmatic statements. Those readers who find ideas colored by predilections of one sort or another may reflect that often it is scarcely feasible to write without expressing a point of view and that sometimes it is not possible to shun questions of personal belief.

Balance and a sense of proportion are obviously important in a work of this kind, and some readers may feel that radical movements like Anabaptism and Quakerism, and such more recent developments as Mormonism, Christian Science, and Jehovah's Witnesses, merit little more than passing comment in an elementary introduction to the history of Christian ideas. In view, however, of my wish to be comprehensive and because of the frequency with which denominations of this kind are referred to in daily conversation, I decided to include brief accounts of their origin and nature. In keeping with the intention of the book, footnotes have been avoided, and source references have been reduced to a minimum, particularly in the parts that deal with the later centuries, where the proliferation of sects and schools of thought creates many complications. Nevertheless, the pertinent writings of the principal thinkers are cited throughout. A short bibliography has been appended to each chapter, and a select book list of a broader nature appears immediately before the Index. Many of the works mentioned themselves offer valuable suggestions for further reading, and in the General Bibliography books containing extensive information about supplementary reading are marked with an asterisk. Readers should not hesitate to use the Index freely, for terms whose meaning may not be immediately clear in one place may be clarified elsewhere.

Much of the content of Chapter 24 appeared in *Les Actes du VIIe Congrès Interamericain de Philosophie*, volume 2 (Quebec, 1968), and for permission to reproduce this material thanks are due to Monsieur Lucien Zérounian, director of Les Presses de l'Université Laval.

My thanks are also due to several scholars in Europe and North America, whose reactions have helped to give final shape to the book; and to Bella, my wife, whose services in the preparation of the manuscript have been invaluable.

T. A. B.

University of Rhodesia
Salisbury, Rhodesia
October 1970

⁝ Contents

Introduction   1

I. ANCIENT CATHOLICISM

  1. The Apostolic Fathers   25
  2. The Apologists   34
  3. Marcion and Montanus   41
  4. Foundations of Catholicism: Irenaeus   50
  5. Western Theology: Tertullian and Cyprian   57
  6. Eastern Theology: Clement and Origen   65

II. THE ORTHODOX CREEDS

  7. The Alliance of Church and State: Constantine   75
  8. Monarchianism   81
  9. Arianism and the Nicene Christology   87
  10. Nestorianism and the Chalcedonian Creed   96
  11. The Monophysite and Monothelite Controversies   102
  12. Iconoclasticism and John of Damascus   108

III. TOWARD THE EAST-WEST SCHISM

  13. Augustine   117
  14. Pelagianism and Semi-Pelagianism   126
  15. Pseudo-Dionysius and Gregory the Great   129
  16. The Emergence of Monasticism   136
  17. The Papacy and the Holy Roman Empire   146
  18. The East-West Schism   152

IV. MEDIEVAL DEVELOPMENTS

19. Monastic Orders   159
20. Earlier Scholasticism   164
21. Later Scholasticism   179
22. The Papacy and Conciliarism   197
23. The Dawn of the Reformation   205
24. Mysticism and Sacramentalism   212

V. THE REFORMATION

25. New Horizons   225
26. Martin Luther   234
27. Zwingli and Calvin   246
28. Anglicanism and Puritanism   259
29. Radical Movements   270
30. The Counter-Reformation   282

VI. RATIONALISM AND PIETISM

31. Science and Philosophy   291
32. Deism   304
33. Pietism and Methodism   315
34. Continental Rationalism   328
35. Catholic Trends   343
36. American Developments   352

VII. RECENT TENDENCIES

37. Kant and His Successors   371
38. Biblical Criticism   398
39. Catholic Modernism   414
40. Tractarianism and Liberalism   424
41. Ecumenism   435
42. Quests for Clarity   450

    General Bibliography   487
    Index   489

THE EVOLUTION
OF CHRISTIAN
THOUGHT

*Evolution is the general condition
to which all theories must conform
and a light that clarifies all facts.*

                       Teilhard de Chardin

‡ Introduction

So far as can be gathered from the earliest gospel records contained in the New Testament, the teaching of Jesus, with its forthright warnings and promises, furthered the prophetic tradition embodied in the Old Testament, the basic sacred writings of the Jewish people. His sayings reflect a firm belief in the nearness of the end of the present order of existence, and, like some of his great prophetic predecessors, he evidently felt that he had been called to prepare his contemporaries for the final judgment on the world which would shortly precede the establishment of the Kingdom of God in a new and more glorious age. His proclamations and counsels were therefore in a considerable measure governed by a doctrine of last things, that is, by an eschatology (Greek: *eschaton*, "end" + *logos*, "word" or "discourse"). Personal guidance in face of the impending crisis was to be found in the Hebrew scriptures, wherein God had declared his will for humanity to Moses and the prophets of old. But it was a matter of urgency that the biblical injunctions should be correctly understood, otherwise the divine purpose would be wrongly construed and divine condemnation would ensue. Ritual performances had their value, yet God fundamentally required the practice of justice and mercy; and human beings had fallen short of the demands of their Maker. So it behooved them to amend their ways, relying on God's lovingkindness, a divine attribute discernible in nature and history, as well as in scripture and, more specifically, in the miraculous

I

healing works of the Galilean ministry itself. These works were a sure sign of the approach of the new age.

The earthly career of Jesus ended in the shame and humiliation of crucifixion (*c.* A.D. 30), but his followers quickly became convinced that he had triumphed over death and that his Spirit was continuously available as a source of present inspiration. It was by virtue of this resurrection faith that the church came to birth: Jesus was the Messiah whose coming had been predicted in the scriptures, and he would soon come again as the triumphant Son of Man to punish the wicked and to receive the righteous into the blessedness of the Kingdom of God. To what extent such Christian doctrine differs from the teaching of Jesus himself is disputed. Some scholars hold that Jesus spoke exclusively in terms of the coming Kingdom of God, never employing such titles as the Messiah and the Son of Man. Others point out that in the gospels Jesus alone uses the expression "Son of Man" and argue that he really did speak of the Coming Judge in terms of the enigmatic figure of the Son of Man. But the majority scholarly opinion goes further: Jesus thought of himself as the promised Messiah in a special sense and was actually convinced that he would soon be exalted as the Son of Man to judge the world in righteousness.

Because of the lateness and character of the extant evidence, the truth in this matter cannot be definitively ascertained. It is generally agreed that the canonical gospels were written during the last third of the first century, some forty to seventy years after the crucifixion; that Mark was probably the earliest and John the latest; and that the authors of Matthew and Luke used Mark in the composition of their works. Moreover, all four gospels contain traditions which developed at different times and in different circumstances, and these would seem to reflect the divergent assessments of Jesus that evolved in the various primitive Christian communities. A clear indication of such differences in interpretation is to be found in the numerous titles ascribed to him in the constituent traditions; he appears as

Prophet, Teacher, Son of Man, as Bridegroom, Messiah, Son
of David. By no means do such designations severally have the
same signifiance; they represent various roles that were assigned
to Jesus in the eschatological drama of early Christian belief
and expectation.

The title that eventually prevailed was *Christos*, which is the
Greek for the Hebrew *Mashiach*, meaning "Anointed One."
In ancient Israelite practice the religious ceremony of anointing
the head was involved in the formalities of inducting a person
to the highest political office, and *mashiach* ("messiah") thus
became a royal title, a way of referring to the king. After the
destruction of the monarchy in 586 B.C., which marks the beginning of the exile and of the dispersion of the Jews in
Babylonia and elsewhere, the kingdom of David was commonly
looked back upon as the high point of Israelite history. And
during the centuries following the long and checkered process
of Jerusalem's restoration (the first exiles returned in about 520
B.C.), the hope spread that one day, when Israel had paid for its
sins, God would send a new Messiah under whose leadership the
people would be enabled to recapture the vanished glories of
the reign of David. If, as seems likely, the Zealots of Jesus'
day entertained an expectation of this kind, it would give the
force of religion to their advocacy of revolutionary action
against Rome.

But confidence in the ultimate vindication of righteousness
assumed different forms. Thus, besides the messianic mode of
expectation, there existed, for example, the vaster hope concerning the advent of the Son of Man, a heavenly Being who
would appear at the end of the whole cosmic process to restore
humanity (or a section thereof) to the ideal state it supposedly
enjoyed prior to Adam's original disobedience. Christianity
emerged within the matrix of Jewish religious aspiration and inherited its variations in thought and expression. But what is
especially noteworthy is that, as early as in the writings of the
Apostle Paul, the terminology of Messiahship, or rather of

Christhood, was exhibiting a faith, the content of which was quite different from a mere yearning for the re-establishment of Israel's political autonomy. This remarkable semantic development can be most readily explained on the hypothesis that it resulted from a compromise between opposing evaluations. The original Christian church was entirely Jewish, and some members took Jesus to be the promised Messiah, while others understood his person in terms of the apocalyptic Son of Man.

The various doctrinal differences would give rise to internal rivalries, and some groups, severally convinced of the unique validity of their own particular mode of interpretation, may have chosen to go their own way; perhaps a number joined the Zealots in their revolutionary activity against Roman rule. But on the whole, a relative doctrinal harmony was reached, a synthesis that combined divergent concepts of the nature and function of Jesus in the awaited eschatological course of events. Thus the title "Christ" was retained, but it now signified a Being endowed with the transcendent dignity of the Son of Man, whose glorious coming to judge the world and inaugurate a new order of existence would be heralded by overwhelming signs of cosmic disintegration. Of course such an important change in the connotation of Messiahship would be facilitated by the diffusion of the church's message among Greek-speaking Gentiles, for in general these latter would have little or no acquaintance with what Messiahship meant among Aramaic-speaking Jews in Palestine.

In the early stages the rapid spread of Christianity in the Gentile world seems to have been due mainly to the inspiring leadership of the Apostle Paul, who identified himself with the new religion within a decade or so of the crucifixion. The base of his missionary operations was apparently located in Syrian Antioch, and from there he journeyed across Asia Minor, Macedonia, and Greece. It is not unlikely that during his travels he usually won his first converts among "God-fearers" (as they are called in the Acts of the Apostles)—that is, among Gentiles

attracted by Judaism, who attended synagogues of the dispersion but refrained from submitting to circumcision and the
other rites of initiation. The efficient organization of the Roman
Empire facilitated travel, and, since Greek had become the
lingua franca of the eastern Mediterranean region, ideas could
be communicated with relative ease. In fact, the Christian
mission to the Gentiles met with such success that by the end
of the first generation the church was overwhelmingly non-
Jewish in its membership.

Paul spoke and wrote in Greek. Before he embraced Christianity, he was an ardent Pharisee (Hebrew: *parush*, "separated"
—the Pharisees tended to hold themselves aloof from the re-
ligiously lax) and, according to the book of Acts, he studied
in one of the rabbinical schools at Jerusalem. But he was born
and brought up at Tarsus of Cilicia in the southeastern corner
of Asia Minor, and there he would doubtless have acquired
some knowledge of Greek philosophy and of the mythological
themes reflected in the cultic dramas of the mystery religions.
He had one foot in the Hebraic world, the other in the field
of Hellenistic culture, and the dual affiliation would help to fit
him for the apostolic task of mediating Christianity to the
Gentiles.

The transition to a new milieu entailed a modification in the
presentation of the new religion, for as in the biological, so in
the sociological sphere, adaptation is a basic condition in the
struggle for survival; and a change in the outward form of the
gospel could hardly take place without affecting its religious
content. That the title "Christ" as used in the extant epistles of
Paul means something quite different from what "Messiah"
must have signified among Jewish groups in Palestine evidences
that the *Christos* had been invested with the transcendent dignity of the Aramaic *Bar-nasha* ("Son of Man"). And there are
indications of other significant developments. For instance,
when undergoing the initiatory rite of baptism, the neophyte is
represented as being assimilated to the incorruptibility of the

risen Lord of the cultus (Rom. 6:4)—a notion that adumbrates a familiar theme in the mystery religions. Moreover, Hellenistic pessimism may be reflected in the assumption that the flesh is inherently evil (Rom. 7:18)—an idea which could have some connection with the Apostle's preference of celibacy to marriage (I Cor. 7:8).

On the other hand, Paul's aversion to marital union may have been conditioned by his eschatological expectation: the end of the world is imminent; hence Christians should avoid unnecessary earthly entanglements. Again, he can on occasion give expression to the current Jewish view that evil was introduced into the continuum of human flesh through man's primordial sin in the Garden of Eden (Rom. 5: 12; and, in the Apocrypha, Ecclus. 25:24), in which case what is bad results from a misuse of moral freedom. Such considerations illustrate the difficulty of determining the precise extent to which Pauline Christianity was affected by Gentile culture. But there can be little doubt that Hellenistic influence was operative. When a sensitive reader of the New Testament passes from the sayings and parables of the synoptic gospels (Matthew, Mark, Luke) to the epistles of Paul (which were addressed to Greek-speaking people), he can scarcely fail to realize that he has moved into another world with a different cultural atmosphere.

The Hellenizing process continued after the Apostle's death, and in the course of time there was some danger that Christianity would lose its distinctive character by being drawn into the vortex of Hellenistic syncretism—that lively mixture of ideas from East and West which went to make up the popular religious philosophy of the Empire's eastern provinces. In the various forms of gnosticized Christianity which flourished in Alexandria and elsewhere during the second century, we are provided with an indication of what Christianity might have become (at least on its more intellectual side), had not the church's traditions been firmly rooted in biblical religion. Our knowledge of gnostic Christianity has been considerably enriched in recent years through the recovery in the sands of Egypt of such works as the *Evangelium Veritatis* ("The Gospel of Truth") and *The Gospel of Thomas*. The authors of these documents shared the general outlook of Hellenistic pessimism, setting matter in dualistic opposition to mind or spirit. Since it is essentially evil, matter could not have been deliberately created by the Supreme Being. There are various realms of existence, and the physical world belongs to the meanest order. The plenitude of divine perfection overflowed and congealed in several inferior spheres of being, and the lowest became the material universe.

Humanity is not wholly lost, however, for it contains sparks of the divine essence: the soul may be liberated from the prison house of the body and restored to the supreme order of being which is its proper home. Such salvation becomes possible through the acquisition of special knowledge (Greek: *gnōsis*), conveyed by a divine Redeemer who descended into the material world through the intervening realms of existence. He became incarnate docetically (Greek: *dokeō*, "seem") and suffered death docetically—that is, he *seemed* to assume human form and *seemed* to die, whereas actually he remained apart from corporeal existence by virtue of the completeness of his divinity. Nevertheless, before returning to the highest realm he imparted the required knowledge of salvation to his closest disciples, and it was this precious gnosis that the exponents of Gnosticism claimed to possess: they had been commissioned by their predecessors to pass it on to the elite capable of assimilating it.

Salvation was not necessarily for all. Some Gnostics divided humanity into three classes, namely, the pneumatical (Greek: *pneuma*, "spirit"), the psychical (*psychē*, "animating soul"), and the sarcinal (*sarx*, "flesh"). The first class could appropriate saving gnosis with ease; the second class could only do so through diligent effort; and the third class were without the capacity to secure salvation. Thus the greatest evil is ignorance, and man's fundamental need is for illumination, the light that comes with genuine knowledge. On the ethical side, perhaps most of the Gnostics advocated the mortification of the flesh; but some may have practiced carnal indulgence, arguing that, because body and spirit are quite disparate, physical acts like those involved in sexual licentiousness could have no real effect on the spiritual life.

Gnosticism in the radical form just outlined was rejected by the end of the second century. In general the church held tenaciously to a belief in the effective universality of the gospel, and the connection between moral evil and the freedom of the will was never completely eclipsed. In a certain measure the outcome of the struggle must be attributed to the church's retention of the Old Testament as sacred literature and its preservation of the synoptic gospels in a new body of canonical works. For these writings were a constant reminder of the fact that the religion of Jesus was rooted and grounded in the prophetic tradition of the Hebrew people—a tradition that bore witness to the essential goodness of the created world and to the dignity of the human individual as a child of the one true God.

The extensive organization of the Empire appears to have engendered widespread feelings of loneliness, and many of the inhabitants of its far-flung provinces seem to have been deeply affected by a poignant awareness of the transience of life. Such psychological reactions may have contributed to the popularity of the mystery religions, which claimed the authority to grant salvation to all who submitted to their rites of initiation. Salvation was predominantly interpreted as victory over death, the attainment of immortality through secret union with the particular savior-god (or goddess) of the cultus. And perhaps it was mainly due to the mystery religions that the notion of the dualism between the seen and the unseen, matter and spirit, the temporal and the eternal, came to prevail among considerable sections of the population.

An easy tolerance existed among the multifarious religious

associations, and any individual could be initiated into several mysteries. Membership in one society did not exclude membership in others; the sociological basis was purely voluntary. On the other hand, the worship of the genius of Caesar was made obligatory throughout the Empire, except in the case of Jews, whose religion was strictly monolatrous, requiring the worship of Yahweh, and of Yahweh alone. The exemption was secured through the good offices of Herod the Great, whose pro-Roman policy had earned for him imperial favor.

Veneration of the genius of the emperor was already established during the reign of Augustus (under whom the Empire was formally founded in 27 B.C.), and a refusal to participate in the official cultus came to be treated as a capital crime—a sign of atheism and serious disloyalty to the state. However, learning of the firmness of Israelite intransigence, Augustus was statesman enough to allow that the Jews might pray *for*, instead of *to*, the emperor (or his genius). This concession eventually benefited the church. For, in the earliest decades of its existence, Christianity was assumed to be a branch of Judaism, the result being that its adherents lived under the protection of Jewish privileges, which included freedom from full military service, as well as exemption from participation in the imperial cultus.

Jewish religious exclusivism aroused resentment and hostility in some quarters; thus, toward A.D. 40, an outbreak of Jew-baiting occurred in Alexandria. Yet in many urban centers there appear to have existed certain Gentiles for whom the worship of the Most High was strangely attractive. As already suggested, such God-fearers found in Judaism something more deeply satisfying than anything they could discover in the numerous forms of pagan religion, and through associating with the synagogue they could readily become acquainted with the fundamentals of the Jewish faith. These involved belief in a single personal God, the Creator of the world, whose will to righteousness was being fulfilled in the processes of history, and who had chosen a particular people to be the special agent of his moral and redemptive purpose; to them he had entrusted the Torah, the written word of his will for man, revealed to Moses on Mount Sinai.

The primitive church inherited beliefs of this kind with the Hebrew scriptures, which were already available in the lingua franca of the eastern provinces. The most important of the Greek versions, the Septuagint (or, more briefly, the LXX), originated in Alexandria during the third and second centuries B.C. and acquired its title from the legend that seventy-two scholars had been appointed for the work of translation. It is not surprising that the New Testament writers, when quoting the Old Testament, frequently betray septuagintal influence in their citations. For example, in Matt. 1:23 the "Immanuel" passage of Isa. 7:14 is reproduced in its septuagintal form. In this case the Septuagint rendering was especially significant since the word 'ǎlmāh ("young woman") of the Hebrew original had been translated as "virgin" (*parthenos* in Greek), and therefore could be used to support the doctrine of the virgin birth. Of course discrepancies between the original and the translation did not usually come to have such doctrinal importance in the evolution of Christian thought.

There are very few allusions to primitive Christianity in extant pagan literature of the century following the death of Jesus. Suetonius, secretary to the emperor Hadrian (who reigned from A.D. 117 to 138), may refer to Christian believers in his *Life of Claudius* (25:4) when he writes: "Since the Jews continually made disturbances at the instigation of Chrestus [perhaps a misspelling of "Christus"], he [Claudius] expelled them from Rome." Presumably this action took place in about A.D. 50 (see also Acts 18:2). In his *Annals*, Tacitus, another Latin historian, refers to the crucifixion of Christ in a passage (15:44) concerning the persecution of Christians at the order of the erratic Emperor Nero, who blamed them for the disastrous fire of Rome in A.D. 64. Tacitus himself did not hold that the Christians were in fact responsible for the destructive conflagration; he had no liking for their religion, however, and viewed it as an abominable superstition.

In A.D. 112, some four years before the publication of the *Annals* of Tacitus, the younger Pliny, the governor of Bithynia in Asia Minor, wrote a letter to the emperor Trajan (*Letters*, 10:96) questioning whether a person should be charged with a criminal offense simply for professing Christianity. By this time Christians were numerous in Asia Minor and were recognized as being quite distinct from Jews. Pliny had conducted investigations, discovering that the accusations of sexual promiscuity and of cannibalism were unfounded. Adherents of the movement met before dawn and sang a hymn to Christ as to a god; they later assembled to partake of ordinary food; they were obstinately persistent in their maintenance of absurd beliefs, but on the whole they seemed harmless enough. In his reply Trajan stated that the governor should neither initiate persecutions nor accept anonymous charges, and that Christians who renounced their religion when brought to trial should be freely pardoned.

With regard to early Jewish allusions, mention must be made of Josephus, the historian who switched his allegiance to the Roman side during the revolutionary war that culminated in the destruction of Jerusalem in A.D. 70. His *Antiquities* (a work published around A.D. 94) contains a passage in which there is reference to Jesus (18:3:3), but this is now generally acknowledged to be a Christian interpolation, in part if not as a whole. Later in the same work (20:9:1) Josephus writes of the execution of James "the brother of Jesus who was called Christ" —along with certain others—at the order of the Sanhedrin (about A.D. 62). This passage may well be substantially authentic. The James concerned was apparently a leader of the church at Jerusalem (see Mark 6:3; I Cor. 15:7; Gal. 1:19— 2:12; Acts 1:14; 12:17; 15:3). He is not to be confused with the James who, like John, was a son of Zebedee (see Mark 3:17) and who (according to Acts 12:2) was the first of the Twelve

to suffer martyrdom, after being condemned to death by Herod
Agrippa I in A.D. 44.

The leadership of James, the Lord's brother, turned out to
be something of a precedent, for, apart perhaps from an interval
in Transjordania, a succession of Jesus' relatives presided over
Christian groups in metropolitan Judea for the next seventy
years or more. But Jewish Christianity was considerably weakened by the disastrous outcome of the revolt against Rome
which broke out in A.D. 66, when, as it seems, many Christians
fled from Judea to Pella, a town that lay to the east of the River
Jordan, thereby offending the patriotic susceptibilities of their
zealotic compatriots (see Eusebius, *Ecclesiastical History*, 3:5:3;
this important treatise was issued in its final edition in A.D. 323
by its author, then bishop of Caesarea). A number of the refugees returned after the fall of Jerusalem, and the reconstituted
church there survived until the emperor Hadrian, after the suppression of the second Jewish revolt (this time under the
messianic leadership of Bar Kokba), banished all Jews from the
Judean metropolitan region (see Eusebius, *Eccles. Hist.*, 4:5:2;
4:5:4; 4:22:4). Jewish Christianity continued to exist for some
centuries, in Transjordania and elsewhere, but only in small
and uninfluential communities.

The Ebionites (a designation derived from a Hebrew word
meaning "poor" or "lowly") represented a type of Jewish
Christianity that persisted chiefly in Transjordania (see Hippolytus, *Refutation of all Heresies*, 7:34; this polemical work was
published in Rome around A.D. 225). In their estimation there
was nothing miraculous about Jesus' birth; he was generated
bisexually in the ordinary manner; the divine Spirit descended
upon him at his baptism, and it was then that he was adopted
as God's unique Son, an act which enabled him to fulfill his
appointed mission in the world (see also the quotation from
Psalm 2:7 in the Western reading of Luke 3:22—"today I have
begotten thee"—a reading cited in the footnote of the Revised
Standard Version, and one that could be understood as a form-

ula of adoption). The Ebionites held tenaciously to the Law of Moses and advocated ascetic disciplines, *inter alia* favoring vegetarianism. Perhaps the Nazarenes, a Jewish-Christian sect that survived in Syria, upheld similar ideas and practices.

Cerinthus, who taught at Ephesus around A.D. 100, showed a marked predilection for theological syncretism, combining an ebionite form of christology with gnosticising speculations (see Hippolytus, *Heresies*, 7:33; Eusebius, *Eccles. Hist.*, 3:28:6). He argued that the world was created out of pre-existent matter, not by the Most High God, but by an inferior angelic being, and that Jesus was born and lived as a natural human being until his baptism at the age of thirty; thenceforward he acted under the inspiration of a divine *dynamis* (Greek: "power"), which miraculous endowment, however, forsook him shortly before the crucifixion (cf. Mark 15:34). According to Eusebius, the doctrines of Cerinthus were held in abhorrence by the genuine Christians of Asia Minor, and he seeks to prove his point by citing a report that one day "John, the disciple of the Lord," ran out of the public baths at Ephesus immediately on hearing that Cerinthus was also taking the waters there; he evidently feared that the whole building might suddenly collapse, since he believed that Cerinthus was a nefarious enemy of the truth and as such liable to God's judgment at any moment (Eusebius, *Eccles. Hist.*, 3:28:6).

An important controversy in the early evolution of Christian thought concerned the position of Gentiles in relation to the Law of Moses. The Apostle Paul (who had not been a disciple of Jesus during his earthly ministry) set forth the radical view that the Law had been superseded by virtue of the coming of the Christ, and hence that Gentiles need not submit to circumcision and other Mosaic regulations before they could be initiated into the fellowship of the church. At the other extreme were Christians at Jerusalem and elsewhere who argued that the Torah was still in force under the new dispensation. Peter seems to have represented this latter view when the Easter faith was first established. But he shifted his position, moving in the direction of the Pauline standpoint on the question. At one stage he may have wavered between the two extremes; and while visiting the mixed Christian society at Antioch, he was sharply rebuked by Paul for succumbing to conservative pressure from Jerusalem and cutting himself off from table-fellowship with non-Jewish members of the community (Gal. 2:11–21).

It ought not to be supposed, then, that primitive Christianity was characterized by a static uniformity of belief. There was a variety of interpretations, not only in the field of christology but in other areas as well. Doctrinal differences obtained between the Aramaic and the Hellenistic churches, and in all likelihood the original Jerusalem community itself was not without its theological tensions and personal rivalries—as, for example, between the Apostle Peter and James, the brother of Jesus. In some measure the existence of such diversities may be detected in the Acts of the Apostles (the sequel to Luke's gospel), which was probably published sixty years or more after the crucifixion. Apparently, however, the author of this work wished to give the impression that the inner development of Christianity was one of steady and peaceful growth. Any conflict was due to opposition from without and, in the providence of God, led surely to the advancement of the new religion. So he reports (Acts 10:15) that Peter, quite independently of Paul, by a divine revelation that came in a dream, arrived at the view that what God had cleansed should not be regarded as common or unclean. He also reports (Acts 15:20) that Peter and James and the elders of the Jerusalem church, to Paul's satisfaction, agreed that it would be enough if Gentile Christians observed three or four Mosaic prohibitions.

It is doubtful, however, whether the Apostle Paul would in fact have been satisfied with the promulgation of any demands on Gentile believers which implied that the Law of Moses was still operative in even a minimum way. As may be gathered from his extant epistles, he firmly held that the Torah had served as a temporary custodian whose rule preceded and prepared for the Gospel (Gal. 3:24). Jesus put an end to the Law, inaugurating a new epoch in God's dealings with the world (Rom. 10:4). Men were now justified by a faith that involved a humble reliance on the divine love revealed in Christ, who renounced his Godlike status and assumed the form of a servant; he became man and humbled himself even to the extent of dying on a cross, wherefore God highly exalted him that all creatures should confess his Lordship (Phil. 2:5–11). But though he was exalted to heaven his Spirit was still available and men could participate in the incorruptibility of his divine life (Rom. 8:11).

Christ had become the head of a regenerated humanity, integrated in a community wherein all racial, social, and sexual distinctions had been nullified (Gal. 3:28). As members of the body of Christ, the faithful were infused with the Spirit that informed and sustained the whole corporate complex (I Cor. 12:13), so that they no longer lived under the subjection of death (Rom. 8:11). It was in Christ that they had their existence, and their common participation in the quickening energies of his divine Spirit found tangible focus in the eucharistic meal, a communion rite which pointed forward to the glory of the *parousia* or second advent of Jesus (I Cor. 10:16; 11:23–26; I Thess. 4:13–17). Hence anyone baptized into the body of Christ was a new creation, restored to fellowship with God and entrusted with the message of reconciliation (II Cor. 5:17–19). The damage done by Adam's primordial disobedience had been made good (Rom. 5:19).

In other words, according to Pauline doctrine, Israel, the elect people, had been eschatologically reconstituted as a spiritual community founded upon divine grace appropriated by faith. This community already manifested the life of the promised age of fulfillment, which had dawned with the coming of Christ and was pressing on toward its triumphant consummation. For the fullness of time had come (Gal. 4:4), and, as a spiritual society established by faith, the reconstituted Israel was quite different from the old Israel founded "after the flesh" (Gal. 6:15–16). Not all Jews belonged to the new Israel, and the new Israel did not exclude Jews (Rom. 2:29; 9:6; Gal. 3:29). All members of the Body of Christ were the spiritual heirs of Abraham, the prototype of the life of faith, to whom the divine promises of the dispensation of grace were first communicated, and so it could be said that the Hebrew scriptures preached the gospel beforehand to the first of the patriarchs in pointing out that through him all nations would ultimately be blessed (Gal. 3:8). All was foreseen because in the last resort the multifarious processes of Israelite history were a continuous realization of God's saving purpose; and now at last God had made the vital intervention in Christ with a view to the reconciliation of an alienated humanity.

The notion that the sands of historical time were sinking, which dominated much of the thinking of the early Christians, deeply affected their attitude to established worldly institutions. Material possessions, for example, tended to lose the value status they normally enjoy among people who take for granted the persistence of existing social structures, and it is not surprising to come across indications that certain Christians surrendered substantial properties to the church for the welfare of the poor (Mark 10:21; Acts 4:36–37). On the other hand, the author of Acts may give a wrong impression when he baldly states that the company of those who believed had all things in common (Acts 4:32). He is probably generalizing from traditions that reported particular instances of extreme generosity among members of the apostolic church, thereby idealizing the situation. For why should Barnabas be singled out and commended for selling a field and giving the proceeds to the ecclesiastical authorities (Acts 4:36–37) if all Christians at that time automatically gave up their property when they were baptized? It should also be noticed that Ananias and Sapphira, in the ensuing passage, were suddenly struck down dead for not telling the truth; presumably, they would not have been condemned for simply retaining their piece of land (Acts 5:4).

Why should the author of Acts have wished to inform his readers that the early Christians were communistic? In all likelihood it was because of an a priori judgment that private property is an evil institution bound up with the corruption of the present world. Such a conception, which was not foreign to Platonic teaching, was involved in the Genesis story of the Garden of Eden, where the first parents of the human race are represented as having equal rights to appropriate the fruits of the earth. The same kind of idealism is evinced in biblical eschatology, for to some extent it gave expression to a conviction that the end of history must be like its beginning. In God's good time the paradise lost would be regained. From this standpoint salvation from evil was understood as a restoration of the original state of affairs, when human beings were vegetarians and without institutionalized private property, when peace and harmony reigned among all animal creatures, and when no human government was necessary. So it is affirmed, in a prophecy attributed to Isaiah, that during the golden age of the future the wolf will dwell amicably with the lamb and the lion will eat straw like the ox (Isa. 6:11–12).

It is in the light of this principle that certain features of early Christianity should perhaps be understood. Among these was the resolution in certain quarters to renounce private property, a determination eventually taken up and perpetuated in Christian monasticism. And, while Mark 10:7–8 (an appeal to Gen. 2:24) suggests that monogamous marriage restores Adam's primordial bisexuality, another primitive tradition states that those destined to enjoy the post-resurrection life of the consummated Kingdom will neither marry nor be given in marriage (Mark 12:25); apparently some took this to imply that Adam's original androgynous state (Gen. 2:22–23) was somehow to be secured without marriage (see Chapter 16). Again, according to the

Gospel of the Ebionites (written *circa* A.D. 175), John the Baptist, being a vegetarian, did not eat both locusts and wild honey (Mark 1:6) but only the latter (Epiphanius, *Refutation of All Heresies*, 30; this work was written late in the fourth century, its author being bishop of Salamis in Cyprus).

As for human government, there was a noteworthy ambivalence of attitude. Thus the Apostle Paul, although persuaded that earthly institutions stood under divine condemnation and were shortly to pass away, could on occasion exhort his readers to respect the existing political authorities as ordained by God (Rom. 13:1). In other situations he could explain that the restraints of law and order held back the free expression of evil forces (II Thess. 2:7). However, the time would soon come when such forces would break completely loose, and then in the ensuing eschatological conflict they would be vanquished by divine power (II Thess. 2:8; I Cor. 15:24). Indeed it was for this triumphant climax that the whole world was yearning (Rom. 8:22).

But in a general way, for a sound assessment of the church's political attitudes, it is important to distinguish between the imperial and the Jewish authorities. Jesus had been put to death for sedition by a Roman provincial court; the superscription on the cross ("The King of the Jews") made it plain that he had been condemned for making claim to royal dignity (Mark 15:26). Hence, for this reason alone, Christianity was from the outset liable to fall under political suspicion as a danger to the Empire, and, in their effort to prevent repressive measures, defenders of the new faith were often concerned to show that there was nothing subversive in the doctrines they proclaimed. Among other things, they argued that the condemnation of Jesus was a miscarriage of justice brought about by the malevolence of the Jewish authorities at Jerusalem (I Thess. 2:14 ff.); they misrepresented Pontius Pilate by depicting him as a docile individual who was easily persuaded (Mark 15:6 ff.); they contended that, in the view of Roman officials in Palestine, the Apostle

Paul had been falsely accused by his Jewish opponents (Acts 23:29; 26:32). Thus primitive Christian thought took on an anti-Semitic coloring—and this despite the facts that Jesus and his first followers were Jews, and that, according to the church's ultimate theological explanation, the whole career of Jesus, including the mode of his death, was predetermined by the counsel of God (Acts 2:23).

On the whole the early Christian apologists met with much success, and it is remarkable that no general and systematic persecution of the church took place until the reign of the emperor Decius in A.D. 250. By that time, however, Christianity had become too strong and pervasive to be eliminated by imperial edict, no matter how ruthlessly the sanctions were applied. In A.D. 303, when the Empire was divided among four territorial rulers, Diocletian, the senior holder of the shared imperium, launched the last and most prolonged of the persecutions. It continued after his retirement in 305, but its intensity varied according to the policies of the different rulers; thus Maximinus in the East favored severity, whereas Constantius in the West inclined to conciliation.

Time and tide were on the side of the latter's policy. Galerius issued an edict of toleration in 311, and Maximinus temporarily relented in the following year. Constantine (the son and successor of Constantius) and Licinius met at Milan in 313 and drew up a rescript for provincial governors, granting complete liberty of religion. After his victory at Chrysopolis in 323 Constantine became sole emperor. He patronized Christianity; Sunday was proclaimed a public holiday, and church-building was liberally endowed. Discounting a brief interruption during the reign of Julian the Apostate (361–63), the tendency to pass from impartial toleration to the integration of Christianity with the state continued to gather strength. And eventually, under the emperor Theodosius I (379–95), the church's leadership finally accepted the principle that orthodoxy should be forcibly upheld and promoted by the secular power of the state.

BIBLIOGRAPHY

Beare, F. W. *The Earliest Records of Jesus.* Oxford: Basil Black-well, 1964.

Black, M., ed. *The Scrolls and Christianity: Their Historical and Theological Significance.* London: Society for Promoting Christian Knowledge, 1969.

Brandon, S. G. F. *Jesus and the Zealots: A Study of the Political Factor in Primitive Christianity.* New York: Barnes and Noble, 1967.

Burkill, T. A. *Mysterious Revelation: An Examination of the Philosophy of St. Mark's Gospel.* Ithaca, N.Y.: Cornell University Press, 1963.

Cross, F. M. *The Ancient Library of Qumran and Modern Biblical Studies.* New York: Doubleday, 1958.

Cullmann, Oscar. *Jesus und die Revolutionären seiner Zeit.* Tübingen: Mohr (Paul Siebeck), 1970.

Dibelius, Martin. *Studies in the Acts of the Apostles.* New York: Scribner's, 1956.

Enslin, M. S. *From Jesus to Christianity.* Boston: Beacon Press, 1964.

Goguel, Maurice. *The Birth of Christianity.* New York: Macmillan, 1954.

Jonas, Hans. *Gnostic Religion.* Boston: Beacon Press, 1958.

Kümmel, W. G. *Introduction to the New Testament.* Nashville, Tenn.: Abingdon Press, 1966.

Martyn, J. L. *History and Theology in the Fourth Gospel.* New York: Harper and Row, 1968.

Pfeiffer, R. H. *History of New Testament Times.* New York: Harper, 1949.

Sandmel, S. *The First Christian Century in Judaism and Christianity.* New York: Oxford University Press, 1969.

Wikenhauser, A. *New Testament Introduction.* New York: Herder, 1958.

Winter, Paul. *On the Trial of Jesus.* Berlin: Walter de Gruyter, 1961.

A Note Concerning Early Sources

The works of Josephus, with the Greek and English on opposite pages, are in The Loeb Classical Library (translated by H. St. John Thackeray and others, 9 vols., Harvard University Press, Cambridge, Mass., 1926–65). Extremely valuable are the English translations of patristic writings in *The Ante-Nicene Fathers* (Edinburgh edition revised by A. C. Cox, Buffalo, 10 vols., 1884–86) and in *The Nicene and Post-Nicene Fathers* (edited by P. Schaff and H. Wace: First Series, 14 vols., New York, 1886–94; Second Series, 14 vols., New York, 1890–95). These three collections have been photographically reprinted since the Second World War and are published by Wm. B. Eerdmans, Grand Rapids, Michigan. Eusebius' *Ecclesiastical History* is the first volume of the Second Series of *N.P.N.F.* This work, in Greek and English, is also included in The Loeb Classical Library (translated by K. Lake and J. E. L. Oulton, 2 vols., Harvard University Press, 1926–32). A new series which should eventually cover all the patristic literature in translation is *Ancient Christian Writers* (edited by J. Quasten and J. C. Plumpe, Newman Press, Westminster, Md., 1946——). *The Library of Christian Classics* (edited by J. Baillie, J. T. McNeil, and H. P. Van Dusen, 26 vols. planned, Westminster Press, Philadelphia, and Student Christian Movement Press, London, 1953——) comprises crucial theological writings from the early Fathers through the Reformation. Useful, too, are *Documents of the Christian Church* (selected by H. S. Bettenson, 2nd ed., New York, Oxford University Press, 1963) and *A New Eusebius: Documents Illustrative of the History of the Church to A. D. 337* (edited by J. Stevenson, London, Society for Promoting Christian Knowledge, 1957).

I ‡ ANCIENT CATHOLICISM

I ✦ *The Apostolic Fathers*

Since the seventeenth century the designation "Apostolic Fathers" has been used of certain Christian writers supposed to have lived in the period immediately succeeding that of the New Testament. The Greek word *apostolos* derives from a verb signifying "to send forth" and in a general sense has a meaning similar to the word "missionary" (Latin: *mittere*, "to send"). But in Christian circles it rapidly acquired a technical denotation and referred to those leaders of the early church who had actually been disciples of Jesus prior to the crucifixion. So it came to be held that there were only twelve apostles. Paul objected to this restriction of the term (I Cor. 9:2), but the net result of his contention was that only he apart from the Twelve came to be regarded as an apostle. The presumption that the Apostolic Fathers had enjoyed some personal contact with one or more of the original apostles has no secure foundation.

The writers concerned are Clement of Rome, Hermas, Ignatius, Papias, Polycarp, Barnabas, and the authors of *The Teaching of the Twelve Apostles* (usually known as the *Didachē*, the Greek word for "teaching"), *The Epistle to Diognetus*, and *II Clement*. Although containing valuable indications of the intellectual climate of Christianity in the second century, their works on the whole do not have the spiritual quality of the New Testament writings. Nevertheless, some of the works, for instance *The Shepherd* (or *Pastor*) of Hermas, seem to have been highly respected in a number of influential churches and were almost included in the canon of the New Testament.

Clement was a bishop (or leading elder or presbyter) of the Roman church and wrote *I Clement* around A.D. 96 to the Christian community at Corinth, where a dispute had led to the deposition of certain elders. Clement, writing in the name of his own church, made an appeal for repentance and argued that it was God's will that the duly appointed leaders should be reinstated. God required order and discipline in the church, and it was for this reason that the apostles had appointed bishops and deacons in every place to direct the perpetuation of the ministry. The higher ecclesiastical officials were charged with the task of administering the eucharist, and the general government of the church had been divinely committed to them. Another work, *II Clement*, really a sermon, was probably not in fact written by Clement; the so-called *Clementine Literature* is also spurious.

From *The Shepherd* we learn that Hermas, its author, was a Christian slave who had been bought and subsequently emancipated by a certain woman named Rhoda. He became a wealthy merchant but was denounced by his children during a persecution and lost all his property; he had not always been honest in his business practices, however, and at length both he and his family did penance. His book is divided into three parts, entitled respectively *Visions*, *Mandates*, and *Similitudes*. In the first part there is much fanciful symbolism; for example, in the fifth vision penance appears in the personal form of an angelic shepherd. The *Mandates* concern Christian ethics, and the *Similitudes* often illustrate Christian principles with vivid imagery. Hermas seems to have held that the divine Spirit and the divine Son were identical prior to the incarnation, and that the threefold distinction within the essence of the Godhead did not emerge until the incarnate Christ had been exalted to heaven. His view that post-baptismal sins could be forgiven, when due penance had been made, induced Tertullian (after he had become an ardent rigorist) to describe the book as "The Shepherd of the Adulterers." On the whole the work was more highly regarded in the East than in the West, and even in the East its prestige declined from about the year 400. It may have been written in the middle of the second century.

Papias (*c.* 50–130) was bishop of Hierapolis in Asia Minor, and, according to Irenaeus (for whom, see Chapter 4), had apostolic connections and was a companion of Polycarp. His treatise *Expositions of the Dominical Oracles,* preserved only in quotations made by Irenaeus and Eusebius, apparently contained much legendary tradition. His statement that Mark's gospel is an accurate but disorderly reproduction of what Peter remembered of Jesus is quite misleading, for (as recent criticism has shown) all the synoptic gospels presuppose a period in which oral traditions concerning Jesus circulated in the primitive Christian communities. Papias is reported to have been a firm believer in millenarianism (Rev. 20:4–6), maintaining that, after the resurrection of the dead, the Kingdom of Christ would be set up on earth for a period of a thousand years. The form of his religious expectation suggests that he had a taste for wine, for he evidently taught that in the millennium each vine would have ten thousand branches, each branch ten thousand twigs, each twig ten thousand shoots, each shoot ten thousand clusters, and each cluster ten thousand grapes, and each grape would be so large that it would yield twenty-five casks of wine (see Irenaeus, *Against all Heresies,* 5:33:3–4; 36:1:2; Eusebius, *Eccles. Hist.,* 3:39:1 ff.).

Polycarp (*c.* 70–155) became a bishop at Smyrna in Asia Minor; Irenaeus saw in him a link with the apostolic age, but little is known of his lengthy career. Toward A.D. 155 he went to Rome hoping to persuade Pope Anicetus to conform with Asian quartodeciman usage, that is, to adopt the practice of always celebrating Easter on the fourteenth day of the Jewish month of Nisan, whatever the day of the week, and not on the following Sunday. His mission failed. After his return he was arrested during a pagan festival; he refused to renounce his religion and was burned at the stake.

The author of *The Epistle of Barnabas* probably lived in Alexandria about the year 100. He was strongly anti-Semitic, arguing that the Jews had perverted the Torah: the worship in the temple at Jerusalem and the attendant elaborate sacrificial system were never intended by God. When properly understood the scriptures revealed quite clearly the truth of Christianity and the falsity of Judaism. The complete Greek text of the *Epistle* first became available to modern scholars with the discovery in 1859 of the Codex Sinaiticus, a fourth-century Greek manuscript of the Old and New Testaments, with some additional material.

The *Didachē* is a short treatise which deals with morals, liturgy, and church polity, and it may have originated among relatively isolated Syrian churches around A.D. 150. It appears to have some connection with *The Epistle of Barnabas* and *The Shepherd* of Hermas. The work makes much of the distinction between "the way of life" and "the way of death." The Lord's Prayer is reproduced, and instructions are given regarding baptism and the eucharist; fasting is required on Wednesdays and Fridays. A local ministry ("bishops" and "deacons") is differentiated from itinerant "prophets" who are apparently given the primacy as "chief priests." In the final chapter there are predictions of the appearance of the Antichrist and the second coming of Jesus. The only manuscript of the work was discovered in Constantinople in 1875, and this was first published in 1883. There also exists an incomplete Latin version.

The Epistle to Diognetus may have been written late in the second or early in the third century. Its author and the person addressed are otherwise unknown. The point is made that Christianity, unlike Judaism and paganism, rests on a valid revelation of God's love, which is the sole ground of human salvation. There are some particularly impressive passages in chapters 5–7, as the following quotations show:

Christians . . . live in countries of their own, but simply as sojourners; they share the life of citizens, they endure the lot of aliens; every foreign land is to them a fatherland, and every fatherland a foreign land. . . . They love all men, and they are persecuted by all; . . . they are put to death, and yet they give proof of new life. They are poor, and yet make many rich. . . . In brief, what the soul is in the body Christians are in the world. . . . The soul dwells in the body, and yet it is not of the body: so Christians dwell in the world, and yet they are not of the world. . . . Immortal itself, the soul abides in a mortal tenement; so Christians dwell for a time amid corruptible things, awaiting their incorruption in heaven. . . . God himself in truth . . . planted among men . . . the holy, inscrutable Logos. . . . He sent him as man to men, he sent him to save, to persuade, not to coerce; for coercion is no part of God's nature. . . . He sent him in love, not in judgment. . . . Do you not see that the more they [the Christians] are punished, the more their numbers increase? These things do not have the appearance of human achievements; they are the power of God; they are the proofs of his presence.

The words in 5:9—"They pass their existence on earth, but their citizenship is in heaven"—echo the Apostle Paul's words in Phil. 3:20—"We are a colony (or commonwealth) of heaven" —and the whole context supplies a valuable piece of evidence for a prevalent Christian attitude to life around A.D. 200. The law by which the communities lived was a divine law, and obedience to it was merely a prelude to the bliss that would be enjoyed as a reward in the consummated Kingdom of God: thought was focused on the world to come. Thus the *Epistle* is of much interest to the student of early Christian doctrine, and it is most unfortunate that the one manuscript which survived into modern times was destroyed at Strasbourg in 1870.

Ignatius represents a type of Christianity rather different from that of the other Apostolic Fathers, and before proceeding to consider his teaching we may conveniently draw attention to certain features common to the writings already listed. While Ignatius followed the Pauline and Johannine mode of interpretation, the other Apostolic Fathers were in line with the kind of representation to be found in the Epistle of James, where we read: "Religion that is pure and undefiled before God and the

Father consists in this: to visit the fatherless and widows in their affliction and to keep oneself unstained from the world" (Jas. 1:27). Man is not, in this view, justified by faith, but by obedience to the divine law as revealed in the Hebrew canonical scriptures and as summed up and confirmed in the ministry of Jesus. Of course this law did not contain the ritual and dietary requirements of Judaism, for the Levitical system had been rendered unnecessary by Christ's sacrificial death on Calvary, and during his life Jesus has summed up the whole of the law by pointing to two great commandments (Mark 12:28 ff.). So we read in the *Didachē* (1:2), "The way of life is this: firstly thou shalt love the God who made thee, secondly thy neighbor as thyself." Whereas obedience to the divine law will bring eternal reward in the life to come, disobedience will bring eternal damnation (cf. *Barn.*, 21:1–2); and Jesus is God's agent both in revelation and in judgment.

The Hebrew scriptures were authoritative because they foretold the advent of Jesus and because the pre-existent Christ revealed himself through the inspired writers (*I Clem.*, 22:1). The New Testament canon had not yet been formally constituted; only in one passage are dominical sayings cited as scriptural (*II Clem.*, 2:4), and it is significant that, according to Irenaeus (*Heresies*, 2:33:3), the elders derived their knowledge of the teaching of Jesus from oral tradition, which had been handed down by the original apostles. Moreover, besides being supplemented by the information received from apostolic times (*I Clem.*, 42), scriptural revelation was further augmented by the disclosures of prophetic teachers who were believed to be present organs of the Holy Spirit (*Did.*, 11; Hermas, *Mand.*, 11). But, as we gather from *The Shepherd* and the *Didachē*, charlatans were liable to make prophetic pretensions, and this encouraged the tendency toward the regularization of the ministry through a hierarchy of officers in which the prophet had no place.

In view of their moralistic or quasi-legalistic emphasis, it is not surprising to find that most of the Apostolic Fathers were anxious to point out that righteousness in this life would be duly rewarded in the approaching era of eschatological fulfillment. The notion that virtue is its own reward seems to have been alien to their way of thinking; and, as we have seen in the case of Papias, their concept of the future rewards of the faithful could be expressed in crudely materialistic terms. Of course in the New Testament itself the doctrine of rewards and punishments, the appointed sanctions attached to divine demands, played an important role. Admittedly, it has been argued that in the synoptic traditions the references of Jesus to future rewards and punishments (e.g., Mark 10:29–30) are metaphorical, and were meant to signify in a vivid fashion the approval or disapproval of God; and there may be some truth in this contention. Nevertheless, the idea of just retribution is intimately bound up with Jewish and early Christian eschatology, and any attempt to explain it away would fly in the face of the plain empirical evidence. Even the Apostle Paul, who could hardly be described as a legalist in his interpretation of Christianity, asserted that those who suffered with Christ would also be glorified with him (Rom. 8:15–17).

But it should be noted that for Paul "glorification" was far from being materialistic, and in one passage he informs his readers that flesh and blood cannot inherit the Kingdom of God (I Cor. 15:50). Also, he sometimes thinks of the Christian life in present experience as a glorification (e.g., II Cor. 3:18); members of the church were baptized into one body and thereby enabled to draw on the vitalizing energies of the divine Spirit (I Cor. 12:13), and among the fruits produced by spiritual inspiration were peace and joy (Gal. 5:22). The trials endured in the practice of the Christian life, then, were not just externally related to future rewards as mere means to an end. A form of immediate satisfaction and an inner spiritual growth were enjoyed by the faithful, and this means that there was a tendency at work in the Apostle's thinking which could induce him to move away from the eschatological idea that virtue is nothing more than the cost of ultimate blessing. Yet it remains that in the great christological statement in Phil. 2:1 ff., the voluntary humiliation of Christ is set forth as though it were a dark passage, the terrible price that had to be paid for his subsequent "superexaltation" by the power of God. On the other hand, in the Fourth Gospel a mystical sense of the immediate reward of virtue is projected into the christology, and the passion is occasionally represented as the hour of Christ's glorification or exaltation (John 12:23, 32; 13:1).

It seems clear, then, that the Apostolic Fathers so far considered give expression to a moralistic or legalistic type of Christianity such as finds New Testament exemplification in the Epistle of James and the Book of Revelation. In the works of Ignatius, however, we discover a different emphasis, which is reminiscent of the mystical and sacramentarian mode of interpretation to be found in the Pauline epistles and in the Fourth Gospel. Ignatius was bishop of Antioch in Syria and was martyred in Rome *circa* A.D. 115. While being escorted to Rome by ten soldiers he was received as a hero of the faith by Polycarp at Smyrna, and in the course of the fateful journey he wrote seven letters, which are still extant: six are addressed to the churches of Ephesus, Magnesia, Tralles, Rome, Philadelphia, and Smyrna respectively, and the seventh to Polycarp. The style is vigorous and often aphoristic.

Ignatius was extremely devout, and he regarded martyrdom as the highest honor that could be conferred upon a Christian; so in his letter to the church at Rome he begs his readers not to intervene on his behalf with the political authorities lest they prevent his obtaining the crown of life, namely, death for the confession of Christ. In the other letters he argues strongly against Docetism—the view that the Christ only *seemed* to have a human nature (*Tralles*, 9); and he condemns ecclesiastical disunity in no uncertain terms. Heresy is evil because it disrupts the Body of Christ, and the institution of episcopacy is good because it safeguards the integrity of the Christian faith. "For those who are of God and Jesus Christ are with the bishop;

and those who in repentance return to the unity of the church shall also be of God" (*Phila.*, 3). It is not merely that heresy makes for conflict in the fellowship of a human society; it disrupts a divine community and breaks the vital connection of the individual member with the source of eternal life.

Ignatius thought of salvation primarily as deliverance from death through union with Christ (*Eph.*, 17–20), and he could refer to the Ephesians as to fellow initiates in a divine mystery (*Eph.*, 12). As such they obtained vitalizing potency. The preexistent Christ (*Mag.*, 6) became truly man (*Tralles*, 9) and in virtue of his resurrection humanity was immortalized (*Smyrna*, 5–7). His victory over death was communicated to others through their participation in the common life of the church, and it was possible to represent the eucharist as supplying a "medicine of immortality" (*Eph.*, 20). Thus the Pauline notion of mystical faith and the Johannine doctrine of liberating gnosis assumed a more definitely institutionalized form in the writings of Ignatius: saving faith and knowledge were objectified in the unity guaranteed by the episcopal authority; and the bishop alone could dispense the sacramental grace that imparts eternal life (see *Eph.*, 5; *Mag.*, 7; *Tralles*, 2; *Phila.*, 8).

BIBLIOGRAPHY

Altaner, Berthold. *Patrology.* New York: Herder, 1960.

Barnard, L. W. *Studies in the Apostolic Fathers and Their Background.* Oxford: Basil Blackwell, 1966.

Goodspeed, E. J. *The Apostolic Fathers: An American Translation.* New York: Harper, 1950.

Kelly, J. N. D. *Early Christian Doctrines.* New York: Harper, 1958.

Meecham, H. G., ed. and trans. *The Epistle to Diognetus.* Manchester: Manchester University Press, 1949.

Torrance, T. F. *The Doctrine of Grace in the Apostolic Fathers.* Edinburgh: Oliver and Boyd, 1948.

2 ‡ *The Apologists*

The term "apologists" is applied to a number of Christian writers of the second century who sought to defend and commend their religion to outsiders. They argued that Christianity was quite innocuous to the imperial government despite the refusal of its adherents to associate themselves with emperor-worship, and that Christian doctrine and practice were superior to Judaism and pagan culture. Much was made of the argument from prophecy, and they elaborated the Johannine doctrine that the Logos or Word of God, the divine agent of creation and revelation, had become incarnate in the person of Jesus the Christ (John 1:1 ff.). Of course the apologetic motive is to be found in Christian literature *ab initio;* it is dominant in the New Testament in the writings of Luke (the third canonical gospel and the Acts of the Apostles), and it is evident elsewhere.

Aristides was an Athenian thinker who, according to Eusebius (*Eccles. Hist.*, 4:3:3), presented his *Apology* to the emperor Hadrian in about A.D. 124. But some modern scholars hold that his work was in fact addressed to the emperor Antoninus Pius about twenty years later. Aristides argued that the Christians alone possess the truth concerning God:

They know God, the Creator and Ruler of all things, through his only-begotten Son and the Holy Spirit, and they worship no other God beside him. They have the commandments of the Lord Jesus Christ inscribed on their hearts, and they observe them, looking forward to the resurrection of the dead and the life of the age to

34

come. . . . If they see a stranger they take him under their roof and rejoice over him as over a brother, for they call each other brethren, not according to the flesh but according to the spirit (*Apol.*, 15).

An ancient Syriac translation of the whole work was printed and published in 1891.

Quadratus may have lived in Asia Minor, and according to Eusebius (*Eccles. Hist.*, 4:3:1–2), he wrote an *Apology* for Christianity addressed to the emperor Hadrian around the year 124. The passage quoted by Eusebius is the only part of the document that survives. In this fragment the writer employs the argument from miracle, claiming that some sufferers cured by Jesus had actually survived into the period of his own life.

The Athenian Athenagoras addressed his *Plea for the Christians* to the emperor Marcus Aurelius and his son and coregent Commodus *circa* A.D. 177. Among other things he argued that there was no ground for certain current slanders against the Christians: 1586703

Three things are alleged against us: atheism, orgies, and incest. If these charges are true, spare none. . . . But if they are merely idle tales . . . it remains for you to make inquiry . . . and thus at length to grant us the same rights (that is all we ask) as those accorded to our persecutors.

In another treatise, *On the Resurrection of the Dead,* he contends that since it is the whole person that does good or evil, the body as well as the soul must be rewarded or punished by God. In certain passages the fact that God requites men according to their deserts is taken to be the ground and motive of Christian benevolence (*Plea,* 12; *Res.,* 19). As for his theory of the Godhead, he clearly differentiated the Son or Logos from the Holy Spirit (*Plea,* 10).

Theophilus, bishop of Antioch in the seventies of the second century, addressed his *Apology* to a certain Autolycus and in it sought to demonstrate the inherent superiority of Christian doctrine by calling attention to the crudities of Greek polytheistic mythology. In this work (2:15) we have the first occurrence in extant Christian literature of the term "trias" with regard to the Godhead. Theophilus prefers the formula "God, Logos, and Wisdom" to "Father, Son, and Spirit." In line with his predecessors generally (but unlike Athenagoras), Theophilus was liable to confuse the second and third persons of the divine Triad, as in the tenth chapter of the second of the three books into which the *Apology* is divided. On the other hand, he developed theological doctrine by distinguishing (2:10, 22) the "endiathetical" Logos (the eternal and inherent rationality of God) from the "prophorical" Logos (the externalized instrument of creation). Among his other writings (not extant) was a criticism of Marcion, whose teaching will be considered in Chapter 3.

Tatian, a native of Assyria, after studying rhetoric and philosophy, went to Rome in about A.D. 150. He there embraced Christianity and became a pupil of Justin Martyr. His *Oration to the Greeks* involves violent attacks on Hellenistic culture; he had eyes only for the corruption and grossness of the pagan world, contending that the Greek myths were immoral and that the Greek gods were demons. So far from being of recent origin, Christianity was extremely ancient; its truth was already proclaimed by Moses and the prophets of the Old Testament, and whatever grains of truth the writers of other peoples may have possessed, these must ultimately have been obtained from the inspired scriptures. Around A.D. 172, some seven years after the martyrdom of Justin, Tatian returned to the East, and there is a tradition that he founded the sect of the Encratites, a gnosticizing group that abstained from wine and meat and (in many cases) from sexual intercourse. His *Diatessaron*, a compilation made from the four canonical gospels, was widely used in the Syriac churches until it was displaced by the Peshitta in the fifth century; this latter was a revision of the old Syriac version of the New Testament, probably made by Rabbula, bishop of Edessa from about A.D. 411 to 435.

Melito, bishop of Sardis, addressed his *Apology* to the emperor Marcus Aurelius, perhaps in the year 175. But, like most of his voluminous writings, the work is no longer extant. Recently his *Homily on the Passion*, a devotional treatise, came to light through the chance discovery of a papyrus, which is now in the library of Michigan University. This document is of christological interest in its dramatic use of the *communicatio idiomatum*, the doctrine that what is true of Christ as man is equally true of him as God. Thus we read: "He who hung the earth is hanged, he who fixed the heavens is fixed." As one would expect, Melito defended Asian Quartodecimanism against the custom, which prevailed in Rome and elsewhere, of celebrating Easter on the Sunday following the fourteenth day of the Jewish month of Nisan.

Minucius Felix may have been a native of North Africa, and his apology *Octavius* was probably published at the end of the second century. Unlike the other apologists considered in this chapter, he wrote in Latin. The work is in the form of a dialogue between a Christian, Octavius, and a pagan, Caecilius, who is eventually persuaded by the force of Octavius' arguments and becomes a Christian. Like Athenagoras, the author seeks to refute popular calumnies against the Christians, criticises pagan mythology, and maintains that the concepts of monotheism and divine providence are not unreasonable. But, taken as a whole, his work does not evince the philosophical penetration exemplified in the writings of such men as Athenagoras and Theophilus. There is evidently a connection between the *Octavius* and Tertullian's *Apology* (published *c.* 197), and it may be that Minucius drew on the latter.

Justin Martyr, perhaps the most colorful of the apologists of the period, was probably born at Samaria during the nineties of the first century, and was successively a Stoic, an Aristotelian, a Pythagorean, and a Platonist before being converted to Christianity. For some years he taught at Ephesus, where, as it seems, he took part in debates with a Jewish thinker named Trypho. At length he moved to Rome and opened a Christian academy there. According to Tatian, who studied at the academy for a while, Justin and a number of his pupils were eventually denounced as Christians by an opponent belonging to the school of the Cynics; and, on their refusal to offer sacrifice to the emperor, they were decapitated (*c.* A.D. 165).

Justin's *First Apology*, which counters popular charges of immorality made against the Christians, was addressed to the emperor Antoninus Pius (*c.* 155). His *Second Apology*, largely a refutation of specific charges, was apparently addressed to the Roman Senate soon after the accession of Marcus Aurelius in the year 161. On the philosophico-theological side he argued that all men are to some extent inspired by God through the agency of the "spermatical" or "germinative" Logos, a fact which is taken to account for the elements of truth contained in pagan writings (*First Ap.*, 46). However, the *entire* Logos became incarnate in Christ (*Second Ap.*, 10), and this clarified the saving truth already revealed: Jesus came to bring light to the darkened minds of men. Justin evidently did not believe (as Paul did) that men had been corrupted by an original sin inherited from Adam, but rather that they had been deceived by demons and had turned aside from the truth through the baneful influence of evil customs (*First Ap.*, 5:54 ff.). Hence the Logos became incarnate to guide men into the way of truth, and Christ was the divine teacher par excellence. He satisfied a need for illumination (*First Ap.*, 6:13:19; *Dialogue with Trypho*, 76).

In his *Dialogue with Trypho* Justin replied to adverse Jewish criticism of Christianity, his main thesis being that Jews and Gentiles alike could now win salvation only by being initiated into the church, the New Israel, which, in compliance with the intention of God, had displaced the Old Israel according to the flesh (that is, founded on physical descent from Abraham).

Jesus, as the fulfillment of the Logos-inspired prophecies of the Hebrew scriptures, had inaugurated a new age in the history of salvation. Thus, like the Apostle Paul, Justin held that the Mosaic Law, with its multifarious ceremonial and dietary regulations, constituted but a temporary dispensation in the divine scheme for the redemption of humanity (*Trypho*, 119; 135 ff.).

On the other hand, Justin's general interpretation of Christianity differed from Paul's in being essentially moralistic rather than mystical or sacramental. He certainly did not lay himself open (as Paul evidently did) to charges of antinomianism or licentiousness. For in his view Christ was not primarily the Spirit that energizes a redeemed society, but the divine Teacher who had come to make plain the basic moral conditions of salvation. Man is a free and responsible being, and to be saved he must repent and obey the Law of God as disclosed in Christ. Jesus was the new Moses who had summed up the Law in the two great commandments to love God and to love one's neighbor (*Trypho*, 93). It is true that on occasion Justin made concessions to the mystico-ecclesiastical tradition and stressed the importance of the sacraments. Baptism, for instance, could be described as a means of regeneration as well as a sign for the remission of sins (*Trypho*, 116; *First Ap.*, 66); but such a concept does not seem to follow naturally from his basic theological position.

The incarnate Logos was God's only-begotten Son (*Trypho*, 105) and was born of a virgin (*First Ap.*, 22; *Trypho*, 43). Apparently, three main theories concerning the origin of Christ's divine status were already current in the apostolic church, and these come to expression in the New Testament: (1) Jesus became the Son of God at his baptism, a notion found in the Western reading of Luke 3:22 (see the footnote in the Revised Standard Version) and perhaps popular among the Ebionites and other early Jewish-Christian groups. (2) Jesus was begotten of God at the very commencement of his earthly life when he was conceived in the womb of his mother, an idea to be found in Matt. 1:18 and Luke 1:35—passages which, however, run counter to the implications of the genealogies in Matt. 1:1 ff. and Luke 3:23 ff., where the ancestry of Jesus is traced through Joseph, to whom Mary was betrothed. The virgin birth is not mentioned elsewhere in the New Testament, and among the Apostolic Fathers only Ignatius alludes to it (e.g., *Eph.*, 19:1). (3) Christ pre-existed as the Son of God, a view expressed in Phil. 2:1 ff. and in John 1:1 ff. In the Johannine passage the only-begotten Son of God is identified with the eternal Logos, the divine agent of creation that became incarnate in the person of Jesus.

As we have already implied, Justin combined the second and the third of these theories, but in so doing he was forced to treat the doctrine of the virgin birth not as a theory of Christ's divine origin but merely as an indication of the fashion in which the eternal Logos assumed human form (*First Ap.*, 33; *Trypho*, 75). Like his predecessors, Justin was prone to confuse the Logos and the Holy Spirit, and in one remarkable passage (*First Ap.*, 33) he asserts that the power of the Most High that overshadowed or impregnated Mary was none other than the Logos, the first-born of God, a doctrine which would seem to signify that Jesus as divine was the father of Jesus as human.

BIBLIOGRAPHY

Barnard, L. W. *Justin Martyr, His Life and Thought*. Cambridge: Cambridge University Press, 1967.

Goodspeed, E. J. *A History of Early Christian Literature*. Chicago: University of Chicago Press, 1942.

Lietzmann, Hans. *The Beginnings of the Christian Church*. New York: Scribner's, 1937.

Little, V. A. Spence. *The Christology of the Apologists*. New York: Scribner's, 1935.

Turner, H. E. W. *The Patristic Doctrine of Redemption*. New York: Morehouse Gorham, 1952.

3 ‡ *Marcion and Montanus*

Anti-Semitic and gnostic tendencies, already evident in Christian thought during the first century, were taken up and made central in the teaching of Marcion, a wealthy shipowner and son of the bishop of Sinope in Pontus. None of his writings is extant, but much can be gathered about his position from the surviving writings of his critics, and especially from Tertullian's *Adversus Marcionem* ("Against Marcion"). He apparently went to Rome about the year 140 and made a generous gift to the church there. But he soon became dissatisfied with the general state of Christianity, and, perhaps partly under the influence of a Gnostic named Cerdo, he began to argue that the principal cause of the church's degenerate condition lay in its continued respect for the legalism of the Jewish scriptures. Hence, to be reformed and purified, Christianity must be purged of those elements that properly belonged to the old dispensation, and the first requirement was the elimination of the Old Testament from the canonical scriptures. New wine ought never to be put into old wineskins.

Marcion began to proclaim his views, and in A.D. 144 he was formally excommunicated. In consequence, he and his followers organized a separate society, and Marcion with much enthusiasm devoted the rest of his life (he died *c.* 160) to the strengthening and extension of the movement. He met with much success. By the end of the century Marcionite communities seem to have existed in most of the Empire's major urban centers, but by the year 300 many of them had turned to Manicheanism—the doctrine of the Persian prophet, Mani (*c.* 210–75), who combined a syncretist-dualist philosophy with a strict ascetic discipline. Nevertheless, a number of small Marcionite groups managed to maintain a precarious existence for some considerable time.

Marcion expounded his main position in a work entitled *Antitheses*. The Demiurge (or creative God) of the Hebrew scriptures was set in contrast with the God of grace revealed by Christ. The former revealed himself in the Mosaic Law and had nothing in common with the God of the New Testament: he was inconsistent, ignorant, capricious, cruel, jealous, devoted to strife and war. Although he was the source of the Law, with its stress on moral retribution, Yahweh was in fact unjust, for he showed special favor to the Jewish people and neglected the rest of mankind. The Supreme Being, however, had no favorites; he was the God of grace who offered salvation to all by faith alone; that is, the divine gift could be appropriated by any penitent person, whatever his racial or national connections.

Christ came to live among men as the true representative of the Supreme Being, and he revealed something that had never been known to humanity previously. He came out of love to save forlorn creatures for whose wretched existence he was in no wise responsible. But he did not actually become incarnate, for a delegate from the heavenly Father could not have contaminated himself by coming into direct contact with matter, which is inherently evil. He was not conceived in a woman's womb, but appeared suddenly as a mature man in the synagogue at Capernaum; and he did not really suffer death or conduct a preaching mission in Hades before returning to the God from whom he had originally proceeded.

In view of Marcion's disparagement of the flesh, it is not surprising to find that he proclaimed an ethic of strict asceticism. He insisted on the importance of complete abstinence from sexual intercourse; carnal lusts were bad in themselves, and the normal consequence of sexual desires was also bad, for it entailed an increase in the number of souls subjected to the nefarious control of the Demiurge.

In his deprecation of carnality, his asceticism, and his christological Docetism, Marcion had obvious affinities with the Gnostics of the second century. On the other hand, he did not hold, as most of the Gnostics apparently did, that salvation from evil and death could only be obtained by a select few, a spiritual elite; God offered salvation to all, and anyone who put his trust in the divine mercy would be redeemed. Also, unlike the leading Gnostics of the period, he seems to have had little or no interest in elaborate cosmological speculations or in the subtleties of allegorical exegesis.

In Marcion's view, Paul alone among the early followers of Jesus properly understood the irreconcilable opposition between the Law and the Gospel. The original apostles were blinded to the truth through persistent Jewish influence, and even the text of the ten Pauline epistles (perhaps he did not recognize the pastoral epistles as Pauline) had been tampered with in an effort to bring them into line with Jewish legalism. But he felt the need for an authoritative body of writings to displace the Old Testament, and for this purpose he took Luke's gospel in addition to the ten epistles of Paul, freely modifying the text in each case, in order to eliminate, as he claimed, the corruption which had been introduced because of the continuing hold of the Demiurge on the Christian mind.

This action on Marcion's part had an important effect, for it stimulated the church to make haste in the work of forming its own canon of sacred documents. By the year 200 the four gospels and the thirteen epistles of Paul seem to have been generally accepted as canonical in Christian circles; that is, they were considered to be as authoritative as the Hebrew scriptures, and they constituted the nucleus of the present New Testament. The *Festal Epistle* of Athanasius (A.D. 369) provides the earliest surviving testimony to the New Testament canon as it eventually came to be established in East and West. The presence of Marcionite prologues to the Pauline epistles in the majority of the better manuscripts of the Vulgate (the official Latin version of the Bible, published *circa* 404) may be due to the circumstance that these works were first put into Latin by followers of Marcion in Rome during the latter part of the second century.

As we gather from the Pauline epistles, which are in all probability the earliest surviving Christian documents, life in the apostolic communities was characterized by a confident belief in the nearness of the end of the world, by stringent ethical standards, and by an assurance that the divine Spirit was an experiential source of personal inspiration for all members of the Body of Christ. But even before the end of the first century there were factors which militated against the notion that the church was a *corps d'élite*, a charismatic community awaiting its imminent vindication at the hands of the living God. The final judgment was delayed, and the world often seemed to go on much as it had before the coming of Christ; there were tares sown among the wheat, and it was not always easy to distinguish the true from the false; there were charlatans who claimed to be divinely inspired, and some dared to say that the eternal Son of God must have been crucified in appearance only.

In consequence of such circumstances as these the church tended to take the early eschatology less literally, to relax the rigorous discipline of the apostolic period, and to lodge authority in the episcopal hierarchy. Hence during the second century it came to be ever more widely held that the vitalizing Spirit and the liberating Truth are exclusively dispensed by the church's duly constituted officers. And Montanism may best be understood as a vigorous protest against a development of this kind; it represents an attempt to return to the Spirit-filled life of the primitive Christian communities, with their apocalypticism and other-worldly ethical orientation. The Fourth Evangelist had written of the coming of the Paraclete or the Spirit of Truth (John 14:15–17; 15:26; 16:7–15), and the followers of Montanus apparently believed that the special dispensation of the Spirit had dawned with the prophetic enthusiasm of their inspired leader.

Like Marcion, Montanus was a native of Asia Minor. He was born in Phrygia and, according to at least one report was a priest of the cult of Cybele before his conversion to Christianity. It was around A.D. 156 (Epiphanius, *Heresies*, 48:1) or 172 (Eusebius, *Eccles. Hist.*, 5:16 ff.) that he began to announce himself as a passive instrument of the Holy Spirit, prophesying that the New Jerusalem (Rev. 21:2) would shortly come down from heaven and establish itself in the region of the Phrygian town of Pepuza. Among his leading disciples were two women, Prisca and Maximilla, who also claimed to prophesy under divine inspiration. An unnamed opponent of Montanism, cited by Eusebius, reports of Montanus:

He lost all control of himself and falling suddenly into a frenzied ecstasy he began to rave and babble and make strange utterances, prophesying in a fashion quite contrary to the constant custom of the church transmitted by tradition from the beginning (*Eccles. Hist.*, 5:16:7).

This report suggests that the emotional excitement of the early days, when prophesyings and speaking with tongues were common occurrences in the life of the Christian communities (cf. I Cor. 14:1 ff.), had ceased to be familiar to many members of the church in the latter half of the second century. Apparently it was widely held that fervid prophesyings were a form of madness or a manifestation of demon-possession.

On the other hand, Tertullian, the first great theologian of the Latin church, who was converted to Montanism around A.D. 206, had a more sympathetic appreciation of the significance of religious ecstasy, and in one passage he writes:

For when a man is possessed by the Spirit, especially when he beholds the glory of God or when God speaks through him, he necessarily loses his senses because he is overshadowed by the power of

God, concerning which there is a point at issue between us [the *pneumatici* or "Spirit-filled" people] and the *psychici* [or "animalistic" people] (*Adv. Marcionem*, 4:22).

Montanist other-worldly asceticism seems to have become particularly prominent in the movement as it developed in North Africa, and it may well have been the strictness of Montanist discipline that especially attracted Tertullian, who attacked the penitential system at Rome for its laxity.

In the course of the controversy Tertullian referred to the official representatives of Roman Christianity as *psychici* in contradistinction to the *pneumatici* of his own rigorous party, who prohibited flight during times of persecution, held that the prevailing regulations on fasting were too lenient, and disallowed second marriages. In his work *De Pudicitia* ("On Modesty") he admonished Callistus, who was bishop of Rome from 217 to 223, for his "animalism" in readmitting fornicators and adulterers into church membership after canonical penance. In Tertullian's view post-baptismal engagement in extramarital sexual intercourse was a mortal sin (cf. I John 5:16–17), and so baptized Christians who committed fornication excluded themselves permanently from the church and the means of salvation.

The distinction drawn by Tertullian between *pneumatici* and *psychici* is reminiscent of the gnostic classification of human beings into three groups—the pneumatical, the psychical, and the sarcinal. It should be observed, however, that Tertullian's basis of division was essentially ethical, whereas with the Gnostics it tended to be intellectual, a question of human capacity for spiritual illumination. This is a point of much interest because it is indicative of an important difference between Montanism and Gnosticism, and, more generally, between Latin patristic thought and Greek patristic thought.

On the whole the ancient Latin theologians were fundamentally practical in their interests, whereas those who wrote in Greek were deeply influenced by the Hellenic spirit and not infrequently took delight in speculative flights of the metaphysical imagination. Thinkers like Tertullian largely sought to prescribe for an ordered ecclesiastical polity, but theologians like Origen of Alexandria, as we shall see in a later chapter, sought spiritual vision and a comprehensive philosophical formulation of Christian truth. If the church's form of organization was a product of the Latin genius, the great ecumenical creeds were a legacy bequeathed by the Hellenistic world.

Montanism was condemned by synods in Asia Minor before the year 200—and also, though he hesitated for a time, by Zephyrinus, the bishop of Rome from 198 to 217. In rejecting Montanism the church strengthened the secularizing tendencies against which Montanus and his followers protested. Like rabbinical Judaism, consolidated Catholic Christianity by the end of the second century came to believe that prophetic revelation was a thing of the past. The apostolic period constituted a closed epoch of revelation, whose divine disclosures had been faithfully recorded in the sacred writings of the New Testament, which had been handed down (and properly interpreted) by bishops who stood in the apostolic succession. Thus order prevailed over the anarchy to which associations of the charismatic type are always susceptible, and in this connection (as will become clear in Chapter 4) the church's reaction against Montanism joined forces with its reaction against Gnosticism.

Two further points need to be made. In the first place, with the repudiation of Montanism, confidence in an imminent second coming of Christ was discredited; and, although eschatological enthusiasm was never formally condemned as heretical, belief in the nearness of the end of the world for the most part ceased to play a central role in the main stream of Christian development. This indeed is a paradoxical truth, for in what was taken to be the normative period of religious history, the period of the apostolic church, a fervid eschatological expectation dominated both thought and practice.

In the second place, the rejection of Montanism meant a reaction against the strictness of the discipline it advocated. The movement within Catholicism toward moderation gathered strength, and it soon came to be officially laid down that no sin is in principle mortal or unforgivable. The opposition between mortal and venial post-baptismal sins ceased to be one between unpardonable and pardonable offenses, and became little more than a differentiation of more serious from less serious defections. As we have seen, in about A.D. 220 Callistus of Rome shocked Tertullian by announcing that he would absolve illicit instances of sexual intercourse after canonical penance had been undergone by the offenders.

Some thirty years later, after the terrible persecution under the emperor Decius, the question of the forgiveness of apostasy became acute. Even Cyprian, the rigorous bishop of Carthage, became more lenient in his attitude toward those who had apostatized under threat of torture. In 251 Cornelius was elected bishop of Rome in preference to Novatian, whereupon the latter joined the rigorists and was consecrated counter-pope, becoming the leader of a schismatic church which persisted into the fifth century. The Novatianists argued that apostasy was strictly mortal, and hence that those who compromised with paganism during a persecution must suffer permanent excommunication. For some time attitudes varied in different centers, but eventually the Roman decision that Novatianism was heretical came to prevail. Also, in the year 314 the Council of Ancyra ruled that homicide is a pardonable offense, and Canon 13 of the Council of Nicea (A.D. 325) affirms that, given due penitence, all capital sins are in principle forgivable.

But it must be noticed that the movement toward moderation in ecclesiastical discipline generally was accompanied by a tendency to exalt the ascetic way of life, a tendency which eventually led to the establishment of a double moral standard, one for the mass of Christians, who were expected to fulfill merely the ordinary requirements of the gospel, the other for the clergy, who had a vocation for a higher life and followed the counsels of perfection, taking vows of poverty, chastity, and obedience. To some extent this development may have been influenced by the not-uncommon Hellenistic view that, matter being inherently evil, to free oneself from the shackles of the flesh is a necessary step to be taken in the salvation of the soul. The Stoic ideal of passionlessness or freedom from desire may also have had an effect in this connection.

Moreover, although biblical cosmology was fundamentally not dualistic in a gnostic sense, there were many scriptural passages that could be cited in support of the view that the Christian life demanded the supersession of egoism in all its forms. Jesus called for self-abnegation (Matt. 10:38–39.), and this entailed vigilance (Matt. 24:42) and fasting (Matt. 9:15): for a chosen few (the "perfect") it even meant the renunciation of private property (Matt. 19:21) and self-castration (Matt. 19:12). It was in accordance with such ideas that monasticism seems to have emerged in Egypt by the year 200, and to have spread in the course of subsequent centuries until at length it came to dominate the life of the church, both in the East and in the West.

BIBLIOGRAPHY

Bethune-Baker, J. F. *An Introduction to the Early History of Christian Doctrine*, 9th ed. London: Methuen, 1951.

Blackman, E. C. *Marcion and His Influence*. London: Society for Promoting Christian Knowledge, 1948.

Cadoux, C. J. *The Early Church and the World*. Edinburgh: Clark, 1925.

Labriolle, Pierre de. *La crise montaniste*. Paris: E. Leroux, 1913.

4 ‡ Foundations of
Catholicism: Irenaeus

Irenaeus was apparently born at Smyrna in Asia Minor, perhaps in the year 130, and as a boy he listened to Polycarp, the bishop of that town. After studying at Rome he became a presbyter at Lugdunum (Lyons) in Gaul, where he eventually succeeded Pothinus as bishop. He had practical as well as theological interests, and he effectively combined characteristically Eastern and Western ways of thinking, producing a theological synthesis upon which subsequent Catholic thought came to be largely based. Despite his resolute opposition to the extravagances of gnostic speculation and to the extremism of the Montanists, he was a man with broad sympathies, and on at least two occasions he made representations to the pope in favor of certain deviationist groups in the East. In 177 he went to see Pope Eleutherus in Rome and advocated toleration for the Montanists of his native country; and in 190 he wrote to Pope Victor on behalf of the quartodeciman churches in Asia Minor that celebrated Easter (the Christian Passover) on the fourteenth day of Nisan, regardless of the day of the week. It was during his visit to Rome in 177 that persecution broke out at Lugdunum; Bishop Pothinus suffered martyrdom, and Irenaeus was consecrated to the episcopal office after his return in the following year. It is not known for certain if Irenaeus also was martyred; he may have died in 200, shortly before the persecution under the emperor Severus.

Adversus Omnes Haereses ("Against All Heresies"), the principal work of Irenaeus, is divided into five books and is primarily directed against Gnosticism, especially the form of it propounded by Valentinus (a native of Egypt who taught in Rome and seceded from the Catholic church perhaps in A.D. 165). The argumentation is not purely negative, and from it one can gather the author's fundamental beliefs concerning the nature of religious truth and authority and the nature of salvation. Parts of the treatise are preserved in Greek (the language in which it was written) and parts in Syriac and Armenian; the whole is extant in a Latin version. An Armenian translation of another work, *The Demonstration of the Apostolic Preaching*, an apology which makes much use of the argument from prophecy, was discovered early in the present century; a German edition was published in 1907, and an English translation appeared in 1920.

Irenaeus found the criterion of truth in apostolicity. In his view, what was apostolic was *ipso facto* sound and authoritative in the religious life. This was no nebulous notion but a divine datum which came to definite expression in a corpus of sacred writings (the New Testament canon), in the credal *regula veritatis* ("rule of truth"), and in the episcopal succession that obtained in the most ancient churches, particularly in that at Rome. All genuine Christian doctrine must have stemmed from the Twelve and the Apostle Paul. As we have seen, exponents of Gnosticism claimed to be conversant with certain secret traditions concerning the incarnate Redeemer, and Marcion had set up a canon of scripture to replace the Old Testament, a canon which consisted of Luke's gospel and ten Pauline epistles in a duly expurgated edition.

Confronted with a situation of this kind, Irenaeus contended that the apostolic gospels of Matthew, Mark, Luke, and John, as commonly received in the churches, and the epistles of Paul, also in their generally accepted form, constituted the basis of any authentic Christian canon; and that such a body of author-

itative writings must be used to supplement, not to replace, the
canon of the Old Testament. Of the four gospels Irenaeus
writes:

The gospels cannot be more or less than these; for since there are
four regions of the world and four principal winds, and the church
is as seed sown in all the earth, and the gospel is the church's pillar
and ground and life-breath, it is natural that it should have four pillars, breathing incorruption from all quarters and kindling men into
life (*Adv. Haer.*, 3:11:8).

The Apostles had perfect knowledge, and their writings could
not possibly be improved upon; hence they must be taken as
they stand (*ibid.*, 3:1:1ff.).

Irenaeus realized, however, that the apostolic literature was
liable to diverging interpretations, and so he argued that for
correct exegesis it was necessary to have a guiding principle.
This he found in the rule of truth or faith (*ibid.*, 1:22:1; 3:4:2),
which seems to have been a brief statement used as a baptismal
creed in the church at Rome. Actually, it is not unlikely that
this *requla veritatis* was of recent origin and an early form of
so-called Apostles' Creed or Symbol; with its stress on monotheism, its antidocetic tendency, its assertion of coming divine
judgment, the confession has all the appearance of having been
devised specifically to exclude Marcionism. But Irenaeus evidently took it to contain the essentials of apostolic doctrine,
and in consequence he could think of the *regula* it supplied
as a normative hermeneutical principle.

But even this was not sufficient as a guarantee that truth
would be preserved, for the *regula* itself could be variously understood and variously applied. Hence Irenaeus contended that
the bishops of the churches of apostolic foundation represented
the final court of appeal. As the divinely appointed successors
of the Apostles they were the ultimate guardians of the genuine
tradition, and the episcopal condemnation of any doctrine
would be meant to protect believers from the baneful influence
of error and falsity. Irenaeus writes:

We are able to name those whom the apostles appointed bishops in the churches and to trace their succession to our own time. . . . If the apostles had known hidden mysteries which they privately imparted to the spiritually mature, they would have transmitted these to those to whom they committed the churches. For they wished their successors whom they entrusted with ecclesiastical government to be perfect and blameless in all things (*ibid.*, 3:3:1).

Clearly it follows from this that whatever new formulations of doctrine might be arrived at in the course of Christian history, the truth contained therein must have been implicit in the apostolic bedrock of the church's tradition.

Irenaeus thought of salvation both as deliverance from sin and as victory over death, and he combined a moralistic interpretation of Christianity (such as is stressed in the writings of Justin Martyr, for example) with a mystico-sacramental mode of interpretation (such as is prominent in the writings of Ignatius of Antioch). Irenaeus held that it was primarily through Christ's perfect obedience that humanity recovered the status it had lost through the disobedience of Adam. If in Adam man made a descent, in the incarnate Logos he made an ascent; and Irenaeus expressed this by maintaining that Christ effected a certain "recapitulation" of the course of human evolution. So he writes:

[Christ] recapitulated in himself the old formation. For as through the disobedience of one man sin entered, and death through sin, so also through the obedience of one man righteousness came in and will give life to those who once were dead (*ibid.*, 3:21:10).

Christ, being the representative of a restored humanity, was a second Adam, a compendious man, whose earthly career evinced "a parallelism with a difference" to the calamitous career of the Adam. As Adam was made of untilled soil, so Christ was born of a virgin woman (*ibid.*, 3:21:10); as Adam was tempted when he was not hungry, so Christ was tempted when he was hungry (*ibid.*, 5:21:2); as Adam fell on the sixth day, so Christ was put to death on the sixth day (*ibid.*, 5:23:2).

Thus the incarnate Logos accomplished an act of compensation that could redound to the benefit of the whole human race and deliver it from the power of Satan. But such an accomplishment could never have taken place had not Christ been inherently divine (*ibid.*, 4:33:4). It was because of his identity with the eternal Logos of God that he could overcome the satanic conqueror of man; and it was for the same reason that he could change human nature by infusing it with a death-negating vitality. Christ united the divine and the human, so that corruptible flesh became incorruptible (*ibid.*, 3:19:1). The transmutation of God into man, exemplified in the incarnation of the Logos, made possible the deification of humanity (*ibid.*, 4:33:4). The Logos became what we are, in order that we might become what he is (*ibid.*, 5, preface). In the view of Irenaeus, therefore, salvation is not only a moral release from the tyranny of sin, but also a substantial transmutation of human nature that makes it immortal and, in that sense, divine.

The likelihood is that in working out such a doctrine Irenaeus had certain Pauline ideas in mind: all things were summed up ("recapitulated") in Christ (Eph. 1:10); as in Adam all die, so in Christ all shall be made to live (I Cor. 15:22; Rom. 5:12ff.). This concept of human solidarity reappears in Irenaeus' doctrine that man's disobedience in the first Adam was made good by man's perfect obedience in the second Adam (*Adv. Haer.*, 5:16:2). Moreover, although Paul apparently did not contemplate man's deification, Irenaeus' further contention that Christ immortalized human nature (*ibid.*, 5:1:3), adumbrates the Pauline notion of the second Adam's quickening spirit (I Cor. 15:45). According to Irenaeus, Christ restored humanity to its pristine condition, enabling human development to resume its proper course. If the first Adam comprehended a fallen race, the second Adam summed up a renewed race. And pursuing this line of thought, Irenaeus felt that Jesus must have reached the age of fifty when he died: as the representative of a renewed mankind, he must have attained full maturity, passing through the various stages of human growth and consecrating them all (*Adv. Haer.* 2:22:4–6).

But there is an important difference in effective status between the two Adams, and this point is sometimes obscured by Irenaeus' mode of analogical reasoning. The effect of the first Adam's disobedience is (on the principles in question) necessarily transmitted in every act of human procreation, but such a transmission does not obtain in the case of Christ's obedience. Otherwise the ministrations of the church could be dispensed with. Unlike the deleterious consequences of the fall, the benefits of the incarnation are not inherited at birth but must be appropriated by each individual through his personal compliance with certain ethical and sacramental conditions. And the renewed humanity, of which Christ is the generative prototype, is a community founded upon faith, not a race in the strictly biological sense.

Irenaeus thought of the required ethical conditions in terms of repentance, faith, and obedience. To be saved from the power of sin the individual must have faith in the reality of God as the moral ruler of the universe, who rewards men according to their deserts, and he must have faith that God truly revealed himself in the scriptures and supremely in Christ. God set forth his requirements in the biblical Law made known to Moses and clarified in the life and work of Christ. The new dispensation inaugurated by Christ made it plain that the ceremonial regulations of the Mosaic Law were merely part of a temporary plan to train people in the practice of obedience. The moral or natural Law, the implications of God's permanent will for men, came to expression in the Ten Commandments, and his will was further elucidated in the ministry of Jesus (*Adv. Haer.*, 4:15ff.). When an individual recognizes all this he apprehends his own shortcomings, and in repentance he seeks to reproduce in his own life the obedience demonstrated in Christ.

The believer is aided in his efforts by the church. Not only do the sacraments communicate divine power through Christ—that is, a divine power which reinforces the will to righteousness; they also regenerate human nature in such a way that man becomes truly a child of the eternal and immutable God. Irenaeus writes:

As the bread of the earth, when it receives the invocation of God, is no longer ordinary bread but becomes the eucharist, being made of two things, an earthly and a heavenly, so also our bodies, when they receive the eucharist, are no longer corruptible but have the hope of resurrection unto eternal life (*ibid.*, 4:18:5; regarding baptism, see 1:21:1).

Thus, according to Irenaeus and to orthodox Christian teaching since his time, the salvation made available through the incarnation of the Logos is a benefit appropriated by the fulfillment of sacramental, as well as of ethical, conditions.

BIBLIOGRAPHY

Bousset, W. *Kyrios Christos.* 3rd ed. Göttingen: Vandenhoeck und Ruprecht, 1926.

Hitchcock, F. R. M. *Irenaeus of Lugdunum: A Study of His Teaching.* Cambridge: Cambridge University Press, 1914.

Wingren, Gustav. *Man and the Incarnation: A Study in the Biblical Theology of Irenaeus.* Philadelphia: Muhlenberg Press, 1959.

5 ‡ Western Theology: ‡ Tertullian and Cyprian

Tertullian was born of heathen parents at Carthage *circa* 155. He qualified in law and practiced in Rome for a time. After returning to Carthage he embraced Christianity and was soon ordained to the priesthood. He inclined to rigorism, and in 206 he definitely identified himself with Montanism, whereupon his disciplinarian principles became still more stringent. He died around the year 223. He was a prolific writer and an ardent controversialist; most of his Latin works survive in ninth-century manuscripts, but his much less numerous writings in Greek (a language he had acquired in the course of his education) have all been lost.

Tertullian was the first significant theologian to write in Latin, and he stands next to Augustine as the greatest thinker of the ancient Western church. His writing is vivid, often violent, in style, but he had a remarkable capacity for devising crisp formulations of Christian ideas. Although he fervidly attacked pagan philosophy in all its forms he was deeply influenced by Stoicism, whereas the great theologians of the East, like Origen, were much more affected by Platonism. Moreover, Tertullian's legalist approach suited the temper of Western Christianity and, partly through the precedent he established, Latin theology came to be permeated with forensic themes. Discussion tended to revolve around such matters as guilt and its transmission (original sin), personal responsibility (free will), man's debt to God (obligation to justice), direct and vicarious satisfaction (compensation)—matters which have obvious affiliations with jurisprudential notions concerning inheritance, contract, credit, and debit. And it is noteworthy that Western theologians came to be largely concerned with the question of the satisfaction to justice entailed by the atoning death of Jesus, whereas in Eastern christology it was the question of the incarnation of the Logos, the union of the eternal with the temporal, that figured as the focus of attention.

In his *Apologeticum* Tertullian refuted popular charges against the church, pointing out that the belief in one and only one God precludes participation in the worship of Caesar, and that "the blood of the martyrs is the seed of the church." The short treatise *De Testimonio Animae* ("On the Testimony of the Soul") defends the thesis that the human soul is essentially Christian by nature. In *De Praescriptione Haereticorum* ("On the Prescription of Heretics") it is argued that the scriptures belong exclusively to the church, the sole recipient of the divine truth handed down from Christ himself via the Apostles. The *Adversus Marcionem* ("Against Marcion") opposes the metaphysical dualism of Gnosticism and upholds the doctrine that Jesus was truly the fulfillment of the messianic prophecies contained in the Hebrew scriptures. In *Adversus Hermogenem* ("Against Hermogenes") much stress is laid on the omnipotence of God, who created the world out of nothing, not out of pre-existent matter.

The *Adversus Praxean* ("Against Praxeas") attacks what Tertullian believes is excessive emphasis on the unity of God in the teaching of Praxeas, an enemy of Marcionism who had migrated to Rome from Asia Minor and who had so much opposed the doctrine of the Logos as to declare that it was God the Father who suffered crucifixion on Calvary (Patripassianism). The term *Trinitas* occurs of God for the first time in extant Christian literature in section 2 of this work, and the formula *tres personae, una substantia* ("three persons, one substance") was taken up by exponents of orthodox doctrine. The three persons of the Trinity are thought of as possessing the same divine substance in common, though in different degrees or measures: "For the Father is the whole substance, but the Son is a derivation and part of the whole" (*Adv. Praxean*, 9). Thus subordinationism is involved: the Father, the Son, and the Holy Spirit are not strictly coequal, although they are all fundamentally divine. When the eternal Son became incarnate, his portion of the divine substance did not coalesce with human flesh; the two natures—the divine and the human—were conjoined in Jesus, not confused, so that he could be said to have possessed genuinely human attributes in their fullness (*ibid.*, 27).

Stoic monism was influential in Tertullian's vigorous opposition to Platonizing gnostic dualism; and in his psychological treatise *De Anima* ("On the Soul") he argues that the soul, so far from being of a wholly different essence from the body, is itself composed of a species of attenuated matter. Indeed, nothing exists that is not corporeal, and God could not have created physical things were he not in some sense material in constitution (*De Anima*, 7; *Adv. Praxean*, 7). As we should expect, Tertullian was a traducianist—that is, he held that the soul, like the body, is inherited from one's parents, not created by a special act of God at the moment of conception, and not eternally existent. But it can scarcely be said that he worked out his general theory with complete consistency: while he affirmed that the soul is indivisible and incapable of death or dissolution, he also argued that it is spatially extended in three dimensions; and on occasion he could so stress the peculiarities of the soul as to suggest that a radical dualism obtains between flesh and spirit (*De Anima*, 9ff.).

Tertullian believed that the fear of God is the spring of the good life (*De Paenitentia*, 7). The Creator is the supreme Lawgiver, and it is the proper function of the human creature to obey the commands of his Maker (*ibid.*, 4). The will of God should be humbly accepted, and to question the validity of a divine command is a sign of pride. Sometimes Tertullian pressed the concept of unquestioning obedience to the point of extreme paradox, as when he stated that the very absurdity of the doctrine that the Son of God died is a sure sign of its being worthy of credence (*De Carne Christi*, 5). Obviously, from such passages as this it is not to be inferred that Tertullian was some irresponsible enthusiast for a cult of Christian irrationalism. The contrary was the case. He frequently sought to demonstrate the reasonableness of Christian belief and practice. For example, in his criticism of Marcionism he contended that it was quite irrational to suppose that the physical universe had been created by an inferior God, and he resorted to the argument from design (the teleological proof) in his efforts to show that the world must have been produced by a supreme creative Intelligence; a single flower of the hedgerow testifies to no mean Creator (*Adv. Marcionem*, 1:11ff.).

Tertullian thought of God in his relation to humanity as the majestic Lawgiver who rewards the good and punishes the wicked, and he inclined to construe salvation as an exemption from the divine punishment that is deserved. He held that salvation is not handed out gratis. Exemption from punishment at the hand of God can be obtained only through repentance and baptism and through a subsequent life of obedience to the divine law. Repentance is not easy, however. Tertullian considered it the price that must be paid for God's forgiveness (*De Paenitentia*, 6). Apparently, true repentance is difficult because of original sin: death and other punishments are sanctions divinely imposed through the guilt of Adam, a guilt transmitted in every human act of procreation. Man is not wholly depraved by Adam's sin, and yet the fact remains that babies come into the world under the condemnation of God (*De Testimonio Animae*, 3).

Nevertheless, Tertullian did not advocate infant baptism. In fact his views on this question were oriented in an opposite direction, namely, that baptism should be postponed until maturity (*De Baptismo*, 3). This belief was not, as it seems, primarily due to a tendency to couple repentance with baptism, but to a conviction that certain post-baptismal sins could not be absolved more than once, even by the severest acts of penitential self-torture. As we saw in our discussion of Montanism, Tertullian was a strict disciplinarian. During his pre-Montanist days he maintained that mortal sins, such as fornication, homicide, and apostasy, committed after baptism, could be pardoned on one and only one occasion, when the requirements of canonical penance had been met (*De Paenitentia*, 7).

But in his Montanist period Tertullian did not even make that minimum allowance: mortal sins were deemed to be strictly mortal, or unpardonable (*De Pudicitia*, 1); and he vigorously attacked Callistus, the bishop of Rome, for declaring that fornication and adultery could be absolved after due compensation had been made through penance. It was in accordance with such stringent ecclesiastical disciplinarianism that some put off baptism until after they had married, feeling that married men are less likely to commit mortal sin than are bachelors. A number of people, including the emperor Constantine, were so anxious to be on the safe side that they even delayed baptism until they lay on their deathbeds, thereby leaving as little time as possible in which they might fall into mortal sin.

Tertullian deeply influenced his fellow countryman Cyprian, who in turn affected the course of Western theology, particularly concerning such matters as the nature of the church, the ministry, and the sacraments. A rhetorician, born around the year 200, Cyprian turned to Christianity when in his mid-forties. He was ordained, gained quick promotion, and became bishop of Carthage in 248. He fled during the autumn of the following year at the onset of the severe persecution under the emperor Decius. Many Christians purchased from the provincial authorities documents certifying that they had made sacrifices to the pagan divinities, when in reality they had not; others openly apostatized. It was widely held that martyrs gained a surplus of merit which they could make available to others, and after the persecution those who had suffered imprisonment and torture for their perseverance in the faith began to offer absolution cheaply to people who had succumbed.

On his return to Carthage Cyprian objected strongly; he called for greater stringency, and two local synods ratified his views. Similar disputes occurred in Rome, and the controversy led to the schism of Novatian, a capable theologian and a man of high principles, who headed the party in favor of strict discipline. Cyprian became involved in the quarrel; and, when the question of the rebaptism of schismatics was raised, he contended that no one outside the Catholic church could administer the sacraments: people who separated themselves from the main ecclesiastical body broke their connection with the episcopacy, through which alone divine grace could be transmitted from the apostolic source of human salvation. Stephen, the bishop of Rome, did not agree that heretics and schismatics should be rebaptised when they sought to return to the Catholic fold, and a lively correspondence between the two men ensued.

Cyprian was beheaded in 258 during the persecution initiated by the emperor Valerian. His collected correspondence (*Epistles*) contains (according to the numeration of G. Hartel's edition in the Vienna series of Latin patristic writings, *Corpus Scriptorum Ecclesiasticorum*, 1868–71) eighty-one letters, sixty-five of which are from Cyprian's own pen, the remainder being letters to him or to persons associated with him. Epistle 63 (by Cyprian) is of special interest in connection with the development of the Western doctrine of the eucharist. Among his treatises, *De Habitu Virginum* ("On the Dress of Virgins") extols chastity and stresses the importance of modesty in dress and behavior; *De Lapsis* ("On the Lapsed") deals with the discipline of apostates; *De Catholicae Ecclesiae Unitate* ("On the Unity of the Catholic Church") expounds the thesis that the unity of the church is realized through the institution of the episcopate in the apostolic succession; *De Opere et Eleemosynis* ("On Works and Alms") commends almsgiving as a means of obtaining divine grace.

At first Cyprian agreed with Tertullian that apostasy was

strictly a mortal sin (*Ep.* 16:2), but he came to adopt a more relaxed position, allowing that the lapsed could be readmitted into church membership after they had done a form of penance acceptable to the bishop. This last point was of great importance in Cyprian's theory, for he held that the episcopacy is the cohesive authority at the basis of the unity of the Catholic church (*Ep.* 55:24), and that the bishops alone, either directly or indirectly through the men they ordained, can mediate God's pardoning grace to the faithful (*Ep.* 63:14). "Outside the church there is no salvation" (*Ep.* 73:21). "No one can have God for his Father unless he has the Church for his Mother" (*De Cathol. Ecc. Unitate*, 6). "If any one is not with the Bishop he is not in the Church" (*Ep.* 66:8).

In some passages Cyprian apparently argued that the Roman bishop was the focal point of ecclesiastical unity, and that valid episcopal authority could be exercised only when a bishop was in communication with the pope (*Ep.* 43:5). But he resented Pope Stephen's demand that the African bishops must conform with the Roman practice of not requiring the rebaptism of schismatics, and in certain passages he seems to imply that the vital unity of the Catholic church is to be found in the regular episcopacy generally, acting through councils (see *De Unitate,* 5; *Ep.* 55:24). Thus, concerning the nature of episcopal authority, Cyprian rendered the teaching of Irenaeus and Tertullian into the definite terms of an ecclesiastical polity: the bishops are the guardians of divine truth and the disposers of the means of salvation, so that the episcopacy is an indispensable condition of the church's continuing existence.

With regard to the sacraments, they could be effectively administered only by the bishops or their duly appointed representatives; and baptism was not completed until the bishop had laid his hands upon the neophyte (*Ep.* 73:7–9). Cyprian agreed with Tertullian on the question of original sin, but, unlike the latter, he did not advocate the postponement of baptism. Doubtless this change was partly due to the fact that, despite the relative rigorism of his teaching, he disbelieved that mortal sins are strictly mortal: the sin inherited from Adam could be dealt with in baptism, and post-baptismal sins could be atoned for by the performance of duly prescribed penitential actions. It should be observed, however, that unlike Callistus and Stephen of Rome, Cyprian maintained that bishops and their vicars who committed mortal sins were *ipso facto* rendered permanently incompetent for the valid exercise of priestly functions (*Eps.* 67–68; see also Eusebius: *Eccles. Hist.*, 6:43:10). Thus something of Tertullian's stringency survived in the teaching of his great successor: while penance could now atone for the mortal sins of the laity, it had not the potency to restore a delinquent clergyman to the sacerdotal office.

Concerning the eucharist, Cyprian was, so far as we know, the first theologian to stress that the officiating priest somehow repeats Christ's sacrificial death (*Ep.* 63:4ff.). He did not repudiate the view prevalent in the East that the eucharist provided nutriment for the soul regenerated by baptism, but it was the rite's connection with the atoning death of Christ that evidently interested him; and this prepared the way for the eventual association of the eucharist with canonical penance.

BIBLIOGRAPHY

Campenhausen, H. E. von. *The Fathers of the Latin Church.* London: Black, 1964.

Faulker, J. A. *Cyprian the Churchman.* New York: Eaton and Mains, 1906.

Fichter, J. H. *Saint Cyprian: Early Defender of the Faith.* St. Louis, Mo.: B. Herder, 1942.

Morgan, James. *The Importance of Tertullian in the Development of Christian Dogma.* London: Kegan Paul, Trench, Trubner, 1928.

Roberts, R. E. *The Theology of Tertullian.* London: Epworth Press, 1924.

Short, C. *The Influence of Philosophy on the Mind of Tertullian.* London: E. Stock, 1933.

6 ‡ Eastern Theology: ‡ Clement and Origen

Clement was born *circa* A.D. 150, probably in Athens. He traveled and studied under Pantaenus, a converted Stoic and head of the catechetical school at Alexandria, the city that had become the cultural center of the Hellenistic world. He succeeded Pantaenus as head of the school in 190, but twelve years later he fled during the persecution ordered by the emperor Septimius Severus and was succeeded by his famous pupil, Origen. He died around the year 215.

His principal works are: *Protrepticus*, an "Exhortation" to the Greeks, in which he commends Christianity and seeks to make clear its superiority to paganism; *Paedagogus* ("Instructor"), a practical treatise on Christian manners and morals, in which he addresses himself to the masses; and *Stromateis* ("Miscellanies"), a number of studies in which he considers various exegetical, ethical, and theological matters.

Although Clement frequently thought of sin in terms of ignorance, and of divine revelation in terms of education, he differed from the radical Gnostics in maintaining that confidence in the validity of the Christian doctrine as proclaimed by the church is in itself sufficient for human salvation (*Paed.*, 1:6). He repudiated the excessive intellectualism of extremist Gnosticism, and he showed that the most ardent of the Gnostics must postulate the validity of their first principles, the unproved assumptions at the basis of their doctrine (*Strom.*, 5:1; 2:4). On the other hand, Clement did not teach that simple faith represents the highest form of the Christian life. While genuinely devout people live by faith in accordance with the rule of the church (*ibid.*, 7:7), philosophical knowledge can fortify trust and can lead to spiritual advancement (*ibid.*, 1:20; 2:6; 6:14). There is definite progress in the transitions from paganism to Christian faith, from faith to knowledge, and from knowledge to charity (*ibid.*, 7:10), and the highest stage of the spiritual life is reached when knowledge is informed and sustained by Godlike love. This means that with the attainment of Christian perfection, the individual is neither restrained by the fear that God will punish the wicked nor motivated by the hope that he will reward the obedient, for devotion has become a free and spontaneous expression of a life wholly consecrated to the divine reality, and as such it is quite disinterested (*ibid.*, 7:11). Clement greatly stressed the importance of asceticism in the process of spiritual advancement: the true Gnostic seeks to be like God (*ibid.*, 2:19), and since passionlessness is a divine characteristic (*ibid.*, 4:23; 6:9) the ideal life involves freedom from desire.

After the fashion of Justin Martyr, Clement sometimes argued that philosophy was a divine gift which, like the Mosaic Law in relation to the Jews, functioned as a tutor to bring the Greeks to the larger truth of Christianity (*ibid.*, 1:5). The Logos was universally operative, revealing God's will to all men (*ibid.*, 1:13). At other times, however, Clement asserted that whatever truth the Greek thinkers possessed they must have obtained from the Hebrew scriptures, a contention to be found in the writings of Tatian and other apologists, as well as in the works of Philo, the influential Jewsh thinker of the first century A.D., who effected a philosophical synthesis of Judaism and Hellenism.

Clement made little of the concept of original sin, although (perhaps under Pauline influence) he did occasionally allude to the deleterious consequences of Adam's disobedience (*Protrept.*,

11). He assumed that man is ignorant (*Strom.*, 1:17) and hence in need of divine education. Man's mind is darkened, and it was pre-eminently to illumine the human understanding that the Logos became incarnate (*Protrept.*, 1). God in himself is wholly transcendent, beyond space and time, and quite outside the range of the defining powers of the human mind (*Strom.*, 5:11); and it is only through the agency of the Logos that the divine Being is creative and can enter into a sympathetic relationship with creaturely existence (*ibid.*, 4:25; 7:2).

Origen was born of Christian parents in Alexandria *circa* 185. He studied under Clement. His father suffered martyrdom in the persecution of the year 202, but Origen was prevented from seeking a like fate by his mother, who hid his clothes while he lay in bed. When the persecution was over he succeeded his master (who had fled Alexandria) as director of the catechetical school. He became extremely ascetical in his manner of life, and eventually he castrated himself in literal compliance with the saying of Jesus recorded in Matt. 19:12.

According to a report preserved by Eusebius (*Eccles. Hist.*, 6:19:5), Origen studied under Ammonius Saccas, the founder of Neoplatonism, but it may well be that the reference is really to another Origen. He traveled widely and went to Rome and Arabia. There were riots at Alexandria in 215, and he visited Palestine, where he received invitations to preach from the bishops of Caesarea and Jerusalem. But he had not been ordained, and Demetrius, bishop of Alexandria, raised objections. Origen returned to his native city and spent the next dozen years or so in writing. In 230 he went to Palestine again, and he took holy orders at Caesarea. Demetrius contended that this was a breach of discipline and took action against him, depriving him of his teaching post. Origen then settled in Caesarea and founded a school there. During the persecution under the emperor Decius (249–50) he suffered imprisonment and tortures which undermined his health. He died *circa* 254.

Origen was an even more prolific writer than his master,

Clement, and he not infrequently put forward ideas which seem to be inconsistent with his fundamental doctrines—for example, his view that the death of Christ was a ransom paid to the Devil (see his *Commentary on Matthew*, 13:8–9). But many of his works have been lost, doubtless owing partly to the fact that he was later suspected of heresy; his doctrines were condemned on more than one occasion by official representatives of Catholicism. Those of his writings that have come down to us usually are extant only in part or in Latin translations. Origen was both a great biblical scholar and a daring speculative theologian in the Platonic tradition. His most important biblical work was the *Hexapla*, an edition of the Old Testament containing the Hebrew text, a Greek transliteration, and four different Greek translations (including the LXX), all arranged in six parallel columns. He also wrote numerous biblical commentaries, most of which have been lost in whole or in part, and a large number of sermons.

Origen's apologetic work *Contra Celsum* ("Against Celsus"), apparently published toward the end of his life, was a reply in eight books to a criticism made in about 178 by Celsus, a Platonist philosopher; the earliest extant manuscript dates from the thirteenth century and is in the Vatican library. Origen's greatest theological work was *De Principiis* ("On First Principles"), in four books, a comprehensive essay in constructive speculation concerning God, creation, and destiny. It is characterized by much metaphysical adventurousness, and the argumentation is diffuse and not always consistent; it largely determined the course of subsequent christological controversy. The Greek text has been almost wholly lost, but we have the Latin translation of Rufinus (which, however, is by no means always satisfactory) and parts of Jerome's more literal rendering. Also extant are considerable sections of Origen's commentaries on the gospels of Matthew and John and (in the Latin of Rufinus) of those on the Song of Songs and the Epistle to the Romans. He freely utilized the allegorical method of exegesis, not only to bring out supposed hidden meanings of scripture (he argued, for instance, that the Song of Songs evinces the doctrine of the church as the bride of Christ), but also to overcome historical discrepancies and moral difficulties, such as the barbarism entailed in parts of the Old Testament.

As we gather from the preface to *De Principiis*, Origen held that saving faith consists essentially in the acceptance of the basic teachings handed down by the church through the apostolic succession, teachings which are more or less covered in the *regula veritatis* of Irenaeus. He thus interpreted faith intellectually, and this was not unnatural for a thinker who stood in the Platonic tradition; he also postulated a mystical faculty of cognition by which the finite individual can come to apprehend God directly (*De Princ.*, 1:1:9). Moreover, Origen agreed with his master that rigorous academic training is necessary for spiritual progress and for the refining of religious discernment. Faith needs to be supplemented by philosophical acumen, and it is the function of the theologian to elucidate the implications of the deliverances of faith and to relate them to first principles. According to one passage (*ibid.*, 4:2:4), scripture has a somatical or surface meaning, a psychical or ethical meaning, and a pneumatical or spiritual meaning; and at the highest stage of the Christian life the individual probes beneath the surface and plumbs the depths of divine truth.

Origen maintained that God in himself is one and indivisible, the spiritual Source of all existence, the Supreme Being who cannot be known per se but only as the Author of the universe (*ibid.*, 1:1:6). The Logos (or Son, or Christ) is a differentiation within the nature of God, necessitated to mediate the transition from the oneness of the Godhead to the manyness of the world in the process of creation (*ibid.*, 1:2:1ff.). That is, the Logos is the agent of God's creating and revealing activities; and since God must have objects on which to actualize or fulfill his omnipotence, he is eternally productive. Hence the world and the Logos must both exist from everlasting to everlasting, and yet they are quite different in inner constitution, for, whereas creatures are made out of nothing, the Logos is continuously generated out of the essence of God: the Son is eternally begotten of the Father.

Besides the Logos, there is a further differentiation within the Godhead, namely, the Holy Spirit, whose function it is to inspire the followers of Jesus to holiness of life (*ibid.*, 1:3:1ff.). Origen's thought tended to be nebulous on the subject of the third person of the Trinity, and he refrained from defining the mode of divine operation by which the Spirit becomes existent (*ibid.*, 1:3:3), Moreover, while (according to Rufinus' rendering) Origen stated that the members of the Trinity enjoy an equal status (*ibid.*, 1:3:7), the Father as unbegotten would seem to be ontologically superior to the Son or Logos; also, the notion of the instrumentality of the Son in the work of creation suggests a certain subordinationism within the Godhead. It was the subordinationist aspect of Origen's teaching that appealed to Arius (see Chapter 9); and the concept of the eternal generation of the Logos out of the essence of God became central in the christology of the ecumenical creeds. So a situation was to arise in which heterodox and orthodox alike could find support in Origen.

Although he held that God's creative activity is everlastingly going on, and that finite creatures always exist, Origen did not believe in the eternity of the material universe. God created a great society of finite spirits, all equal in endowment and status. Some used their freedom aright and are the good angels, but the rest went astray, and it is such precosmic disobedience that is symbolized in the biblical story of Adam (*C. Celsum*, 4:40). The very bad became demonic, while the not-so-bad became human beings, the physical world having been created for their discipline and correction. Thus life in the flesh is a form of purgatory, and apart from the material universe there are other purgatorial spheres (*De. Princ.*, 2:9:1; 3:5:1ff.).

Origen argued that the Logos became flesh in order to aid

man in the recovery of his pristine state of unblemished communion with God (*ibid.*, 4:31:1ff.). The Holy Spirit also promotes salvation by inspiring men to holiness of life (*ibid.*, 1:3:8). Before becoming incarnate the Logos coalesced with an angel, and the result of this union was the soul of the human Jesus; through living an earthly life of obedience his soul became wholly divine; that is, presumably, the deity of the pre-existent Logos was recovered (*ibid.*, 2:6:3ff.).

Origen believed neither in the resurrection of the flesh nor in the everlastingness of the material world; in true Platonic style he was convinced that the things which are seen are temporal and that the things which are not seen are eternal—a notion expressed in the writings of the Apostle Paul (II Cor. 4:18); and it should also be noticed that Paul had asserted that the resurrection body is of a spiritual, not a carnal, nature (I Cor. 15:42 ff.). Accordingly, Origen was opposed to the materialism of millenarian expectation—the belief that there would be a golden age on earth under the rule of the returned Messiah (*De Princ.*, 2:11:2). But it is not to be supposed that Origen was pessimistic in any final sense. On the contrary, he had a lively eschatological hope and envisaged a time when the precosmic paradise would be regained, when reformatory action of every kind would be at an end, and when all men and all demons—including the Devil himself—would be redeemed (*ibid.* 1:6:1 ff.).

BIBLIOGRAPHY

Armstrong, A. H., ed. *The Cambridge History of Later Greek and Early Medieval Thought.* Cambridge: Cambridge University Press, 1967.

Campenhausen, H. E. von. *The Fathers of the Greek Church.* London: Black, 1963.

Chadwick, H. *Early Christian Thought and the Classical Tradition.* Oxford: Clarendon Press, 1966.

Daniélou, J. *Origen.* New York: Sheed and Ward, 1955.

Osborn, E. F. *The Philosophy of Clement of Alexandria.* Cambridge: Cambridge University Press, 1957.

Rahner, Hugo. *Greek Myths and Christian Mystery.* New York: Harper and Row, 1963.

Rist, J. M. *Eros and Psyche: Studies in Plato, Plotinus, and Origen.* Toronto: University of Toronto Press, 1964.

II ‡ THE ORTHODOX ‡ CREEDS

7 ‡ The Alliance of Church and State: Constantine

After a relatively long period of peace (beginning in 260), during which the church continued to gain in numbers and strength, Diocletian, the senior of the four imperators, initiated in the year 303 the last and most prolonged of the persecutions. Three edicts against Christianity were issued, in February, May, and November, and a fourth was published by Maximian in April of the next year, while Diocletian was ill. The persecution continued after Diocletian's retirement in 305, and Maximinus Daia issued a fifth edict of persecution in 308. But the repressive action varied in intensity according to the attitudes of the different emperors; thus in the West Constantius was lenient, and in the East Maximinus was severe.

The church as a whole withstood the onslaught, and people generally sickened of the cruelties. Galerius issued an edict of toleration in 311, shortly before his death, and Maximinus temporarily relented in 312. Constantine (the son of Constantius) and Licinius tended to join forces, and so did Maximinus and Maxentius. In 312 Constantine, having crossed the Alps, defeated Maxentius in a battle near the Milvian Bridge, and early in the following year he conferred with Licinius in Milan, where a rescript (popularly but erroneously known as the Edict of Milan) was drawn up, granting complete religious toleration and the restoration of all confiscated ecclesiastical property (see Eusebius, *Eccles. Hist.*, 10:5:2–14). Licinius vanquished Maximinus later in 313, so that the provisions of the rescript became effective in the East as well as in the West, and, with the overthrow of Licinius in 323, Constantine became sole emperor. Thus the church had come triumphantly through nearly three centuries of storm and stress, but it was now destined to become increasingly involved in the affairs of the world. Its whole temper suddenly underwent a profound change. The sense of a heavenly citizenship, so characteristic of primitive Christianity, weakened, and ecclesiastical concerns were more and more subjected to state direction.

Constantine's policy was to achieve strength through unity, and with this end in view he sought to fortify the cohesive forces of Catholicism. There was one imperium, and there should be one religion solidly behind that one secular authority. Hence the impartial tolerance evinced in the rescript of 313 rapidly gave way to discrimination against paganism and heresy, and this kind of process—apart from a brief interruption during the reign of Julian the Apostate (361–63)—continued until the orthodox Christian state was established under Theodosius I (379–95). But even under Constantine imperial sanctions, both negative and positive, were applied against those who persisted in dissenting from prevailing Catholic belief and practice.

Soon after the conference with Licinius at Milan early in 313, Constantine began to patronize the church, and in return the church was doubtless expected to be the religious support and stay of the Empire. Under imperial favor the number of church adherents grew rapidly. By an edict of 319 the clergy were exempted from burdensome taxation, and in 321 Sunday was proclaimed a holiday throughout the Empire. Churches were built or repaired at public expense; action was taken against heathenism; preference was shown for Christians in the appointment of provincial governors. Byzantium, in the most Christianized region of the Empire, was reconstructed on a magnificent scale and, under the name Constantinople, became the imperial capital in 330.

The great persecution had divided the church in Latin North Africa, and this quickly led to imperial intervention. Rigorists there, whose thinking was in the tradition of Tertullian and Cyprian, argued that the consecration of Caecilian as bishop of Carthage in the year 311 was invalid, on the ground that the ceremony had been conducted by Felix of Aptunga. They contended that Felix was a *traditor*—that is, a churchman who on demand had handed over ecclesiastical documents to the persecutors. As in the case of the Novatianist controversy in Rome some sixty years earlier (after the Decian persecution), the advocates of stringency elected a counter-bishop whom they considered to be the true holder of the office. This was a man named Majorinus; Donatus was his successor, and the movement came to be designated by his name.

Constantine's favors excluded the Donatists, and they protested. A synod assembled at Arles in southern Gaul, and Donatism was condemned. A further appeal was made, and in 316 Constantine himself decided against the Donatists. But they stood by their conviction, whereupon the emperor resorted to compulsive action. This involved a remarkable change of roles: within three years of the enunciation of the principle of toleration at Milan, the persecuted had become persecutors. The repressive measures were renounced five years later, but they were taken up again in 347 under the emperor Constans, and yet again in 405, when Augustine had become involved in the controversy. The Donatists refused to yield, maintaining that the Catholic church was infected with mortal sin and that they alone represented valid Christianity. They claimed the support of Cyprian for their rulings, and converts from Catholicism to Donatism were baptized afresh. Donatism survived until the Moslem conquest of North Africa in the years around 700, and Christianity in the region was considerably weakened by the internal strife.

Dissension in the East on more purely speculative matters led to further intervention on the part of the state. There were several reasons for the outbreak of the controversy, which concerned christology, and these included the rivalry between the theological schools of Antioch and Alexandria, and the fact that the Trinitarian teachings of Origen contained conflicting tendencies, one subordinationist, the other egalitarian. At the center of the dispute was Arius, a presbyter in Alexandria, who had studied under Lucian of Antioch and who worked out a form of subordinationist christological theory, according to which the Logos is less than God. The conflict intensified. Constantine was appealed to, and in consequence a general council was convened and held at Nicea in Asia Minor in the year 325. Although only six out of about three hundred delegates present at the conference were from the West, the gathering came to be known as the first of the seven ecumenical ("world-wide") councils of the church.

Constantine (though unbaptized) presided, and he hoped for a credal formulation on which the rival factions could agree. He wanted conciliation, recognizing that strength lies in unity. But his hopes were not to be fulfilled; from the standpoint of his political purpose, the council ended in complete failure, for, so far from effecting a conciliation, the creed finally adopted intensified antagonisms by excluding the Arians as exponents of a spurious type of Christianity. The fact is that none of the ecumenical councils held between 325 and 787 promoted the cause of unification. What they did was largely to propound and ratify credal statements that were directed against certain tendencies of thought operative within the Christian sphere. Hence the ecumenical creeds of the church cannot be properly understood without some acquaintance with the doctrines they were originally meant to repudiate.

There were several ways in which Constantine's policy profoundly affected the subsequent course of doctrinal development.

In the first place, under imperial patronage it became easy— even advantageous—to be a Christian, and all too soon perhaps the majority of church members were Christian in name only. By way of reaction, many of the more devout took to the ascetic life, and monasticism grew. This in turn contributed to the establishment of a dual standard: there were certain minimum requirements for the mass of adherents, but for the minority (the "religious") there existed the so-called counsels of perfection. The spiritual elite took the vows of poverty, chastity, and obedience and thereby sought to recapture something of the seriousness that had characterized Christianity generally during the earlier centuries.

In the second place, the *disciplina arcani* ("discipline of the secret") was gradually relaxed, and by about 500 it seems to have disappeared altogether. When Christianity was a minority movement in a hostile world the rule seems to have been that only members of the church could be present at the eucharist, and so the noninitiated who attended services were sent away before the sacred rite actually began (hence perhaps the term "mass" from the Latin verb *mittere*, "to send"). But with the alliance of church and state, it became widely held that imperial citizenship entailed allegiance to the church, and the idea apparently gained ground that Christianity of the average type was ethnic—that is, something which, like one's mother tongue, is acquired through birth and upbringing, rather than by a personal decision involving repentance and faith.

In the third place, Constantine's resolve to shift the imperial capital from Rome to Byzantium left the bishop of Rome as the most important figure in the West, and from 330 onward the papal office came to have increasing temporal or secular importance. Eventually, in the eighth century, the Western hierarchy allied itself with the powerful Frankish monarchy, and on Christmas Day in 800 Pope Leo III crowned Charlemagne the first emperor of the Holy Roman Empire, an act which could be construed to signify that the bishop of Rome had the God-given authority to make and unmake kings. The foundation of a Western imperium contributed to the stresses and strains of the relationship between East and West, and it was probably during the ninth century that the Donation of Constantine was drawn up, obviously with a view to strengthening the claims of the papacy to secular dominion. Constantine is represented as handing over to Pope Sylvester I (314–35) and his successors—besides ecclesiastical primacy over the ancient Eastern patriarchates of Alexandria, Antioch, Constantinople, and Jerusalem—temporal authority over Italy and all the Western provinces. This fabrication helped to further papal power and prestige during the middle ages; and it was not until the fifteenth century that the document was proved to be a forgery (by Lorenzo Valla and Nicholas of Cusa).

In the fourth place, the process of defining orthodoxy came to be largely determined by the extraecclesiastical pressure of the state, so that the outcome of theological discussions often had an immediate political significance. Those who failed to conform with official standards of belief were not merely placed under the ban of the church but were exposed to charges of treachery to the state—as were *all* Christians prior to the reign of Constantine. In the action against the Donatists of North Africa and in the rejection of Arianism at Nicea, one may discern the beginnings of a development which culminated in the forcible establishment of the orthodox Christian state under Theodosius I in the later years of the fourth century.

BIBLIOGRAPHY

Foakes-Jackson, F. J. *The History of the Christian Church from the Earliest Times to A.D. 461*. 8th ed. Chicago: W. P. Blessing, 1927.

Lietzmann, Hans. *From Constantine to Julian*. New York: Scribner's, 1950.

Stevenson, J., ed. *Creeds, Councils, and Controversies: Documents Illustrative of the History of the Church, A.D. 337–461*. London: Society for Promoting Christian Knowledge, 1966.

8 ‡ *Monarchianism*

Jewish faith is strictly monotheistic: God is essentially one, and there is no other God than he. Christianity arose within Judaism and originally shared its rigorous belief in the unity of the Supreme Being, although very soon, with the emergence of the idea that Christ was a divine Savior who had descended into human life, a theistic complication was introduced into Christian thought. Already the Apostle Paul could testify that Christ existed in the heavenly sphere prior to his assumption of human form in the person of Jesus of Nazareth (Phil. 2:1 ff.); hence at an early date the church exposed itself to the possibility of a Jewish charge that its doctrine was in some sense idolatrous, calling for the worship of a being other than the one true God. As we have seen, certain early Jewish Christians, the Ebionites and the Nazarenes, evidently did not share the high christology of Paul and others. Besides abiding by the regulations of the Mosaic Law, they maintained that Jesus, who was born in the ordinary manner, came to enjoy a unique filial relationship with God at his baptism (cf. the quotation from Psalm 2:7 in the Western reading of Luke 3:22—"today I have begotten thee"—which may be a formal declaration of adoption, and which appears in the Revised Standard Version in a footnote).

As the etymology would lead us to expect, monarchian theology stresses the unity of God's governance of the world; and it was ultimately rejected by the church because of its failure to recognize the distinctive personal reality of Christ as the eternal Son or divine Logos. Modern historians usually distinguish two species of the monarchian type of teaching, namely, Adoptionist (or Dynamic) Monarchianism and Modalist Monarchianism. According to the former, a divine power (Greek: *dynamis*) invaded the personality of Jesus in a way which made him God's Son in a special sense, whereas according to the latter, the incarnate Christ was a mode of God's self-manifesting activity in the world. The Ebionites and Cerinthus were early representatives of Adoptionist Monarchianism.

The term "monarchianism" was first employed with a christological meaning by Tertullian in a polemical work (*Adv. Praxean*, 3–4); and for him, an exponent of a Logos christology, the expression designated a heretical doctrine that exalted the unity of God at the expense of the trinity of persons subsisting within the essence of the Godhead. Moreover, as we gather from Epiphanius (*Heresies*, 51), the word *alogi* was used of certain Monarchians. These people were apparently flourishing in Asia Minor in the seventies of the second century, and they strongly attacked the Montanists, who made much of the Johannine conception of the Spirit of Truth; the *alogi* rejected the Fourth Gospel as nonapostolic, and with it repudiated not only the doctrine of the Spirit of Truth but also the Logos christology which comes to its earliest expression in John 1:1 ff. The term *alogi* could signify "irrational (or stupid) men" as well as "men who disbelieve in the Logos christology"—a double meaning that was not overlooked by supporters of the Johannine doctrine.

Among the leading Dynamic Monarchians of the second and third centuries were Theodotus, Artemon, and Paul of Samosata; and the most famous Modalists were Noetus, Praxeas, and Sabellius. Unfortunately our knowledge of the teaching of these thinkers is fragmentary and indirect, based largely upon evidence supplied by writers of the opposite camp, whose doctrines came to be officially regarded as orthodox.

Theodotus, a leather merchant, apparently traveled to Rome from Byzantium in the nineties of the second century, and he publicly argued that Jesus was an ordinary human being upon whom the divine Spirit descended at his baptism, thereby equipping him for his saving mission as the supernatural Christ. Such teaching was condemned by Pope Victor (189–98), and followers of the leather merchant (among whom was a banker, also named Theodotus) were excommunicated by Pope Zephyrinus (198–217). Toward 235 Theodotianism was again prominently represented, this time by Artemon, and he also suffered ecclesiastical condemnation (Hippolytus, *Heresies*, 7:35–36; 10:23–24; Eusebius, *Eccles. Hist.*, 5:28–29; Epiphanius, *Heresies*, 54–55).

Paul of Samosata became an important official in the administration of Zenobia, queen of Palmyra, and about the year 260 he was appointed bishop of Antioch. He emphasized the reality of Christ's human nature, and he anticipated Nestorian teaching in maintaining that, although there can be agreement of will and purpose between different personalities, two self-conscious individuals cannot merge into one as, for example, two drops of water can coalesce to form one drop. Jesus was ethically, not substantially, one with God, his will acting in harmony with the divine will. On the other hand, the eternal Logos or Reason was taken to be an impersonal faculty of the same essence of God, but not differentiated so as to constitute a separate divine personality or hypostasis. Through the activity of the Logos, Jesus was endowed with divine potency in a superabundant measure; this enabled him to conduct his life in complete accord with the divine purpose, and thereby qualified him for his exalted mission as the Savior and Judge of humanity.

Paul's teaching was condemned at synods held in Antioch around 260, but through Zenobia's support he retained his office until 272, when the queen's forces were defeated by Emperor Aurelian. On the advice of the bishops of Italy, Aurelian approved the Antiochene verdicts, and so Paul had to vacate his see. The use to which the latter had put the term *homoousios* ("of the same essence as") brought this epithet into disrepute in certain circles, for it came to be supposed that an assertion of a sameness of essence within the Godhead meant a oneness of hypostasis or personality, and this conflicted with the Trinitarianism of the prevailing Logos christology (Eusebius, *Eccles. Hist.*, 7:27–30; the relevant fragments are collected in H. de Riedmatten, *Les Actes du procès de Paul de Samosate*, pp. 135 ff.).

Turning now to Modalist Monarchianism, we learn from one of Tertullian's polemical works (*Adv. Praxean*) that in Rome during the nineties of the second century Praxeas, a native of Asia Minor and a persuasive opponent of Montanism, so stressed in his teaching the essential unity of God as to argue that the heavenly Father had himself suffered on Calvary: the fullness of the Godhead became incarnate in Jesus, temporarily assuming a redemptive role for the salvation of humanity. "*Patrem crucifixit*" ("He has crucified the Father"), declared Tertullian with characteristic vividness. Noetus also represented Patripassianism in Rome a few years later, according to Hippolytus (*Heresies*, 9:7–10; *Contra Noetum*). He rejected the Logos doctrine and understood the teaching of the prologue to the Fourth Gospel in an allegorical sense.

The most important of the Modalist Monarchians was Sabellius, who taught in Rome around 215. In his view the only differentiations within the Godhead were successive and diverse modes of divine activity: in the *prosōpon* (or role) of the Father, God operated creatively; in the *prosopon* of Christ, God operated redemptively; in the *prōsopon* of the Holy Spirit, God operated sanctifyingly. Sabellius' teaching was condemned, and after his excommunication he went to Libya and Egypt, where he attracted a not uninfluential following.

Hippolytus (*c.* 166–236), like Tertullian, was a rigorist, and opposed the bishops of Rome—especially Pope Callistus (217–23)—in their relaxation of the penitential system; also, like Tertullian, he vigorously opposed Monarchianism. A presbyter in Rome, he was the last important theologian living in the capital to write in Greek, and during the earlier part of the third century he was the city's ablest exponent of the Logos christology. Popes Zephyrinus and Callistus were evidently Modalists, and Callistus sought to evade the charge of Patripassianism by arguing that since God incarnate alone is the divine Son, and God unincarnate alone is the heavenly Father, it would be wrong to say that the Father died on the cross (Hippolytus, *Heresies*, 9:2).

This attempt at compromise failed to settle the issue, and so Callistus proceeded to take practical action, excommunicating both Sabellius and Hippolytus, the latter being accused of ditheism (a belief in the existence of two gods). Hippolytus, however, seems to have had enough support to set himself up as counter-pope, and after the death of Callistus he continued to attack his papal successors, namely, Urban (223–30) and Pontianus (230–35). During the persecution under Emperor Maximinus (235–38) Hippolytus and Pontianus were both banished as slaves to the mines in Sardinia, where they died. Hippolytus' prestige may have increased after his enforced exile, and under Pope Fabian (236–50) his body (along with that of his rival) was brought back to Rome, where he was soon venerated as a martyr of the Catholic faith.

Hippolytus' most important theological treatise was his *Refutation of All Heresies*. He regarded the Logos as the divine instrument of creation, and he seems to have held that it was originally impersonal. Personality was somehow acquired when the Logos became flesh—in which case the intrinsic character of the Godhead is not such as to exclude change or development. Thus Hippolytus did not wholly anticipate orthodox teaching.

Novatian, the founder of the rigorist schism after the Decian persecution (249–50), was the first considerable theologian at Rome to write in Latin, and in about 245 he published a work entitled *De Trinitate* ("On the Trinity"), which furthered the cause of the Logos christology in the West. He was seemingly much under the influence of Tertullian who, as we have seen, had defined the Trinity in terms of "three persons" and "one substance."

Dionysius, bishop of Alexandria (247–64), in his polemics against Sabellianism, had inclined to subordinate the Logos to the divine Creator and Father, and this aroused adverse criticism from his namesake, Dionysius, bishop of Rome (259–68). In the course of their correspondence, the latter used the term *homoousios* of the Logos in what came to be recognized eventually as the orthodox sense: Father, Son, and Holy Spirit are distinct individualities within the divine essence, and they are such as to enjoy an equality of status within the economy of the Godhead.

Thus it was principally through the writings of Tertullian, Hippolytus, Novatian, and Pope Dionysius that a nonsubordinationist form of the Logos christology triumphed over Monarchianism in the doctrine of the Western church.

BIBLIOGRAPHY

Bardy, G. *Paul de Samosate, étude historique.* Louvain: Spicilegium Sacrum Louvaniense, 1923.

Loofs, F. *Paulus von Samosata.* Leipzig: J. C. Henrichs, 1924.

McGiffert, A. C. *The God of the Early Christians.* New York: Scribner's, 1924.

9 ‡ *Arianism and the Nicene Christology*

The general meeting of church representatives convened by Emperor Constantine in 325 was the first of a series of ecumenical councils, which may be conveniently listed at this point: (1) The First Council of Nicea, 325; (2) The First Council of Constantinople, 381; (3) The Council of Ephesus, 431; (4) The Council of Chalcedon, 451; (5) The Second Council of Constantinople, 553; (6) The Third Council of Constantinople, 680; (7) The Second Council of Nicea, 787. The first six councils were concerned with christological problems, the last one with Iconoclasticism—that is, with the question of the legitimacy of the use of images in Christian worship. Besides being dominated by theologians of the East, the discussions in each case were subjected to political pressures, and it is noteworthy that all the meetings took place in or near the Eastern seat of the imperial government.

Constantine sought strength through unity, and when acute christological controversy broke out in the East he strove to conciliate the contending parties. Attempts at personal mediation failed, and in consequence he called the council which produced the Nicene Creed (325). This statement became the basic standard of orthodoxy in East and West, but only after a struggle that lasted for several decades. It interpreted the Logos christology in such a way as to exclude both Monarchianism and Arianism.

Arius (born about 250, perhaps in Libya) studied under Lucian of Antioch, and in 312 he was ordained to the priesthood at Alexandria, where he became a popular preacher. Toward 320 he began to argue for a radically subordinationist form of the Logos christology. Controversy broke out, and Arius appealed to other former pupils of Lucian. Although he secured the support of Eusebius of Nicomedia, an important figure in the Eastern church, he was condemned at a synod held in Alexandria.

The emperor tried to mediate a settlement and sent Hosius, bishop of Cordova, to Alexandria for this purpose. The attempt failed—hence the convening of the First Ecumenical Council at Nicea in 325. Mainly through the efforts of Athanasius, a deacon and the able secretary of Alexander (bishop of Alexandria), Arius was condemned and banished. But Eusebius of Nicomedia had much influence in the imperial court, and Arius was recalled from exile. Athanasius (who had succeeded Alexander in 328) was ordered to receive him back into the church, but he refused to do so and was punished by being exiled to Trier (336). However, Arius collapsed suddenly and died on the eve of the day appointed for his official readmission into the church.

According to the central thesis of Arius, the Logos is not eternal, but was created out of nothing at a certain point in time to be an instrument for the creation of the world. Hence it is not *homoousios* with (of the same essence as) God, but rather shares the ontological status of creaturely existence. The Logos emerged into being to become a *tertium quid* between God and the world, and eventually assumed human embodiment in the person of the historical Christ, whose mind or soul the Logos was. Because of Jesus' surpassing righteousness God honored him with the title "Son of God," and he could be venerated as such, despite the fact that he was not strictly of the divine essence. For there was a time when the Logos did not exist.

Constantia, Constantine's sister, inclined to Arianism, and through her influence, and that of Eusebius of Nicomedia, Constantine turned against Athanasius in 334.

Athanasius was born at Alexandria *circa* 295 and was educated at the catechetical school there. As we have seen, he became bishop of Alexandria in 328. He consistently opposed Arianism, and in consequence his career was a checkered one, and his official standing varied in accordance with prevailing imperial attitudes. He was exiled under Constantine in 336, but returned in 337 when Constantine died. In 339 he fled to Rome, where he found support among the Italian bishops. He returned in 346 through the influence of the Western emperor Constans, but Constantius, the Eastern emperor, banished him in 356. Julian the Apostate, discovering that Athanasius was back in Alexandria, exiled him in 362. He returned on Julian's death in 363, but suffered a further period of banishment in 365–66 under the Eastern emperor Valens. Thus Anthanasius showed great tenacity of purpose. And it was largely due to his influence that, eight years after his death in 373, the Nicene christology secured confirmation at the Second Ecumenical Council in Constantinople.

In 318 Athanasius wrote his most famous work, *De Incarnatione Verbi* ("On the Incarnation of the Word"), which shows the influence of Irenaeus and Origen: the incarnate Logos was divine and restored what humanity had lost through Adam's sin; the image of God was regained for the faithful and death was overcome. Throughout his career Athanasius was mainly concerned to uphold the essential divinity of the Logos, and through his persistence he eventually won over the Semi-Arians to the Nicene christology, these latter being somewhat reluctant to accept the concept of *homoousios*, partly because of its connection with the heretical doctrines of Paul of Samosata, and partly because it was unscriptural. He also argued for the reality of Christ's manhood and for the reality of the Holy Spirit's essential divinity. And he was instrumental in introducing the Western church to monasticism.

In opposing Arius' doctrine that the Logos was created *ex nihilo* (see his Epistle to Eusebius of Nicomedia in Theodoret,

Eccles. Hist., 1:4), Athanasius, following Origen, maintained that the Logos was begotten of the essence of God, although, unlike Origen, he was much preoccupied with the mystical theory of salvation from mortality such as we find in the writings of Irenaeus. In addition to *De Incarnatione Verbi*, especially notable are Athanasius' treatises *De Decretis Nicaenae Synodi* ("On the Decrees of the Nicene Council"), *Orationes Contra Arianos* ("Orations against the Arians"), and his *De Synodis*, which deals with the synods of Ariminum and Seleucia. His fundamental contention stands out clearly: salvation was made possible only through the coalescence of the divine and the human in Christ, and this is a merging that can transmit divine qualities to man—in particular, immortality. If the Logos incarnate were merely a creature, such salvation could not have been made available (*II Oration*, 70). God became man, that man might become God (*De Incarn.*, 54). The incorruptible united with corruptible humanity and imparted deathlessness to it (*ibid.*, 9); for the Son is everlastingly generated by the Father (*I Oration*, 14). The Logos did not merely take the place of the human mind in Jesus but became man mentally as well as physically, deifying human nature completely (*III Oration*, 30; *II Oration*, 70).

There were three main parties at Nicea in 325, namely, the Arians, led by Eusebius (bishop of Nicomedia); the Anti-Arians, led by Alexander, Athanasius, and Hosius of Cordova; and the moderates, who included Eusebius of Caesarea. An Arian creed put forward by Eusebius of Nicomedia was rejected. Eusebius of Caesarea then submitted the baptismal creed of his church, and it was accepted by the majority, with the addition of *homoousios*. It would seem, however, that the creed finally promulgated (the original Nicene Creed) was not the revised Caesarean Creed, but a revised form of the baptismal creed of the Jerusalem church. It includes *homoousios* and four anathemas against Arianism. The text may be translated as follows:

We believe in one God, Father Almighty, Maker of all things visible and invisible; and in one Lord Jesus Christ the Son of God, begotten of the Father, uniquely-begotten, that is from the substance [or essence] of the Father, God of God, Light of Light, true God of true God, through whom all things were made, both the things of heaven and the things on earth; who for us men and for our salvation descended and was made flesh, was made man, suffered and rose again on the third day, ascended into heaven, and comes to judge quick and dead; and in the Holy Spirit. But those who say "There was once when he was not" and "Before his generation he was not" and "He was made out of nothing"; or pretend that the Son of God is of another *hypostasis* or *ousia* ["substance" or "essence"], or created or alterable or mutable, the Catholic church anathematizes.

In this way Arianism was excluded, but the victory, as we have seen, was short-lived. Constantine's sons, Constans and Constantius, shared the Empire, the latter inheriting the East, the former the West. Constantius was pro-Arian, and when he became sole ruler in 350 the Arians came into the ascendency. But they weakened their position by splitting into three main groups: the Anomoeans stressed the differences between Father and Son; the Homoeans preferred vagueness, arguing the Father and Son were similar; the Homoiousians spoke of similarities and differences between Father and Son, and they favored the epithet *homoiousios*, which means "of like essence to."

Athanasius died in 373. His work was taken up by three Cappadocians, Basil of Caesarea, Gregory of Nyssa (Basil's brother), and Gregory of Nazianzus, and they prepared for the victory of the Nicene christology under the emperor Theodosius I at the Council of Constantinople in 381. They addressed themselves particularly to the Homoiousians and explained *homoousios* in such a manner as to make it clear that oneness of essence did not obliterate the distinctions among the members of the Trinity. They employed the formula "one *ousia* in three *hypostaseis*," which means "one essence in three substances." In the Latin, however, *substantia* was used for *ousia*, and *persona* for *hypo-*

stasis, so that the formula became similar to that previously employed by Tertullian.

The Cappadocian thesis meant that the common essence of the Godhead was possessed by the three individual members of the Trinity, just as three men, though numerically distinct, share a common human essence or nature (Basil, *Epistles,* 38). This kind of interpretation, which definitely excluded Modalist Monarchianism, eventually prevailed among the Homoiousians, and thereby achieved victory for the Nicene christology in the East. In the West, however, the Athanasian interpretation tended to persist. Athanasius had used *ousia* and *hypostasis* as synonymous and thought of one divine essence or substance as existing in three kinds of relation, and this line of interpretation was followed by Augustine who, for instance, compared the members of the Trinity not to three men who partake of one human essence, but to memory, understanding, and will, which belong to a *single* human personality (*De Trinitate,* 14:8). That is, Western doctrine was more inclined to Sabellianism, although of course the concept of the eternal generation of the Son prevented pure Modalism.

Doctrine concerning the Holy Spirit was relatively amorphous, for the expression was frequently used in an impersonal sense of the divine presence as an inspiration to holiness of life. As we have seen, Origen expatiated on the Logos and developed the idea of the eternal generation of the Son, but his theorizing concerning the Spirit gives the impression of being something of an afterthought. Although he connected the activity of the Spirit with the life of the church, as the informing and sanctifying power, one feels that this function could just as well have been ascribed to the Logos, the instrument of creation and the agent of revelation. Seemingly, Origen was endeavoring to bring his thought into line with the traditional baptismal formula ("in the name of the Father, the Son, and the Spirit") and with the Pauline benediction (II Cor. 13:14). It is also significant that the original Nicene Creed contented itself with a simple affirmation of belief in the Holy Spirit.

In general, followers of Arius evidently tended to think of the Spirit as they thought of the Logos or Son. In the course of time, however, some Arians came to put the Logos on the divine side of reality and yet persisted in thinking of the Spirit as a *tertium quid* between God and the world. Basil (in his *De Spiritu Sancto*—"On the Holy Spirit"), opposed the upholders of such teaching; and they were condemned as *Pneumatomachoi* ("Spirit-fighters") at the Second Ecumenical Council, convened by Emperor Theodosius I at Constantinople in 381. This council ratified the Nicene christology, and provided the credal basis of the orthodox Christian state which Theodosius was concerned to establish.

Since the time of the Fourth Ecumenical Council, held at Chalcedon in 451, what is usually known as the Nicene Creed has been commonly understood to be the original Nicene Creed (325) as revised at Constantinople in 381. But this view is without secure foundation. No extant authorities before 449 associate the statement with the Second Ecumenical Council of 381, and especially noteworthy is the fact that it refrains from aplying *homoousios* to the Holy Spirit. The text may be translated as follows:

We believe in one God, Father almighty, Maker of heaven and earth and all things visible and invisible; and in one Lord Jesus Christ, the uniquely-begotten Son of God, who was begotten of the Father before all worlds, Light of Light, true God of true God, begotten not made, of one essence [or substance] with the Father, through whom all things were made; who for us men and for our salvation came down from heaven and became incarnate of the Holy Spirit and Mary the Virgin, and was made man, and was crucified for us under Pontius Pilate, and suffered and was buried, and rose on the third day according to the scriptures, and ascended into heaven, and sits at the right hand of the Father, and comes again with glory to judge the quick and the dead, of whose kingdom there shall be no end; and in the Holy Spirit, the Lord, the Giver of life, who proceeds from the Father, who with the Father and the Son is worshiped and glorified, who spoke through the prophets; in one holy catholic and apostolic church. We confess one baptism for remission of sins; we expect the resurrection of the dead and the life of the age to come.

Because of its traditional association with the Second Ecumenical Council, this creed has come to be frequently referred to among scholars as the Niceno-Constantinopolitan Creed. It is very similar to the original Nicene Creed, and perhaps both were revisions of the pre-Nicene baptismal creed of the church at Jerusalem. Its explanations respecting the Holy Spirit suggest that it is a later revision than the Nicene Creed proper, and this, coupled with the absence of anathemas, would help to account for its eventual widespread adoption as an element in the liturgy of the eucharist.

Cyril, bishop of Jerusalem (349–86), was exiled on three occasions because of his opposition to Arianism. But for some time he objected to the word *homoousios* because of its nonscriptural origin, and this gave rise to suspicions that he did not subscribe to the Nicene christology defended by Athanasius and by the three Cappadocians. He was present at the Council of Constantinople in 381, and it may be that, to demonstrate his orthodoxy, he formally presented the creed currently in use at Jerusalem. The council recognized the validity of his statement, and perhaps a copy of the creed was included in the official records of the meeting. Such a circumstance would account for the rise of the belief some seventy years later that the Niceno-Constantinopolitan Creed was the Second Ecumenical Council's revision of the Nicene Creed of 325.

After 381 Arianism was largely a lost cause, except among the Germanic tribes, who had been evangelized primarily through Ulfila, a man of Cappadocian ancestry who had been born and brought up among the Goths. In about 340 Eusebius (patriarch of Constantinople, earlier bishop of Nicomedia) had consecrated him to the episcopacy, and subsequently he became a highly successful missionary among the Teutonic tribes. He translated the Bible into Gothic, prepared a Gothic liturgy, and composed a confession of faith which gave expression to a *homoian* form of Arian christology. These works were destined to have an important effect, and when the Germanic tribes occupied wide regions of the Western empire they persecuted the Catholics who upheld the Nicene christology, especially in North Africa and Spain. The Visigoths, the Ostrogoths, the Vandals, the Burgundians, the Franks, and the Lombards were all under Ulfila's influence. The Salic Franks were the first of these tribes to accept the *homoousios* of the Nicene christology (*c.* 495), and the Lombards the last (by about 650).

BIBLIOGRAPHY

Bindley, T. H., ed. *Oecumenical Documents of the Faith*. London: Methuen, 1899.

Burnaby, John. *The Belief of Christendom: A Commentary on the Nicene Creed*. London: Society for Promoting Christian Knowledge, 1959.

Gwatkin, H. M. *Studies of Arianism*. 2nd ed. Cambridge: D. Bell, 1900.

Kelly, J. N. D. *Early Christian Creeds*. New York: Longmans, Green, 1950.

10 ‡ *Nestorianism and the Chalcedonian Creed*

The Nicene problem basically concerned the relation of the divine Logos in Christ to the Father, whereas the Chalcedonian problem fundamentally concerned the relation of the divine Logos in Christ to the humanity of Jesus. With regard to the latter question, there were two main tendencies of thought, one represented by theologians of the Alexandrian school, the other by theologians of the Antiochene school. In line with the teaching of Athanasius, the Alexandrians were inclined so to stress the unity of Christ's theanthropic personality as to imply that his humanity was somehow taken up and absorbed in his divinity; such a view was subservient to a mystical theory that construed salvation in terms of a deification of humanity through the union of God and man. In line with the teaching of Paul of Samosata, the Antiochenes were inclined so to stress the reality of Christ's human nature as to leave the unity of his personality in doubt; such a view was subservient to an ethical soteriology that construed salvation in terms of moral renewal through the example set by Jesus.

Even before 381 Apollinaris (*c.* 310–90), bishop of Laodicea and a friend of Athanasius, had argued that if a fusion of the divine and the human in Christ had really occurred, the Logos must have assumed an embodiment that was devoid of human personality. Normally the human individual is composed of body, soul, and mind (or spirit), and it is this third element that constitutes the active noetic or intellectual core of the personality. In the case of Christ, however, the Logos took the place of the mind, it being impossible for two personalities essentially to merge into one. Such teaching was rejected at synods in Rome and Antioch before being finally condemned at the Second Ecumenical Council held in 381 at Constantinople. Thereafter Apollinarianism was proscribed. Nevertheless, Apollinaris to some extent foreshadowed the ultimate teaching of the church. For at the Fifth Ecumenical Council (Constantinople, 553) the interpretation of Leontius of Byzantium, with its concept of the *enhypostasia*, was approved: the relation of the human to the divine in Christ, so it was held, must have been enhypostatic, his manhood finding its noetic personal center or *hypostasis* in the incarnate Logos.

Theologians of the school of Antioch strongly opposed the doctrine of Apollinaris, contending that the divine and the human in Christ were ethically conjoined through a harmony of will or purpose; there was no essential merging such as Apollinaris had contemplated. Christ's humanity was complete, and properly Mary was the mother of this human nature only. Nestorius, patriarch of Constantinople (428–31), soon after his appointment to this important office, began openly to condemn the use of the term *Theotokos* ("Mother of God") as a designation of Mary, and this quickly led to violent controversy.

Nestorius had probably studied under Theodore of Mopsuestia (*c.* 350–428), an extremely perceptive exegete who had opposed the characteristically Alexandrian method of allegorical hermeneutics and who had vigorously opposed all that savored of Apollinarianism. Nestorius proceeded to denounce the exponents of Alexandrian christology as heretical, whereupon Cyril, patriarch of Alexandria (412–44), at once arose to the counterattack. The dispute was deeply affected by personal ambitions and regional differences; on the one hand, there was the theological rivalry between Antioch and Alexandria, and, on the other hand, there were the political rivalries between

Alexandria and Constantinople and between Rome and Constantinople. Cyril argued that in Christ there was a single divine-human or theanthropic nature which had resulted through a coalescence of divinity with humanity, so that Mary was *Theotokos*, her Son being a deified Man. Clearly, such a conception was fundamentally Apollinarian, as Nestorius had declared, but Cyril evaded the objection by asserting that Christ's manhood was an integral humanity, composed of body, soul, and spirit, and not merely of body and soul.

Cyril was a typically successful politician, being astute and unscrupulous; *inter alia* he may well have been responsible for the lynching of Hypatia (perhaps the most competent woman mathematician and philosopher of the ancient world), who had been suspected of inciting the prefect of Alexandria against the Christians. He prevailed upon Pope Celestine in 430 to call a synod in Rome to condemn Nestorius, and he had the condemnation repeated at a synod in Alexandria.

But the controversy spread, and in 431 the emperor Theodosius II convened the Third Ecumenical Council at Ephesus. Cyril and his friends arrived promptly, and before the Antiochenes got there he held a meeting at which Nestorius was denounced as a heretic. When the Antiochenes arrived they held a further meeting at which the christology of Cyril was repudiated. In face of the deadlock Theodosius deposed both Nestorius and Cyril, but the latter was clever enough to secure his rapid reinstatement, and under imperial pressure the moderate Antiochenes and the Alexandrians were forced into a compromise, Nestorius being dispatched to his monastery in Antioch. The bishops supporting Nestorius, who refused to accept the proposed Formula of Union in 433, went on to found a separatist Nestorian church; it came to have its center in Persia, and an influential Nestorian school developed at Edessa in Syria. The Nestorians became active missionaries during the sixth century, and the movement spread into Arabia, Turkestan, India, and China; the Malabar Christians of southern India are present-day survivors of Nestorianism.

In 436 Nestorius was exiled to southern Egypt, and it was there that he died. His letters and sermons have survived only in fragments, and the precise nature of his teaching is disputed. During the nineties of the last century his *Bazaar of Heracleides* was discovered, and it was printed and published in 1910; in this document the author makes claim for the orthodoxy of his critique of the monophysite (one-nature) form of christology propounded by Eutyches and his followers. For Nestorius, however, as for the Antiochene school generally, the bond between the divine and the human nature of Christ was of a volitional or ethical character, a conjunction rather than a coalescence. It should also be observed that Nestorius' refusal to describe Mary as *Theotokos* ran counter to the increasing popular tendency to venerate the Virgin, a tendency which, according to some scholars, represented a progressive Christian adaptation of the pagan mother-goddess.

A further outbreak of controversy centered around the forthright teaching of Eutyches (*c.* 378–454), archimandrite of a monastery in Constantinople, who maintained that Jesus had a single nature, a deified human nature, so that all Christ's human attributes belonged to the one hypostatic subject, the humanized Logos. He admitted that there were two natures in Christ before the incarnational union, but believed that there was only one after the union, namely, the nature of the deified humanity. Despite his approach to Cyril's mode of interpretation he was accused of heresy. Flavian, patriarch of Constantinople (446–49), convened a synod there, and the teaching of Eutyches was condemned, Flavian inclining to the Antiochene interpretation. Both Eutyches and Flavian presented the issue to Leo I, bishop of Rome (440–61), and in his reply (Leo's *Dogmatic Epistle* or *Tome*) judgment was given in favor of Flavian.

Leo argued that there were two natures in Christ, each preserving its properties in such a way as to make possible a *communicatio idiomatum*, so that what was true of the human nature could be attributed to the divine nature, and vice versa. But Dioscorus, patriarch of Alexandria (444–54), with the support of Emperor Theodosius II, rallied to the support of Eutyches, and in 449 Dioscorus presided over the Latrocinium (the "Synod of Robbers," as Pope Leo subsequently described it in his letter to Empress Pulcheria), at which gathering Flavian was deposed. The meeting appears to have been a violent one, and it seems that Flavian suffered injuries there from which he died a few days later.

With the death of Theodosius in 450, however, the fortunes of Dioscorus underwent a sudden reversal. Theodosius was succeeded by his sister Pulcheria and her husband Marcian, and they at once supported the doctrinal position of Pope Leo. The Fourth Ecumenical Council was called and met at Chalcedon, a small town near Constantinople, in the year 451, and at the third session Dioscorus and Eutyches were excommunicated and banished. The Niceno-Constantinopolitan creed and the *Dogmatic Epistle* of Leo were approved, and a mediating statement of faith was arrived at, which, however, tended more toward the Antiochene than to the Alexandrian manner of interpretation. A close reading of the text of the creed can scarcely fail to show that beneath its carefully chosen phraseology opposing views lay concealed:

Following the holy Fathers we all with one consent teach men to confess one and the same Son, our Lord Jesus Christ, the same perfect in divinity and perfect in humanity, truly God and truly man, of a reasonable soul and body, of one substance [or essence] with the Father in his divinity, and of one substance with us in his humanity, in all things like us but without sin; begotten before all ages of the Father in the matter of his divinity, in the last days for us and for our salvation born of the Virgin Mary, the Mother of God in the matter of his humanity; one and the same Christ, Son, Lord, uniquely-begotten, acknowledged in two natures, inconfusedly, unchangeably, indivisibly, inseparably, the distinction of the natures being by no means taken away by the union, but rather the property of each nature being preserved, and concurring in one person [*prosōpon*] and one hypostasis ["personality"], not divided or separated into two persons, but one and the same Son and Uniquely-begotten, God, Logos, Lord, Jesus Christ; as from the beginning the prophets and the Lord Jesus Christ himself taught us concerning him, and the creed of the Fathers handed down to us.

Thus the oneness of Christ's personality was asserted against Nestorianism, and the unchangeableness of the distinction between the two natures in Christ was asserted against the Monophysitism of Eutyches.

But the differences were too deep-seated to be settled by a verbal compromise. Despite the fact that the council confirmed Cyril's condemnation of Nestorianism at the Ephesian synod of 431, a number of Eastern theologians came to regard the Chalcedonian Creed as a veiled expression of Nestorian belief, with the result that monophysite separatist churches were ultimately established in Egypt and elsewhere. And it may be noticed here that the Copts of Egypt and the Amharic Christians of Ethiopia are still monophysite.

BIBLIOGRAPHY

Bethune-Baker, J. F. *Nestorius and His Teaching.* Cambridge: Cambridge University Press, 1908.

Grillmeier, Alois. *Christ in Christian Tradition from the Apostolic Age to Chalcedon (451).* London: Mowbray, 1965.

Raven, C. E. *Apollinarianism: An Essay on the Christology of the Early Church.* Cambridge: Cambridge University Press, 1923.

Sellers, R. V. *The Council of Chalcedon: A Historical and Doctrinal Survey.* London: Society for Promoting Christian Knowledge, 1953.

11 ⁝ The Monophysite and
⁝ Monothelite Controversies

Emperor Justinian (527–65) was the most successful of the early Byzantine rulers. He conquered the Goths in Italy and the Vandals in North Africa, and made strenuous efforts to establish political and religious unity throughout the empire. He initiated a comprehensive legal reformation. The code of Theodosius II, comprising all general constitutions (with due adaptations) enacted from the beginning of the reign of Constantine I up to the year 438, was updated and published by Justinian in 529. Among other things it legalized the domination of the church by the state and set forth the principle of the supremacy of the monarch's will. Justinian also launched many great building projects, including the renowned Santa Sophia in Constantinople. He compelled the baptism of many pagans, ordered the closing of the Athenian philosophical schools, and took sternly repressive measures against the Montanists.

With regard to the Monophysites (those holding that Christ had one deified human nature), he adopted a policy of conciliation, making determined attempts to win them back to orthodoxy. This may have been partly due to the fact that his wife Theodora had monophysite leanings; and it should also be borne in mind that Monophysitism was a relatively young and growing movement, seriously threatening to divide the empire in Egypt and elsewhere. Justinian worked on the Chalcedonian christology, which the Monophysites and others regarded as

Antiochene or Nestorian, and he evidently sought an interpretation that would bring the Creed more into line with the christology of Athanasius and Cyril of Alexandria. In this connection he was greatly assisted by Leontius of Byzantium (*c.* 485–
543), who argued that, while Christ's humanity was not strictly
impersonal, it nevertheless possessed no independent hypostasis
or personality. We have seen that Leontius introduced the concept of the *enhypostasia:* the relation of the humanity to the
divinity in Christ was enhypostatic, Christ's manhood finding
its personality in the humanized Logos. This interpretation of
the Chalcedonian christology received official approval in Constantinople at the Fifth Ecumenical Council in the year 553.

In pursuance of his policy of conciliating the Monophysites,
Justinian in 543 issued an anti-Nestorian edict, the so-called
Three Chapters, condemning Antiochene doctrine under three
headings: The works of Theodore of Mopsuestia, the polemics
of Cyrus Theodoret against the christology of Cyril of Alexandria, and the epistle of Ibas of Edessa to Maris. The Eastern
patriarchs assented, but Justinian had difficulties with Pope Vigilius, who, besides resenting state interference, wished to uphold the Chalcedonian decisions as they stood. The emperor
tried to compel obedience, but without success, and the conflict
dragged on. Vigilius refused to attend the ecumenical sessions of
553, knowing that the predominant feeling would be against
him, and perhaps even fearing violence. At the council the
Three Chapters was formally approved, and Vigilius, in his
Constitutum, issued the following year, expressed qualified
agreement. But this submission caused considerable controversy
in the Western church, and it was not until about 700 that the
Latin authorities generally accepted the ecumenical status of
the Constantinopolitan sessions of 553.

Justinian's conciliatory policy was a total failure; it led to
disaffection in the West, and in the East the Monophysites were
not reconciled to orthodoxy. For some time nationalist sentiments in Egypt and Syria had given force to the deviationist

theological doctrines represented there. Syria came to be grievously split between Nestorianism and Monophysitism. The
Armenian church, reacting against Persian Nestorianism, had
moved in a Monophysite direction and in 491 had officially
condemned the Chalcedonian decisions. Thus, by helping to
give rise to widespread separatist movements, the prolonged
christological disputes did not strengthen the political structure
of the Eastern empire, and it is not altogether surprising that
its provinces fell an easy prey to the advancing Moslems during
the seventh century. In the meantime Egyptian Monophysitism
persisted and eventually spread into Ethiopia.

The restoration of imperial power under Justinian was short-
lived. From about the year 568 the Lombards advanced into
Italy and went on to occupy most of the peninsula. The Visigoths had conquered the whole of Spain by 624. Persian armies
overran wide areas of the East, and Avars and Slavs penetrated
the Danube regions and had reached the neighborhood of Constantinople by 625. The empire was saved from collapse mainly
through the inspired leadership of Heraclius (*c.* 575–642), the
emperor who established his reputation by winning a notable
victory over the Persians in Palestine (629). But before his
death Islam had arisen. Mahomet died *circa* 630, and under the
caliphs Oman and Othman the new religion entered upon a period of remarkable expansion. Damascus was taken in 635, Antioch and Jerusalem in 638, Alexandria in 641, Persia in 651.
The followers of the Prophet surged westward across North
Africa and had secured a footing in Spain by 711. They tra-
versed the Pyrenees and pressed on toward Paris. But their progress in the West was permanently stemmed near Tours in 732
by Frankish forces under the leadership of Charles Martel. Constantinople was seriously threatened in 718 but after a desperate
struggle succeeded in repelling the invaders.

As a result of the Persian and the subsequent Moslem invasions, Emperor Heraclius, following the precedent of his great
predecessor Justinian, sought to unite the Monophysites with

the orthodox church. The policy of conciliation failed again, and this time it led to a further heresy: Monothelitism, the doctrine that Christ had but one will. In 624 Heraclius conferred with Monophysite leaders, and the meeting decided that a formula which could reconcile the factions would assert that Christ had two natures but only one mode of motivating energy. The matter was referred to Sergius, patriarch of Constantinople (610–38), who, having found a similar concept in the works of Cyril of Alexandria, accepted the emperor's proposal, and on its basis a number of Monophysites in Egypt were received into the orthodox church.

Sophronius of Jerusalem, however, protested that the formula was heretical, whereupon in 634 Sergius consulted Pope Honorius (625–38) who, while concurring with the conciliatory policy, replied that the term "energy" was unscriptural and should be dropped in favor of "will" (Greek: *thelēma*). Honorius' proposals were taken up in the *Ecthesis,* presumably written by Sergius, and promulgated by Heraclius in 638: Christ had one will only, and the word "energy" should not be employed. The *Ecthesis* was approved at two synods in Constantinople, but the four popes who followed Honorius all rejected it as heretical. To conciliate the Western church the emperor Constans II repudiated the *Ecthesis* in 648 and issued the *Typos,* which condemned all use of the term "will" in christological expositions, thereby excluding Dyothelitism (the doctrine that Christ had two wills), as well as Monothelitism. But the *Typos* was no more acceptable to the West than the *Ecthesis,* and Pope Martin I (649–55) presided over the Lateran Synod of 649 which proclaimed the dogma that Christ had two wills, and denounced the Eastern patriarchs. Martin was subsequently imprisoned at the order of the emperor and finally banished to the Crimea; he was the last of the popes to be officially venerated as a martyr.

By the reign of Emperor Constantine IV, the provinces where Monophysitism was strong had been invaded by Moslems, and earnestly desiring peaceful relations with the Western empire, Constantine entered into negotiations with Pope Agatho (678–81), who, after synodal discussions, sent delegates to the emperor with an epistle setting forth the Western doctrine. Constantine at once convened the Sixth Ecumenical Council (Constantinople, 680). Macarius, patriarch of Antioch, was condemned as a Monothelite, and all the leading representatives of the heresy, including Pope Honorius, were anathematized. The Chalcedonian formulation was approved, and Christ was said to have possessed two natures and two wills, his human will always following his divine will; there was no coalescence of the two natures, but rather his personal unity realized itself through an operative harmony between the two wills. Thus, owing to Latin support, the Antiochene mode of christology in this case triumphed over the characteristically Alexandrian doctrine. On the other hand, thanks to the notion of the *enhypostasia* propounded by Leontius of Byzantium, it was still possible for theologians of the East to interpret the Chalcedonian christology so as to agree with the conception of the deification of humanity as propounded by Ignatius, Irenaeus, Athanasius, and Cyril.

Despite the Moslem invasions Monophysitism survived in four principal churches—the Coptic, the Ethiopian, the Syrian (or Jacobite, after Jacob Bardaeus consecrated bishop of Edessa in 542), and the Armenian.

BIBLIOGRAPHY

Franks, R. S. *The Doctrine of the Trinity*. London: Duckworth, 1953.

Luce, A. A. *Monophysitism Past and Present: A Study in Christology*. London: Society for Promoting Christian Knowledge, 1920.

Mackintosh, H. R. *The Doctrine of the Person of Christ*. New York: Scribner's, 1912.

Relton, H. M. *A Study in Christology: The Problem of the Rela-*

tion of the Two Natures in the Person of Christ. London: Society for Promoting Christian Knowledge, 1917.

Wolfson, H. A. *The Philosophy of the Church Fathers.* Vol. I: *Faith, Trinity, Incarnation.* Cambridge, Mass.: Harvard University Press, 1956.

12 ‡ Iconoclasticism and John of Damascus

Imperial strength was renewed under the able leadership of Emperor Leo III (717–40), whose fame was assured at the outset of his reign through his decisive victory over strong Moslem forces that besieged Constantinople. He subsequently turned his attention to administrative and legal reform, issuing the *Ecloge*, a new code of law, in 726. During the years 726–29 he published a series of edicts directed against image worship, a practice that was taken to contravene the second of the Ten Commandments (Exod. 20:4) and thereby to hamper the church's missionary work among Jews and Moslems.

Germanus I, patriarch of Constantinople, opposed Leo's iconoclastic policy and appealed to Pope Gregory II (715–31). The emperor took vigorous action. He removed Germanus from office in 730 and proceeded to persecute monastic groups that were particularly devoted to images. Synods at Rome in 727 and 731 denounced Iconoclasticism.

Leo's son and successor, Constantine V (740–75), was also averse to the veneration of images, and the Synod of Hieria in 753 ruled that, by paying homage to objects representative merely of Christ's humanity, the votaries of images necessarily fell into heresy: either they became Nestorian by dividing Christ's personal unity, or they became monophysite by confounding his manhood with his divinity. As for icons of the Virgin and the saints, the synod ordered that they should be destroyed as instruments of idolatry. Repressive measures followed, and many monks (who in general were more ardently in favor of images than the secular clergy) suffered martyrdom.

Persecution all but ceased under Emperor Leo IV (775-80), and after his death his widow, Irene, when acting as regent for her juvenile son, began definitely to oppose Iconoclasticism. In 784 she secured the patriarchate of Constantinople for her chief secretary, Tarasius, who at once sought to establish harmonious relations with the Western church. He negotiated with Pope Hadrian I (772-95), and the latter expressed his willingness to send official delegates to a proposed general council, provided that the rulings of the Synod of Hieria would be condemned. The result was that the Seventh Ecumenical Council (after being broken up by iconoclastic military detachments at Constantinople in 786) gathered at Nicea in 787, Tarasius presiding. The decrees of the Synod of Hieria were declared null and void, and the Iconoclasts were anathematized. The council ratified the papal doctrine set forth in Hadrian's letter to Irene; it was laid down that absolute worship could be addressed to God alone, and that the veneration of sacred objects, including images and pictorial representations of Christ, was of a relative character, the honor attributed to them passing over to the divine reality they symbolized. God became truly man in Christ, and so it could not be improper to portray him in visible forms.

Despite these official pronouncements Iconoclasticism was revived in the East (mainly through the influence of the military) during the period 814-43. Interestingly enough, its progress was again arrested through the agency of a woman—this time by Theodora, the widow of Emperor Theophilus (829-42), who, like Irene, acted as regent for her son after the death of her husband.

There was resistance to the decrees of the Seventh Ecumenical among the Frankish theologians under Charlemagne. The decrees in question were condemned at the Council of Frankfurt in 794 and at an episcopal synod held at Paris in 828. This opposition was not wholly due, as has sometimes been suggested, to a mistranslation of the Greek acts of the Seventh Ecumenical Council, which led to a confusion of veneration (*proskunēsis*) with absolute worship (*latreia*). Apart from political rivalry and a possible aversion to the flamboyant refinements of an old civilization, Frankish iconoclastic tendencies may have been partly due to a persisting Arian influence. If Christ himself did not enjoy a divine status, how much more was this the case with pictorial representations of his incarnate person!

John of Damascus (*c*. 675–745) was the most significant of the theologians who controverted Iconoclasticism. He belonged to a prominent Damascus family and succeeded his father as the church's representative to the caliph; in 716 he retired to the monastery of St. Sabas near Jerusalem and was eventually ordained to the priesthood. He remained a recluse to the end of his life, studying and writing. He was extremely learned and systematized the principal tenets of consolidated orthodoxy. The tenor of his thought is often reminiscent of Origen, a thinker he adjudged to be heretical. It should be borne in mind, however, that in condemning the great Alexandrian theologian John was merely following tradition; for example, at the Fifth Ecumenical Council (Constantinople, 553) Origen was denounced for upholding such doctrines as the pre-existence of souls, metempsychosis (or transmigration), and the ultimate salvation of all rational creatures.

In the years around 728 John published three treatises in which he defended the veneration of images. He maintained that material things can subserve and symbolize spiritual realities. To deny this, and to regard matter as being necessarily opposed to the life of the spirit, would be tantamount to embracing the Manichean heresy (see Chapter 13). The emperor had no right to impose his belief upon the church, for he was without competence in such matters. The prohibition of images in the

Decalogue could have no application to pictures of Jesus, who represented God in visible form. There is a difference between veneration and worship. The highest type of adoration, worship in an absolute sense, can be directed only to God, but finite things may be venerated in so far as they signify the transcendence of the Divine. Respect for sacred objects has its justification in what they symbolize, the honor paid to them passing on to God, the heavenly Being beyond the sensible world. Images also have a subjective justification, for man is so constituted that his faith in the unseen is enlivened by sensuous representations of the eternal object of his faith.

John's most important work, *The Fount of Knowledge,* is divided into three parts: the first deals with general philosophy, and the principles involved are Aristotelian and Neoplatonic; the second concerns heresies and is largely based on the works of Epiphanius and Theodoret, the most notable addition being a discussion of Islam; the third expounds the principal doctrines of the orthodox faith in four books, which are devoted respectively to God, Creation, Christ, and Miscellanea. This third part has remained the basic standard of the theology of the Eastern church down to the twentieth century.

In contradistinction to Origen, John was a traditionalist and feared unbridled speculation (*Fount,* 3:4:11). Theology should elucidate the principles underlying what has been revealed. It is on the basis of revealed truth that we know of God's triune nature: God is one essence (*ousia*) in three hypostases (*ibid.,* 3:1:6–8). Choosing to bestow his grace on other beings, God went forth in creative activity, producing angels and men out of nothing, through the mediation of the Logos. John reflected a not uncommon inconsistency in his treatment of the problem of evil, sometimes suggesting that it is merely an absence of good, at other times arguing that it emerged through a revolt of the creature against the Creator. The former interpretation is in line with Neoplatonism, the latter with biblical teaching (*ibid.,* 3:2:1–4). God in his omniscience knows the future, and yet he does not entirely predestinate, for man is free and responsible, just as angelic beings are (*ibid.*, 3:2:25–30).

John was at pains to clarify and defend Chalcedonian christology. The Logos, the eternally generated Son of God, became flesh and lived a genuinely human life in the physical world. Christ, the incarnate Logos, was one person and yet had two natures, divine and human, which remained quite distinct. Each nature had a will of its own; that is, Jesus had two wills, the human will always harmoniously following the behests of the divine will. At the cost of endangering the completeness of Christ's manhood (cf. the doctrine of Apollinaris), John took up the thesis of Leontius of Byzantium, contending that the relation of the human to the divine nature was enhypostatic, so that Christ's humanity found its noetic ego or governing personality (its hypostasis) in the incarnate Logos (*ibid.*, 3:3:3–19).

Moreover, John contended that Christ, by offering himself as a ransom to the Father (not to the Devil, as Origen and others had proposed), delivered man from the consequences of Adam's sin, which included the corruption of mortality. As the incarnate Logos, he constituted a model of virtue, so that the faithful who reproduced his ethical character might become by adoption what he was by nature (*ibid.*, 3:4:13).

It is characteristic of the nonlegal approach of the Greek church that there was little elaboration of the doctrine of penance, and John had nothing significant to say about it. On the other hand, he placed much stress on the reality of the miraculous change of the eucharistic elements: the bread and wine are actually transmuted into the divine body and blood of Christ (*ibid.*, 3:4:13).

John's systematization of orthodoxy exercised influence in the West as well as in the East. In the twelfth century it was translated into Latin and in certain circles came to be highly regarded; among the Western theologians who studied it was Thomas Aquinas.

BIBLIOGRAPHY

Adeney, W. F. *The Greek and Eastern Churches*. New York: Scribner's, 1908.

Alexander, P. J. *The Patriarch Nicephorus of Constantinople: Ecclesiastical Policy and Image Worship in the Byzantine Empire*. Oxford: Clarendon Press, 1958.

Martin, E. J. *A History of the Iconoclastic Controversy*. London: Society for Promoting Christian Knowledge, 1930.

Tisserant, E. *Eastern Christianity in India*. London: Longmans, Green, 1957.

III ‡ TOWARD THE EAST-WEST SCHISM

13 ‡ *Augustine*

Augustine was the greatest figure in the ancient Western church. Like his important theological predecessors, Tertullian and Cyprian, he was a native of North Africa. His influence on Eastern theology was slight, but in the West he largely determined the shape of medieval thought, and he also to some extent inspired the Protestant Reformation. A dynamic personality, he was deeply affected by diverse philosophical and theological doctrines. His voluminous writings exemplify opposing interests, and his numerous theses scarcely form a wholly consistent system of ideas. His conception of the church as the hierarchical organization which alone can mediate saving grace to humanity, prepared the way for the claims of the medieval papacy to supreme authority in spiritual and temporal affairs. On the other hand, he anticipated the Protestant distinction between the invisible and the visible church: the former is the congregation of the elect, whereas the latter is a mixed society composed of good and bad alike.

Augustine was born at Tagaste in Numidia in 354. His mother was Christian, but his father did not identify himself with the church until late in life. Augustine studied rhetoric at Carthage; originally he had intended to become a lawyer, but he soon turned to writing and teaching. He fell away from the limited Christianity of his upbringing and, according to the reports (perhaps somewhat exaggerated) in his *Confessions*, gave himself over to a dissolute life. He took a mistress and begot a child by her. When nineteen years of age he read Cicero's *Hortensius* (not extant), and he became more serious. The problems of philosophy began to fascinate him, and it was not long before he became a Manichean, an adherent of the religious system of Mani (Latin: Manichaeus), a Persian teacher and prophet who had flourished in the third century (*c.* 210–75).

Like Gnosticism, Manicheanism was a syncretistic religious philosophy, founded upon a radical dualism between good and evil, or light and darkness. The Devil, who embodied the evil principle, had imprisoned fragments of light in the bodies of human beings; and the great religious leaders, such as Gautama, Jesus, and Mani himself, had been commissioned to show how the divine sparks could be liberated from the shackles of the flesh. The Manicheans further showed affinities with Gnosticism by taking delight in elaborate cosmological speculations and by practicing asceticism. They abstained from meat and regarded the begetting of children as essentially the work of Satan, who was ever on the look-out for suitable carnal prisons in which to incarcerate the particles of light he had stolen from the divine sphere.

When he approached the age of thirty Augustine began to doubt the validity of Manichean principles, and after moving to Rome in 384 he was somewhat attracted by the moderate scepticism of the so-called Academics, who denied that man could attain a knowledge of absolute reality. Dissatisfied with his associates as well as with his own existence, he proceeded to Milan, where he took up a teaching post. The preaching of Ambrose, the bishop there (374–97), impressed him, but he turned to Neoplatonism before eventually being baptized by the bishop in 387. He was actually converted during the summer of the previous year, when, after listening to one of Ambrose's sermons, he was deeply moved while reading a passage from the Epistle to the Romans (13:13–14); and Paulinism continued to exercise a formative influence on the development of his thought. He returned to North Africa in 388, was ordained a presbyter in 391 and became bishop of Hippo a few years later. He died in 430, when the city was being besieged by the invading Vandals.

A large proportion of Augustine's surviving works are polemical. Treatises against Manicheanism include *Contra Faustum Manichaeum* ("Against Faustus, the Manichean"); among his anti-Donatist works is *De Baptismo contra Donatistas* ("On Baptism, Against the Donatists"); his literary attacks on Pelagianism (see Chapter 14) are more numerous and include *De Peccatorum Meritis et Remissione* ("On the Guilt and Remission of Sins"), *De Spiritu et Littera* ("On the Spirit and the Letter"), *De Nuptiis et Concupiscentia* ("On Marriage and Concupiscence"), *De Natura et Gratia* ("On Nature and Grace"); four works critical of Semi-Pelagianism should also be mentioned, *De Gratia et Libero Arbitrio* ("On Grace and Free Will"), *De Correptione et Gratia* ("On Corruption and Grace"), *De Praedestinatione Sanctorum* ("On the Predestination of the Saints"), and *De Dono Perseverantiae* ("On the Gift of Perseverance"). Of all his writings the best known are his *Confessions* and his *De Civitate Dei* ("On the City of God"); the former gives an account of his life to the time of his conversion to Christianity, the latter (occasioned by the fall of Rome to the Visigoths under Alaric in 410) is a consideration of the relation between Christian and secular society. Among his other works, perhaps the most important are *De Trinitate* ("On the Trinity") and *Enchiridion ad Laurentium* ("An Enchiridion Addressed to Laurentius"). Certain early dialogues, for example, his *Soliloquia* ("Soliloquies"), have survived, and also exegetical works and numerous epistles and sermons.

Rejecting the Manichean concept of an evil principle at work in nature, Augustine maintained that the world was created by one supremely good Creator and that the physical universe is basically good. Evil does exist, but its existence is due to the finitude of creaturely entities and to their associated tendency to lapse into nothingness; evil also arises through the misuse of freedom on the part of self-conscious moral creatures. Against the Donatist thesis that the church (as the divinely founded society which mediates salvation to men) must be pure and holy, Augustine argued that the church necessarily includes good and bad members, and that the validity of the sacraments in no way depends upon the moral character of the officiating priest. Also, the state may on occasion legitimately apply force to suppress heretical doctrines, although capital punishment should not be inflicted upon heretics and schismatics.

Controverting Pelagianism, Augustine contended that man, so far from being born free and guiltless, suffers from an inherited moral disability. The whole human race as it actually exists constitutes a *massa peccati et perditionis*, a mass of sin and perdition, out of which God in his loving-kindness has elected certain individuals to be recipients of his saving grace. God cannot be accused of injustice in this connection, for the descendants of Adam were potentially in him and must therefore share in the guilt of his disobedience. All men deserve damnation, and the choice of some men for salvation is an expression of the loving-kindness of God. The damned have no ground for complaint since they get what they justly deserve, and the saved have no ground for self-congratulation, since the salvation they obtain is quite unmerited.

In a considerable measure, then, Augustine's doctrines were set forth and elaborated in opposition to teachings he regarded as heretical, and, like the ecumenical creeds, they cannot be thoroughly understood apart from the controversies in which they were involved.

Despite his view that humanity is a mass of perdition, Augustine was basically an optimist in his primary ontology. Being is good and nothingness is evil (*Enchirid.*, 11), and empirical evidence of this is the widespread fear of death among living creatures. Like Spinoza, Augustine held that the will to live is a universal feature of creaturely existence (*De Civit.*, 11:6). Existence as such is intrinsically valuable, and even when corrupted it is better than nonexistence (*Enchirid.*, 12). Nothingness is at once an absence of being and an absence of value (*Confess.*, 7:12). God is the *Ens Realissimum*, the most real of all entities (*De Trinit.*, 5:2), and hence supremely good. He is immutable and self-dependent, for he himself called time into being when the world was created (*De Civit.*, 11:6).

The divine activity that resulted in the production of the temporal universe out of nothingness, was necessarily good, and God continues to act upon the world to maintain it in existence. What is creaturely cannot be self-dependent; it has an inherent tendency to slip back into nothingness, and it is only through God's continuous sustaining activity that finite existence can persist (*De Civit.*, 14:11). Thus God is omnipresent; the whole universe is pervaded with the preservative activity of God, so that certain unusual occurrences cannot be in a strict sense more miraculous than regular natural processes. Properly interpreted, everything that happens in the world bears witness to the sustaining power of the *Ens Realissimum*.

To some extent, however, the tendency of finite beings to lapse into nothingness is given free play, the consequence being that in varying degrees evil enters the world. The universe is a rich synthesis of mutually opposing parts; as light in a painting is brought out through contrasting it with shadow, so the value of goodness is displayed through contrasting it with evil (*ibid.*, 11:23). God does not directly promote evil, but rather evil is permitted to arise for the sake of what is ultimately a greater good or larger value (*ibid.*, 14:11).

The principles of Augustine's ontological optimism bear witness to the continuing influence of Neoplatonism in the formation of his thought. On the other hand, Augustine was also affected by the biblical and patristic tradition, and he overlaid his primary ontology with the Hebraic doctrine of God as the personal Creator who rules the world with his sovereign will.

The *Ens Realissimum* is the righteous God of the Old Testament prophets; and the Trinity itself is thought of, not so much as three *hypostaseis* with one *ousia*, but rather as a single Personality who manifests himself in three faculties or relations (*De Trinit.*, 10:12). As for the presence of evil in the world, this is not merely due to the general inclination of created things to relapse into nothingness, but has a positive significance, arising from a creaturely determination to rebel against the will of the Creator (*Epistle* 166). Humanity was endowed with reason and freedom, and the primordial progenitor of the race had the audacity to contravene the commandment of his Maker. Justice had to be done, and so Adam's nature became corrupt as a result of his sin, the corruption being necessarily transmitted to his offspring. All men were potentially in Adam, and they share in his guilt; unbaptized infants are therefore liable to damnation (*De Corrept.*, 10).

Augustine argued that the corruption of human nature must mean that, to practice the good life, men need the spiritual reinforcement of divine grace. The natural human will is *de facto* ineffective; and in the course of the Pelagian controversy Augustine so stressed the necessity of the infusion of a divine dynamic for the conduct of the Christian life that he arrived at the notion of the irresistibility of grace: God saves whom he will (*De Corrept.*, 14). Some he predestines to salvation, others to damnation (*Enchirid.*, 100). The elect have been endowed with the gift of perseverance (*De Dono Persev.*, 8), and their number is permanently fixed (*De Corrept.*, 13).

If Neoplatonism made a permanent imprint upon Augustine's teaching, the same would seem to be true of Manicheanism, for he held that sexual pleasure is one of the factors involved in the corruption of human nature. He maintained that concupiscence, the ardor of lust and passion, is the emotion through which original sin is transmitted to the offspring of Adam (*De Nupt.*, 1:27). Prior to the rebellion of Adam and Eve against the will of their Creator, the generation of children took place at the behest of the will, like the movement of a hand or the turning of the head. But after their audacious disobedience, man's first parents felt shame, for they noticed that their sexual organs began to act independently of mental control, and henceforth the functioning of the genitals had to wait on sexual excitation. This brought the blush of shame over embodied freedom and induced Adam and Eve to cover their sexual organs with fig leaves (*ibid.*, 1:7). Man could no longer reproduce his kind at the prompting of reason, but only through the emotional stimulation of lust.

Thus, concupiscence is evil in itself, a mark of human depravity that remains even after baptism; it lingers like languor after an illness (*ibid.*, 1:28), and Christian parents necessarily transmit to their children the condition of their own carnal birth, not that of their spiritual new birth (*ibid.*, 1:37). In face of this situation the relatively perfect man of faith will preserve his chastity; the next best thing is to turn concupiscent evil into good by begetting children in legitimate wedlock (*ibid.*, 2:1 ff.).

According to Augustine's teaching, it is through the infused grace of God that the process of sanctification is effected; those who are sanctified in this life will be transported after death directly to enjoy the blessings of heaven, whereas those who are not completely sanctified by the time of their death will have to spend a period in purgatory (*Enchirid.*, 69). Heavenly joys are the ultimate rewards of the saved, and the torments of hell are the punishment awaiting the damned. And yet, because God is really the source of all human virtue, it should be said, in the interests of clarity, not that God rewards certain men for their noble achievements, but rather that he crowns bestowed gifts with further blessings (*De Grat.*, 6).

Augustine made no significant contribution to christology or to the doctrine of the work of Christ. With regard to the latter, he commended Jesus as a model for all who would exemplify in their own lives the divine spirit of neighborly love (*De Catechizandis Rudibus*, 4). He also followed Origen and others in the argument that Christ, by sacrificing his life, paid a ransom to the devil for the deliverance of man from the bondage of sin (*De Civit.*, 7:31). And sometimes he reproduced the idea, much stressed by Irenaeus, that in Christ God became man that man man might become God (*Sermo* 192).

In his doctrine of the church Augustine followed Cyprian, maintaining that the church is a divinely ordained institution governed by the bishops in apostolic succession. As such, it is the seat of authority in religion and the sole dispenser of the grace that guarantees salvation. But it should be noticed that Augustine recognized the fallibility of individual bishops as well as of general councils (*De Bapt.*, 2:3). In his treatise *De Civitate Dei* he made a fundamental distinction between the *civitas terrena*, the earthly city, and the *civitas Dei*, the City of God, which is composed of angels and humans destined for salvation. The two opposing communities originated prior to the creation of the world in a strife that took place among the angels (*De Civit.*, 11:1); and in this world the City of God is represented by the true church, the earthly city by the Roman Empire. The former city is grounded in the love of God, the latter in the love of self. The earthly city has its *raison d'être* in the maintenance of law and order; but terrestrial political states are fated to pass away with the expansion of the *civitas Dei*, whose members are God's chosen. The processes of history have conspired to produce the *civitas Dei*, and they are still conspiring to strengthen and extend its sway (*ibid.*, 18:51). The organized church is actually the Kingdom of God on earth, and Christ's sovereignty will be finally demonstrated to the world through the mediation of the saints (*ibid.*, 20:9).

This mode of thought was taken up by those who in subsequent centuries supported the claims of the papacy to temporal rule. But it seems to be inconsistent with Augustine's other conception of the organized church as an imperfect or mixed society, the organ of whose divine authority cannot always be discerned with certainty.

BIBLIOGRAPHY

Battenhouse, R. W., ed. *A Companion to the Study of Saint Augustine.* New York: Oxford University Press, 1955.

Brown, P. *Augustine of Hippo, a Biography.* London: Faber and Faber, 1967.

Cochrane, A. N. *Christianity and Classical Culture.* New York: Oxford University Press, 1944.

D'Arcy, M. C., and others. *St. Augustine, His Age, His Life and Thought.* New York: Meridian Books, 1957.

Gilson, E. *The Christian Philosophy of Saint Augustine.* London: Gollancz, 1961.

Widengren, G. *Mani and Manichaeism.* London: Weidenfeld and Nicolson, 1965.

14 ‡ *Pelagianism and*
‡ *Semi-Pelagianism*

Pelagius, a monk from Britain, settled in Rome *circa* 400 and quickly acquired a reputation for learning and serious moral concern. He came to feel that Augustine's predestinarianism, besides being intellectually unsound, was liable to rob people of the sense of moral responsibility, and he proceeded to attack the doctrine. He won many supporters for his critique, among whom was a capable fellow countryman named Celestius. Soon after Rome had been occupied by Alaric's forces (410) the two men migrated to North Africa, and Celestius sought ordination at the hands of Aurelius, bishop of Carthage. There were difficulties, however, and in the ensuing controversy Aurelius received a list of six complaints against Celestius, which had been prepared by Paulinus, a deacon of Milan.

The document accused Celestius of proclaiming the following erroneous doctrines: (1) that Adam was mortal quite independently of his disobedience; (2) that Adam's sin had an injurious effect upon himself only, not upon his offspring; (3) that new-born babies are innocent, just as Adam was before his disobedience; (4) that men do not die because Adam sinned, nor will they rise from the dead on account of Christ's resurrection; (5) that the Law, like the Gospel, points the way to the Kingdom of God; (6) that even before the coming of Christ some men lived without sin. Celestius was found guilty of these errors at a synod held at Carthage in 412, whereupon he moved to Ephesus. Pelagius himself went to Palestine. In response to their appeals for authoritative rulings, synods were held at Jerusalem and at Diospolis of Lydda in 415; and in neither case was Pelagianism declared obnoxious.

In 412 Augustine vigorously entered into the controversy, and he condemned Pelagius for denying that man can attain salvation only through the infusion of divine grace (which overcomes the moral weakness of original sin), and for maintaining that a man is capable of living without sin. Two synods which met in North Africa in 416 condemned Pelagianism, and in the following year Pope Innocent I (401–17) ratified these synodal condemnations. Pope Zosimus (417–19), however, declared Pelagius innocent of heresy, but after a further synod, held at Carthage in 418, the pope changed his mind and Pelagianism was condemned. This synod declared that Adam became mortal as a result of his disobedience, that babies are in need of baptism for the remission of original sin, that divine grace is necessary for the practice of the Christian life, and that men cannot live without sin. It seems that Pelagius died in 420, presumably in Palestine.

Pelagianism was taken up by Julian, bishop of Eclanum in southern Italy. He violently attacked Augustine, contending that his doctrine was a form of Manicheanism, and controversy again flared up. Emperor Honorius intervened and called upon the Western bishops formally to condemn Pelagianism. Julian and several associates refused to do so, and some of the recalcitrants sought refuge in the East. Nestorius, patriarch of Constantinople (428–31), added to his own difficulties by pleading the cause of Julian and those associated with him, and at the Third Ecumenical Council, held at Ephesus in 431, both Nestorianism and Pelagianism were formally condemned.

Although Augustine had gained much prestige before his death in 430 and was highly respected, especially in the West, his radical views were not by any means generally accepted; Jerome, for instance, rejected the doctrine of irresistible grace, and the question of the part played by divine grace in the work of salvation continued to be a subject of earnest debate.

The Vandals were overrunning Latin North Africa at the time of Augustine's death. As a consequence of their conquest the intellectual leadership of the Western church tended to shift across the Mediterranean from Africa to southern Gaul, and it was in the Marseilles region that Semi-Pelagianism came to have it most ardent representatives. They argued that while divine grace is necessary to the conduct of the Christian life, human effort also has its part to play; that is, their position mediated between the contrasting extremes of Augustinian predestinarianism and of Pelagian individualism. Outstanding exponents of such Semi-Pelagianism were Cassian of Marseilles (*c.* 360–435), Vincent of Lérins (*c.* 390–450), and Faustus, bishop of Riez (*c.* 460–90).

In 470 Faustus published *De Gratia* ("On Grace"), and in it he came nearer to the position of Pelagius than Cassian did, but his theses were accepted at a synod held at Arles in about 472. He maintained *inter alia* that the human will is weakened but not enslaved by original sin, and that God can foresee the future without predestinating. More than half a century later, however, the work was denounced as heretical both in Rome and in Constantinople; and Caesarius (*c.* 470–542), who inclined more to Augustinianism than Cassian had, convened a synod that took place at Orange in 529. The Semi-Pelagianism of Faustus was formally condemned, and the synodal decrees were ratified by Pope Boniface II two years later. Although the teaching approved was Augustinian in tenor, the concept of the irresistibility of grace found no official ratification.

BIBLIOGRAPHY

Ferguson, J. *Pelagius: An Historical and Theological Study*. Cambridge: Heffer, 1957.

Jauncey, E. *The Doctrine of Grace up to the End of the Pelagian Controversy, Historically and Dogmatically Considered*. London: Society for Promoting Christian Knowledge, 1925.

15 ‡ Pseudo-Dionysius and ‡ Gregory the Great

The development of medieval Christianity was much affected by Pseudo-Dionysius (*c.* 500), who made a sustained attempt to interpret Christianity in terms of Neoplatonism, and by Gregory the Great (*c.* 540–604), who set forth an institutionalized form of Augustinianism adapted to the needs of the ordinary believer. The two men were very different, however; Pseudo-Dionysius devoted himself to the promotion of the contemplative life and mystical union with God, whereas Gregory was primarily a man of action and an able administrator who sought to relate theological doctrine to the demands of common social existence. While the former was influential in both East and West, Gregory's influence was mainly exercised upon the habits and thoughts of the Latin church.

The name "Dionysius" was falsely given to the writer of a number of works on mystical theology published in the years around 500. Perhaps the author himself was responsible for the nom de plume, hoping that by attributing his writings to one of the alleged converts of the Apostle Paul (Dionysius the Areopagite), he would increase their chances of gaining acceptance in church circles. Subsequent history justified his hope. Some authorities (for example, Hypatius of Ephesus, *c.* 530) questioned the apostolic authorship of the writings, but such sceptical arguments were generally disregarded, and for a thousand years the view prevailed that the author was in fact the Dionysius mentioned in Acts 17:34. This is somewhat surprising, for the writer obviously relies upon Proclus, the Neoplatonist who died in 485; and there is no evidence that the works were ever referred to prior to the time of Severus of Antioch (*c.* 512). It is not impossible that the author had been a disciple of Proclus before embracing a tempered form of monophysite Christianity. This would help to explain why representatives of Monophysitism appealed to his apostolic authority in 533, at a synod held in Constantinople.

The corpus of Pseudo-Dionysius contains four treatises and ten letters purporting to be addressed to various members of the apostolic church, one of whom is the Apostle John. The treatises are: (1) *The Celestial Hierarchy*, which maintains that the incomprehensible and transcendent God is made known through the mediation of three orders of angelic beings; (2) *The Ecclesiastical Hierarchy*, a work that concerns sensible signs of divine reality: the three sacraments of baptism, eucharist, and chrism (or anointing), and the threefold ministry, bishop, priest, and deacon (for which unusual terms are used); it is further argued that the three categories of believers (catachumens, baptised, and monastic) correspond to the three phases of the spiritual life (purification, illumination, and perfection) in the soul's ascent to deified oneness with God; (3) *The Divine Names*, which deals with the essence and attributes of God and, among other things, upholds the view that evil is nothing positive but simply an absence of good; the finite mind may come to a knowledge of God in three ways: the "linear" way, by proceeding from sensible things to their Cause and Ground; the "spiral," by discursive intellection; and the "circular," by directing the mind away from the external world and the exigencies of rationality; (4) *The Mystical Theology*, the shortest of the four treatises, which delineates the soul's passage along the *via negativa* ("negative way") to the ecstatic experience of union with the One that is beyond all finite knowledge and being; the soul, duly purged of limited rational concerns, then contemplates "the superessential splendor of the divine darkness" in a state of unmitigated rapture.

The works of Pseudo-Dionysius soon became standard authorities in the Eastern church, and in the West Gregory the Great, before the end of the sixth century, referred to them with approval. They were used in connection with the repudiation of Monothelitism at the Lateran Council in 649, and knowledge of them greatly increased after John Scotus Erigena (*c.* 810–77) had translated them into Latin. Thomas Aquinas and other important scholastic theologians of the West held Pseudo-Dionysius in high esteem, and medieval mystics in particular (Meister Eckhart, for example) drew on the writings freely. In the sixteenth century the apostolic origin of the corpus began to be seriously questioned, but scholarship had to wait until the last decade of the nineteenth century for a systematic demonstration that the author must have flourished somewhere around the year 500.

Gregory the Great (Gregory I) is counted as one of the four Doctors of the Western church, along with Ambrose, Augustine, and Jerome (the scholar responsible for the revised Latin translation of the Bible known as the Vulgate, who died *c.* 420). Gregory was born of a wealthy senatorial family (*c.* 540), and became prefect of Rome in 573 but soon decided to renounce the world. He sold his property, and proceeded to found seven monasteries, six in Sicily, and one, named after St. Andrew, at Rome. He took the monastic vows, but a few years later he was called upon to become the papal representative at Constantinople. He returned to Rome about ten years later (*c.* 585) and assumed the office of abbot at St. Andrew's. In 590 he attained the distinction of being the first monk to occupy the papal see. Italy was much troubled at the time, languishing under famine, pestilence, and Lombard aggression. In 592, perceiving the weakness of the imperial authority, he took the initiative and successfully negotiated a separate peace with the Lombards, thereby asserting in a practical way the temporal authority of the papacy. He maintained that the bishop of Rome, as the rightful successor of the Apostle Peter, was juridically supreme, and he declined to recognize the legitimacy of the title "Ecumenical Patriarch," which had been adopted by the occupant of the Constantinopolitan see.

Gregory was responsible for sending Augustine (the prior of St. Andrew's) and some forty other monks as missionaries to Britain. The Celtic church there had recently been driven westward and northward by the invading Saxons. Augustine's mission prospered, and he became the first archbishop of Canterbury (*c.* 598). However, he did not succeed in securing an agreement with the Celtic church; and even after the *rapprochement* effected at the Synod of Whitby in 664, Celtic Christianity, some of whose usages were distinctive, survived for some time in Wales and Ireland.

Gregory was no creative thinker, but he had a remarkable capacity for formulating the common belief of the Western church of his day. Despite his political astuteness, his basic attitude was other-worldly; he regarded the present life as a preparation for the life to come, and he did much to promote monasticism and its ascetic disciplines. His understanding of Christianity was generally legalistic, and he represented the spirit of the Latin church as it had been exemplified in the works of Tertullian, Cyprian, and Augustine of Hippo. The scholarship and the speculative adventurousness of Origen were alien to his temper, although of course he subscribed to the ecumenical creeds of Nicea and Chalcedon. He postulated that the Catholic church is the sole mediator of saving grace, and that its teachings should be accepted without question: faith is meritorious precisely because it entails a certain something which man's puny intellect cannot comprehend (*Homilies on the Gospels,* 26:1). He freely used the allegorical method in his exegesis of the scriptures, and not infrequently he betrayed a childlike naïveté in the *Dialogues,* a work which recounts the adventures of Benedict and other saints of the Western church; many of the tales concern the machinations of the Devil and his demonic subordinates, and they are often amusing in their unconscious whimsicality.

Gregory's most important theological treatise, frequently cited as the *Moralia*, is a popular exposition of Christian doctrine in the form of an interpretation of the book of Job. Gregory's basic doctrinal position was in line with the mediating decrees of the Synod of Orange (529). The human will is weakened by original sin, and in order to turn to God in repentance man needs to be inwardly moved by prevenient grace. But the corruption inherited from Adam does not involve the complete enslavement of the human will, and grace is not irresistible. Infused grace does not transmute man into an automaton; by faith the individual becomes a co-worker with God and is enabled to perform good works that are genuinely his own; it is erroneous to suppose that God rewards merely his own gifts (*Moralia*, 16:30). God predestinates, but to salvation only, not to damnation, and perhaps predestination is conditional—that is, dependent upon God's foreseeing the possible future merits of an individual (*ibid.*, 20:18).

On the other hand, Gregory agreed with Augustine that baptism, while removing the guilt of original sin, does not remove the corrupt condition of man's inherited nature. Depravity lingers into the Christian life, and forgiveness for post-baptismal sins can be obtained by the performance of atoning acts involving repentance, confession, and self-sacrifice. The church has made provision for such offences in the institution of penance, which presupposes that self-punishment acts as a substitute for punishment inflicted by God (*ibid.*, 9:54). Although one can never be absolutely certain that adequate penance has been made, this circumstance is not without value since it prevents people from becoming unduly complacent (*ibid.*, 5:21). Penitents who have not atoned for their post-baptismal sins at the time of their death must go to purgatory for the completion of their penance; then they will proceed to heaven. But the wicked, who are without the credit of atoning or meritorious works, will be subjected after death to the everlasting torments of hell (*Dialogues*, 4:39).

Christ's life, which culminated in his crucifixion, was a continuous sacrifice offered for the good of all men (*Moralia*, 1:32); and (as Cyprian had insisted) the eucharist is a repetition of Christ's sacrifice. Unlike the one atoning archetype, however, eucharistic sacrifices benefit not every human soul, but only the communicants themselves and others definitely cited at the services. These latter could be souls in purgatory; and the offering of a eucharistic sacrifice on their behalf has the effect of shortening the period of their disciplinary sufferings.

Through Adam's sin, so Gregory argued (following Augustine and others), humanity was subjected to corruption and death; man lost his freedom and came under the rightful control of Satan. But through the incarnation of the Son of God the Devil was tricked out of his rights. Satan assumed that Christ was an ordinary man and engineered his crucifixion, not realizing that in fact Jesus was sinless. In this crucial instance the Devil went too far; hence he forfeited his right to enslave the descendants of Adam, and God can now forgive sinful men without doing violence to the requirements of justice.

Ideas of this kind had already been expressed by Augustine, as well as by Origen (*C. Celsum*, 7:17) and others. But Gregory set them forth more systematically. He also advised his fellow Christians to implore the holy martyrs to intercede on their behalf before the judgment seat of Christ (*Moralia*, 16:64), and he promoted the veneration of sacred relics. He improved the liturgy and composed the original Gregorian Chant. His interest in the writings of Pseudo-Dionysius may well have been mainly due to the elaborate angelology they contain.

BIBLIOGRAPHY

Dudden, F. H. *Gregory the Great: His Place in History and Thought*. 2 vols. London: Longmans, Green, 1905.

Jones, R. M. *Studies in Mystical Religion.* London: Macmillan, 1909.

Rolt, C. E. *Dionysius the Areopagite on the Divine Names and the Mystical Theology.* London: Society for Promoting Christian Knowledge, 1920.

16 ‡ The Emergence
of Monasticism

Etymologically, "monastic" and "monk" (Greek: *monos*, "alone") mean much the same as "hermit" (Greek: *erēmitēs*, "desert recluse") or "anchorite" (Greek: *anachōrētēs*, "one who retires"), and should be applied to individuals who separate themselves from ordinary society to live a solitary existence. As things have developed, however, those who lead what is commonly called a monastic life are not isolated hermits; they are members of communal orders, and hence, from one point of view, the term "cenobite" (Greek: *koinos*, "common" + *bios*, "life") would be more appropriate, as signifying a person belonging to a society whose members own their goods in common. The word "asceticism" is also of Greek derivation (*askēsis*, "exercise" or "training"), and is used of any system of austerities voluntarily undertaken for the promotion of the spiritual life.

Christian monasticism, which apparently had its beginnings in Egypt during the third century, spread rapidly into the Sinai peninsula, Palestine, and Syria. An influential anchorite in the early days was Antony of Egypt (*c.* 270–360), who, prompted by the dominical saying in Matt. 19:21, sold his property and distributed the proceeds to the poor. He then retired to the desert and surrendered himself to a life of strict asceticism. About twenty years later (*c.* 305) he gathered several hermits together and introduced a rule of discipline; but the organization appears to have been relatively loose. He emerged from retirement to support Athanasius (*c.* 295–373) in the Arian controversy and, according to tradition, the latter wrote the widely-read biography *Vita Antonii*, a work that enhanced Antony's reputation. Besides promoting the monastic movement in Egypt, Athanasius used his influence to expedite its diffusion in the West.

Pachomius (*c.* 292–346) seems to have developed the cenobitic ideal more systematically than Antony. He lived for a while as a hermit, but toward 320 he built a monastery at Tabennisi on the Nile in southern Egypt. By the time of his death he had established nine monasteries and two convents. Basil of Caesarea in Cappadocia (*c.* 330–79) furthered the work of Pachomius and greatly contributed to the regulation of monastic discipline in both East and West; he formulated two rules, and these were translated into Latin by Rufinus (*c.* 345–410). But it would be wrong to suppose that the spread of cenobitic monasticism crowded out the hermits; many still preferred to practice their asceticism alone, and in certain instances their austerities were most spectacular. Simeon Stylites (*c.* 390–459), for example, sat on a pillar near Syrian Antioch for over thirty years, absorbed in prayerful contemplation most of the time, and he attracted a great deal of attention; people flocked to him for consultations, and he corresponded with a number of ecclesiastical authorities. Some sought to emulate his achievement, spending their lives on the tops of pillars or amid the branches of trees; these latter were the so-called dendrites. On the whole, however, such extravagances were discouraged in Christian circles, and competitive extremism in the practice of austerities never gained there the respect it achieved in India.

As we have seen, following in the wake of the *rapprochement* between church and state under Constantine, Athanasius aroused Latin interest in monasticism, and earnest souls tended increasingly to react against growing ecclesiastical secularization by choosing to take up the ascetic way of life. Martin of Tours (*c.* 325–97) seems to have been the first person to found a monastery in Gaul; he traveled widely in Italy, and then, with the assistance of Hilary, bishop of Poitiers, established an ascetic community at Ligugé (360). The institution he subsequently founded at Tours (after his appointment as bishop there) became especially influential. The work of John Cassian (*c.* 360–435) was also significant in this general connection. His birthplace is unknown. After spending several years at a monastery in Bethlehem, he went to Egypt before settling in the region of Marseilles, where he proceeded to found two communities secluded under special vows. He set out regulations for the monastic life in his *Institutes*, and in his *Conferences* he reported on the contacts he had made with leaders of Eastern monasticism. Besides all this, he was a Semi-Pelagian and initiated the theological discussions that culminated in the decisions of the synod held at Orange in 529.

It was Benedict (*c.* 480–550), however, who laid the foundations of monastic legislation in the Latin church. He was born at Nursia and educated in Rome. Disgusted with the low moral standards prevalent in the capital, he retired to Subiaco as a hermit toward the year 500. Gradually, an interested group gathered about him, and he eventually founded twelve monasteries, each with a membership of twelve. But rivalry and disobedience finally induced him to move again. In 527, with a few faithful followers, he went to Monte Cassino (between Rome and Naples), and it was there that he drew up the famous rule that bears his name. His sister, Scholastica, formed a community of women ascetics in the same vicinity. Apparently, he had not been ordained, and the order he established was not originally intended for the clergy.

In the compilation of his rule of discipline Benedict drew on the earlier regulations formulated by Cassian and Basil (the latter in the translation of Rufinus) and on proposals made by Caesarius, the archbishop of Arles, who played an important role in the condemnation of Pelagian tendencies at the Synod of Orange (529). Besides poverty and chastity, the rule required *stabilitas loci* ("fixity of location"). But on the whole it was characterized by reasonableness and moderation; the monk's activities were carefully scheduled, and his time was divided between sleep, work, and devotions. The rule came to be widely adopted, and within a hundred years of Benedict's death it dominated Western monasticism and continued to do so into the thirteenth century—the period which saw the rise and spread of the mendicant orders of the Dominicans and the Franciscans.

The reasons for the emergence and consolidation of Christian monasticism are as complicated as they are interesting, for numerous motives and influences were doubtless at work. The ascetic ideal never became dominant in Judaism, and in this respect Christianity provides a striking contrast to the religion from which it sprang. According to the Old Testament, the world, as God's creation, was fundamentally good; the sexes were part of God's handiwork, and primordial humanity was exhorted to be fruitful and multiply (Gen. 1:1 ff.). Hence any notion that sexual intercourse was evil would be quite contrary to basic biblical teaching. On the other hand, there are elements in the vast range of the Jewish scriptures which could be used for support by people who were already predisposed to asceticism. For one thing it could be argued that the sin which led to the dispatch of Adam and Eve from paradise (Gen. 3:1 ff.) profoundly changed the human situation: the flesh had been corrupted, and in consequence carnal desires should be mortified by strenuous self-discipline. Such was the view of the Apostle Paul, and it became extremely influential in the early development of Christian thought.

Moreover, the great prophets from about 750 B.C. onward tended to react negatively against Canaanite civilization. Amos, Hosea, and Jeremiah referred nostalgically to a nomadic past: during the desert sojourn Israel lived truly as the people of God (Amos 5:25; Hos. 9:10; Jer. 2:1 ff.), but degeneration set in with the settlement in Canaan, and increased wealth turned the people aside from the path of rectitude and the worship of the

one true God (Hos. 10:1; 11:1–2). In a well-known passage
Jeremiah commends the faithfulness of the Rechabites, a group
that sought to recapture the simplicities of the desert life by
living in tents and abstaining from wine (Jer. 35:1 ff.). While
Jeremiah recognized that what was really required for the people's salvation was a change of heart, rather than a change of
habitat or of social institutions (Jer. 4:3–4), the fact remains
that he saw in the austere simplicities of the old bedouin life a
standard by which he could condemn the corruptions of current civilization (Jer. 6:16).

Moreover, during the Maccabean period in the second century B.C. there were certain Jewish groups that cut themselves
off from ordinary society. Perhaps the Essenes and the community at Qumran (the sect that produced and treasured the
so-called Dead Sea Scrolls) were Israelites who to some extent
had been moved to react against the Hellenizers (those Jews
who wished to assimilate Israelite to Greek culture) by with-
drawing into the wilderness. In an effort to reconstitute the true
Israel of God, they held themselves aloof from the corruptions
of secular existence and led a monastic life. Moreover, may it
not be that John the Baptist had belonged to the sect at Qumran? The gospels report that he preached in that region (in the
wilderness, not far from the fords of the Jordan) and that he
lived on a scanty diet of locusts and wild honey (e.g., Mark
1:4 ff.). Also, Jesus himself must have been affected by John,
for he even submitted to his baptism for repentance (Mark 1:9).
Thus the austerity of the Israelite desert tradition could have
been made a part of the Christianity of the earliest days, and it
was largely in monasticism that such rigorism eventually found
expression.

It must be observed, however, that the majority of scholars
tend to deny that the Baptist ever adhered to the sect of the
Scrolls. Also, there are passages in the gospels which suggest
that Jesus came to oppose John's asceticism (Mark 2:18–22;
Luke 7:33–34); and it is not impossible that a conflict had en-

sued between Jesus and the Baptist on the matter of purification (John 3:25). Furthermore, we have no certain evidence that the community of Qumran regarded carnal desires as inherently evil or that they considered celibacy to be superior to marriage. The skulls of women have been discovered at the Qumran cemetery—an indication that the group there was not exclusively masculine; and (as in Mark 10:7–8) in one of their writings (*Zadokite Fragments*, IV:20–21) Gen. 2:24 is cited to authorize the permanence of the (monogamous) marriage vow.

Indeed, according to basic Jewish belief, an unmarried person is incomplete or imperfect. For one thing, in singleness no human individual could fulfill the primordial divine command that humanity should be fruitful and multiply, whence it follows that wedlock must have divine sanction. Even Ben Sira, the Jewish sage of the second century B.C. and author of the book of Ecclesiasticus, who often appears to have been something of a misogynist, maintained that a good wife is a man's best possible possession (Ecclus. 36:24). Although Ecclesiasticus is in the Apocrypha (the works included in the Greek translation of the Hebrew scriptures but not finally accepted as canonical in the rabbinical schools) it was widely read in the early Christian centuries, and the practical wisdom of its ethical teachings probably had a moderating effect upon tendencies toward extreme asceticism. Ben Sira could even declare that Eve's sin brought mortality upon humanity, and that a man's wickedness is better than a woman's goodness (Ecclus. 25:24; 42:14); and yet he was convinced that a harmonious married life is far superior to a bachelor's existence (Ecclus. 36:18 ff.).

As was observed in the introductory chapter, the notion that the end of the present world was drawing near dominated the thinking of the early Christians, deeply affecting their attitude to material possessions and to such institutions as marriage and existing forms of civil government. The last judgment was imminent; the powers of evil would soon be vanquished and the Kingdom of God finally constituted. The church itself, with its charismatic powers, was a standing witness to an approaching vindication of the faithful that would inaugurate the joys of the age to come and bring to an end the trials and tribulations of the present age.

Hence apostolic ethics demanded singleness of purpose; all interests were to be subordinated to one supreme spiritual concern —namely, preparation for a divine judgment that was shortly to take place. So the Jesus of the synoptic gospels frequently called for rigorous self-discipline. For example, the wealthy could be instructed to give their goods to the poor, and thereby make sure of treasure in heaven (Luke 12:32 ff.). What really mattered was richness toward God (Luke 12:21). The dead should be left to bury their dead (Matt. 8:22), and loyalty to the Christ must take precedence over all mundane family affections (Luke 14:26). The Son of Man gave his life for the salvation of many (Mark 10:45), and self-abnegation was demanded of his followers (Mark 8:34). There were some who had gone so far as to mutilate themselves for the sake of the Kingdom of Heaven (Matt. 19:12). The same sort of moral stringency found exemplification in the writings of the Apostle Paul, who, in his advocacy of freedom from worldly entanglements, could argue that marriage necessarily distracts a person from the service of the Lord, since any husband or wife becomes anxious about mundane things in an effort to please his or her spouse (I Cor. 7:32 ff.).

Accordingly, eschatological expectation had an important bearing upon the ethical rigorism and other-worldliness of apostolic Christianity. The appointed time was short; and apparently men and women sometimes lived together without engaging in sexual intercourse (I Cor. 7:36 ff.), while others would sell their property and give what accrued to the church or to the poor (Acts 4:36–37; cf. Mark 10:21). But the author of Acts probably gives an idealized picture of the situation when he baldly asserts that the early believers had all things in common (Acts 4:32). In all likelihood, such a representation was due to an a priori judgment of his own, according to which, private property is one of the evils bound up with the fallenness of the present human situation. Similar idealization is evident in Acts 2:1 ff., where it is related that, after the outpouring of the divine Spirit at the first Christian Pentecost, the followers of Jesus were enabled to speak in a language that was universally comprehensible; the *glossalalia* ("speaking with tongues") is in this case no unintelligible gibberish, as it is in I Cor. 14:1 ff., but a mode of utterance representative of a return to a supposed original state of affairs prior to the destruction of the Tower of Babel, when men were not divided by differences of language (Gen. 11:7). Thus the motif is reminiscent of the Pauline contention that faith in Christ restores mankind to a fellowship in which there is neither Jew nor Gentile, neither bond nor free, neither male nor female (Gal. 3:28).

Hence actual Christian existence was in some measure understood as a restoration of primordial conditions; the paradise lost was being regained. As at the beginning, so at the end, peace would reign, and no human government would be needed to restrain man's selfish passions; the goods provided for man's benefit would be held in common; and humanity, recovering an androgynous constitution, would neither marry nor give in marriage (Mark 12:25). In other words, an eschatological principle helps to explain certain features of early Christian valuations; and the tendency to renounce private property, which was taken up and perpetuated in monasticism, is a case in point. Perhaps the same principle also affected apostolic views on matrimony, although the evidence in this instance is somewhat indirect. In any event, according to Gen. 2:4 ff., Adam and Eve were originally one flesh, and only after the separation of the woman from the man was paradise lost through the commission of sin. And (despite the exaltation of marriage in such passages as Mark 10:7–8) it was apparently taken to be harmonious with this line of thought that Saying 23 in the recently discovered gnostic work *The Gospel of Thomas* represents human beings as entering the Kingdom when man and woman became "single"—that is, presumably, when humanity, without marriage, somehow recovers its androgynous character in bisexual individualities.

Of course the Gnostics shared the characteristic outlook of Hellenistic pessimism, regarding matter and spirit as being dualistically opposed to each other. Matter was essentially evil, and salvation consisted in the deliverance of the soul from the prison house of the body. Such liberation was to be obtained by a special mode of secret knowledge (Greek: *gnōsis*) possessed solely by the gnostic teachers. As one would expect, they generally advocated the mortification of the flesh; and it is not impossible that ascetic tendencies within the church were strengthened through influences that came from gnostic quarters. A metaphysical dualism between matter and spirit was basic in Neoplatonism and Manicheanism, as well as in Gnosticism, and it was inevitable that Christianity should have been affected by its cultural environment. Already in the writings of the Apostle Paul there are suggestions that the flesh is inherently evil (e.g., Rom. 7:18)—and this despite the fact that his basic theology was essentially Jewish. The question of the extent to which Paul was influenced by Hellenistic pessimism is disputed, but there can be little doubt that some of the statements in his epistles could easily be construed in a dualistic sense, and thus be used to encourage the development of asceticism and monasticism.

A further factor that must be taken into account concerns the relaxation of church discipline. As we have seen, Tertullian strongly protested against the view (which was becoming increasingly prevalent) that the church is a mixed community containing good and bad alike. He insisted that certain postbaptismal sins were truly mortal; but time and tide were against him, and during the third century the belief gained ground that penance could take care of all mortal sins. On the other hand, Tertullian was by no means the last of the rigorists, and kindred spirits who came after him found a place in the church by taking the monastic vows. Moreover, with the *rapprochement* of church and state under Constantine it became easy, even advantageous, to belong to the church, and all too soon perhaps most of those who had been baptized were Christian in name only. By way of reaction, many of the more serious-minded took to the ascetic life, and monasticism grew. This in turn contributed to the acceptance of a dual standard: there were certain minimum requirements for the masses, but for a minority the so-called counsels of perfection were operative obligations (cf. Matt. 19:21). The spiritual elite took vows of poverty, chastity, and obedience, and thereby sought to recapture the heroic virtue which had so often characterized the practice of Christianity in the earlier years. (See Chapter 19 for medieval monastic developments.)

BIBLIOGRAPHY

Bailey, D. S. *The Man-Woman Relation in Christian Thought.* London: Longmans, Green, 1959.

Chadwick, W. O. *John Cassian: A Study of Primitive Monasticism.* Cambridge: Cambridge University Press, 1950.

Chitty, D. J. *The Desert a City: An Introduction to the Study of Egyptian and Palestinian Monasticism under the Christian Empire.* Oxford: Basil Blackwell, 1966.

Farag, F. R. *Sociological and Moral Studies in the Field of Coptic Monasticism.* Leiden: E. J. Brill, 1964.

Harnack, Adolf von. *Monasticism: Its Ideals and History and the Confessions of St. Augustine.* London: Williams and Norgate, 1913.

17 ‡ The Papacy and the
‡ Holy Roman Empire

In 726 Emperor Leo III precipitated the iconoclastic controversy, and in 732 Frankish forces under Charles Martel conquered the invading Moslems near Tours on the River Loire. Popes Gregory II (715–31) and Gregory III (731–41) vigorously opposed the emperor's iconoclastic policy, and for a time Italy was in a state of revolt. Leo reacted by annexing the Papal Patrimonies in southern Italy and the province of Illyria. In addition, the Lombards had become aggressive and were pressing southward with a view to the conquest of the whole of Italy. In 739 Pope Gregory III tried to secure Frankish help by appealing to Charles Martel. Although the appeal was made in vain, it may be regarded as the first step in the formation of the alliance between the papacy and the Frankish kings, which eventually led to the establishment of the Holy Roman Empire and the virtual liberation of the popes from political subordination to the Byzantine emperors.

In 751 the Lombards captured Ravenna, the seat of the exarch, the Western representative of the Constantinopolitan emperor. In the same year Pippin the Short, the son of Charles Martel, was proclaimed king by the nobles (in place of the Merovingian, Childeric III), and with the approval of Pope Zacharias (741–52) he was anointed by Boniface, the archbishop of Mainz. This ritual act could easily be so interpreted as to imply that the papacy enjoyed supreme temporal authority, and had the right to create kings, a dogma that was to be promoted by the spurious Donation of Constantine (see Chapter 7) and the Forged Decretals (to be explained shortly). A year or two later the Lombards were threatening to take Rome. Pope Stephen III (752–57), failing to secure assistance from Constantinople, turned to Pippin, who reacted favorably. In 754 Stephen himself anointed Pippin afresh, and conferred upon him the title *patricius* which had formerly been held by the exarch of Ravenna. Pippin was true to his word; he proceeded to fulfill his part of the bargain, conquering the Lombards and thereby delivering Rome from the threat of invasion. The exarchate became a Latin possession, and thus began the papal rule over "the states of the church"—a sovereignty that grew in the course of time and was perpetuated until 1870. Throughout his reign Pippin endeavored to increase the prestige of the church among his subjects, and he did much to implement reforms introduced by Boniface.

After Pippin's death in 768, his sons, Charlemagne and Carloman (both of whom had undergone papal annointing in 754), divided the kingdom between them. Carloman died in 771, whereupon Charlemagne became sole ruler, and during the next twenty-eight years he devoted himself mainly to enlarging his kingdom. He more than doubled his father's territorial possessions, extending his sway over France, Belgium, Holland, Austria, Hungary, a part of northern Spain, and about half of Germany. Pope Hadrian I (772–95) furthered the policy of his predecessor, Stephen III, and sought to maintain good relations with the Frankish monarch. But Charlemagne's greatly increased power somewhat limited the effective authority of the papacy; for example, Charlemagne refused to sanction the anti-iconoclastic decision of the Seventh Ecumenical Council (Nicea, 787), defying Pope Hadrian's demands that he should publicly express agreement with them. This conflict foreshadowed the struggles to come.

Charlemagne's career reached its high point on Christmas

Day in the year 800, when he was crowned at St. Peter's in Rome, thereby becoming the first of the Holy Roman Emperors. The old imperium was now politically divided, and tensions between East and West were aggravated. Pope Hadrian had been succeeded by Leo III (795–816), a man of humble birth, and the latter's election to the papal office aroused the jealousy of Hadrian's noble relatives. They conspired to have him castrated, and during a ceremonial procession in 799 Leo was violently attacked and seriously injured. But he recovered and escaped to Charlemagne, who promised his assistance. Leo was provided with a protective escort for his return to Rome, and Charlemagne followed him in December 800. The antipapal accusations were declared unfounded, and two days later the coronation was carried out at the hands of Leo. A new imperium was born, a Western authority destined to have a long history; for its death did not occur until Napoleon took lethal action in 1806, and even then its ghost, the Austrian empire, lingered on until the victory of the Allies in 1918.

Charlemagne centralized the administration of his kingdom and did much to standardize the laws by issuing capitularies (that is, ordinances divided into chapters; Latin: *capitulum*, "chapter" or "section"). Like his father, he encouraged ecclesiastical reform. He was a great patron of learning, initiating what came to be known as the Carolingian Renaissance. He seems to have had a genuine interest in theological matters; he opposed the veneration of images, and also Spanish Adoptianism, a form of christology reminiscent of Dynamic Monarchianism, which may have been regarded as less objectionable to the Moslem Moors in Toledo than the Chalcedonian doctrine. Alcuin (*c.* 730–804) was the agent of the educational reform. Born at York in England, he studied and taught at the cathedral school there, becoming an accomplished scholar well acquainted with the writings of Augustine. In 796 he was appointed abbot of Tours, and there he established an important school and library.

Charlemagne was succeeded by his son Louis the Pious (814–

40), and the Empire declined in strength. By the Treaty of Verdun, concluded in 843, the three sons of Louis divided the territory among themselves; and from that date, France and Germany were to go their separate ways, with momentous consequences. The general deterioration continued, and by the end of the ninth century educational standards were perhaps as low as they had ever been in Latin Christendom.

It should be noticed here that in the middle of the ninth century, perhaps at Tours, was produced a remarkably clever collection of documents, the Forged Decretals. The corpus consists of the following items: fraudulent letters of ante-Nicene bishops of Rome; canons of councils, mostly genuine; and letters by bishops of Rome from Silvester I (d. 335) to Gregory II (d. 731), of which thirty-five are definitely spurious. Pope Nicholas I in 865 appealed to the authority of the collection, although evidently aware that it was not historically reliable. The forger probably belonged to a group that saw in the papacy the guarantor of church unity and that wished to uphold the rights of the diocesan (as opposed to the metropolitan) bishops. In the material assembled, the earlier popes already claim the right of general ecclesiastical jurisdiction and assert that any bishop may appeal directly to the papal incumbent; also, they stress that the hierarchy is properly quite independent of all secular control. The genuineness of the corpus was widely accepted until after the Reformation, its falsity being exposed by the Centuriators of Magdeburg, who produced the Lutheran *Historia Ecclesiae Christi* ("The History of the Church of Christ") at Basel in 1559-74.

Simony and nicolaitanism became increasingly common during the closing decades of the ninth century. Each of these terms had come to have a technical meaning in the language of the church: nicolaitanism signified clerical marriage or concubinage, and simony referred to lay investiture, which so often involved the sale of ecclesiastical benefices to the highest bidder. Such practices were disturbing to the more devout, who had come to the conclusion that the church would never be able to put its own house in order so long as it remained in subjection to secular powers. What was needed was a papacy strong enough to overrule external authorities; then, and only then, would the hierarchy be in a position to eliminate abuses and to impose a strict discipline upon the clergy.

Such was the kind of reform contemplated by certain outstanding individuals who, during the tenth and eleventh centuries, were associated with the influential monastery founded in 910 at Cluny (near Mâcon in Burgundy) by William the Pious, Duke of Aquitaine. A serious attempt was made there to regularize monastic life: the abbots aimed at a rigorous application of the Benedictine rule and sought to establish an economic autonomy that would free the institution from all secular domination. Under Abbot Odilo, whose period of office extended for over fifty years (994–1048), the number of Cluniac houses more than doubled, to reach sixty-five; and the administration was largely centralized, most of the affiliated institutions having priors under the direct control of the abbot of Cluny.

The most significant Cluniac reformer of the eleventh century was Hildebrand, born in Tuscany about 1020. He became chaplain to Pope Gregory VI, and when the latter was banished in 1046, Hildebrand took up residence at Cluny, where he remained for three years. Returning to Rome in 1049, he deeply influenced papal policy until he was himself elected bishop of Rome, as Gregory VII, in 1073. He at once made a determined effort to put the ideas of the Cluniac reformers into effect. In 1074 he published decrees denouncing simony and nicolaitanism, and in 1075 he prohibited lay investiture. There was opposition in Germany, France, and England, and a tremendous struggle ensued between Gregory and Emperor Henry IV. *Prima facie* the Pope's career ended in shame and defeat. Rome was besieged, and Gregory had to flee to Monte Cassino. Henry set up a counter-pope in 1084: he was Clement III, who duly played his part by confirming Henry in his office and presiding at a coronation ceremony. As for Gregory, he died at Salerno in the following year.

But Gregory's influence survived him, and his followers gathered strength; eventually, the Concordat of Worms was concluded in 1122 between Emperor Henry V and Pope Callistus II (1119–24); essentially a compromise, it was meant to regulate the appointment of bishops in Germany, Burgundy, and Italy. The agreement provided that the pope had the right of investiture with the ring and staff (the symbols of religious authority), and that the emperor had the right of investiture with the royal scepter (the symbol of temporal authority). Although this settlement by no means represented a complete victory for the Cluniac reformers, it did in any event confirm the church's equality with the state in the important matter of episcopal appointments.

BIBLIOGRAPHY

Gavin, F. S. B. *Seven Centuries of the Problem of Church and State*. Princeton, N.J.: Princeton University Press, 1938.

Kelly, J. N. D. *The Athanasian Creed*. London: Black, 1964.

Wallach, Luitpold. *Alcuin and Charlemagne: Studies in Carolingian History and Literature*. Ithaca, N.Y.: Cornell University Press, 1959.

18 ‡ *The East-West Schism*

It may be recalled that the original Nicene Creed merely affirmed belief in the Holy Spirit, whereas the Niceno-Constantinopolitan Creed contained certain explanations respecting the third member of the Trinity: "We believe . . . in the Holy Spirit, the Lord, the Giver of life, who proceeds from the Father, who with the Father and the Son is worshiped and glorified, who spoke through the prophets . . . ." Certain passages in the New Testament, however, connect the Holy Spirit with the Son (for example, John 16:13–15; Gal. 4:6); and, in accordance with a line of thought to be found in the writings of Cyril of Alexandria, Augustine (*De Trinit.*, 15:17) asserted that the Holy Spirit proceeds from the Father "and from the Son" (Latin: *filioque*). In all likelihood, therefore, it was through Augustine's influence that in 589 at the Third Council of Toledo the expression *filioque* was incorporated into the Latin form of the Creed. The addition came to be widely accepted in the West, and in 809 the Spanish interpolation was formally approved (under the authority of Charlemagne) at the Synod of Aachen, and this decision became regulative for the newly-constituted Holy Roman Empire. About fifty years later, Photius, as patriarch of Constantinople, charged Western theologians with heresy for taking it upon themselves to tamper with an ecumenical creed.

Actually, much more was involved in the great schism be-

tween the Greek and Latin churches than the question of the
filioque addition; there were differences in liturgical usage, in
discipline, and in theological outlook; and, over and above all
this, there was the deep-seated political rivalry between Rome
and Constantinople.

Controversy broke out at Constantinople in 858. The Eastern
ruler at the time, Emperor Michael III (commonly known as
Michael the Tippler because of his intemperate habits) lived
largely under the domination of his uncle Bardas, a gentleman
who was far from being a paragon of virtue. Ignatius, the Constantinopolitan patriarch, scandalized by Bardas' dissolute ways
and sinister influence, eventually served him with an excommunication order. This incensed Michael, who deposed Ignatius
forthwith; and Photius (*c.* 810–95), the chief secretary of state,
was appointed to fill the patriarchal vacancy, although he was a
layman. Ignatius appealed to Pope Nicholas I (858–67), whereupon Roman legates were dispatched to a synod held at Constantinople in 861; but, apparently under court pressure, they
played false to their papal instructions and went so far as to
support the synod's confirmation of Ignatius' deposition. Nicholas responded by declaring their action null and void, and asserting the restoration of Ignatius to the patriarchate.

This Roman move was greatly resented in Constantinople,
and Michael promptly communicated his feelings to Nicholas in
no uncertain terms. The Pope replied that he was willing to re-
open the discussion, but in 867 Photius publicly condemned the
presence of Latin missionaries in Bulgaria as an illegitimate
Roman intrusion into Eastern territory. He went on to accuse
the Western church of heresy for accepting the *filioque* interpolation, and proceeded to denounce a number of Latin practices, namely fasting on Saturdays, consuming dairy products
during Lent, requiring complete celibacy for the clergy, and
restricting the conduct of baptismal confirmation to holders of
the episcopal office. At a Constantinopolitan synod that met
later in 867 the Pope was deposed, anathematized, and excom-

municated. However, Nicholas died before he could take further action.

The controversy flared up again in the eleventh century, when Rome was being threatened by Norman aggression. At the time, Pope Leo IX was persistently interfering with churches in Sicily that followed the Eastern rite, and Michael Cerularius, patriarch of Constantinople (1043–58), joining forces with Leo, the metropolitan bishop of Bulgaria, closed all the Latin churches in their regions. The Bulgarian Leo wrote a strongly-worded letter to Rome, in which he repeated the Photian accusations and, in addition, condemned the employment of unleavened bread at celebrations of the eucharist, a usage that had become widespread in the West during the ninth century. The result was that in 1054 emissaries from Rome officially placed the fateful bull of excommunication on the high altar at the renowned church of Santa Sophia in Constantinople. And Cerularius lost no time in replying with anathemas.

In his work *De Processione Sancti Spiritus* ("On the Procession of the Holy Spirit") Anselm, archbishop of Canterbury (1089–1109), sought a reconciling formulation of the doctrine of the double procession of the Holy Spirit; he argued that the Spirit must proceed from the Father and the Son, not as from independent persons, but as from the single divine essence that is both Father and Son. However, the breach was far too deep to be healed by verbal manipulations, and it was widened by acrimonious conflicts that came with the Crusades. In 1182 the Byzantines massacred Latin residents in Constantinople; in 1191 King Richard I of England subjugated Cyprus; and in 1204 French and Venetian adventurers on the Fourth Crusade sacked Constantinople. Violent exchanges of this character were hard to forget.

Nevertheless, on two occasions representatives of the Eastern church did seek reconciliation with the West and, in the discussions that ensued, actually accepted the validity of the *filioque* credal addition. In both instances, however, the Eastern delegates were prompted by political considerations: at the Council of Lyons in 1274 they feared the aggressive designs of Charles of Anjou, who wished to become the first Latin Emperor of Constantinople; and at the Council of Florence in 1439 they were seeking support from the West against Turkish forces that were approaching Constantinople. In neither case had the agreements any real backing in the Eastern church. Constantinople finally fell to the Turks in 1453; the magnificent Santa Sophia was converted into a mosque, and so it remained until recent years; now a museum, the glory of its mosaics are again exposed to public view.

The Turks had endangered the Eastern empire for many years prior to 1453; they captured Jerusalem and almost the whole of Asia Minor in 1071. Repeated appeals for help were made to the West, but it was not until 1095 that Pope Urban II delivered the stirring speech that led to the first of the eight Crusades. The last took place in 1270 under the leadership of Louis of France and Charles of Anjou. However, all the Palestinian holdings gained by the crusaders had been lost by the end of the thirteenth century.

It should be noticed here that Photius, the man who played such an important part in the division of East and West, seems to have taken the first steps for the Christianization of Russia (*c.* 865). The Russian Queen Olga was baptized at Constantinople in 957; and in 988 Emperor Vladimir I declared Christianity to be the official religion of his kingdom. A metropolitan episcopal see was established at Kiev, but this was transferred to Moscow in 1328; and it was not until 1461 that a second metropolitan bishopric came into existence at Kiev. The elevation of the Moscow see to patriarchal status was due to the action of the Constantinopolitan patriarch, Jeremias II, in 1589.

BIBLIOGRAPHY

Geanakoplos, D. J. *Byzantine East and Latin West.* Oxford: Basil Blackwell, 1966.

Hussey, Joan M. *Church and Learning in the Byzantine Empire, 867–1185.* London: Oxford University Press, 1937.

Runciman, Steven. *The Eastern Schism.* Oxford: Clarendon Press, 1955.

——. *The Great Church in Captivity: A Study of the Patriarchate of Constantinople from the Eve of the Turkish Conquest to the Greek War of Independence.* Cambridge: Cambridge University Press, 1968.

IV $\ddagger$ MEDIEVAL
$\ddagger$ DEVELOPMENTS

19 ‡ *Monastic Orders*

The relaxation of ecclesiastical discipline (see Chapter 16), which first affected the church as a whole, influenced monasticism itself with the passage of the centuries. The Benedictine rule came to be applied with increasing freedom, and, as already observed, the foundation of the famous monastery at Cluny in 910 was inspired by a desire for a rigorous application of the rule of Benedict. But with success, laxity at length overtook the Cluniacs, and a further reformation was called for during the later decades of the eleventh century. The need was filled in 1098 by Robert de Molesme who, along with a few other Benedictines, founded an institution at Citeaux, where the austerities went far beyond the common monastic requirements of the time. Its influence grew rapidly throughout the West, and by 1250 the abbot of Citeaux controlled over six hundred houses. Stringent rules concerning diet and periods of silence were set forth, and manual work was emphasized (as it was in the original Benedictine rule), a consequence being that the Cistercians made an invaluable contribution to agriculture.

Bernard (1090–1153), the outstanding ecclesiastical figure of his day, had been a monk at Citeaux for a time (1113–15) before he founded a monastery at Clairvaux. He was a mystic, as well as a statesman of unusual ability. In 1130 he supported Innocent II against Anacletus, and, with the latter's defeat, official favor was shown to the Cistercian Order. Bernard's influence increased when his pupil, Eugenius III, was appointed to the papal office in 1145. Bernard played an important role in the organization of the disastrous Second Crusade (1147–49). He practiced an extreme asceticism, and combined mysticism with remarkable political acumen and efficiency. He was mainly responsible for the condemnation of Abelard at Sens in 1141.

Bernard made strenuous efforts to convert the Cathari ("purists"), who gathered in considerable numbers in southern France during the twelfth century. They showed similarities of outlook with the Bogomiles, an other-worldly sect that originated in Bulgaria some two hundred years earlier. Perhaps the Cathari had their beginnings in the same region; they were extremely stringent in their asceticism, repudiating marriage and the secularism of the church. Although historical connection with Manicheanism is seriously questioned, there were obvious doctrinal affinities. Pope Innocent III (1198–1216) made war on the heretics in 1208, but they (with support from sections of the nobility) held out for twenty years. Not infrequently, the Cathari showed a closer acquaintance with the scriptures than the representatives of Catholic orthodoxy, and at the Synod of Toulouse in 1229 it was decreed that the laity should not be allowed to possess unauthorized copies of the scriptures, and all translations of biblical passages into vernacular languages were condemned.

The same synod also formally established the Inquisition for the systematic suppression of unorthodoxy by ecclesiastical courts. In 1197 Peter of Aragon had ruled that heretics should be burned at the stake, and Pope Innocent III had pronounced heresy to be a most heinous offence: it was treason against God, and therefore much more serious than secular subversive activity. Pope Gregory IX (1227–41) entrusted the Inquisition to the Dominicans in 1232, thereby carrying the sentiments officially expressed at Toulouse a step further. The proceedings against any alleged heretic (which required at least two witnesses) were not conducted in open court, and, by the bull *Ad*

Extirpanda of Innocent IV, issued in 1252, the accused could be subjected to torture.

The Dominican Order grew out of a sustained attempt to meet the Cathari with an orthodoxy that could match the heretics in learning and enthusiasm. In 1203 Dominic (1170–1221), with his friend Diego (the bishop of Osma), moved into the south of France to convert the Cathari, and in 1206 at Prouille, near Toulouse, they founded a convent for women who had been exposed to the heresy. A few missionary friars were sent to the institution, and the idea of establishing a special order of missionary educators became more definite. Diego returned to Spain, however, and died soon afterward; but Dominic pressed on with the missionary work despite difficulties and dangers, and in 1214, when a château was handed over to him by Count Simon IV de Montfort, he was enabled to carry out his project of constituting a special order of preachers. Two years later he went to Rome, and the new order received formal sanction from Pope Honorius III (1216–27).

Unlike the monks in the Benedictine tradition (but like the Franciscans), the Dominicans were not bound by the vow of *stabilitas loci* (which meant confinement to a particular monastery). Also, they practiced corporate as well as personal poverty, and so, apart from residences and churches, they could not hold property in common, and were thereby committed to beg for their livelihood. Hence the appellation "mendicant friars" (Latin: *mendicus*, "beggar"). The fact that they were not subject to local episcopal jurisdiction caused resentment in certain quarters, as at Paris in the fifties of the thirteenth century. The Dominicans substituted learning and teaching for manual work (such as agriculture and building), and education in a broad sense continued to be their primary concern. By the time of Dominic's death (1221) there existed more than sixty Dominican houses, and the order rapidly grew in importance. Among its outstanding members during the middle ages were

Albertus Magnus and Thomas Aquinas, the renowned scholastic theologians, and Johannes Tauler, the German mystic whose writings influenced Martin Luther.

The Franciscan Order was founded by Francis of Assisi in 1209, five years before Dominic's establishment of the Order of Preachers. The Franciscans were also mendicant, demanding the renunciation of both collective and private ownership. Among the Franciscans, however, controversy broke out between those who took the prohibition of possessions literally and those who adopted a more liberal view, recognizing that their community could scarcely survive without, among other things, permanent buildings. It was chiefly owing to the wise "generalship" of Bonaventura (d. 1274) that a serious rift in the order was prevented. In 1318 Pope John XXII decided against the rigorists and allowed corporate ownership. Francis himself was not an efficient administrator, and the original rule of 1209 was revised in 1221, and again in 1223, when it was approved by Pope Honorius III.

In stressing poverty as a prerequisite of missionary activity among the masses, the Franciscan Order demonstrated loyalty to its founder, who in 1208 (applying the words of Jesus in Matt. 10:7 ff. to himself) forsook his earthly possessions and went off to preach the gospel and serve the needy. He was a man of great personal charm, generous and humble, inspired with a romantic love of nature and utterly captivated by the Spirit of Christ, so that he eventually reproduced in his body the stigmata, the alleged wounds of the Lord's passion (John 20:25). But it must not be supposed that the Franciscans were so devoted to prayer and practical piety that they produced no outstanding thinkers; Bonaventura was extremely learned in the Augustinian tradition, and John Duns Scotus and William of Ockham were to make significant contributions in the development of Christian thought.

BIBLIOGRAPHY

Knowles, David. *From Pachomius to Ignatius: A Study in the Constitutional History of the Religious Orders.* Oxford: Clarendon Press, 1966.

Runciman, Steven. *The Mediaeval Manichee: A Study of the Christian Dualist Heresy.* Cambridge: Cambridge University Press, 1947.

Williams, W. W. *Monastic Studies.* Manchester: Manchester University Press, 1938.

Workman, H. B. *The Evolution of the Monastic Ideal.* 2nd ed. London: Epworth Press, 1927.

20 ‡ *Earlier Scholasticism*

The term "scholasticism" commonly refers to the general theological procedure of the medieval schools (especially those in Latin Christendom), a procedure that sought to elucidate the relation between knowledge and faith and to systematize the basic principles of ecclesiastical doctrine. The data of faith were supplied by the scriptures and the patristic writings of East and West. These data were largely taken for granted, and the function of the theologian was to elaborate upon them by using the available intellectual resources of the ancient Greek philosophers. Platonism in a broad sense tended to predominate until the middle of the twelfth century, when a change of emphasis ensued; Aristotelianism came to the fore, and this led to a new theological synthesis which found its greatest expression in the writings of Thomas Aquinas. Even in the earlier centuries, however, the thought of Aristotle was in some measure made use of. This was partly owing to Boethius (*c.* 480–524), the statesman and thinker, whose work *On the Consolation of Philosophy* was widely read; written in prison, it argued that by philosophical study one could come to enjoy the blessedness of the vision of God. Boethius' Latin translations and his commentaries on the *Categories* of Aristotle and on Porphyry's *Isagōgē* (an introduction to the *Categories*) were often used by Western scholastics in their formulations of logical method.

Especially important in determining the temper of scholastic theology was the teaching of Augustine as interpreted by Gregory the Great. A quasi-Platonic despair of life in the natural world joined forces with concepts taken from the scriptures and the patristic writings. Thought moved within a philosophical framework that was generally presupposed, so that doctrinal differences may often give the impression of being but variations on a theme. Of course controversies took place; not all scholastics thought alike, but with certain notable exceptions they inclined to share the same basic orientation. As previously pointed out, it was postulated that man is a fallen creature, corrupted by original sin, and that salvation is attained solely through the church and its sacraments. Man cannot save himself; and to argue that he can is a sign of pride, a further indication of racial depravity. It is only because God took the initiative in Christ that human salvation has become possible. By the incarnation a regenerating potency was infused into human nature, enabling man to achieve spiritual wholeness again. But the restoring dynamic, introduced into the world by the union of the divine and the human in Christ, does not automatically spread to the whole of humanity. The church as a hierarchical and sacramental institution is the appointed instrument of its diffusion among men; that is, saving grace is appropriated by participation in the continuing body of Christ.

Moreover, according to a doctrine that received much emphasis in Latin theology, man can now be saved and forgiven by virtue of a superabundant compensation realized in Christ's sacrificial death. Satan rightly held the sinful human race in bondage; but in the case of Jesus, who was sinless, he went too far, inflicting a punishment that was undeserved, and this made it possible for God to forgive and renew mankind without contravening the requirements of justice. Again, however, the offer of pardoning grace is not made independently of the ecclesiastical hierarchy; it is only by incorporation into the church that an individual can avail himself of the atoning benefits accruing from Christ's passion.

The baptismal rite of initiation brings the forgiveness of inherited sin and the cancellation of congenital guilt; it also transmits a divine grace that can renew man's corrupt nature. But regeneration is not effected all at once. It is a prolonged process, further grace being continually imparted by other appointed means, such as the eucharist, for example. Hence sins are liable to be committed after baptism, but these may be atoned for by meeting the requirements of canonical penance; should a penitent die before meeting all the stipulated obligations, he will have to spend a period in purgatory before being admitted to the immediate presence of God in heaven. Thus sacramental grace dispensed by the church, through the mediation of bishops in the apostolic succession, ultimately serves to fit men for everlasting life in the world to come.

Such doctrines dominated the institutions of learning in Western medieval Christendom, a civilization whose culture transcended the linguistic barriers of the rising European vernaculars. The language of the schools was Latin, and the scholastic theological enterprise was international.

The outstanding theologian of the ninth century was John Scotus Erigena (*c.* 810–77). A native of Ireland, he eventually became head of the Palace School in Paris, under the auspices of Emperor Charles the Bald. He was one of the few Western thinkers of the period who could read Greek, and his Latin translations of the works of Pseudo-Dionysius greatly contributed to the spread of mysticism during the later middle ages. Among the Eastern fathers, he drew particularly on Gregory of Nyssa. His greatest work *De Divisione Naturae* ("On the Division of Nature") reveals him as an adventurous philosophical thinker in the manner of Origen. This work was not appreciated by his contemporaries and attracted little attention until the twelfth century. Its teaching ran counter to prevailing trends, however, and it was officially condemned at Paris in 1210 and at Rome, by Pope Honorius III, in 1225. The treatise displays pantheistic tendencies, and in some respects it anticipates the philosophical systems of Spinoza and, more especially, of Hegel.

But Erigena was not so out of step with the ideas of his time that he failed to make a contribution to contemporary discussions. Although the relevant document has not survived, apparently he opposed with vigor the realistic interpretation of the eucharist propounded by a Benedictine monk of Corbie, Paschasius Radbertus (*c.* 785–860), whose theory seems to have been roughly equivalent to what later came to be known as the doctrine of transubstantiation. Radbertus argued that the bread and wine became the flesh that was born of Mary, the flesh that was crucified and subsequently resuscitated; this was a miraculous transmutation that took place at every consecration of the eucharistic elements. Erigena, on the contrary, argued that the eucharistic rite had a symbolic value, adumbrating the ultimate union of the finite with the infinite.

Erigena also opposed the Augustinian view set forth afresh by Gottschalk of Soissons (*c.* 800–870) that God elects certain souls to damnation. Gottschalk's radical predestinarianism eventually involved him in great difficulties. He was condemned at Mainz in 848, and at Quiercy in the following year a juridical order assigned him to imprisonment in the monastery at Hautvillers, where he died some two decades later in a state of mental aberration. Erigena's counterdoctrine was published in his work *De Predestinatione* ("On Predestination"), where be maintains that evil, being really an absence of good and of being, cannot be predestined in any way whatsoever.

The *De Divisione Naturae* consists of five books, and the argument is presented in the form of a dialogue between a teacher and his pupil. In it Erigena upholds the thesis that nature is all-inclusive and falls into four principal categories, namely: (1) what creates and is not created—God; (2) what is created and creates—the realm of (Platonic) archetypes or ideas; (3) what is created and does not create—the sensible world of things in space and time; (4) what neither creates nor is created—God.

Thus nature embraces the divine Source of existence, the sphere of universal archetypes, and the world of sensible appearances. And, as we should expect, Erigena went on to argue that the scriptures need to be interpreted allegorically (*De Div.*, 1:163–64). God is transcendent and beyond human definition (*ibid.*, 1:14; 4:5), and yet he is immanent in the world. He is the sustaining principle of all things (*ibid.*, 1:72). God goes forth out of himself into the world of creation, which in turn tends to return to him as its productive source. Nothing is made out of nothing, and all created things have the kind of ontological status as that which, according to Origen, is enjoyed by the Logos alone (*ibid.*, 3:19 ff.); creation proceeds from the universal forms (or archetypes) to finite individuals (angels, human beings, animals, and material things). In the beginning the sensible world was a blank sameness; then came differentiation, the emergence of diverse species, and the distinction between the sexes. With variety, strife and sin appeared on the scene (*ibid.*, 2:6 ff.).

But the multifarious modes of creaturely existence are not ultimately real. Without the capacity for self-sustainment, creatures tend to relapse, not into nothingness as Augustine supposed, but into the divine source whence they ultimately emerged. Hence the transition from the unity of God, through the sphere of universal archetypes, to the spatiotemporal sphere of particular entities, is destined to be followed by a reverse movement from multifariousness to the original unity of being (*ibid.*, 5:1 ff.). The externalization of God gives way to a process of internalization, and this dual cosmic transition found adumbration in the career of Christ, whose descent into an inferior order of being preceded an ascension that typified the ultimate restoration of all creatures to the matrix of the divine nature (*ibid.*, 5:22).

Obviously a pantheistic system of this kind was much more radically Neoplatonic than the theology of Augustine. Erigena left little place for the prevailing Jewish-Christian idea of God as the sovereign Lord of history, who rewards men according to their deserts. But Augustine, despite the Neoplatonic affiliations of his primary ontology, took this idea much more seriously; and the same may be said concerning his treatment of the typically biblical concept of sin as a positive force arising from the willed revolt of the creature against the Creator. Nevertheless, it would be wrong to suggest that Erigena was indifferent to biblical and ecclesiastical tradition. Doubtless he personally believed that he was penetrating beneath the surface meaning of revealed truth, and such an assessment is confirmed when one considers the tortuous arguments in the final book of his magnum opus. Again and again he endeavors to make plain that his doctrine of the cosmic return to God is quite compatible with the underlying significance of the received dogma concerning the everlasting punishment of the wicked (*ibid.*, 5:14 ff.).

Much of the theological discussion among the scholastics was bound up with the philosophical question of the ontological status of universals. For instance, does the essence of humanity subsist apart from its embodiment in particular human beings? Or, do beauty and truth exist apart from specific exemplifications of those values? Plato had given the affirmative answer that the universal is logically prior to any particular entity whose structure it provides. In medieval times this view was known as realism: the reality of a thing fundamentally belongs to the universal form (or essence) of which it is a transient expression. The opposite view was presented by the nominalists, who contended that universals are merely abstract designations of the similarities that certain particular things may hold in common. Humanity, for example, is an abstract name; not enjoying any independent substantial existence, it is simply a verbal sign of the fact that human beings are similar to one another in certain basic respects. A mediating position was adopted by the moderate realists who, following Aristotle, maintained that universals do possess objective reality, but only in individual entities. There is, for instance, a universal structure designated by the word "humanity," but it has no existence independently of the particular things that give it concrete embodiment.

Accordingly, three possibilities were debated with regard to the status of universals: the realists held that universals exist *ante rem* (before the particular thing), the nominalists that universals exist *post rem* (after the particular thing), and the moderate realists that universals exist *in re* (in the particular thing).

To some extent the attitude adopted by the scholastics on this ontological question determined the shape of their theology, so that a realist's formulation of ecclesiastical doctrine differed from a nominalist's. On the other hand, an agreement on this ontological matter did not necessarily guarantee theological agreement. Erigena and Anselm were both in the Platonic tradition and definitely realists, and yet their interpretations of Christian truth differed profoundly. Erigena freely indulged in speculative extravagances, whereas Anselm was much more restrained in his thinking and, while making important contributions, he remained fundamentally in the Western theological tradition.

Anselm (*c.* 1030–1109) was born in Lombardy, and in 1059 he entered the monastic school at Bec in Normandy. Four years later he succeeded Lanfranc as prior, and in 1078 he became the abbot. He visited England a number of times, renewing his personal acquaintance with Lanfranc, and, having won the respect of William the Conqueror, he succeeded Lanfranc as archbishop of Canterbury. However, his strenuous defence of ecclesiastical autonomy involved him in conflict with the monarchy (Rufus and Henry I), a consequence being that he suffered two periods of exile (1097–1100 and 1103–7). *Inter alia* he opposed lay investiture.

Anselm held that the Christian accepts by faith the truths of Christianity on the authority of the church, and that the primary act of faith issues in a life of charity and in an intellectual concern to understand what one's religion entails. He greatly respected Augustine and agreed with him that faith must precede knowledge: *credo ut intelligam* ("I believe that I may understand"), he wrote (*Proslogium, 1*). Nevertheless, Anselm argued that certain basic Christian truths can be demonstrated without resorting to the authority of the scriptures or to that of the church; and in his view it is the function of the theologian, not merely to clarify ecclesiastical teaching, but also to demonstrate the validity of its fundamental affirmations.

Anselm defended ontological realism in his dialogue *De Veritate* ("On Truth"), upholding the thesis that truth is a unity, a substantial existence reflected in particular truths: these latter are true only in so far as they participate in the one eternal principle of truth itself. In his work *De Fide Trinitatis* ("On Faith in the Trinity") he attacked the nominalism of Roscellinus of Compiègne (*c.* 1070–1125), accusing him of tritheism (the heresy of believing in the existence of three gods). Holding that the universal is not *in re* but only *in nomine* or *in voce*, Roscellinus had apparently taught that the assertion of a *homoousia* ("sameness of essence") among the members of the Trinity must imply that the Father begot himself and that the Father and the Holy Spirit became incarnate with the Logos or Son: there exists no such thing as a common essence which the divine Persons could share, and hence the doctrine that the members of the Trinity are one necessarily signifies that they are personally identical. A view of this kind clearly has affinity with the Nestorian contention that a oneness between persons always signifies a oneness of will or a harmony of purpose, never a merging into a common substance. Two drops of water may unite to form one drop, but such coalescence cannot characterize the interrelationship between two or more personalities.

In his reaction against tritheism, however, Anselm inclined to

the opposite extreme of Sabellianism (Modalist Monarchianism), the essential unity of God sometimes being so construed
as to suggest a *personal* unity or a hypostatic oneness. Thus, like
Augustine, he could draw a comparison between the Trinity
and three faculties of a single personality (memory, intelligence,
and love), and yet, on the other hand, he could postulate the
distinctions among the Persons: he argued, for instance, that
the masculine terms "Father" and "Son" are justifiable because
in bisexual generation the man, not the woman, is the primary
cause of offspring (*Monologium*, 42 ff.). A tendency towards
Modalism is also present in his work *De Processione Sancti
Spiritus* ("On the Procession of the Holy Spirit"), in which
he maintained that the Son is involved with the Father in the
productive operation from which the Holy Spirit must proceed.
But, we may ask, if the Father and the Son are entailed in the
procession of the Spirit, why should not the Father and the
Spirit be implicated in the incarnation of the Son?

One of Anselm's principal theological concerns was to demonstrate the existence of God. Historically, five main types of
argument have been used in this connection. The *cosmological*
proof proceeds from the principle that every effect has a cause:
the world is a complicated network comprising effects of causes
which in turn are the effects of other causes, and so on; since
an infinite regress is impossible, ultimately there must be an uncaused First Cause. The *teleological* proof starts from the notion
of order or design: there is ample evidence of design (mutual
adaptation) among species in the world, and this implies the
existence of a Supreme Designer, an all-powerful Architect of
the universe. The *ontological* argument proceeds from the concept of perfection: all men have the idea of an absolutely perfect
Being, and since it is greater to exist in fact than merely in
thought, the idea of a supremely perfect Being must represent
what is actually the case. The *ethical* proof is based upon man's
moral consciousness; value standards may vary, but the existence
of an inward ethical imperative is inescapable and must entail

the existence of God, whose will comes to expression in man's rational constitution. The *historical* argument takes its stand on humanity's ceaseless quest for the highest: as man's physical appetites are not directed toward nonexistent objects of satisfaction, so in a general way his spiritual aspirations cannot be vain hallucinations, but are destined to find their fulfillment through the existence of a supremely perfect Being.

In his *Monologium* Anselm resorted to the cosmological proof, and he also contended that there must be one Supreme Good of which all empirical values are limited manifestations. He maintained that an infinite regress of causes is inconceivable and therefore impossible, the logical consequence being that the universe has its ground in the effective will of a self-originating Creator (*Monologium,* 15). Further, in his *Proslogium* Anselm gave the classic formulation of the ontological argument. God is passionless, without any weakness or deficiency (*Proslogium,* 8). He is That-than-which-a-greater-cannot-be-conceived (*id quo nihil majus cogitari possit*); and, with the aid of the postulate that it is greater to exist both in thought and in reality than to exist in thought only, the conclusion is reached that God necessarily exists. In other words, the real existence of God follows directly from the idea or definition of him as That-than-which-a-greater-cannot-be-conceived (*ibid.,* 2). A monk, Gaunilo of Marmoutiers, raised objections to the argument, declaring among other things that one cannot infer the existence of a perfect island from the mere idea of such an island. Anselm replied in his *Liber Apologeticus,* observing that to talk of perfect islands is quite irrelevant, since the ontological argument applies uniquely to God as That-than-which-a-greater-cannot-be-conceived.

Having, as he thought, demonstrated the existence of God in the *Monologium* and the *Proslogium,* Anselm in his treatise *Cur Deus Homo?* ("Why God-Man?") addressed himself to the task of proving that the incarnation of the Son of God was necessary for human salvation. Like Gregory the Great, he used the principle involved in the doctrine of penance, but applied it in a different way. He dismissed the theory that Christ's death was a ransom paid to the Devil for man's release (*Cur Deus Homo*, 1:7), as well as the view that the crucifixion represented a miscarriage of justice involving a penal substitution (*ibid.*, 1:8). Christ did not suffer for human sin in man's stead, but rather performed of his own free will an all-surpassing act of penance, which made it possible for God to forgive men without injury to his honor. Christ was sinless; even his mother had been purged of her sin before she conceived him (*ibid.*, 2:16), and in the course of his earthly career he lived a life of matchless obedience to the will of God. Nevertheless, he suffered death, the penalty of sin, and thereby offered to God something he did not owe, an offering that was more than enough to atone for the sins of the whole world. He was entitled to reward, but as the *Deus-homo* ("God-man") he already possessed everything, and so the reward that was due could be given in the form of an offer of salvation to sinful men.

Peter Abelard (1079–1142) had neither the speculative boldness of Erigena nor Anselm's confidence in reason, but he was perhaps the most colorful figure among the scholastic theologians. A native of Brittany, he studied under Roscellinus, William of Champeaux, and Anselm of Laon, with all of whom he disagreed on theological questions. He was a brilliant lecturer and attracted large numbers of students to his classes in Paris. Elected a canon of Notre Dame in 1115, he eventually fell in love with Heloise, a niece of a fellow canon named Fulbert. On learning of the affair, the latter was infuriated and resorted to violence by having him forcibly emasculated (1118).

Abelard retired to the monastery of Notre Dame, but further trouble came in 1121 when the Council of Soissons condemned him for allegedly heretical teaching concerning the Trinity; and subsequently he had difficulties at St. Denis because he had questioned the historicity of the legend of Dionysius the Areopagite, the patron saint of that institution. In 1125 he became abbot of the monastery of St. Gildas in Brittany, but the harshness of the discipline he imposed induced the monks to revolt against him. About ten years later he resumed his teaching in Paris, and again he attracted widespread attention among the students.

But this time he invoked the wrath of Bernard of Clairvaux, the most influential ecclesiastic of the period, and it was mainly through Bernard's determined hostility that Abelard was condemned at the Synod of Sens (1141), and that the decision was ratified by Pope Innocent II. Bernard's opposition was highly emotional: he accused Abelard of Arianism for distinguishing grades in the Trinity, of Pelagianism for preferring free will to grace, and of Nestorianism for excluding Christ's humanity from the Trinity (*Epistles*, 331). While Abelard undoubtedly repudiated the Augustinian notion that men inherit Adam's guilt, and in that respect inclined to Pelagianism, the charges are by no means to be taken at their face value. Bernard was evidently incensed by Abelard's audacious individualism; and it is noteworthy that Abelard's tendency toward Modalist Monarchianism (Sabellianism), which is unorthodox by Chalcedonian standards (and which is present in the works of Augustine and Anselm, as well as in those of Abelard), is not so much as mentioned in Bernard's invectives.

Abelard found a good friend in Peter the Venerable, the abbot of Cluny, who welcomed him at that renowned monastery. But he died during the following year (1142) at the Cluniac priory of St. Marcel near Chalon-sur-Saône. Before the end he was apparently reconciled to Bernard: but did he submit merely for the sake of peace?

Abelard was a talented individualist. He did not elaborate a new system of theology, but his manner of treating important problems revealed an intellect of unusual power and penetration. He was a popular lecturer, and his extraordinary success when still quite young may have encouraged the development of a latent arrogance. He had broad sympathies. He admired the Greek philosophers, and he contended that they frequently had a fineness of character that made them morally superior to many Christians (*De Unitate et Trinitate Divina*, 1:5). In his *Dialogus* he to some extent anticipated the modern comparative study of religions. In this work a philosopher, a Jew, and a Christian present themselves to Abelard in a dream and ask him to pronounce judgment on the discussions in which they proceed to engage. While it maintains that Christianity is superior to Judaism and to natural religion, the work displays a spirit of tolerance remarkable for the age in which it was produced. Unfortunately, the document was for some reason never completed. As we should expect, Abelard opposed the use of force to compel religious belief, and in his work on morals he goes so far as to assert that, if opponents of the church are convinced that they do right when they put Christians to death, they cannot be condemned for performing sinful acts (*Ethica*, 13).

Although Abelard did not share Anselm's confidence in man's capacity for demonstrating the basic beliefs of Christianity, he held that valid doctrine must be reasonable (*Introductio ad Theologiam*, 2:3), and hence that the Christian should try to perfect his faith with understanding. Blind faith was unacceptable to him. He believed in a general way that the scriptures are authoritative, but so far as the patristic writers are concerned, he held that they could scarcely be regarded as infallible. In his work *Sic et Non* ("Yes and No") he undertook to prove this point by listing 158 themes in the form of propositions, and subsuming under each heading patristic quotations for and against. In the prologue Abelard stated that he compiled the work to stimulate the spirit of inquiry; but some of his opponents were apparently convinced that in fact he published the document in an effort to undermine the Christian faith.

His treatise *De Unitate et Trinitate Divina* ("On the Divine Unity and Trinity"), which was condemned at the Synod of Soissons, contains passages that show Sabellian tendencies, as when the Father, the Son, and the Holy Spirit are represented as power, wisdom, and goodness. This kind of representation suggests that the Persons in the Trinity are really attributes of one divine Personality, and this, as we have seen, accords ill with the orthodox Chalcedonian christology, with its one *ousia* and three *hypostaseis*. It is therefore rather curious to read in Abelard's autobiographical work (*Historia Calamitatum*, 9) that at Soissons he was accused of teaching tritheism. Perhaps the explanation is to be found in the ignorance of some of his opponents, who took it for granted that he must have upheld tritheism because he had vigorously attacked the ontological realism of William of Champeaux. The inference might have been hastily drawn that he was a nominalist after the manner of Roscellinus, and since the latter had propounded a form of tritheism the same must have been true of Abelard. Actually, Abelard was not a nominalist; he was an Aristotelian or moderate realist, holding that the universal always exists *in re*, and yet that the universal does exist. As Abelard informs us later in the same chapter (*ibid.*, 9), he was finally denounced at Soissons, not for a doctrinal offence, but on the ground of breach of discipline: the verdict was based on the charge that he had published his treatise without having first obtained official permission.

In his dissertation on morals Abelard revealed his firm belief in individual responsibility. He opposed indulgences and argued that to secure divine forgiveness the essential thing is genuine repentance, not the performance of certain prescribed penitential acts. He greatly stressed the inwardness of morality, contending that what makes an action good or bad lies in the character of the motive or intention behind it (*Ethica*, 3 ff.).

In accordance with his general ethical principles Abelard propounded a moral-influence theory of the atonement, an interpretation he set forth in his commentary on Paul's Epistle to the Romans (2:3, 5). He argued that God is love, and therefore always ready to forgive the repentant sinner; what prevents fellowship between God and man lies in the creature (human pride or stubbornness), not in the Creator or in some abstract principle of justice. Abelard therefore rejected the view that Christ's sacrificial death was a ransom paid to Satan, as well as the view that it was a satisfaction paid to the outraged honor of God. Christ became flesh in order to reveal God's willingness to forgive and to move men to repentance; so far as Christ's disclosure of the divine nature is effective, fellowship with God is achieved in the responsive love of the human heart.

BIBLIOGRAPHY

Gilson, Etienne. *A History of Christian Philosophy in the Middle Ages.* New York: Random House, 1955.

Knowles, David. *The Evolution of Medieval Thought.* Baltimore, Md.: Helicon Press, 1962.

MacIntyre, John. *St. Anselm and His Critics.* Edinburgh: Oliver and Boyd, 1954.

Murray, A. V. *Abelard and St. Bernard.* New York: Barnes and Noble, 1967.

Rashdall, Hastings. *The Universities of Europe in the Middle Ages.* Rev. ed. Oxford: Clarendon Press, 1936.

Taylor, H. O. *The Medieval Mind.* 2 vols. 4th ed. Cambridge, Mass.: Harvard University Press, 1949.

Weinberg, J. R. *A Short History of Medieval Philosophy.* Princeton, N.J.: Princeton University Press, 1964.

Weingart, R. E., *The Logic of Divine Love: A Critical Analysis of the Soteriology of Peter Abailard.* New York: Oxford University Press, 1970.

21 ‡ Later Scholasticism

The twelfth century saw the rise of the universities, first in Italy and then north of the Alps. Since the Carolingian period education had been almost exclusively conducted in the monastic and cathedral schools, although in Italy there also existed institutions of learning at which lay philosophers gave instruction in the seven liberal arts. A university was originally a corporation of scholars who had banded together for self-protection, and the first to be formed was at Bologna, where students of law from various parts of Europe had congregated. The majority being aliens and possessing no citizenship rights in the locality to which they had come, the students sought to consolidate their position by forming a *universitas scholarium* ("guild of scholars"). Different educational centers tended to specialize in different subjects; thus Bologna was strong in law, Salerno in medicine, Paris and Oxford in theology. The Paris system became especially important and provided a model for other universities, particularly those that developed in northern Europe; in 1207 a guild of masters (*universitas magistrorum*) was formed and it received its statutes from Pope Innocent III in 1215. The organization was technically independent of local monarchical and episcopal jurisdiction.

The university in Paris really had its unofficial beginnings in the first half of the twelfth century, when Abelard was at St. Geneviève, Hugh at St. Victor, and Peter Lombard at the cathedral school of Notre Dame. The large numbers of scholars who gathered to attend the lectures of these famous teachers made possible the emergence of the *universitas* soon after the year 1200. Between 1215 and 1225 the organized "Four Nations" (Gallicans, Normans, Picards, and English) developed; this grouping according to nationality included both masters and scholars. A little later the *universitas* that had been formed for the so-called *studium generale* was divided into four faculties, namely, Arts, Theology, Law, and Medicine. Arts offered a preparatory curriculum and included the *trivium* (grammar, rhetoric, and logic) and the *quadrivium* (astronomy, arithmetic, geometry, and music). Scholars who graduated in Arts could proceed to one of the higher faculties: the degrees of Master and Doctor signified qualifications to teach. Both instructors and students usually lived in colleges, the most famous of which was the Sorbonne (founded in 1252 by Robert de Sorbon in an effort to relieve student poverty). Monastics or "regulars" resided in the houses of their orders. A dispute that arose between the regulars and the secular clergy (who were resentful of the growing influence of the mendicants) was eventually settled in favor of the former by Pope Alexander IV (1256).

The establishment of a university at Oxford may have been an indirect consequence of an edict of 1167 which forbade students to travel abroad. The *studium generale* followed the pattern of that at Paris; it was a secular foundation, the chancellor deriving his authority from the bishop at Lincoln, in whose diocese Oxford then lay. Out of the hostels or residences (some monastic, some secular) emerged the colleges, among the earliest being University (1249) and Balliol (1263). In 1209 a number of scholars from Oxford joined the canons of All-Saints-in-the-Castle at Cambridge to form a new educational institution, and by 1233 a university was established there, with a chancellor licensed by the bishop of Ely to grant degrees.

Abelard, Hugh of St. Victor, and Peter Lombard were important in the development of scholasticism, not only because they were stimulating teachers who attracted large numbers of students to Paris, but also because they undertook to write systematic compendia of Christian theology. Abelard's work in this connection is incomplete, but from his *Introductio ad Theologiam* we may assume that he had planned a comprehensive exposition of ecclesiastical doctrine under the headings of faith, love, and the sacraments. The most important works of Hugh and of Lombard were theological compendia, and these prepared the way for the greatest literary production of medieval scholasticism, namely, the *Summa Theologica* of Thomas Aquinas.

Hugh (*c.* 1095–1141) was a younger contemporary of Abelard (1079–1142). A native of Saxony, in 1115 he entered the monastery of St. Victor at Paris, an institution whose school had acquired considerable prestige under William of Champeaux. He became prior in 1133. Educated in the Augustinian tradition, he was also much influenced by the writings of Pseudo-Dionysius. In his compendium *De Sacramentis Christiane Fidei* ("On the Sacraments of the Christian Faith") he maintained that all sensible things are signs or concrete expressions of divine ideas. Hence in a broad sense every created entity is sacramental, a sign of the active thought of God, so that the eucharist, for instance, is but a specialization of a general mode of religious symbolism.

Hugh's treatise is composed of two books, the first dealing with God's saving operations prior to the advent of Christ, the second with God's remedial activity in the incarnation, the church, the hierarchy, and the sacraments. The various discussions are held together by their common reference to the theme of redemption. Moreover, rational theology is combined with a form of mysticism. To some extent divine truth may be apprehended by reason, but in the more advanced stages of the religious life pure intellection is supplemented by a direct mode of cognition that results from disciplined contemplation. The depths of religious knowledge are beyond reason (*supra rationem*), but not contrary thereto; they are *secundum rationem* ("according to reason").

Peter Lombard (*c.* 1100–1160) studied at Bologna and Rheims, and from 1139 he taught at the cathedral school in Paris; twenty years later he was appointed bishop of Paris but died in the following year. His compendium *Sententiarum Libri Quatuor* ("Four Books of Sentences") was, as the title indicates, divided into four main sections, a partition that was perhaps derived from John of Damascus, whose exposition of the orthodox faith had recently been made available in Latin. The first book deals with God, providence, and predestination; the second with creation, original sin, grace, and free will; the third with Christ, virtues, and vices; and the fourth with the sacraments and the end of the world.

The treatise contains many quotations from the fathers, including John of Damascus, whose writings hitherto had been virtually unknown in the West. Some readers argued that the work was heretical, but, after its orthodoxy was officially recognized at the Lateran Council of 1215, it became a standard textbook in Western schools and so it remained until superseded by the *Summa Theologica* of Thomas Aquinas; the last commentary on it (by the Jesuit J. M. de Ripalda) appeared in 1635. The compendium evinces nothing of Hugh's mysticism; divergent patristic pronouncements are not left standing side by side, as they were in Abelard's *Sic et Non*, but rather attempts are made to bring out their essential harmony. *Inter alia* Lombard maintained that there are seven sacraments, adding penance and ordination to the five recognized by Abelard (baptism, confirmation, the eucharist, extreme unction, and marriage).

Of great significance in the second half of the twelfth century was the translation into Latin of numerous Aristotelian works. A new intellectual interest had developed, and certain Arabic commentaries on Aristotelian writings by the Moslem philosophers Avicenna and Averroës were also put into Latin.

Avicenna (980–1037) was a physician in the Persian court and an Aristotelian with pronounced Neoplatonic tendencies. He believed in the subsistence of a system of divine emanations that mediate between God and the world. One such emanation is the active intellect, a universal form in which the passive intelligence of the finite individual must participate, human thinking being a limited expression of a transcendent cogitation. Averroës of Cordova (1126–98) understood the Koran allegorically and, like Avicenna, was an Aristotelian with Neoplatonic affiliations. He argued that matter is eternal, and he denied the immortality of the soul. The Prime Mover wholly surpasses finite reality, and yet there is intercommunication among all orders of the cosmic hierarchy through the mediation of intelligent beings that have emanated from the overflowing perfection of the Supreme Being. In the epistemology of Averroës, as in the teaching of Avicenna, one substantial form of intellection is operative in the whole of mankind (monopsychism), and human instances of thinking are particularized expressions of the informing activity of a universal mind.

Also influential in the Latin schools of the thirteenth century was Moses Maimonides (1135–1204), a Jewish scholar and philosopher. Born at Cordova, he wrote in Arabic as well as in Hebrew. In 1149, because of an outbreak of anti-Semitism, he moved to Morocco, but eventually he traveled eastward and became the leader of the Jewish community in Cairo. His principal philosophical treatise, *Guide for the Perplexed*, written in Arabic, deals with the existence and nature of God, the creation of the world, the problem of evil, and the significance of divine providence. The question of the relationship between reason and revelation was fundamental for him, and he sought to effect a synthesis between the metaphysics of Aristotle and the deliverances of the traditional biblical faith of Jewish religion.

In the academic circles of Western Christendom there were three principal reactions to these new intellectual influences: certain traditionalists vigorously opposed all Aristotelian doctrines that were at variance with the teaching of Augustine; some theologians whole-heartedly embraced Averroistic interpretations; and certain highly gifted Dominicans, notably Albertus Magnus and Thomas Aquinas, endeavored to synthesize basic Aristotelian principles with ecclesiastical dogmatics. The ensuing struggles among the representatives of these conflicting theological tendencies were largely localized at the University of Paris, and for a short time Averroism gained the ascendency. In 1255 the study of Aristotle's writings was prescribed in the faculty of Arts, but Albertus Magnus was prompted to attack Averroism in the following year. The Averroists were led by Siger of Brabant who, in his defence of monopsychism, denied the freedom of the will and the immortality of the soul, arguing that what is true in theology may not be true in philosophy.

In 1257 Aquinas began to write his *Summa contra Gentiles*, a work that was partly meant as a criticism of Averroism; and in 1263 Pope Urban IV went so far as formally to forbid the study of Aristotle's writings. Similar orders had been issued in 1210 (specifically against the *Physics*), in 1215 (against the *Metaphysics*), and in 1231 (when Pope Gregory IX commissioned William of Beauvais to produce an acceptable edition of Aristotle's works). The controversy continued. In 1270 Aquinas published his polemical *De Unitate Intellectus contra Averroistas* ("On the Unity of the Intellect against the Averroists"), and the bishop of Paris excommunicated defenders of Averroist doctrines. Seven years later there was another condemnation, and thereafter the power of Averroism was broken, although it continued to have its representatives (particularly at Padua) until the time of the Renaissance.

The ultimate acceptance and adaptation of Aristotelianism by the Latin church was mainly due to Albertus Magnus (*c.* 1200–1280), a Dominican who taught at Hildesheim, Ratisbon, and Cologne, as well as in Paris. He was a man of great erudition, and a prolific though unsystematic writer. He was deeply versed in the works of Aristotle and in the relevant Jewish and Moslem commentaries and expositions. Most important of all, he stimulated the interest of his still more famous pupil, Thomas Aquinas (*c.* 1225–74), who was destined to lay the foundations of orthodox Roman Catholic theology.

Thomas was born at Roccasecca in central Italy. As the youngest son of Count Landulf of Aquino, he had connections with the emperor and the king of France. His earlier education took place at the Benedictine monastery of Monte Cassino and at Naples. Against the wishes of his parents he decided to become a Dominican. In 1245 he went to Paris, where he came under the spell of Albertus Magnus, and he was soon eagerly studying the available works of Aristotle. Three years later Albertus was appointed to the new Dominican school at Cologne, and Aquinas followed him thither, not to return until 1252 when he took up a teaching post at the Dominican monastery of St. Jacques. Subsequently he traveled to Italy, again returning to Paris in 1269. In 1272 he was commissioned to establish a Dominican school at Naples, where he did extensive work on his *Summa Theologica*. But he died before the treatise was completed, when on his way to attend the council of Lyons in 1274.

Aquinas was a voluminous writer and much more systematic than Albertus Magnus. He wrote several commentaries on Aristotelian works and on various biblical books, as well as a number of polemical treatises and two *summae*. The word "*summa*," earlier used to designate works of reference, had come to be applied to any theological, philosophical, or legal compendium, designed as a textbook for students. In the *Summa contra Gentiles* Aquinas was writing primarily for missionaries, and the work contains the most lucid exposition of his thought on natural theology. It is divided into four books. The first deals with the being, nature, and attributes of God: divine existence may be demonstrated by arguments from experience, and the Creator is passionless because he is pure actuality.

The second concerns the production of the world out of nothing: all matter and all species emerged at once, and creation (motivated by God's goodness) did not modify God's character. The third deals with man's final happiness in the contemplation of God: the present life is a preparation for the beatific vision in the world to come. The fourth and last book concerns the data of revelation, such as the Trinity, original sin, the sacraments, eschatology, rewards and punishments.

In the later compendium, the *Summa Theologica*, natural and revealed theology are not considered in separate books, although in the first part the emphasis is on the former and in the third part on the latter. The work constitutes the greatest achievement of scholastic theological systematization. The dialectical method is applied, each topic being divided into a number of questions and the thesis developed by way of a discussion of opposing opinions in so-called articles. Despite the massive proportions of the compendium, it was intended as an introduction; altogether there are more than three thousand articles, and the argumentations are marked throughout by a singular clarity of style. The work is divided into three main parts. The first (*Prima*) deals with God's existence, nature, and attributes, creation, providence, predestination, and angels. The second is a lengthy treatment of ethics, and covers more than half of the total extent of the work. It is subdivided into two sections: the first (*Prima Secundae*) concerns man's final goal, the will, good and evil, law and grace; the second (*Secunda Secundae*) concerns the natural virtues, excellencies attainable by man's unaided efforts (wisdom, justice, fortitude, and temperance), and the theological virtues, excellencies unattainable by man without divine grace (faith, hope, and charity). The third and last part (*Tertia*) deals with the incarnation and the sacraments. Aquinas died when engaged on the subject of penance, and the compendium was completed by Reginald of Piperno, who utilized the deceased author's *Commentary on the Sentences* (of Lombard) for this purpose.

Although Aquinas was not a slavish follower of Aristotle, the latter's principles provided the basis for his reconstruction of ecclesiastical doctrine. Aristotle had insisted that human knowledge is derived from sense experience, and so far as life in this world is ordinarily concerned, Aquinas agreed with him. Unlike Platonists and Neoplatonists, Aristotelians were empiricists, denying that man possesses a faculty of supersensuous intuition by which he can directly apprehend the transcendent reality of God. Aquinas sought to reconcile the church's teaching with such a denial by limiting the scope of its application: natural man does not possess a faculty of supersensuous intuition, and yet there have existed certain human beings (the prophets and apostles) who were chosen to be special instruments of God's self-revelation. Their knowledge was not wholly mediated by the senses, and the fruit of their privileged experience has been made available to others in the records of sacred scripture. Thus Aquinas was led to distinguish natural from revealed theology, a distinction that had no place in the philosophy of Aristotle himself: natural theology starts with the creature and ascends to God, whereas revealed theology starts with God and descends to the creature. Aristotelian empiricism applies to the natural sphere, but the natural sphere is not coextensive with the whole of experience. The data of revelation have to be taken into account, as well as the functionings of the soul in the noncorporeal life beyond the physical world.

Moreover, Aristotle held that universal ideas (forms or essences) do not subsist per se in an eternity above sense, but only in their individual embodiments. Everything experienced is a form individualized in matter. The notion of matter without form is a limiting conception; it is an abstraction, no less than the thought of form without matter. Also, in the world of experience things are subject to motion of various kinds, and in the biological sphere processes of growth are especially characteristic. In any such process the form of an entity is progressively united to matter it appropriates and, for the sake of clarity, the potential has to be distinguished from the actual. For example, an acorn is potentially an oak tree; that is, the form of the oak is potential in the acorn and actual in the full-grown tree. Thus, in a philosophical interpretation of existence, besides the differentiation of form from matter, account needs to be taken of the opposition between potentiality and actuality.

Aristotle further observed that biological growth begins in an activity of generation, and in this connection he maintained that four types of determination are operative, namely, efficient, material, final, and formal causation. This was held to be clearly discernible in instances of bisexual generation, where, as Aristotle thought, the male agent (or efficient cause) produces as the end (or final cause) of his action another being having the same form as himself, though realized in a matter distinct from his own that is supplied by the female. Therefore, in human reproduction the begetter is the efficient agency that supplies the form; the woman who conceives is the responsive agency that supplies the matter; and the child, as a fresh individualization of the human form (or essence), is the final (or generative) cause of the total reproductive activity.

Of course Aristotle recognized that generation, growth, and decay are not the only types of motion: in addition there are alteration (change of quality), augmentation and diminution (change of quantity), transition and rotation (change of place). He also recognized that motions are linked to form chains of indefinite extent, and that no empirical instance of motion is self-complete or independent of other instances. A man begets a child, and his action presupposes a previous begetting of his own existence, and so on, endlessly. Matter is an inert substratum in which motions take place; and, for its total explanation, motion has to be referred to a transcendent source, namely, the Unmoved Mover that moves the world as the object of a desire. Ultimately it is through the lure of God's perfection that matter receives its multiplicity of shapes and that ideas are individualized.

Aquinas took over important Aristotelian concepts and distinctions such as matter and form, actuality and potentiality, and the fourfold notion of causation. Thus he held that God alone, being absolutely perfect, is devoid of potentiality and is incapable of change. He is *actus purus*, the Unmoved Mover and the First Cause. But he is not merely the efficient, formal, and final cause of the world, as Aristotle thought, since he created the world *ex nihilo*, and hence he must also be the ultimate material cause of sensible existence, and not a Creator who simply introduced forms or essences into pre-existent material.

Aquinas further differed from Aristotle in allowing a legitimate place for revealed theology, as well as in maintaining that the immortality of the soul, like the existence of God, may be demonstrated on rational grounds (*Summa contra G.*, 2:55, 79). While the question of God's existence belongs to natural theology, such doctrines as those of the Trinity and the incarnation, although not contrary to reason, are arrived at through the divine revelation recorded in the scriptures. The prophets and the apostles were privileged to obtain special knowledge of the Divine; they were under supernatural control and, without the mediation of the senses, they came to direct acquaintance with God, the result being that they enjoyed even in this life a foretaste of the beatific vision which is proper to the noncorporeal life of the righteous in heaven (*Summa Th.*, 2b:171–175; cf. *Summa contra G.*, 3:37–63).

Despite his rationalism Aquinas did not accept the validity of the ontological argument. Since God is pure actuality without potentiality, his essence must be identical with his existence. According to Aquinas, Anselm rightly insisted on this point; but man does not in fact possess the clear and distinct conception of the Supreme Being such as the argument takes for granted. The notion of God is neither innate nor self-evident, and man in this life, being a corporeal creature, has ordinarily to rely on experience for his knowledge of reality; even his acquaintance with the scriptures, the record of divine revelation, is based on sense perception. Nevertheless, although man in this world cannot demonstrate the existence of God a priori, there are five ways (*quinque viae*) in which that existence can be proved a posteriori from the data of sense experience (*Summa contra G.*, 1:12–13; *Summa Th.*, 1:2:3).

The first three of the *quinque viae* are variations of the cosmological proof (the argument from effect to cause), the fourth takes its stand on comparative valuations, and the fifth is a form of the teleological proof (the argument from design). (1) Motion is datum of experience, and sensible instances of motion ultimately imply the existence of an Unmoved Mover; in developing this argument, which he evidently believed to be the strongest, Aquinas contended that an infinite regress is impossible, that sensible entities remain at rest unless affected by a force *ab extra*, and that the argument would be valid even if the world had not been created at an assignable date in the past (a point that cannot be proved but has to be accepted on scriptural authority). (2) The manifold sequences of causes and effects in nature have their productive ground in an uncaused First Cause. (3) The things of common experience are without aseity; that is, their being is not self-derived, but conditional; and in the last resort such contingency must entail the existence of a Necessary Being as the unconditional ground of things as they are in fact. (4) Finite beings may be compared according to the degree of perfection they exemplify (as when it is said that one entity is better than another), and this implies the existence of an absolutely Perfect Being to supply the ultimate criterion of comparison. (5) The mutual adaptation of objects in the world of experience requires for its explanation reference to a supreme Designing Intelligence or purposive Creator.

Since in God every perfection is completely realized, he transcends time and motion. The divine essence is identical with the divine existence. In God nothing is potential. His action gives direct expression to the superlative goodness of his essence. He wills nothing arbitrarily; what he wills is not of value because

he wills it, but he wills it because of the intrinsic goodness of
his nature. He created a great variety of creatures, multiplying
kinds and individual differences to display the glory of his perfection in all possible manners and degrees (*Summa contra G.,*
2:41 ff.). God's creative will is also expressed in a purely spiritual world of finite entities; for there is no justifiable reason for
doubting the existence of angelic beings; matter exists without
spirit in inorganic nature, and so it is eminently appropriate that
spirit (the superior substance) should exist independently of
matter in the bodiless being of the angels (*Summa contra G.,*
2:91; cf. *Summa Th.,* 1:50:1). God is the Lord of creation, and
his purpose presides over cosmic history, and yet his providence
is such as to permit human freedom. There is divine reprobation
as well as divine predestination; the latter signifies a divine decision to confer saving grace upon men, and the former represents his will to allow human beings to fall into sins deserving
damnation (*Summa Th.,* 1:23:3). So, while Aquinas did not subscribe to the doctrine of irresistible grace, his general theory of
providence inclined to Augustinianism rather than to Pelagianism.

Like Aristotle, Aquinas tended to adopt mediating positions
between opposing extremes. This is shown not only in his discussions of natural theology (to which, for example, the questions of providence and predestination belong), but also in his
expositions of revealed theology. Thus, in his soteriology he
followed Anselm in holding that Christ offered a satisfaction for
sin, and at the same time he followed Abelard in maintaining
that Christ's sacrificial obedience was a divine manifestation that
awakens men to a responsive love for God (*Summa contra. G.,*
4:53–55; *Summa Th.,* 3:46–50). But he differed from Anselm,
and agreed with Augustine, when he argued that in principle
Christ's having suffered and died for man's redemption was not
necessary. God could have chosen some other means to that end,
and the most that may be said in this connection is that the
method actually adopted was eminently fitting and superlatively

efficient. By his passion Jesus not only freed man from sin; he also set forth a supreme moral example and revealed God's loving-kindness.

Because of Christ's transcendent dignity as human and divine, his sacrificial death constituted a superabundant satisfaction for human sin, and the rewarding grace due to (but not needed by) him was freely bestowed upon all members of the church which is his body (*Summa Th.*, 3:48). Renewed by grace, men and women are enabled to practice the theological and not merely the natural virtues, and to fulfill the counsels of perfection as well as the precepts (or basic requirements) of the gospel, thereby contributing through works of supererogation to the stored-up merits of Christ and the saints. Reinforcing grace is thus transmitted to fallen humanity via the church and its sacraments. At his baptism the neophyte's sins are forgiven and his nature is regenerated, and by his subsequent participation in the eucharist his soul continues to receive spiritual nutriment. But the believer is not normally made perfect in the present world. He yields to temptation, and his resulting sins have to be atoned for, a circumstance for which provision is made in the sacrament of penance. Sometimes indulgences may be granted and the imposed temporal penalties mitigated, or remitted entirely; such a recourse is possible because of the church's treasury of merits (surplus satisfactions) which representatives of the hierarchy can dispense to any offending believer who has confessed his sins and is duly contrite (*Summa contra. G.*, 4:56; *Summa Th.*, 3:62).

Opposition to the doctrine of Aquinas persisted in certain circles after his death. Some of his theses were condemned in 1277, and again seven years later; for a time members of the Franciscan Order were forbidden to read his works. Among the Dominicans, however, his teaching was formally accepted in 1278. He was canonized in 1323, and pronounced a Doctor of the Church by Pope Pius V in 1567. A period of relative neglect terminated with the publication of the bull *Aeterni Patris* in

1879. So the study of Aquinas' writings became the official basis of Roman Catholic theological education, and outstanding exponents of Neo-Thomism have since appeared in Belgium, Germany, France, and elsewhere.

It is not to be supposed that all the early critics of Aquinas were blindly opposed to Aristotelianism. The influential Franciscan, Bonaventura (*c.* 1221–74), was to a limited extent attracted by Aristotelian principles, but he objected to the view that man's knowledge of God on this side of the grave has to be mediated by sense perception. He set forth a mystical theory of divine illumination and maintained that the noneternality of creation could be proved. Other Franciscans were more vigorous in their adverse criticism of Thomism. John Duns Scotus (*c.* 1265–1308) stressed the importance of volition as opposed to intellection, and still more radical was William of Ockham (*c.* 1300–1350), who pressed nominalism to an extreme. Some of the latter's followers were induced by his formulations to defend the concept of the Double Truth (what is true in religion may be false in philosophy), thus reviving a doctrine rejected in the Parisian condemnation of Averroism in 1277. This dualist mode of teaching seems to have reflected a concern to bring out the supernatural nature of Christianity, regarding the Divine as the "Wholly Other" and as such quite unamenable to interpretation in ordinary intellectual terms.

A native of Scotland (as "Scotus" implies), Duns joined the Franciscans and studied at Oxford. Subsequently he went to Paris, and thence to Cologne, where he died. His works include the *Opus Oxoniense* ("Oxonian Work"), a diffuse commentary on Lombard's *Sententiarum,* and *Reportata Parisiensia* ("Parisian Reports"), a smaller one; and *De Primo Principio* ("On the First Principle"), a short treatise on natural theology. His voluntarism led him to give the primacy to active love, not to knowledge or contemplative intuition, in the attainment of man's final beatitude. But his opposition to Thomism has been exaggerated by historians through the attribution to him of certain writings that were in fact produced among his followers. Thus, while he objected to the argument from empirical instances of motion to an Unmoved Mover (*Opus Oxon.*, 1:2:2), he believed in the ultimate accord of reason with revelation, and agreed that man's knowledge of God is arrived at through experience, evidently accepting the theistic arguments from contingency and from the notion of perfection. Again, while he differed from Aquinas in holding that God's will ultimately determines what is good (*Opus Oxon.*, 3:19), he agreed that in the sphere of human existence the rightness of a line of conduct is not established by its being decreed; no finite authority could make wrong right by any amount of legislation (*Reportata Paris.*, 2:22).

Duns Scotus was an acute thinker, though sometimes inconsistent, and generally negative rather than constructive. Not infrequently he allowed his main contentions to lose themselves in intricate discussions of minutiae and fine distinctions. But of the perspicacity of his mind there can be no doubt (he was popularly called *Doctor Subtilis*), and so it may seem strange that the word "dunce" should have come to signify a dull-witted person. The term was originally applied to followers of Scotus, and eventually humanists of the Renaissance period began to employ it of schoolmen generally, whom they derided for their alleged sophistry and preoccupation with pointless verbal quibbles; and it was from such derogatory usage that the word came to acquire its current meaning. However, in one matter at least Scotism prevailed over Thomism: Duns differed from Aquinas in holding that the Virgin Mary was born without original sin, and this became official doctrine in 1854 when Pope Pius IX pronounced that she was immaculately conceived.

The English Franciscan William of Ockham (a village in Surrey) studied and taught at Oxford. His doctrine fell under suspicion, and he was summoned to Avignon where he had to answer charges of heresy. Belonging to the rigorous section of the Franciscan Order, he soon involved himself in a violent con-

troversy with Pope John XXII on the question of the apostolicity of voluntary poverty, maintaining that Jesus and his disciples possessed no property, either individually or collectively.
Ockham was excommunicated in 1328, but he had the good fortune to find refuge with Louis of Bavaria, who also was at odds
with Pope John. He continued to defend his position in various
polemical works, and his writings generally were destined to
exercise an important influence upon the conciliar movement,
as well as upon the Protestant Reformation.

Unlike Duns Scotus, a moderate realist, Ockham was a nominalist. One of his chief principles is commonly known as "Ockham's razor": *Entia non sunt multiplicanda praeter necessitatem*
("Entities are not to be unnecessarily multiplied"). Beauty as
such does not exist, but only particular beautiful things; humanity as such does not exist, but only individual human beings. On the other hand, like Duns Scotus, Ockham defended a
form of theological voluntarism; that is, he took up the notion
of the primacy of volition over intellection, and argued that divine choices are entirely uncaused, God's will being the ultimate
ground of all existence and value.

In other words, the Creator determines what is good and
therefore cannot himself be determined by any anterior good.
Divine decisions have their own intrinsic sufficiency; they are
entirely unconditioned, and any course of action the Creator
has undertaken could have been otherwise had it been his pleasure. Hence what God does cannot be deduced from a supposedly rational divine character or essence. His action shows
what he is, and the deliverances of such self-revelation have to
be accepted in trust. Moreover, since God's action imposes received intellectual standards, attempts to prove the reasonableness of Christian truth (as in natural theology) are quite futile.
Divine revelation is communicated by the church, the authority
of which is founded upon the scriptures.

Ockham's thesis that God's active will is known solely by
faith proved congenial to Martin Luther, as did his appeal to

the scriptures in the dispute concerning apostolic poverty. More immediately, Ockham's refusal to regard the papacy as the organ of valid ecclesiastical authority gave strength to the conciliar movement, which is to be considered in the following chapter.

BIBLIOGRAPHY

Gilson, Etienne. *The Philosophy of St. Thomas Aquinas.* Cambridge: Heffer, 1929.

Grabmann, M. *Thomas Aquinas, His Personality and Thought.* New York: Longmans, Green, 1928.

Harris, C. R. S. *Dun Scotus.* 2 vols. Oxford: Clarendon Press, 1927.

Moody, E. A. *The Logic of William of Ockham.* New York: Sheed and Ward, 1935.

Ryan, J. K., and B. M. Bonansea, eds. *John Duns Scotus, 1265–1965.* Washington, D.C.: Catholic University of America Press, 1965.

22 ‡ *The Papacy and Conciliarism*

The rift between East and West that occurred during the eleventh century considerably weakened the power of Christendom, and sporadic attempts were made to effect a reconciliation. Differences of language and outlook, as well as variances on doctrinal and liturgical matters, were involved in the controversy, but perhaps most important in practice were opposing views on the vexed question of the seat of authority in the religious life. In prevailing Western thought the pope was supreme, subservience to his rule being commonly regarded as an essential element in Christian discipline. At the Council of Lyons in 1274 (whose proposals for reunion were quickly repudiated in the East) certain Latin theologians cited a short treatise *Contra Errores Graecorum* ("Against the Errors of the Greeks"), a work written by Thomas Aquinas a year or two earlier at the suggestion of Pope Urban IV.

In it the great Dominican had maintained that obedience to the papacy is necessary for the achievement of man's salvation, a doctrine that accords with views he expressed elsewhere. On rational grounds he held that unity and peace, the ultimate aims of all human government, can best be attained when political authority is centralized in a single ruler. And on scriptural grounds he held that Christ had commissioned the bishop of Rome as head of the church in succession to the Apostle Peter (*Summa contra Gentiles*, 4:76). Thus, as in other connections, the findings of reason harmonized with the data of revelation;

and from the general principle propounded in this case it could be argued that the pope had a right to intervene whenever secular political policy was calculated to impede the individual citizen in his efforts to fulfill the requirements of faith, the essential content of which was defined by the papal authority (*Summa Theologica*, 2b:1:10).

It has already been observed that Hildebrand, as Pope Gregory VII (1073–85), made a determined attempt to put the ideas of the Cluniac reformers into effect, condemning simony and nicolaitanism and prohibiting lay investiture. There was much opposition from the secular side, especially from the emperor Henry IV, and Gregory was eventually forced to flee from Rome. But his cause was not wholly lost, and in 1122 Emperor Henry V and Pope Callistus II concluded the Concordat of Worms, in which the equality of church and state in the making of episcopal appointments was formally recognized.

Despite this compromise, however, the rivalry between church and empire persisted. Emperor Frederick I Barbarossa (1152–90), who evidently thought of himself as a second Charlemagne, regarded the concordat of 1122 as a betrayal of rightful imperial authority. His family connections, political astuteness, and personal charm enabled him to infuse a new dynamism into Germany, and he determined to make the church subservient to the imperial throne. In a spirited statement (published in 1157) he denied that the imperium is a benefice conferred by the pope, arguing that the supremacy of the emperor is presupposed in the commandment given (as was assumed) by Peter himself: "Fear God, honor the king" (I Pet. 2:17). But his schemes for the conquest of Italian territory were frustrated by the resistance of the Lombards, while his prolonged periods abroad weakened his power and influence at home. On the other hand, the marriage of his son (the future Henry VI) to the heiress of Sicily gave added strength to the empire. And the struggle went on.

After the death of Emperor Henry VI (1197) rival claims to the throne brought confusion into the political situation. Immediately after his election, Pope Innocent III (1198–1216) intervened, showing remarkable adroitness in his actions. He supported in turn Otto IV, Philip of Swabia, and Frederick II; and the last-mentioned was crowned only because he acceded to papal demands. Innocent also made his presence felt in Scandinavia, Spain, and the Balkans, as well as in France and England. He urged the suppression of the Cathari, and at the Lateran Council of 1215 Catharism and other heresies were formally defined and denounced.

Thanks to his statesmanship and to the historical circumstances of his reign, Innocent III was more successful than any of his predecessors in translating the high papal doctrine into practice. In a decretal of 1202 he asserted that the appointment of emperors comes within the province of the pope's jurisdiction, the Western empire itself being a creation of the papacy. Firmly maintaining that princes and bishops alike are instruments of the pope's will, he was the first to apply the designation "Vicar of Christ" to the bishop of Rome. Whoever holds the papal office is the divinely appointed mediator between God and man, and no secular prince can rightfully fulfill his functions unless he serves Christ's earthly representative.

Like his predecessors Gregory VII and Innocent III, Pope Boniface VIII (1294–1303) made strenuous efforts to make a reality of the high papal theory. But the forces of nationalism had gathered strength during the thirteenth century, and he incurred the wrath of the French king, Philip the Fair. The conflict was arduous, and in 1303 Boniface was taken prisoner and died a few weeks afterward. Nevertheless we owe to Boniface the classic statement of the doctrine of papal supremacy, the bull *Unam Sanctum*, published in 1302. According to this pronouncement, subjection to papal rulings is necessary for salvation, for outside the church there is no remission of sins, and to reject the pope's authority is to exclude oneself from the means of redemption. As the soul is superior to the body, so the church is superior to the state, and is therefore ordained to control secular politics. The temporal sword and the spiritual sword alike are ecclesiastical instruments, and the former is wielded by princes only because the hierarchy (represented by the Roman pontiff) has chosen to delegate some of its powers. Thus all political rulers—emperors, kings, and princes—ultimately derive their rights from the supreme spiritual authority, and they immediately forfeit their prerogatives when they defy the will of the papacy.

Clement V became pope in 1305, succeeding Benedict XI. He was under the domination of Philip the Fair, and in 1309 he transferred his residence to Avignon in southern France. So began the so-called Babylonian Captivity of the papacy, which was to last until 1378, when, according to official Roman Catholic judgment, the papal seat was restored to Rome.

The high papal doctrine was opposed, not only by force of arms, but also by intellectual means. In the manifesto of 1157 Frederick Barbarossa had argued that secular rulers derive their authority directly from God, not through the mediation of the papacy, and he appealed to the scriptures in support of his contention. Others took a similar view, but it was not until the early part of the fourteenth century that arguments against the absolute power of the papacy were developed and elaborated. Especially important in this regard were the Florentine poet Dante (*c.* 1265–1321), the English Franciscan William of Ockham (*c.* 1300–1350), and Marsiglio (Marsilius) of Padua (*c.* 1275–1342).

Dante set forth his political doctrines in a Latin work *De Monarchia* (*c.* 1313). He argued that the state, no less than the church is divinely ordained and has its own separate sphere, for the exercise of its authority. Two governmental institutions exist because there are two fundamental goals in human life: the state is ordained to promote happiness in this world, and the church is meant to facilitate the attainment of blessedness in the world to come. And he contended that these functions can best be fulfilled if there are two independent realms, each governed by a single ruler. A universal empire should have its counterpart in a universal church, emperor and pope having complete control over temporal and spiritual affairs respectively. William of Ockham agreed in a general way concerning the supremacy of the two authorities in their separate spheres, but laid down the provision that one could interfere with the other in extreme situations. For example, if a pope turned out to be incurably unorthodox, the emperor had the duty to enter the spiritual realm and relieve the heretic of his office.

Marsiglio, who studied at Padua and Paris and was elected rector of the latter university in 1313, holds the distinction of being the first Christian thinker to formulate what is in principle a democratic political philosophy. His magnum opus, *Defensor Pacis* ("The Defender of Peace"), appeared in 1324. It aroused papal hostility, and when the identity of its author became known he sought refuge with the emperor, Louis of Bavaria—a course to be repeated two years later by William of Ockham. Five theses of the book were condemned by Pope John XXII, and Marsiglio was excommunicated.

According to *Defensor Pacis*, all political power, both sacred and secular, derives from the people who, out of a desire for peace in their interrelationships, appoint a prince to whom is delegated the business of government. The chosen leader proceeds to exercise authority on their behalf, but they always have the right to restrain or depose the monarch if he becomes tyrannical. In the service of the people's material needs the prince selects leading officials for the civil administration, and in the service of their spiritual needs he chooses bishops for the ecclesiastical administration. All officials, both civil and ecclesiastical, are subject to the prince, and all bishops are on an equal footing. In the apostolic church Peter had no more authority than the other disciples, and existing papal claims have their historical basis, not in a commission given by Christ, but largely in the action of the first Christian emperor, Constantine I (Marsiglio did not question the authenticity of the Donation of Constantine). Strictly, the church has no rights of ownership, and *de jure* it merely uses certain properties that have been entrusted to it by the state. Also, any policy pursued by the hierarchy may be rejected by the people, the prince being empowered to call a conference in cases of serious dispute. As in the ancient church, ecumenical councils, composed of clerical and lay members, are the proper authority in ecclesiastical affairs, and are the only instrument with the right to define the content of faith.

Chiefly because of the papacy's failure to maintain a unified order in Christendom, Marsiglio's basic thesis came to practical expression in a number of general councils that met in the course of the fifteenth century. As we have seen, Pope Clement V transferred his residence to Avignon in 1309, and he was the first of seven popes to reign from that city. Late in 1377 efforts were being made to restore the papacy to its ancient seat, and in the spring of the following year the cardinals, meeting at Rome, succumbed to local pressure and appointed an Italian to the papal office, the autocratic Urban VI. A few months later, however, they repented of their action and proceeded to elect a Frenchman, Robert of Geneva, who assumed office as Pope Clement VII. Thus began the Western Schism, and for over thirty years Europe was seriously divided in its allegiance. Some countries supported the popes at Rome—Urban VI (1378–89), Boniface IX (1389–1404), Innocent VII (1404–6), Gregory XII (1406–15); while others supported the popes at Avignon—Clement VII (1378–94) and Benedict XIII (1394–1417).

Plans for the settlement of the dispute and for the reformation of the church were propounded by men who were much under the influence of the ideas of Ockham and Marsiglio. Outstanding among these were Jean Gerson, chancellor of the university at Paris, and another French cardinal, Pierre d'Ailly. It was argued that the papacy had proved itself ineffective and that unity could be restored to Christendom only by means of a general council. Unfortunately the council that met at Pisa in 1409 fell prey to the wiles of Balthasar Cossa, an Italian adventurer, and Alexander V (1409–10) was elected to the papal office. Cossa succeeded him as John XXIII (1410–15). Thus matters were further complicated by the emergence of a third pope.

The papal divisions were terminated by the Council of Constance (1414–18), the greatest ecumenical gathering of the middle ages, which aimed at structural unity, reform, and the suppression of certain heresies. It was convened by Emperor Sigismund. So far as the popes were concerned, John XXIII was deposed and Gregory XII resigned, but Benedict XIII fled to Spain, where he survived as an exile for several years. Martin V was appointed in 1417. Before the proceedings came to an end it was ruled that a similar conference should be called five years later, and that subsequently a general council should meet every seven years.

Because of plague the proposed seat of the next council (1423) was changed from Pavia to Siena; but strife between France and England (Joan of Arc was burned at the stake at Rouen in 1431) and between the Spanish and the Moors ruined the attendance and no business was transacted. Under pressure, Martin V (1417–31) convened the Council of Basel (1431–49), but he died soon afterward, and Eugenius IV (1431–47) was elected pope in his stead. Conflicts between rival factions seriously affected the deliberations, and a split ensued. Moreover, Turkish forces were approaching Constantinople and an appeal for help from the Greek church led to more disagreement. A conference to consider the possibility of a reunion between East and West was proposed, and, after a majority had voted against moving to a location more convenient for the Greeks, Pope Eugenius took the initiative and convened the Council of Florence (1438–45), at which a decree of union was signed by Greek and Latin delegates in 1439. But this was not confirmed by the Eastern synods, and Constantinople fell to the Turks in 1453. At later sessions of the Florentine council the supremacy of papal authority was affirmed and the delegates conferring at Basel were denounced as heretics.

A strengthening of the nationalistic spirit in Europe seems to have been largely responsible for the failure of the conciliar movement to bring about ecclesiastical reform. And it is significant that the two outstanding religious enthusiasts of the period, John Huss (*c.* 1370–1415) and Joan of Arc (1412–31), each in his or her own way, combined devotion to Christianity with great intensity of patriotic feeling.

BIBLIOGRAPHY

Elliott-Binns, L. E. *Innocent III*. London: Methuen, 1931.

Gewirth, Alan. *Marsilius of Padua: The Defender of Peace.* 2 vols. New York: Columbia University Press, 1951–56.

Turbeville, A. S. *Medieval Heresy and the Inquisition.* London: C. Lockwood, 1920.

23 ‡ The Dawn of the Reformation

John Wycliffe (*c.* 1327–84) was born near Richmond in Yorkshire and studied at Oxford, where he eventually became master of Balliol College. Later he was successively the incumbent in three different parishes—Fillingham, Ludgershall, and Lutterworth—though he continued to spend much of his time in Oxford. Well versed in scholastic philosophy, he defended realism against the nominalism of Ockham and others, but his doctrine of the church betrays a mind that would doubtless have sympathized with Ockham's exaltation of the ideal of apostolic poverty, and with his concern to limit the temporal authority of the hierarchy.

Wycliffe was scandalized by the church's abuse of its power, and he largely blamed excessive wealth for the corruption that had eaten its way into the Body of Christ. He felt that the situation called for drastic action: the church must be deprived of its substantial endowments and the clergy made to depend on the voluntary offerings of the people. Such a contention found elaboration in his treatise *De Dominio Divino* ("On Divine Dominion"), where it was argued that in the last resort the only absolute owner of property is the Creator himself. The earth is the Lord's and the fullness thereof. However, God delegated a limited right of ownership when he gave human beings a certain control over their environment; and it was initially assumed that they would hold in common what they had been permitted to appropriate for their use.

This line of thought reaches back to the ancient idea, reflected in a number of biblical passages, that before man's lapse into sin, society was communistic. And, in accordance with the same idea, Wycliffe held that original sin led to private ownership and the need for some form of political authority to restrain fallen humanity's inordinate acquisitiveness. But it was no part of the hierarchy's business to assume such temporal authority; the church's proper function was to proclaim the gospel of salvation, a divine work that had been impeded by secular entanglements. Also, while the clergy must have the means of livelihood, luxury makes for spiritual inefficiency; hence Wycliffe concluded that the state should confiscate all undue ecclesiastical endowments and devote them to the sacred cause of social welfare.

For all-too-human reasons, teaching of this kind was congenial to the more ambitious representatives of the nobility, and it is not surprising that Wycliffe should have been faithfully protected by John of Gaunt. His doctrine also appealed to active elements in the unprivileged classes; and some critics (apparently without good ground) held him directly responsible for the Peasants' Revolt of 1381—a charge that seems to have cost him considerable support among the lay nobility.

With the outbreak of the papal schism in 1378, Wycliffe became still more bitterly opposed to the hierarchy, contending that the Bible alone provides the standard for Christian thought and practice, and that papal claims even to spiritual hegemony have no scriptural warrant. He further anticipated the Protestant Reformation in condemning such practices as the granting of indulgences and the veneration of the saints, and in maintaining that the scriptures should be made available in the vernaculars. Parts of the Bible had previously been rendered into Anglo-Saxon and Norman French, but it was mainly through the influence of Wycliffe that the scriptures as a whole were translated into English.

In his work *De Eucharistia* ("On the Eucharist") Wycliffe

attacked the doctrine of transubstantiation (a theory that first received official approval at the Lateran Council convened by Pope Innocent III in 1215). Duns Scotus had taught that whenever the eucharist is duly administered God performs a miraculous volitional act: at the moment of consecration, the substance of the bread, for instance, disappears into nothingness through a fiat of the divine will, a supernatural decision that issues in a reversal of the creative process. This basic idea was taken up and developed by followers of Scotus, who interpreted his teaching in a nominalist sense. Thus William of Ockham argued that God's omnipotence can create naked essences—that is, substances divested of accidents, or sensible qualities (see his *De Sacramento Altaris*—"On the Sacrament of the Altar"— ed. T. B. Birch, pp. 223 ff.); and this enabled him to contend that the underlying substances of the eucharist elements may cease to exist (being replaced by the substances of Christ's flesh and blood) while their accidents, such as taste and smell, remain intact absolutely.

Wycliffe, however, stood in the tradition of Platonic realism, holding, for example, that "humanity" is not merely a general name for a group of distinct entities possessing certain similar properties or accidents, but signifies a substantial form that is embodied in all existing human individuals. To be what it is (with the pertinent characteristics) a finite being must inhere in the changeless essence of which it is a particular exemplification. Whence it follows that, since any assignable loaf participates in the transcendent substance of universal bread as such, the essential annihilation of even the smallest crumb would mean the immediate removal of all bread from the world of actuality. Wycliffe therefore repudiated the doctrine of transubstantiation, contending that Christ is present among sincere communicants, not physically, but virtually, as a monarch is present among all the inhabitants scattered throughout the territory under his sovereignty.

It should further be noticed that Wycliffe foreshadowed the

teaching of the Protestant reformers in reviving the Pauline-Augustinian concept of predestination. Man is free in appearance only, and the church is ultimately composed of those whom God has elected for salvation. The Creator's inscrutable decision guarantees the church's oneness, hierarchical distinctions of status being quite irrelevant; and ultimately it is the same transcendent decision, not the rites and ceremonies of an earthly institution, that conditions the distribution of saving grace.

A number of Wycliffe's doctrines were denounced by Pope Gregory XI in 1377; further condemnations were successively made at Oxford (1381) and at the so-called "earthquake" synod at Blackfriars in London (1382). But Wycliffe survived these censures and died a natural death in his parish at Lutterworth in 1384. Later, however, the Council of Constance (1414–18), after declaring 267 of his theses to be heretical, ordered that his writings be destroyed and his earthly remains exhumed and burned. The second order was not executed until 1428.

Wycliffe disseminated his ideas after the Franciscan manner, sending forth mendicant preachers (clerical and lay) to evangelize the people, and his followers came to be popularly known as Lollards, a term whose origin has not been definitely ascertained. It may be connected with the old Dutch verb *lullen* or *lollen* ("to sing"), signifying that the persons so designated were chanters of prayers or mumblers of complaints. Another possibility is that the term derives from the Latin word *lollium* ("tare"); thus Adam of Usk in his *Chronicon* wrote that Wycliffe polluted the faith "with tares of his pestilential teaching."

Lollardry included various elements—ambitious nobles, disgruntled peasants, eschatological enthusiasts with communist tendencies, and so on. They stressed personal faith, as did Wycliffe, and claimed to base their teaching on the scriptures, repudiating sacerdotalism, hierarchical authority, transubstantiation, indulgences, and clerical celibacy. Harsh measures were taken against the movement during the early years of the fifteenth century, and by 1450 Lollardry seems to have become virtually extinct. Its direct influence was mainly exercised upon the Hussite insurgency in central Europe.

John Huss (*c.* 1370–1415), a native of Husinek in Bohemia, distinguished himself at the University of Prague. Like Joan of Arc, he combined an eminently subjective form of Christianity with nationalistic enthusiasm and, thanks to the works of Wycliffe, was induced to base his religious faith on the scriptures, rejecting the authority of the hierarchy. Ordained in 1400, he quickly became a popular preacher, and in 1402 he was appointed rector of the university. The marriage in 1398 of the sister of King Wenzel (Wenceslaus IV) to Richard II of England had aroused an interest in things English, and Wycliffe's writings were soon circulating in Prague. Huss was impressed by the force of the Yorkshireman's arguments, and in his sermons he began to attack the clergy for their dissolute ways. Archbishop Zbynek von Hasenburg was offended and took action against him. But Huss had the support of the king.

The conflict intensified. In 1409 a third pope was elected, and Prague was divided in its allegiance. Huss and Wenzel supported Alexander V, whereas Zbynek supported the pope of longer standing, Gregory XII. In the same year Huss's position was strengthened by Wenzel's decision so to modify the constitution of the university that the Bohemian constituency would have a voting power superior to that of the foreign elements (Bavarians, Saxons, and Poles). The latter seceded and founded a new university at Leipzig.

Wycliffite doctrines rapidly became dominant in Prague, and Zbynek forsook the ineffective Gregory XII, appealing to Alexander V, who promptly ordered the suppression of heretical teachings. In 1411 Alexander's successor, John XXIII, excommunicated Huss, and during the following year he placed Huss and his followers under an interdict. Wenzel saw the seriousness of the situation, and Huss was forced to retire to the country, where he wrote his principal work *De Ecclesia* ("On the

Church"), the contents of which were mainly derived from the writings of Wycliffe. The controversy continued. Huss asserted his right to a hearing before a general council, and it was under the protection of Emperor Sigismund that he went to Constance in 1414. Nevertheless, despite Sigismund's solicitude, he was condemned and burned at the stake (1415).

Patriotic feelings were stirred, and Huss became the martyred hero of the Bohemians. After King Wenzel's death (1419) fighting broke out, and for fifteen years the country was torn by civil war. In the course of the ensuing struggles and disputes the Hussites divided into two main parties, the extremists and the moderates. The former were known as Taborites, for their fortified headquarters lay on Mount Tabor to the south of Prague. They demanded the abolition of all earthly dignities and a complete break with the Roman hierarchy. Like the Zealots of Jesus' day they passionately sought to establish the Kingdom of God by military means. The moderates, on the other hand, campaigned for the reformation of the church without the destruction of its unity. Their demands included the right freely to preach the word of God, the confiscation of undue ecclesiastical endowments, and the right of the laity to receive the eucharist in both species or kinds (the wine, as well as the bread).

This last demand figured prominently in discussions with the church authorities, and they came to be known as Calixtines because of their objection to the withholding of the cup (Latin: *calix*) or as Utraquists because of their advocacy of communion under each species (Latin: *sub utraque specie*). After the defeat of the Taborites they had power enough to induce the Council of Basel to enter into an agreement with them (1436). Twenty-six years later the agreement was declared void by Pope Pius II, but the Calixtines nonetheless maintained their position, and communion in both kinds for all communicants was recognized in Bohemia until 1567. By this time, however, many of the more radical elements had turned to Protestanism.

A distinct group, the Bohemian Brethren, emerged among the Calixtines in the middle of the fifteenth century and broke away from the main body in 1467. Its members were pacifist, held property in common, and refused to take oaths. In about 1575 they moved their headquarters into Moravia and came to be known as the Moravian Brethren or as the Unitas Fratrum ("Unity of Brothers").

BIBLIOGRAPHY

Oberman, H. A. *Forerunners of the Reformation: The Shape of Late Medieval Thought.* London: Lutterworth Press, 1967.

Spinka, Matthew. *John Hus and the Czech Reform.* Chicago: University of Chicago Press, 1941.

Stacey, J. *John Wyclif and Reform.* London: Lutterworth Press, 1964.

Workman, H. B. *John Wyclif: A Study of the English Mediaeval Church.* 2 vols. Oxford: Clarendon Press, 1926.

24 ‡ *Mysticism and Sacramentalism*

Mysticism normally entails a belief in the possibility of attaining a knowledge of truths that elude discursive intellection, and it may include procedures by which, as it is claimed, man comes to a direct apprehension of the creative Source of all things. Stress is laid on a form of cognition that liberates the soul from the transient and illusory world, and the goal of the mystic's quest is not infrequently represented as a beatific vision, an untrammeled contemplation of ultimate reality. Indeed, emphasis upon the intimacy of the final ecstatic encounter may be so great as to imply that the noetic relation gives way to an ontic union (or "spiritual marriage") in which the distinction between subject and object is transcended through the absorption of the finite individual into the all-encompassing *Ens Realissimum* ("Most Real Being").

Mysticism, however, is not necessarily world-negating, but may be romanticist or world-affirming, in which case typical asceticism is repudiated on the ground that God is discernible precisely in the sphere of sense perception. Thus it may be argued that man's blindness to the presence of the Divine is commonly due, not to his sensuous and appetitive nature, but rather to the deadening effect of his excessive concern with the artificialities of intellectual abstraction. For example, was it not through the liveliness of his susceptible faculties that the poet Wordsworth came to enjoy "a sense sublime / Of something far more deeply interfused, / Whose dwelling is the light of setting suns"? A rapturous experience of this kind is clearly sensuous and also mystical, having a spontaneity and (in subjective conviction) a self-authenticating immediacy that distinguish it from the type of knowledge reached by the tortuous path of reasoned argumentation. To use the technical terminology of the church, in such romanticist ecstasy the grandeur of physical nature becomes sacramental, "an outward and visible sign" of the sustaining grace that pervades the inner world of thought and the outer world disclosed by the senses.

But it must be noticed that there are certain important differences between romanticist and ecclesiastical sacramentalism. In the first place, a very limited number of sensible objects can become sacramental in the orthodox meaning of the term—and these only when they are dealt with in the ways canonically prescribed. In the second place, according to accepted ecclesiastical doctrine, the material objects concerned in the eucharist, for example, undergo a transubstantiation on being consecrated, an essential change that matches the regeneration of human nature affected by the incarnation of the Logos. In the third place, the grace appropriated via the ordinances of the church is not the universal power by which the cosmos is sustained, but something more specific: it is a divine energy, released at the incarnation and transmitted by the hierarchy to fit the souls of the faithful for eternal life.

The development of sacramental dogmatics was profoundly affected by a conception of salvation which apparently prevailed in the early Greek-speaking churches. As was pointed out in the introductory chapter, a poignant awareness of the transience of life seems to have been widespread in the Hellenistic world, and this may help to account for the popularity of the secret associations known as mystery religions, which offered salvation to all who submitted to their elaborate rites of initiation. Evidently the Platonic belief in the essential immortality of the soul was not held with any degree of confidence among the masses, and salvation was popularly construed as the attainment of immortality through the soul's mystic union with the savior-god of the mystery cultus concerned.

The words "mystic" and "mystery" are both derived from the Greek verb *myo* ("to close the lips or eyes"). A *mystēs* ("initiate") refrained from divulging to outsiders the *mystēria* ("mysteries" or "secrets") he had experienced as a member of his association; he kept his lips sealed regarding such holy matters when in the presence of the uninitiated. Both the sacred forms and their attendant divine revelations were *mystēria*— and so it was with the church's distinctive rites and their attendant disclosures of divine grace. In the West, however, the Latin term *sacramentum*, which ordinarily signified an oath (especially the military oath of allegiance to the emperor) was eventually taken over and applied to the ritual mysteries of Christianity. Nonetheless, the notion of secrecy in this connection was never wholly forgotten.

Although the Apostle Paul may to some extent have been affected by the Pharisaic doctrine that all the dead, good and bad alike, will rise from their graves to appear at the last judgment, it was his evident conviction that eternal life in any real sense belongs only to those who have been inwardly renewed by faith in Christ. He held that man had become mortal through Adam's original disobedience, and that Christ's resurrection finally broke death's power over humanity. Although Jesus ascended to heaven after the crucifixion, his life-giving Spirit remains available and its vitalizing potency may be appropriated by faith. The church is his body, and those initiated into its membership by the rite of baptism are inwardly regenerated, so that they become new creatures. Their common participation in the corporate life of the fellowship finds its center and focus in the eucharist, the mystic communion of Christ's body and blood. Thus, in Pauline teaching, the saving work of the Lord's earthly ministry is continued in the ministrations of the church, and believers are spiritually prepared for eternal life in the age to come.

It will be recalled that, side by side with the mystico-sacramental assessment of Christianity, there existed from apostolic times a moralistic interpretation. According to the latter, Jesus was a second and superior Moses who came to clarify God's will for men, and salvation is achieved by obedience to the divine law as thus revealed. Of course the two kinds of interpretation were far from being mutually exclusive; some thinkers stressed the ethical, others the sacramental. And in the thought of Irenaeus, who may be said to have laid the foundations of orthodoxy in East and West, although mystico-sacramentalism predominates in his soteriology, ethics has an important role to play. For, in his view, when a person seeks to reproduce the kind of moral piety exemplified by Christ, personal effort receives assistance from the sacraments. But the ritual mysteries of the church not only reinforce the will to righteousness; they also regenerate corrupt human nature, enabling man to regain the health he supposedly enjoyed prior to his original disobedience. Just as bread is transmuted in the eucharist, becoming both heavenly and earthly, so the bodies of sincere communicants are inwardly renewed in a fashion that guarantees their resurrection to eternal life. Hence, according to Irenaeus, God became man that man might become divine and thereby share in the incorruptibility of the transcendent Lord of all things.

In the Chalcedonian Creed, the classic statement of christological orthodoxy, the word *homoousios* ("of the same essence as") found employment to give more precise expression to the same general idea: Christ was consubstantial (Greek: *homoousios*) with God so far as his divinity was concerned, and he was consubstantial with men so far as his humanity was concerned. As indicated in an earlier chapter, this twofold union of essence (Latin: *substantia*) was held to have established a vital contact between God and man, whereby human flesh was immortalized. With Christ's resurrection a new era had dawned, and the saving effect of the incarnate union was perpetuated in the continuing sacerdotal activity of the mystic body of Christ, whose sacramental ordinances were validated by the apostolic succession.

Among medieval theologians there was a tendency to give the term "sacrament" a relatively wide denotation; for example, Hugh of St. Victor (*c.* 1095–1141) listed no fewer than thirty sacraments. Peter Lombard, however, limited them to seven (baptism, confirmation, the eucharist, penance, extreme unction, ordination, and matrimony), and this enumeration eventually prevailed in both East and West. It was accepted by Aquinas (*c.* 1225–74) and subsequently ratified by the councils of Florence (1438–45; cf. the bull *Exultate Deo* issued by Pope Eugenius IV) and of Trent (1545–63). According to a decree of the latter council (Session 7), Christ instituted all seven. Three of them (baptism, confirmation, and ordination) were asserted to have an indelible effect on the soul, and as such could not be conferred more than once on the same individual.

William of Auxerre (*c.* 1170–1231), successively archdeacon of Beauvais and a professor in Paris, was one of the first Christian theologians to utilize the recently discovered writings of Aristotle, and the way in which he employed Aristotelian concepts in his sacramental doctrine helped to pave the way for a new development in scholastic philosophizing. With regard to the eucharist, he argued that the bread and the wine are the *matter*, while the consecratory pronouncements, *Hoc est corpus meum* ("This is my body") and *Hic est calix sanguinis mei* ("This is the cup of my blood"), constitute the *form* of the rite. The new terminology involved a change of emphasis; and, taken up by Thomas Aquinas, among others, it was destined for incorporation into official sacramental dogma. Scholastic discussions came to center largely on the problem of the precise nature of the difference in the eucharistic elements before and after consecration, and solutions were proposed and defended at length in terms of the form-matter and substance-accident distinctions. Aquinas maintained that the eucharist is perfected, not in its use by the faithful, but by the "formation" of the

matter on its consecration. In consequence, the Augustinian
tradition of the virtue of the sacrament (*virtus sacramenti*) suffered a partial eclipse. Although it was never wholly lost sight
of, the concept of the sacrament as a visible sign of an invisible
grace, appropriated in an act of communion, did not come to
the forefront again (unless some exception is made for Scotus
and Wycliffe) until the Protestant Reformation of the sixteenth
century.

It may be gathered from the official definitions of the councils of Florence and Trent that there are four basic requirements
for the validity of any sacrament: appropriate matter must be
used; the form must be as prescribed; the minister (except for
baptism) must be in regular orders, and for ordination (and in
the Latin church, confirmation) he must have episcopal status;
the intention must be right in the sense that the officiating priest
must have the purpose of doing "what the church does" (*quod
facit ecclesia*—Trent, Session 7, Canon 11). When these requirements are fulfilled a sacrament is valid *ex opere operato*,
"from the work done"—that is, by virtue of the ritual performance itself, independently of the moral character of the minister. To be both efficacious and valid the sacrament must also
(according to the Florentine ruling) be received worthily, or
(according to the Tridentine ruling) the recipient must not
present an obstacle to it (as he would if he were without penitence and faith).

The mention of subjective factors in this connection serves
as a reminder that the sacraments, according to orthodox doctrine, do not operate effectively apart from some measure of
spiritual responsiveness on the part of the persons involved.
Despite the frequent use of the phrase *ex opere operato* in theological expositions, the sacred mysteries are not a set of purely
mechanical contrivances working objectively. When they are
properly valid and efficacious, the sacraments transcend sense
perception, and they are *supra rationem* ("above reason") if
not *contra rationem* ("contrary to reason"). The matter and the

form are sensuous and yet, through the act of consecration which brings them together, the physical result normally communicates divine grace. Indeed the entire system has its *raison d'être* in the spiritual ends it is meant to subserve.

Those who uphold the romanticist thesis might object that ecclesiastical sacramentalism imposes too much restriction on the sensuous, and in so doing defeats its own ends. The whole of nature is permeated with the creative presence of God, and any attempt to direct divine power into certain artificial channels is to misunderstand the character of the spiritual life and to overlook the ubiquity of the Divine. The Spirit bloweth where it listeth, and divine grace cannot be captured and distributed by the art and device of man. The letter kills, the Spirit gives life.

A criticism of a contrary kind might be made by purist mystics, like those in the Neoplatonic tradition, who oppose spirit to matter and Creator to creature. In their view, God is the supreme spiritual reality, and as such he cannot be sensuously apprehended. The finite individual who would know God must therefore turn his back on the material world and, by prayer, meditation, and ascetical austerities, sharpen his powers of spiritual perception. Only by mortification of the flesh can man become directly acquainted with the *Ens Realissimum*. Accordingly, whereas churchly sacramentalism is too detached from the world to suit romanticism, it is not other-worldly enough for adherents of purist mysticism.

The Neoplatonic writings of Pseudo-Dionysius (*c.* 500), which profoundly affected the course of Christian mysticism, argue that the ultimate goals of human life are *henōsis* ("union") and *theiōsis* ("deification"). The sacraments possess but symbolic or instrumental worth; and although the writer uses sacerdotal terminology in his speculative explorations of the transcendent spheres, he clearly holds the sacraments in low esteem. They belong to the sensuous sphere, and whatever religious value they may possess is limited to the fact that they point beyond themselves to something higher. So in his exposition of the soul's progress to union with God, Pseudo-Dionysius emphasizes that the individual must first of all rid his mind of everything that appertains to the material world. There are three main stages in spiritual advancement, namely, purgation, illumination, and union. As a prerequisite of its ascent the soul must be purged of all it has acquired in the ordinary processes of education. The spiritual interior can then become a dark vacuity that is eventually illuminated by rays from the divine Reality. This leads on to the soul's final deification through its ecstatic union with the Supreme Being—the Absolute that transcends all finite distinctions. Clearly, for such a purist form of mysticism, the sacraments can have but a subordinate part to play in the higher phases of the religious life.

Some support for the purist attitude could be found in the scriptures. For instance, the Apostle Paul seems to have viewed sacramentalism with a certain ambivalence, for he was apparently an ecstatic who enjoyed moments of unmediated communion with the Divine. On the one hand, he believed that saving contact with the living Spirit of Christ may be achieved in and through the church with its sacramental rites. On the other hand, there are certain passages in his extant epistles which might be taken to imply that, quite apart from the corporate life of the church, he knew God directly, to the glorification of his inmost being. Thus in II Cor. 3:18 he alludes to an unveiled contemplation of the divine glory, a supernormal experience capable of changing men into likenesses of the Lord; and in II Cor. 12:2–4 he writes of his ecstatic transport into the third heaven, where he received unutterable communications.

It should be borne in mind, however, that Paul, unlike Pseudo-Dionysius, nowhere refers to *henōsis* or to *theiōsis*. For him, the ecstatic experience is a peculiarly intimate communion with the Transcendent, and, while this effects a transfiguration of the soul, the human personality is evidently not deified or absorbed into the divine essence. In a typically Hebraic fashion, the Apostle envisaged the goal of piety as a harmony of will and purpose between God and man; and in his extant writings he never clearly implies that the perfected finite personality will be finally submerged in the ocean of Infinite Being.

For obvious reasons, institutional Christianity has tended to frown upon purist mysticism as dangerously liable to be infected with heresy; manifestly, if God can be known directly by such personal disciplines as prayer and fasting, it may be claimed that ecclesiastical sacerdotalism is ultimately dispensable. Doctrine of this kind was vigorously attacked by Aquinas—which is not surprising in view of his philosophical affiliation with Aristotelianism: for him, man's knowledge in this life is necessarily based on sense experience (*Summa contra Gentiles*, 1:12), and to argue that ordinary men can know God without sensible mediation is to contradict biblical teaching (*ibid.*, 3:54). The vision of God properly belongs to the post-resurrection life (*ibid.*, 3:37 ff.), the only exception being provided by those prophets and apostles who received the revelations recorded in the scriptures. Moses and Paul did see God (*Summa Theologica*, 2b:175:3), but direct intercourse between the Divine and the human in this world ceased with the death of the last of the Apostles (*ibid.*, 1:1:8). Accordingly, from that time forward, so far as corporeal souls are concerned, faith and reason can never be superseded by a personal enjoyment of the beatific vision.

However, the judgment of Aquinas on this question by no means won general acceptance. His basic thesis was opposed not only by such an eminent Franciscan as Bonaventura (*c.* 1221–74), who stood in the tradition of Augustinian and Dionysian mysticism, but also by certain influential members of the Dominican order. Thus Meister Eckhart (*c.* 1260–1327), while making much use of Thomist terminology, was fundamentally a mystic after the fashion of Bonaventura. He did not actually repudiate the traditional sacramental system, and doubtless to the end of his days he thought of himself as a loyal member of the church. But the language of his sermons not infrequently suggests that he felt a need for sacramental aids in the spiritual life is a sign of religious immaturity, and it would have been extremely remarkable had he escaped charges of heresy. Accusations were duly made, and at his trial in Cologne he appealed to the pope, but he died before the inquiries were concluded. Two years later, a number of his theses were condemned by Pope John XXII, who denounced him for developing a form of spiritual pride in seeking to know more than befits a mere human being.

Despite this verdict Eckhart's influence persisted. The Dominicans, Johannes Tauler (*c.* 1300–1361) and Henry Suso (*c.* 1296–1366), were among his outstanding followers; also, the German Gottesfreunde ("Friends of God") and the Dutch Fratres Communis Vitae ("Brethren of the Common Life") owed much to his teaching.

The Gottesfreunde spread extensively in the Rhineland and in Switzerland and were led by a group of mystics who sought personal union with God by total self-abandonment to the divine will. They reacted against the externalities of ecclesiastical sacramentalism, and some actually broke with Catholicism to form independent sects. Through the mediation of Jan van Ruysbroeck (*c.* 1293–1381) and Geert de Groote (*c.* 1340–84) the movement gave rise to the Fratres Communis Vitae, a society that promoted mystical piety and founded a number of important schools in Holland and Germany. Among its members was Thomas à Kempis (*c.* 1380–1471), the author of *The Imitation of Christ*, a widely read work which extols the virtues of humility and poverty. Distinguished alumni of schools established by the Fratres were Nicholas of Cusa (*c.* 1400–1464) and Erasmus (*c.* 1466–1536), both of whom greatly contributed to the humanism of the Renaissance.

An important mystical treatise, the *Theologia Germanica*, was produced among the Gottesfreunde in the later years of the fourteenth century. Drawing liberally on the writings of Eckhart and Tauler, it exalts humility and self-abnegation as means of achieving oneness with God. Martin Luther (1483–1546) greatly prized the work and was influenced by it, as he was by the teachings of Paul, Augustine, and Ockham.

BIBLIOGRAPHY

Dugmore, C. W. *The Mass and the English Reformers*. London: Macmillan, 1958.

Huxley, Aldous L. *The Perennial Philosophy*. New York: Harper, 1945.

Jones, R. M. *The Flowering of Mysticism: The Friends of God in the Fourteenth Century*. New York: Macmillan, 1939.

Leclercq, J., and others. *The Spirituality of the Middle Ages*. London: Burns and Oates, 1969.

MacDonald, A. J. S. *Berengar and the Reform of Sacramental Doctrine*. New York: Longmans, Green, 1930.

Otto, R. *Mysticism East and West: A Comparative Analysis of the Nature of Mysticism*. New York: Macmillan, 1932.

Quick, O. C. *The Christian Sacraments*. New York: Harper, 1927.

Spencer, S. *Mysticism in World Religion*. London: Allen and Unwin, 1966.

Underhill, Evelyn. *Mysticism*. 12th ed. London: Methuen, 1930.

Watkins, O. D. *A History of Penance*. 2 vols. New York: Longmans, Green, 1920.

V ‡ THE REFORMATION

25 ‡ New Horizons

The modern period in the evolution of Christian thought may be dated from 1517, when Martin Luther nailed up his ninety-five theses on the door of the castle church at the University of Wittenberg. The protest gave expression to widespread tendencies of the age; hence its effectiveness. As a rejection of absolute papal authority, it had the backing of the increasing strength of nationalistic feelings; as an appeal to the apostolic sources of Christianity, it had connections with the humanism of the Renaissance; as an assertion of the rights of private judgment based on personal experience, it has affinities with the spirit inspiring the rise of the empirical sciences and the momentous geographical discoveries of the time.

The growth of nationalism tended to be accompanied by a reinforcement of royal authority at the expense of the feudal nobilities. Thus in France and England the trend was toward the centralization of power in the monarchy, the consequence being that Francis I (1515–47) and Henry VIII (1509–47) virtually controlled both temporal and ecclesiastical affairs in their respective countries.

In Spain nationalism combined with a passionate zeal for Catholic orthodoxy. This was perhaps partly due to a desire to match the religious intransigence of the Moors. A militant Islam had established itself in Spanish territory by 711 and had spread rapidly across the country. It marched on northward across the Pyrenees until its progress was finally stemmed by the Franks under Charles Martel in 732. Spanish resistance persisted and increased; by 1200 the Moors were restricted to Granada, and the four Christian kingdoms of Castile, Aragon, Portugal, and Navarre were established. A large measure of centralization came about through the marriage in 1469 of Ferdinand of Aragon to Isabella of Castile, the "Catholic sovereigns" who paved the way for Spanish political greatness. In 1480 the Inquisition was reorganized and brought under royal jurisdiction, the property confiscated from heretics going to the crown. Two years later, acting under pressure, Pope Sixtus IV confirmed the right of the two sovereigns to exercise control over key appointments in the Spanish hierarchy. The military forces were improved, and Granada fell in 1492, the year in which Columbus discovered America. Naples was taken in 1503.

Isabella supported Ximenes, archbishop of Toledo (1495–1517), in his efforts to raise the educational standards of the Spanish clergy. He founded and endowed the University of Alcalá (Latin: "Complutum") in 1500, and scholars from Paris and other centers of learning were encouraged to take positions there. Although opposed to making the scriptures generally available, Ximenes held that biblical studies should constitute the basis of clerical education, and he made a significant contribution to scholarship by directing the preparation of the Complutensian Polyglot. This contained the Old Testament in Hebrew, Greek, and Latin, with a Targum (Aramaic translation) of the Pentateuch, and the New Testament in Greek and Latin. The printing of the New Testament section was completed in 1515, but since papal permission for its publication was not obtained until 1520, the redaction prepared by Erasmus had the distinction of being the first printed and published edition of the Greek New Testament (Basel, 1516).

Like Italy, where political power was mainly shared among five states (Venice, Milan, Florence, Naples, and the Church), Germany was divided. Regional authorities (such as those of Saxony, Bavaria, Brandenburg, and Hesse) tended to gain in power, and the importance of the larger cities increased through the weakness of imperial rule. Emperor Maximillian I (1493–1519) sought to strengthen his position, but with only limited success. Ecclesiastical taxation was widely resented, and a number of peasant risings occurred in the decades around the year 1500.

The Renaissance was encouraged by the political conditions of the time. It originated in Italy when the papacy was located at Avignon (1309–78). The Crusades had promoted commerce with the East; this gave rise to the intellectual stimulation of cultural crosscurrents, while the weakening of imperial and papal rule seems to have encouraged local initiative in the city-states. The Renaissance was characterized by a fresh enthusiasm for classical literature and by a new emphasis upon the intrinsic importance of life in this world.

The first outstanding figure of the Italian Renaissance was Petrarch (1304–74), who spent seven years traveling from one center of learning to another and copying classical manuscripts. Himself a considerable poet, he revived an interest in Cicero, the classical Latin rhetorician. His writings reflect a conflict in his nature between an other-worldly longing for the eternal and a mundane concern for the things of time and sense. Petrarch's friend Boccaccio explored the field of Greek mythology and promoted the study of classical Greek in Florence and Naples. After the fall of Constantinople in 1453, numerous Byzantine scholars found refuge in Italy and elsewhere, bringing precious manuscripts with them. John Bessarion (1395–1472) played a significant role in this connection. Archbishop of Nicea, and an ardent advocate of reunion between East and West, he attended the Council of Florence in 1438. But Eastern reaction against the Florentine formula of union disappointed him, and he decided to settle in Italy, where he was made a cardinal in 1439. He encouraged Greek studies and bequeathed his valuable library to the senate at Venice. Semitic scholarship was promoted by Pico della Mirandola (1463–94), an erudite mystic who studied Hebrew, Aramaic, and Arabic, as well as Latin and Greek. He influenced Johannes Reuchlin, the German humanist and the father of modern Old Testament criticism.

The this-worldly tendency in the Italian Renaissance came to typical expression in Lorenzo Valla (1405–57), a man endowed with keen intellectual ability, who argued that supreme value attaches to pleasures of the senses; as one would expect, he was strongly opposed to the other-worldliness of the monastic ideal. He demonstrated the falsity of the Donation of Constantine, severely attacked the papacy for its assumption of temporal power, and scorned the scholastics for their interminable disputations about trivialities. Of course the Renaissance was not confined to letters; great contributions to the visual arts were made by such men as Leonardo da Vinci (1452–1519) and Michelangelo (1475–1564). Leonardo also showed a remarkable creative interest in the fields of natural science and technology. Humanism found its way into the court of Pope Nicholas V (1447–55), who founded the Vatican library and made efforts to reconcile the new learning with traditional theology, besides patronizing the arts and restoring numerous church buildings.

The new ideas spread into Switzerland, France, Germany, the Netherlands, England, and elsewhere, and their diffusion was facilitated through the invention of printing from movable type (cast in separate letters) by Johannes Gutenberg of Mainz (*c.* 1396–1468). The Mazarin (or Gutenberg) Bible came from the press in 1456, and before the end of the century more than thirty thousand printed publications had appeared.

Oustanding representatives of humanism in Germany were Nicholas of Cusa (*c.* 1400–1464) and Johannes Reuchlin (1455–1522). Nicholas studied at Heidelberg, Padua, and Cologne. At first he was a conciliarist, but, disappointed with the attitude of the Council of Basel to the Eastern overtures for reunion, he supported the papacy from 1437, becoming a cardinal in 1448. He was a mathematician and philosopher of unusual acumen, and (independently of Valla) he came to deny the authenticity of the Donation of Constantine. Philosophically, he stood in the Platonic tradition under the influence of Bonaventura and Eckhart. For him, God was the *coincidentia oppositorum* ("coincidence of opposites"), the Absolute Being in whom all contradictions are taken up and reconciled. At once the beginning and the end, the center and the circumference, of existence, God cannot be comprehended by discursive reason (which works on the principle of contradiction), but only by a mode of transintellectual intuition.

Reuchlin was extremely versatile; among other things he wrote two lively Latin comedies and two mystical works based on doctrines of the Jewish cabala (occult lore). He studied classics at Freiburg-im-Breisgau, Paris, and Basel, and subsequently devoted himself to jurisprudence at Orléans and Poitiers. At the age of thirty he turned his attention to Hebrew literature and sought the guidance of Jewish scholars. His Hebrew grammar and lexicon *Rudimenta Hebraica* (1506) opened a new era in Old Testament scholarship. However, in 1512 he became involved in a prolonged controversy. Johan Pfefferkorn, a vociferous convert to Christianity from Judaism, called for the destruction of all Jewish books on the ground that they desecrated Christendom. He took the matter to the archbishop of Mainz, and the latter consulted Reuchlin and Jakob von Hochstraten, the Dominican inquisitor at Cologne.

The two men took opposite sides on the question, and Hochstraten, who was averse to the new learning, accused Reuchlin of heresy. Reuchlin was convinced of Pfefferkorn's folly and confidently appealed to the pope. Sympathizers rallied to his support, and during 1515–17 appeared the satirical *Letters of Obscure Persons*, which did much to discredit scholastic ideas and methods. The case dragged on, and it was not until 1520 that Pope Leo X finally decided against Reuchlin, a verdict which may well have helped the Lutheran cause in Germany. Nevertheless, Reuchlin himself remained within the Catholic fold, and he tried to persuade his grandnephew, Philipp Melanchthon, to break his connection with the Protestant reformers.

Humanism was represented in France particularly by Jacques Lefèvre (*c.* 1455–1536) and in England by Thomas More (*c.* 1478–1535) and John Colet (*c.* 1465–1519). Colet studied at Oxford and Paris, and later acquired a knowledge of Greek in Italy. When in his early thirties he delivered a course of lectures at Oxford on the Pauline epistles, in which he contrasted the stringency of early church discipline with the moral laxity of the hierarchy of his day. Erasmus and More were among his friends. He became dean of St. Paul's Cathedral (1505) and subsequently founded a school (St. Paul's), at which boys were to be taught Greek and Latin.

The most celebrated humanist scholar of the time was Erasmus (*c.* 1466–1536), who combined extensiveness of erudition with keenness of intellect. He vigorously opposed the alleged abstruseness of scholasticism and the externalism of conventional piety. While not denying the validity of the creeds and sacraments, he held that Christianity is primarily a practical philosophy, founded upon the ethical principles enunciated by Jesus; and it was in order to clarify the true nature of Christianity that he prepared his edition of the Greek New Testament with his own Latin translation. He felt that the primary documents of the faith reveal Christianity in its original purity.

The illegitimate son of a priest, Erasmus was born in the vicinity of Rotterdam. He received his early training at Gouda and at the school in Deventer founded by the Brethren of the Common Life, an institution that had become an important center for classical studies. With some reluctance he entered the Augustinian house near Gouda in 1486 and was ordained in 1492, while continuing to steep his mind in classical and patristic literature. After securing permission to leave the monastery, he went to Paris in 1495. Four years later he crossed the Channel and met John Colet, who stimulated his interest in the

Greek New Testament. In 1500 he resumed his journeyings, visiting Paris and Louvain among other places, and after a further brief sojourn in England, he proceeded to Italy. In 1509 he returned to London and stayed with Thomas More at his house in Chelsea, where he wrote his satirical *Praise of Folly;* and then for a few years he taught at Cambridge. After another period of travel, he settled at Basel as a guest of John Froben, the renowned printer (1521). When the town went Protestant in 1529 he sought refuge in Freiburg-im-Breisgau, where, despite attractive offers from Paris, London, and elsewhere, he remained for six years, working all the time for the peace and unity of the church. He died at Basel in 1536, whither he had returned to be near his chosen printing press.

The works of Erasmus include *Adagia,* a compilation of classical adages, which appeared in several editions (the first in 1500); *Enchiridion Militis Christiani* ("A Handbook of the Christian Soldier"), an exposition of the true nature of the Christian life (1504); *Egkōmion Mōrias seu Laus Stultitiae* ("Praise of Folly"), a satirical exposure of corruptions in church and state (1509); an edition of the Greek New Testament with an original Latin translation (1516); *Diatribe de Libero Arbitrio* ("A Diatribe on Free Will"), an attack on Luther's predestinarianism (1524); and many editions of patristic writings, all coming from Froben's press at Basel (beginning in 1516).

Unsympathetic with the monastic ideal, Erasmus rejected the double standard—the notion that some Christians are called to fulfill the counsels of perfection (poverty, chastity, and obedience), while the rest have to be content with a lower ethical criterion. In his view, every Christian should endeavor to be perfect (*Enchiridion,* 15). Although not denying that a few may have a vocation for a life apart from the world, he felt that, as a general rule, members of the church can best improve the world by living in it. Jesus did not cut himself off from his fellows.

Erasmus was also averse to those scholastics who strained out the gnat and swallowed the camel, concentrating on theoretical trivialities at the expense of important matters. For the Apostle Paul, charity was not just a subject for theological discussion but something eminently practical (*Stultitiae,* 53). Christianity does not essentially consist in an external attachment to forms and ceremonies, but in an inner resolution to make Christ one's pattern for thought and conduct. Charity and service are the indispensable ingredients of religious devotion (*Enchiridion,* 13–14). The Christian soldier wages a continuous war against evil, and in his efforts to live rightly he is aided by knowledge and prayer (*ibid.,* 2).

In his essays *Querela Pacis* ("Complaint of Peace") and *Bellum* ("War"), Erasmus pleaded for the application of Christian principles to international relationships, maintaining that a true follower of Christ is committed to nonviolence and pacifism. Armed conflict between nations is always wrong and harms both victors and vanquished. Like Luther and his associates, Erasmus held that fundamental Christianity, as it is exemplified in the New Testament, had been obscured by secondary developments, and he lamented the widespread ignorance of the scriptures among the people, both clerical and lay. But he disliked Luther's emotionalism and objected to his radical predestinarianism, contending that human effort is a necessary factor in the work of salvation. He also believed that the church would be reformed, not by violence or forcible separation, but rather from within, by quiet and unspectacular processes of education.

Accordingly, the views of Erasmus were acceptable neither to the reformers nor to the rigorous upholders of tradition. Luther denounced him as an unbelieving pleasure-seeker, while the university at Paris decided against his doctrines in 1527, and his works were placed on the church's index of prohibited books in 1559.

BIBLIOGRAPHY

Cassirer, E., P. O. Kristeller, and J. H. Randall, Jr., eds. *The Renaissance Philosophy of Man.* Chicago: University of Chicago Press, 1948.

Flick, A. *The Decline of the Medieval Church.* 2 vols. New York: Knopf, 1930.

Huizinga, J. *Erasmus.* New York: Phaidon, 1952.

Kristeller, P. O. *Eight Philosophers of the Italian Renaissance.* Palo Alto, Calif.: Stanford University Press, 1965.

Randall, J. H., Jr. *The Making of the Modern Mind.* Rev. ed. Boston: Houghton Mifflin, 1940.

26 ✠ Martin Luther

Martin Luther (1483–1546), the son of a miner, was born at Eisleben and studied at Magdeburg, Eisenach, and at the University of Erfurt, where he became interested in classical Latin literature and in the doctrines of Ockham. He had originally planned to do post-graduate work in jurisprudence, but through a dramatic decision he made after narrowly escaping death by lightning, he entered the monastery of the Augustinian friars at Erfurt (1505). He was ordained in 1507 and two years later graduated from the University of Wittenberg (founded in 1502 by Elector Frederick III of Saxony). In 1510 he went to Rome on official business and was subsequently elected professor of scripture at Wittenberg, where he proceeded to lecture on the Psalms and the Pauline epistles. In 1515 he became vicar of his order, an appointment that put him in charge of more than a dozen monasteries in the region.

But Luther was far from happy despite his rapid promotion. A deep feeling of his own inherent unworthiness obsessed him, and a scrupulous fulfillment of religious duties seemed only to intensify his anxieties. He felt that he stood under divine condemnation and was liable at any moment to be smitten by the avenging God of righteousness. But perhaps toward 1515 Luther passed through a spiritual crisis (although there has been much controversy about the precise data and significance of his so-called *Turmerlebnis*—German for "tower-experience"), which brought him inner peace and engendered a firm conviction that he had received God's forgiveness through faith and faith alone. On the basis of this new consciousness of personal freedom he went on to work out his interpretation of Christianity, confirmation for which he found in the writings of Paul, Augustine, and Tauler, as well as in the *Theologia Germanica* of the Gottesfreunde. He argued that, because of man's inherited depravity, salvation cannot be earned by meritorious actions but solely by a divinely awakened trust in the validity of the gospel of God's pardoning love in Christ. Thus a true Christian is fundamentally a forgiven sinner, not a self-made moral hero, and any virtue he possesses springs spontaneously from a profound sense of gratitude for the God-given grace he now enjoys, unworthy though he is.

Luther evidently came to such conclusions during the controversy between Reuchlin (representing the new humanism) and Hochstraten (representing the upholders of the scholastic tradition), and it was on the eve of All Saints in 1517 that he made his momentous attack on the authority of the Catholic hierarchy.

Albrecht of Brandenburg became archbishop of Mainz in 1514, and the appointment was recognized by Pope Leo X (1513–21) on the payment of a large sum of money. This involved Albrecht in serious debt, and it was formally agreed that, to reimburse himself, he should appropriate half the proceeds that accrued in Brandenburg and Saxony from the sale of the indulgence Leo had issued (in 1516) for the rebuilding of St. Peter's in Rome. Johann Tetzel (*c.* 1465–1519) officially organized the sale in the districts of Magdeburg and Halberstadt, and he conducted the campaign after the manner of a vulgar advertising agent, proclaiming that a small payment could guarantee the soul's safe passage to paradise after death. Scandalized by the whole affair, Luther was prompted to post ninety-five theses on the door of the *Schlosskirche* ("castle-church") at the University of Wittenberg. Within a few weeks the entire country was astir. Humanists and others rallied to Luther's side, while Tetzel replied with countertheses.

Luther was called before the general chapter of the Augustinian Order at Heidelberg in 1518, and in the course of the disputations he gained additional followers among his fellow monks, including Martin Bucer (Butzer in German; 1491–1551), who was destined to play a significant role in the progress of the reform. Among Luther's supporters at Wittenberg were Andreas Bodenstein of Karlstadt (1480–1541), who had been on the university staff since 1505, and Philipp Melanchthon (1497–1560), a grandnephew of Reuchlin, appointed professor of Greek in 1518, who was to become the most scholarly exponent of Lutheran ideas.

Also in 1518 Luther was summoned for trial to Rome, and Sylvester Prierias, the Dominican inquisitor and an opponent of Reuchlin, prepared the official statement of the doctrinal position of the accused. But, through the intervention of Elector Frederick of Saxony, the hearing was transferred to Augsburg before the judgment seat of Cardinal Cajetan. However, the verdict went against Luther, who forthwith fled to Wittenberg, where he proclaimed his right to state his case before a general council.

In response to a challenge made by Johann Eck (1486–1543), a professor of theology at Ingolstadt, to Luther's colleague, Bodenstein of Karlstadt, a public debate took place at Leipzig in 1519. Luther himself attended, and by skilful cross-examination Eck forced him to admit that John Huss had been unjustly condemned, an admission which implied that general councils are not infallible.

But Luther was far from being perturbed by Eck's logical dialectics and, with unswerving devotion, gave himself to what he now definitely believed to be his divinely appointed task, namely, the deliverance of Germany from the tyranny of the papacy. The hierarchical court at Rome had become for him a sink of iniquity, and he was fond of likening it to Babylon and even to Sodom. He continued to use his great literary gifts in the service of the cause he had made his own, and in 1520 he wrote three influential tractates.

In the first of these, *An den christlichen Adel deutscher Nation* ("To the Christian Nobility of the German Nation"), he called upon the princes to assume responsibility for the reformation of the church; *inter alia* they should abolish all tributes to Rome, the requirement of clerical celibacy, masses for the dead, pilgrimages, and the monastic orders; they should also reduce the number of holy days, improve theological education, and prohibit prostitution and beggary. In the second work, *Von der babylonischen Gefangenschaft der Kirche* ("On the Babylonian Captivity of the Church"), he contended that Christians should be freed from subjection to communion in one kind, and from subscription to the doctrines of transubstantiation and of the sacrifice of the mass; only baptism and the eucharist (or Lord's supper) are genuine sacraments. In the third treatise, *Von der Freiheit eines Christenmenschen* ("On the Freedom of a Christian"), he maintained that men can be justified solely by faith and must therefore be liberated from the obligation to perform so-called meritorious works.

Charles V came to the imperial throne in 1519 and was potentially the most powerful man in Europe. As the grandson of Emperor Maximillian I and Mary of Burgundy, and of the "Catholic sovereigns" Ferdinand and Isabella, he inherited Austria, the Spanish territories in Europe and America, Burgundy, the Netherlands, and the kingdom of Naples. But, as fate would have it, his influence was much curtailed through the persistent opposition of the papacy, the French monarchy, and the Lutheran princes—to say nothing of the Turks who were gaining strength in southeastern Europe.

In 1521 Charles presided over the Diet of Worms to which Luther had been summoned, and the emperor hoped to settle the religious differences once and for all. But Luther steadfastly upheld his position; refusing to retract, he was placed under the ban of the empire. But opinion among the members of the Diet was far from unanimous, some holding that the case should come before a general council. Elector Frederick of Saxony, fearing for Luther's safety, took him into protective custody at Wartburg Castle near Eisenach. He remained secluded there for about ten months and seized the opportunity for literary activity. He wrote some brief polemical works and, more important, began his translation of the scriptures. This was the first German version from the original languages, and its vivid style brought the Bible alive to the people; and, apart from its religious value, the translation greatly contributed to the formation of modern literary German.

During his absence Luther's ideas took increasing effect in Saxony. Traditional practices were abandoned; priests married, and monks and nuns vacated their monasteries. Bodenstein of Karlstadt sought to destroy all altars, images, and crucifixes, and much tumult ensued. Luther was recalled to facilitate the restoration of peace. Karlstadt withdrew under pressure; and it was agreed to retain infant baptism, candles, crucifixes, and sacred pictures; Luther prepared new orders of worship, both general and sacramental.

Further conflicts developed in 1524. From the humanistic side Erasmus published his refutation of Luther's predestinarianism, and Karlstadt (who had come into action again) accused Luther of inconsistency and compromise. Luther quickly rose to the counterattack, describing Erasmus as a sceptic and pleasure-seeker, while Karlstadt—"the new Judas," as Luther called him —was banished from the territory. Perhaps more serious in its consequences for Lutheranism was the peasants' uprising, which to some extent was precipitated through the excitement occasioned by Luther's emotionally-charged oratory. Thomas Münzer (*c.* 1490–1525), an Anabaptist who felt that the Lutheran reform was not radical enough, became the leader of the rebels, and they stated their demands in twelve articles (1525). Luther tried to mediate between the landlords and the insurgents, but without success, and he finally recommended a policy of extermination. Münzer was captured and executed after the crushing defeat of the rebels at Frankenhausen in 1525. Luther's handling of this affair cost him much support, especially in the south.

Elector Frederick of Saxony died in 1525, whereupon Luther married Katherine von Bora, a former Cistercian nun; it has been argued that the marriage was delayed because Frederick strongly disapproved of marital unions between people who had taken the monastic vows, but this is disputable.

Following the Diet of Worms in 1521, Emperor Charles V was largely occupied with affairs outside Germany, and in 1526 the Speyer Reichstag could defy his instruction that the Edict of Worms must be carried out. Luther was not arrested, and Lutheran princes were authorized to govern the churches in their respective territories as they severally thought fit. In 1529, however, Pope Clement VII (1523–34) was forced to make peace with the emperor, and Francis I capitulated, a consequence being that Charles could turn once again to the Lutheran problem; and at the Speyer Reichstag of 1529 it was ruled that church properties in Lutheran lands should be restored to the Roman hierarchy.

The Lutheran powers at once registered a formal protest (hence the use of the term "Protestant" to designate supporters of the Reformation), and Philip of Hesse sought to establish a defensive union of German and Swiss Protestants. With this end in view, Luther and Melanchthon held a colloquy with Zwingli of Zurich and others at Marburg in the autumn of 1529. Agreement was reached on fourteen of the fifteen articles of faith which had been drawn up by Luther, but his eucharistic doctrine of consubstantiation was unacceptable to the Zwinglians. Assisted by Melanchthon and others, Luther expanded the Marburg Articles into the seventeen Articles of Schwabach, which in the following year were to be made the foundation of the first section of the Augsburg Confession. Thus, within quite a short period, Lutheranism was quickly elaborating an intricate theological system of its own; the exigencies of the developing situation were making it increasingly clear that the premise of justification by faith implied much that called for clarification.

The emperor was to be crowned at Augsburg; and the Lutheran confession to be presented there, as a step toward reunion, was prepared by Melanchthon, who made a serious effort to conciliate the various factions. Such controversial topics as the sole authority of the scriptures and the priesthood of all believers were not expounded in the statement. Nevertheless, the theses proved unacceptable to Eck and other representatives of Catholic orthodoxy, and they condemned the confession in an official document *Confutatio Pontificia*.

Charles rejected Melanchthon's apology for the Confession, and in the following year (1531) the Lutheran princes met at Schmalkalden to form a defensive alliance against imperial policy. The so-called Schmalkaldic Articles were drawn up by Luther for presentation to a projected general council to be convened by Pope Paul III (1534–49). In this document the language is far from being conciliatory, and the pope is explicitly identified with the Antichrist. The articles were formally accepted at Schmalkalden in 1537.

The Colloquy of Ratisbon (Regensburg) between three Catholic and three Protestant theologians was arranged by the emperor in 1541, and a large measure of agreement was reached on certain doctrinal issues. But any hope that a lasting settlement might be reached was destroyed by powerful opposition from various quarters. Luther considered the Colloquy to be a patched-up affair, and Caraffa (the future Pope Paul IV), on the opposite side, was of much the same opinion, while Francis I felt that a religious settlement would make the emperor too powerful.

Luther did not help the Protestant cause when he sanctioned the bigamous marriage of Philip of Hesse in 1539; intrigue and controversy increased. Luther died in 1546, and the emperor determined so to weaken the Lutheran powers that they would be forced to submit to the rulings of a general council. But the plan was brought to nought, partly through French opposition and the lack of papal support. Imperial forces were defeated in 1552, and the principle of *cuis regio eius religio* ("whose realm his religion") was basic in the Peace of Augsburg, signed in 1555. Both Catholicism and Protestantism received official recognition, and it was laid down that the inhabitants of any territory should conform with the religion of its ruler; those not satisfied with the religious order established in their own land could migrate to another. The Peace of Augsburg remained regulative in German affairs until the conclusion of the Treaty of Westphalia in 1648, at the end of the Thirty Years' War.

It must be observed at this juncture that Lutheranism spread rapidly in the Scandinavian countries. It was introduced into Denmark as early as 1520; church property was expropriated in 1531, and a Danish translation of the scriptures appeared in 1550. The reform was imposed upon the Norwegians by the Danes. In Sweden the Reformation was not so radical, the episcopal succession being maintained after the break with Rome in 1524. Lutheranism entered Finland in 1523; Catholicism was forcibly suppressed, and its profession continued to be illegal there until 1869.

Luther was a dynamic individualist, a man of deep religious feeling, and a gifted preacher and writer, whose tracts, sermons, hymns, and biblical translation greatly affected German attitudes. Like the Apostle Paul, he was not a systematic thinker, his theological works being occasional writings prompted by particular situations. His persistent melancholy as a young man doubtless helped to determine his basic theological emphasis upon human depravity, while his fear that the converted would misuse their Christian liberty may to some extent have inclined him to resort to the arm of the state for the defense of his doctrines. And perhaps this in turn facilitated the growth of the quietistic view that religion is in essence a purely personal matter, the broad issues of social or national activity being the concern of the civic authorities.

Luther's exposition of his fundamental doctrines of human depravity, justification by faith, and divine predestination reflect Pauline and Augustinian influence. Since man is spiritually impotent and utterly worthless he cannot earn divine forgiveness but can only accept it by faith as a gift from God. But whereas for Paul salvation is essentially the emancipation of the personality from the power of death and the corruption of the flesh, for Luther it is the deliverance of the soul from the fear of divine wrath. God justifies the sinner while he is still sinful, and inner peace ensues through the consciousness of God's pardoning favor. Such a supreme attainment, in the last resort, is an outcome of divine election; salvation is achieved by those to whom God wills to be gracious. It is true that God discloses himself in the scriptures, but it is also true that people may read the Bible without being spiritually moved; the written record of revelation remains external to them. Thus spiritual vision, the required responsiveness of the heart, is granted to some and not to others; and Luther therefore concluded that human salvation is determined beforehand for those whom God has chosen.

Luther proceeded to make further deductions from his basic conception of God's pardoning love. Since the Christian is essentially a forgiven sinner, the good deeds he performs are spontaneous expressions of his thankfulness for a present enjoyment of God's graciousness. He is delivered from all ultimate fear about his own personal destiny and can give himself freely, without ulterior motives, in the service of his fellows. He practices love for his neighbor unstintingly. But he is still a sinner as judged by the standard of God's perfection, and whatever virtue he displays derives from the one creative Source of all finite being. There can exist no merit in what he does, and therefore in principle one vocation is just as good as any other. Nothing especially holy belongs to monastic detachment from the world, so that, for example, a domestic servant who cooks a good meal may be no less saintly than all the monks and nuns in the world. Indeed, if what she does in the kitchen springs from a deep sense of God's loving-kindness, God has revealed himself to her personally, and she is a priest for others in her own right.

Since all true believers are priests, the church can scarcely be constituted by a special class of ordained persons, standing in a supposed apostolic succession. The church is rather the fellow-ship of the faithful who rejoice in their common experience of God's forgiveness, and who organize themselves for the proc-lamation of the gospel through word and sacrament. And from this sort of stance it might be inferred that neither sermons nor sacraments convey grace in the orthodox sense; they are merely the appointed occasions, so to speak, upon which God reveals himself inwardly to the elect.

As already suggested, Luther did not carry out radical ideas of this kind with anything approaching perfect consistency. In some respects he was a traditionalist. Thus, while, like the Apostle Paul, he was averse to a legalistic interpretation of Christianity, his teaching adumbrated the juridical notion of compensation which underlies the Catholic doctrine of penance. He held that God is the avenger of sin, and that, before he could fully reveal himself as love, a supreme act of penance had to take place. The required atoning act was performed by Jesus, who suffered the penalty of human sin, although he was sinless. In sacrificing himself Christ went beyond all the possible re-quirements of justice and, since he was divine, an infinite super-abundance of merit accrued. Hence, without infringing the de-mands of moral retribution, from that time forward God could forgive sinful men by drawing on the store of surplus merit produced by the crucifixion.

Again, whereas his fundamental attitude might seem to imply that the sacraments can be nothing more than visible confir-mations of an already existent faith, Luther's thinking on the subject betrays the continuing influence of the traditional notion of sacramental channels of grace. Apparently, he could rule that baptism actually transmits faith to the infant, and with regard to the eucharist he could put forward the theory of consubstantiation. While rejecting the doctrine of transubstantiation, he maintained that, after the pronouncement of the words of consecration, the bread and wine and Christ's body and blood are "substantially" present with each other in a state of coexistence. Thus, as in Catholic teaching, it could be said that communicants feed materially on Christ by faith for the eternal preservation of their souls.

It should also be borne in mind that, although Luther resorted to New Testament standards in his condemnation of current ecclesiastical doctrine and practice, he was no bibliolater. He did not hold that all parts of the Bible were of equal religious worth, nor did he believe that the epoch of revelation had really come to an end with the last of the canonical writers. For him, the word of God was a living agency of communication which far transcended the records of past revelation, and as such it was still addressed to human beings amid the welter of present experience. Nonetheless, Luther's tendency to treat the scriptures as a final court of appeal in controversy facilitated the development of a dogmatic identification of the word of God with the letter of scripture. Hence in certain Protestant circles the Bible came to be regarded as verbally and uniformly inspired, and the inadequate idea gained ground that the Reformation of the sixteenth century consisted simply in the substitution of the external authority of the scriptures for that of the papacy.

BIBLIOGRAPHY

Bainton, R. H. *Studies on the Reformation.* London: Hodder and Stoughton, 1964.

Bornkamm, H. *Luther's World of Thought.* St. Louis, Mo.: Concordia, 1958.

Cochrane, A. C., ed. *Reformed Confessions of the Sixteenth Century*. London: Student Christian Movement Press, 1966.

Fife, R. H. *The Revolt of Martin Luther*. New York: Columbia University Press, 1957.

Gerrish, B. A. *Grace and Reason: A Study in the Theology of Martin Luther*. Oxford: Clarendon Press, 1962.

Harbison, F. H. *The Age of the Reformation*. Ithaca, N.Y.: Cornell University Press, 1955.

Swihart, A. K. *Luther and the Lutheran Church, 1483-1960*. London: Owen, 1961.

27 ‡ Zwingli and Calvin

Luther's protestations hastened the Reformation in Switzerland. This may be dated from 1519, when Zwingli delivered a course of lectures in Zurich on the New Testament, in which he put contemporary Catholicism in an unfavorable light by contrasting it with what he believed to obtain in the apostolic church. Luther's contentions seem to have helped to crystallize some of Zwingli's ideas and may have finally convinced him of the necessity of a break with Rome. It is true that the Swiss theologian often asserted his independence of Luther, and, while this may have been partly due to a certain personal resentment at what he conceived to be Luther's excessive influence, there can be little doubt concerning the fundamental truth of his insistent claim. Before he had even heard of the German reformer he had come to feel that the church of his day was in dire need of reformation. Unlike Luther, he was a humanist and, despite his patriotism, thought highly of Erasmus.

Huldreich Zwingli (1484–1531) was born at Wildhaus, St. Gall, and studied at Bern, Vienne, and Basel. During his years at Basel (1502–6) he was a pupil of Thomas Wyttenback (1472–1526), a humanist, who, besides doubting the validity of the penitential system, had come to believe in the supreme authority of the scriptures. The young Zwingli determined to acquaint himself thoroughly with the basic literary sources of the faith. But he was a man of action as well as a scholar. Ordained in 1506, for the next ten years he was parish priest at Glarus. In 1513 and again in 1515 he acted as chaplain to those of his compatriots who were employed as hired soldiers in the armed forces of the pope, and he received a pension for his cooperation; but he became increasingly opposed in principle to the practice of mercenary service.

While at Glarus Zwingli devoted his leisure to humanistic studies. He worked at Greek and Hebrew, read widely in patristics, and even learned the Pauline epistles by heart. He greatly admired Erasmus, with whom he corresponded. In 1516 he moved to the parish of Einsiedeln and was shocked by some of the rituals connected with pilgrimages to the popular shrine of St. Meinrad, a hermit of the ninth century. In the same year Erasmus' edition of the Greek New Testament appeared, and Zwingli at once began to study it. His sermons tended to become openly critical of contemporary ecclesiastical practices.

In 1518 he was appointed people's priest at Zurich, and his addresses immediately aroused widespread popular interest. He argued that the one sure basis of Christian truth is to be found in the scriptures, and, using biblical criteria, he proceeded to condemn such beliefs and observances as purgatory, the liturgy of the mass, and the keeping of regular fasts. In 1520 he renounced his papal pension, and two years later there was much commotion in the city when a number of his sympathizers broke the Lenten fast. Disturbances continued, and the bishop of Constance had to take action. But Zwingli held his ground; at a public disputation with Johann Faber, the bishop's representative, he won a signal triumph by victoriously sustaining sixty-seven theses, and within a few weeks a break was made with the hierarchy. The reform was consolidated in subsequent months, and Zwingli celebrated his triumph by getting married (1524).

During the next few years he had a harassing time with certain Anabaptists, whom he found especially difficult to deal with, partly because, like himself, they were concerned to apply biblical standards in the regulation of Christian thought and conduct. Eventually stringent measures were taken, and in

1527 the local council ordered an execution by drowning, a form of capital punishment deemed appropriate for an ardent upholder of adult baptism.

While disputing with Anabaptists, Zwingli was also much occupied with the elaboration of a symbolical interpretation of the eucharist. He held, for instance, that the pronouncement "This is my body" means "This signifies my body," and he therefore rejected the doctrine of Christ's corporeal presence at celebrations of the rite. The eucharist, he contended, is really of the nature of a memorial ceremony, a dramatic reminder of the Lord's sacrifice and a communal attestation of loyalty to the church's founder. Clearly, this interpretation was at variance not only with the orthodox conception of transubstantiation but also with the Lutheran doctrine of consubstantiation. Actually, Luther considered Zwingli's arguments a sinful exaltation of human intellection—and this despite the fact that he himself indulged in abstruse argumentation on the question. Thus at one stage Luther resorted to the notion that Christ's divine attributes, which include ubiquity, were communicated to his human nature, and hence that his flesh could be on a plurality of altars at the same time. On the other hand, Zwingli felt that Luther's teaching in this connection was more unbiblical than the orthodox doctrine of transubstantiation. Although several points of agreement were registered, the Colloquy of Marburg in 1529 made it quite obvious that deep-seated differences existed between the Lutheran and the Zwinglian theological orientation.

Zwingli won an important victory at Bern in 1528 when, before an influential gathering of clergy and laity, he succeeded in sustaining ten theses that he had propounded as a rejoinder to seven theses put forward by that untiring protagonist of received tradition, Johann Eck of Ingolstadt. The canton became reformed, and other cantons (including Basel) quickly followed suit. But vigorous resistance developed in the cantons around Lake Lucerne; war broke out in 1531, and in that year Zwingli was killed on the field of battle.

Much more of a systematic thinker than Luther, Zwingli worked out a theology based on the concept of the sovereignty of God. While he subscribed to such characteristically Lutheran doctrines as justification by faith and predestination, a humanistic strain is present in his teaching, and on occasion his sympathies had a relatively wide range. Thus he could argue that the Creator's will is supremely, but not exclusively, revealed in the Bible, and that there have existed true worshipers of God outside the sphere of Christianity. Genuine religion consists in bringing one's life into conformity with the declared will of God, and Christ came into the world primarily to clarify the divine criteria for human conduct.

But such a moralistic interpretation, which presupposes the reality of human freedom and betrays an affinity with the teaching of Erasmus, seems to be inconsistent with Zwingli's theology of justifying faith. He maintained that the latter is fundamentally a confidence in the universality of divine providence, and in his treatise *De Providentia Dei* ("On the Providence of God") he stressed the all-encompassing character of God's omnipotence. Men are creaturely and can perform no meritorious works because it is God who activates the totality of existence. He is the Creator and Lord of all things, and his will presides over the entire course of cosmic history.

In the last resort, therefore, God is the only effective cause, and yet, being transcendent as well as immanent, he is above mundane laws and cannot be judged by merely human standards. He shows forth his mercy in predestinating some to salvation, and he displays his justice in predestinating others to eternal damnation. God possesses all things, and so his favor cannot be won by any action on man's part, not even by faith in his loving-kindness. Salvation has no creaturely conditions; its sole ultimate ground lies in divine election. Thus Zwingli came to echo the doctrine so greatly stressed by Wycliffe, that the invisible church is the whole company of God's chosen; not all who outwardly profess faith in Christ are members of the true church, and not all so-called heathens belong to the company of the damned.

Partly in consequence of Zwingli's premature death, the center of the non-Lutheran Reformation shifted from Zurich to Geneva. In the process of this transition an important part was played by Guillaume Farel (1489–1565). Already suspected of Lutheranism while still a student at Paris, in 1524 he was banished from Bern for persistent attacks on the Catholic establishment. But his enthusiasm could not be damped. As we have seen, Bern became reformed in 1528; and in 1530 the authorities at Neuchâtel were persuaded by his spirited preaching. Thus encouraged, he soon turned his attention to Geneva.

For some time there had been local opposition to the dukes of Savoy regarding the possession of French-speaking areas in the vicinity of Geneva, and in 1527 the Genevan municipality, having allied itself with Bern and Freiburg, ejected the bishop, who represented Savoyard interests in the region. By 1531 it seemed to Farel that Geneva was ripe for reform, but, owing to the alliance with Catholic Freiburg, it was not until 1533 that he could gain admission to the city. His strenuous efforts eventually had their reward; in 1534 Geneva's alliance with Freiburg was repudiated under Bernese pressure, and in 1536 the Reformation was formally accepted by the general assembly.

In July of that year Farel met Calvin (who happened to be visiting the city) and suggested that he should remain and co-operate in the work of consolidating the Reformation there. Calvin assented to the proposal, but not without hesitation, for he had earlier decided that it was his vocation to devote himself to scholarship.

John Calvin (1509–64) was born at Noyon in Picardy, and his father early intended that he should be ordained. He received his first ecclesiastical benefice in 1521, and two years later he went to Paris for theological training. But from 1528 he studied jurisprudence at Orléans and then at Bourges, where he came under Protestant influence. The switch from theology seems to have been due to his father's quarrel with the cathedral chapter at Noyon, but, quite independently, young Calvin himself could have come to entertain doubts about his prospective ordination within Catholicism. His father died in 1531, and soon afterward he was back in Paris, studying Latin and Greek at the Collège de France, the new humanist institution founded by Francis I (1530). Proof was given of his erudition in 1532, when he issued a Latin commentary on Seneca's work *De Clementia* ("On Clemency").

Calvin's acceptance of Reformation principles, like Zwingli's, gradually developed from his humanistic sympathies, and humanism in France derived much of its inspiration from Jacques Lefèvre (1455–1536), whose general attitude had much in common with that of Erasmus. In his commentary on the Pauline epistles Lefèvre had stressed the regulative authority of scripture, repudiating the notion that man is capable of performing works that are meritorious in God's sight. Nevertheless, although some of his doctrines were censured at the Sorbonne in 1521 and he had to flee to Strasbourg in 1525, he never renounced Catholicism, evidently holding that reform should come from within. Calvin, on the other hand, decided upon secession.

In November 1533 Nicholas Cop, a prominent sympathizer with humanistic learning, made a public plea for reform in his inaugural lecture as rector of the University of Paris. The authorities were disturbed. Like certain others, Calvin discreetly left the city. He made his way to Noyon, where he renounced his benefices, and he may have suffered imprisonment there for a while. With the threat of persecution still in the air he found refuge at Basel in 1535, and his famous theological treatise *The Institution of the Christian Religion* (Latin: *Christianae Religionis Institutio*)—commonly known in English as the *Institutes*

—appeared in March 1536, with a defensive prefatory letter addressed to Francis I. It was the most systematic statement of Protestant principles that had hitherto been published, and its author quickly acquired fame. Within a few months he had the fateful meeting with Farel.

At Geneva Calvin at once took the initiative, publishing a set of disciplinary articles which he sought to impose upon the whole community. The stringency of his demands aroused opposition, and after much disputation both he and Farel were forced to leave (1538), one going to Strasbourg, the other to Neuchâtel. At Strasbourg Calvin served the French Protestant congregation, acting as minister and lecturer. He there made the acquaintance of Martin Bucer, who, while emphasizing the doctrine of predestination, represented a mediating position between Lutheranism and Zwinglianism. Bucer's influence is discernible in the enlarged edition of the *Institutes*, issued in 1539. Calvin's prestige continued to grow, and he attended several important congresses; at the colloquy of Ratisbon in 1541 he met and became a friend of Melanchthon, Luther's influential colleague and scholarly supporter.

In the same year Calvin was recalled to Geneva, and in cooperation with Farel he renewed his efforts to enforce a strict discipline upon the population. He held that the church is composed of God's elect and that (as the New Testament was taken to indicate) there are properly four classes of ecclesiastical officers, namely, pastors, teachers, elders (or presbyters), and deacons (charged with the care of the poor and the sick). Their vocation in each instance derives from an inner divine call whose validity has to be outwardly confirmed by the approval of the congregation as a whole through its appointed representatives. The pastors should meet weekly for public discussions, biblical exegesis, and the examination of ministerial candidates.

Calvin provided that a consistory, with a membership divided between ministers and elders, should function as the principal organ of church government, with the right to enforce general

conformity with the adopted ecclesiastical discipline. The rigorism entailed is shown in the fact that persons caught indulging
in frivolous activities, such as games and dancing, were liable to
punishment; and for serious heresy it could mean the imposition
of the death penalty.

Calvin's struggle for municipal recognition of the church's
autonomy was by no means an easy one. He maintained that
the state was divinely intended to subserve the requirements of
a *corps d'élite*, the earthly organization of the people of God,
protecting it against heretics and applying sanctions (such as
banishment or death) in the case of offenders adjudged by the
consistory to deserve more than excommunication per se. In this
regard Calvin differed from Luther and Zwingli, both of whom,
while agreeing that the state should serve the church, actually
assigned a large measure of responsibility to civic rulers in defining what is right and proper according to the word of God.
And his insistence on the independence of the church, as led by
trained ministers, was destined to have important political consequences in countries like Holland, Scotland, England, and
North America, where Calvinistic forms of Protestantism became especially influential.

Opposition to the regime persisted for about fourteen years,
and a number of recalcitrants were put to death. But gradually
the power of resistance was broken, and by 1555 Calvin was
undisputed master of the situation. The stringent discipline was
legally established, and the municipal council acted obediently
in accordance with the directives laid down by the ecclesiastical
consistory. Foreigner though he was, Calvin finally triumphed,
and Geneva became increasingly a haven of refuge for persecuted Protestants from many countries. So his fame, both as
scholar and as statesman, became increasingly international, and
his influence spread across geographical frontiers.

Calvin was a talented writer, clear and precise in his expression, a systematic if not a creative thinker, and an excellent organizer. Although his narrowness and imperiousness alienated

some, he had close friends, and his disinterestedness commanded respect. He was extremely industrious, and, despite his active participation in matters of practical polity, he continued to engage in literary activity, producing commentaries on most of the books of the Bible. Among other things, he wrote two Genevan catechisms, and a service book (based on that of the French congregation at Strasbourg), which allowed for extempore prayer as well as for congregational singing. The final and greatly enlarged edition of the *Institutes* appeared in 1559, the year in which he founded the Academy, an institution that was to become the chief center of theological learning for the Reformed, as distinct from the Lutheran, churches; with the establishment of a medical faculty in 1872, it became the University of Geneva.

When the first edition of the *Institutes* appeared in 1536, it was issued as an introduction to the Bible and as a concise statement of the Protestant case. Apart from the preface (addressed to Francis I), it contains six chapters: the first deals with law, especially the Decalogue; the second concerns faith, principally the Apostles' Creed; the third treats of prayer, particularly the Lord's Prayer; the fourth concerns the sacraments of baptism and the Lord's supper; the fifth is a criticism of the Catholic doctrine that there are seven sacraments; and the seventh deals with ecclesiastical polity. There is little stress on the notion of divine predestination, although it is implied in the basic idea that man can have no justifying merit in God's sight.

On the other hand, in the larger second edition of 1539, the fourteenth of the seventeen chapters is entirely devoted to the subject of predestination, and this change of emphasis was probably due to Bucer's influence. God is represented as the ultimate cause of all things, and no place is allowed for divine self-limitation or for permissive providence. God predetermined the disobedience of Adam and its baneful consequences; and man, a mere creature, is in no position to question the inscrutable decrees of the Creator, the infinite source of power and majesty. Thus the concept of God's glorious omnipotence became definitely fundamental in Calvin's theological thought. Thanks to Bucer's mediation, the Frenchman approached Zwingli's orientation; but he was averse to the latter's metaphysical speculations, preferring to remain close to the language of scripture; and his theology as a whole had greater comprehensiveness.

The final edition of the *Institutes* appeared in 1559. The treatise comprises eighty chapters, divided into four parts: the first part deals with God the Creator; the second with God the Redeemer; the third with God the Holy Spirit; and the fourth with the sacraments and ecclesiastical polity. Calvin continued to stress the majesty and omnipotence of God and, by way of contrast, the depravity of man; the supreme virtue is humility, and man's first duty can only be to give praise to God (*Institutes*, 1:1:2–3; 2:3:4). The Creator reveals himself in all his works, but man was so blinded by original sin that a special mode of revelation was required. God foresaw this and duly met the requirement, the results of the decisive divine action being recorded in the scriptures. Hence those chosen for salvation necessarily bring themselves into the captivity of obedience to the divine will as it is made known in the word of God (*ibid.*, 4:10:7).

But the Christian life cannot begin with obedience because man's nature is totally corrupt. It begins with a realization of God's redeeming love in Christ, a recognition that arouses repentance and faith; and God in his mercy justifies believing sinners by imputing to them the superabundant merits of Christ, who suffered the punishment of sin on man's behalf. Thus the first step in the soteriological process secures divine forgiveness through Christ by means of repentance and faith; and when justification is attained, the life of obedience commences, so that thenceforth the soul is progressively sanctified in preparation for the eternal blessedness of heaven. The present world, with all its carnal allurements, comes to be despised as a place of exile, the Christian having his citizenship in a celestial country; and advancement in holiness has its correlative in an increasing disengagement from all earthly entanglements (*ibid.*, 3:9:4).

Calvin further maintained that in the work of salvation ecclesiastical ministrations are indispensable, and he could echo Cyprian's mot that he who has not the church for his mother cannot have God for his father (*ibid.*, 4:1:1). As the visible company of the elect, the society of believers is the community in which the word of God is proclaimed and the sacraments are duly administered. Initiation into the Christian life comes about through an inner response engendered by attending to the word of God, and even when repentance and faith have done their foundation work, obedience and sanctification cannot be achieved by man's efforts alone. The forgiven sinner needs to be inwardly fortified in his struggles against temptation, and this implies that he must continually avail himself of the church's sacramental aids, which impart nourishment to the believing soul.

Thus, while Calvin repudiated the dogma of Christ's physical presence at the eucharist, rejecting Luther's doctrine of consubstantiation (as well as that of transubstantiation), he nonetheless maintained that the sacraments are more than visible signs testifying to the love of God. They are means of grace, instruments for the transmission of reinforcing divine energy to the souls of the faithful, and the church, as the only body appointed to administer them, must keep itself pure by holding its members together in the strictest discipline (*ibid.*, 4:1:12).

Perhaps the most important credal expression of strict Calvinism is the Second Helvetic Confession, prepared in 1566 by J. H. Bullinger (of Zurich) for Elector Frederick III of the Palatinate; it came to be accepted by Reformed churches in Switzerland and elsewhere. As already observed, Calvinism spread into many countries. The French Protestant (or Huguenot) church was constituted on a Calvinistic basis in 1559. (The term "Huguenot" seems to have originated as a nickname derived from a certain King Hugo who figured in a medieval tale.) Calvinism was officially adopted in Scotland (largely through

John Knox, a friend of Calvin) in 1560 and in the Netherlands in 1622. The Thirty-nine Articles of the Anglican church (1563–71) were affected by Calvinistic ideas, and Calvinism became the recognized theological basis of the English dissenting churches—Presbyterian, Congregational, and Baptist. From England Calvinism spread to the New England colonies (the Pilgrim Fathers were Calvinistic Congregationalists), and it was destined to play a momentous part in the formation of the American tradition. In the German empire Calvinism found its way particularly into Brandenburg and the Palatinate.

It should be noticed at this point that Calvin was the first important Christian theologian to allow the general legitimacy of lending money on interest. Usury was prohibited (in the case of Jewish clients) in the Old Testament (Exod. 22:25). The same kind of prohibition was applied to the Christian clergy at the Council of Nicea (325) and to the laity at the Third Lateran Council (1179); but the practice of usury was permitted to the Jews in Western Christendom by the Fourth Lateran Council (1215). Accordingly, Calvin's ruling in this connection was a remarkable departure from tradition, and certain scholars in recent decades have detected a close connection between Calvinistic ethics and the rise of modern capitalism; and it is perhaps significant that England and the United States, which have so greatly contributed to the growth of modern capitalism, are countries in which Calvinism has been quite influential.

BIBLIOGRAPHY

Farner, O. *Zwingli the Reformer.* New York: Philosophical Library, 1952.

Kingdon, R. M. *Geneva and the Consolidation of the French Protestant Movement.* Geneva: Droz, 1967.

McDonnell, K. *John Calvin, the Church, and the Eucharist.* Princeton: Princeton University Press, 1967.

McNeill, J. T. *The History and Character of Calvinism.* New York: Oxford University Press, 1954.

Milner, B. C. *Calvin's Doctrine of the Church*. Leiden: E. J. Brill, 1970.

Nelson, B. N. *The Idea of Usury*. Princeton, N.J.: Princeton University Press, 1949.

Rilliet, J. *Zwingli: Third Man of the Reformation*. London: Lutterworth Press, 1964.

Tawney, R. H. *Religion and the Rise of Capitalism*. 2nd ed. New York: Harcourt, Brace, 1937.

Wendel, F. *Calvin: The Origins and Development of his Religious Thought*. New York: Harper and Row, 1963.

28 ‡ *Anglicanism and Puritanism*

It would be gross oversimplification to attribute the emergence of the modern *ecclesia anglicana* entirely to Henry VIII's passion for Anne Boleyn. A number of other factors were involved. As in Continental countries, so in England, during the fifteenth century nationalism had gained in strength, and papal exactions aroused widespread resentment. The clergy, often avaricious and largely ill educated, were far from popular, and their exemption from trial by secular courts was felt by some to be a flagrant injustice. In the early decades of the sixteenth century Lollardry as a force was almost spent; yet Wycliffe's teachings concerning apostolic poverty and the authority of scripture were not wholly forgotten. Indeed among certain intellectuals the latter doctrine regained currency owing to the spread of the new humanistic learning.

John Colet, dean of St. Paul's from 1505 to 1519, was a humanist of considerable influence; and it should be remembered that Erasmus was in London when he wrote his satirical *Praise of Folly* (1509), and that for a few years he taught at Cambridge, where he completed his Latin translation of the New Testament from the Greek. Moreover, there was a rapid infiltration of Lutheran ideas after 1517, and in 1521 Henry VIII himself was prompted to publish his *Assertion of the Seven Sacraments* (a criticism of Luther's thesis that there are but two authentic sacraments), which won for him the title "Defender of the Faith" (Latin: *Defensor Fidei*) from Pope Leo X. In

many quarters there seems to have been an insistent yearning
for a more personal form of religion, while the intrigue and inordinate ambition of Thomas Wolsey, who was designated a
cardinal and lord chancellor of England in 1515, brought further discredit upon the papal system.

Henry VIII (1509–47) married Catherine of Aragon, the
widow of his elder brother Arthur, in 1509; for the wedding a
papal dispensation had been given, removing the impediment
arising from the prohibited degrees. Of the six children born
of the union only Mary survived infancy, and Henry became
concerned about the Tudor succession. He began seriously to
doubt the validity of the marriage, and at length he applied to
the pope for a formal declaration of nullity. But his case was
not a strong one; in the first place, Catherine was an aunt of the
powerful Emperor Charles V (1519–56); and in the second
place, she maintained that her first marriage had not been consummated. Wolsey failed to secure the required certification,
and this led to his downfall in 1529. Exasperated, the king decided upon the repudiation of papal authority, and by a series
of parliamentary and ecclesiastical acts (1530–34) royal authority in England was substituted for that of the pope. Thomas
Cranmer (*c.* 1489–1556), who had secretly married a Lutheran
while visiting the Continent, succeeded William Warham as
archbishop of Canterbury in 1532; and during the following
year he pronounced the king's marriage with Catherine to be
invalid; shortly afterward Anne Boleyn was crowned queen.
Pope Clement VII replied by excommunicating Henry and declaring his divorce and remarriage null and void.

Despite the fact that Henry initiated a fundamental change
in ecclesiastical polity, on the whole he resisted changes in doctrine. Theologically he was basically conservative, although for
a short period, when seeking German favor, his legislation did
move in a Protestant direction. In 1536, the year in which he
ordered the dissolution of the monasteries, he issued the Ten
Articles, to whose composition Cranmer contributed. These

posit three sacraments—baptism, penance, and the eucharist—but they make no reference to transubstantiation, and they affirm justification by contrition, faith, and charity. Much more significant was the order that the English Bible should be made available to the public in every parish church of the country. This represented a remarkable change in policy, for the translation of the New Testament by William Tyndale (*c.* 1494–1536), printed in Germany in 1525, had to be smuggled into England from 1526, its dissemination in the country having been prohibited. But the king soon repented of his pro-Protestant actions, and in 1539 he promulgated the Six Articles, which superseded those of 1536: clerical celibacy was imposed (the archbishop had to banish his wife), and denial of the doctrine of transubstantiation was made a capital offense.

During the reign of the youthful Edward VI (1547–53), the son of Henry's third wife, Jane Seymour, Cranmer became more influential than he had been hitherto, and Protestantism was vigorously promoted. The Six Articles Act was repealed, communion in both kinds was enjoined, and clerical marriage legalized. Cranmer's first Book of Common Prayer, a masterly production, appeared in 1549, and the revised (more Calvinistic) edition in 1552. The archbishop had invited a number of Continental theologians (among them, Martin Bucer) to settle in England, and it was with their assistance that the Forty-two Articles were formulated—partly based on the Augsburg Confession prepared by Melanchthon in 1530—and issued in 1553.

But the Forty-two Articles were never enforced, for soon after their promulgation Mary Tudor, the daughter of Henry's first wife, Catherine of Aragon, came to the throne. As we should expect, during her reign (1553–58) there was a violent reaction against Protestantism: papal supremacy was re-established, and many people suffered martyrdom. Cranmer and others were burned at the stake in Oxford (1556).

With the accession of Elizabeth I (1558–1603), the daughter of Henry's second wife, Anne Boleyn, there was a return to moderation. Although she had discreetly conformed during Mary's reign, Elizabeth was not sympathetically disposed toward Rome, for she resented Catholic assertions of her bastardy. On the other hand, Calvinism did not appeal to her; for one thing, she believed that episcopacy was indispensable for a stable monarchy. Parliament passed a new Royal Supremacy Act in 1559, and in the same year she appointed Matthew Parker (1504–75) as archbishop of Canterbury. His consecration was conducted by four bishops who had been initiated to the episcopacy in the reigns of Henry VIII and Edward VI, and its validity has been the subject of much disputation. (It may be noted here that Pope Leo XIII in 1896 formally pronounced Anglican orders to be invalid because of a defect in intention.) But there can be little doubt that Elizabeth found in the archbishop of her choice a faithful ally and a competent exponent of moderate reform.

The queen reigned with astuteness and managed to formulate a *via media* between Rome and Geneva that proved workable, partly because on many questions it lacked doctrinal precision. The settlement was a compromise, and the church continued to conform with the old ways so far as they were deemed compatible with temperate Protestant sentiment. Before Parker's appointment the second Prayer Book of Edward VI (1552) had been slightly revised and republished (1559); the changes were of a minor character and mainly intended to make the work more acceptable to Catholic orthodoxy, as is seen, for example, in the omission of the prayer against the papacy. Parker contributed to the production of the Thirty-nine Articles, which in 1563 substantially became the doctrinal basis of the newly-constituted church. They were a revision of the Forty-two Articles of 1553; at the last minute the twenty-ninth article (asserting that the wicked who partake of the Lord's supper do so to their condemnation) was omitted, obviously as a concession to Catholic teaching; and it was not until 1571 that this article was restored.

This restoration in fact marked a change in Elizabethan policy. In 1570 Pope Pius V (1566–72) had excommunicated the queen in the bull *Regnans in Excelsis,* and she hardened her will against those who continued to profess loyalty to the Roman hierarchy. The celebration of the mass was proscribed, and Catholics were increasingly subjected to persecution. When invasion from Spain threatened, the Catholic Mary Stuart ("Queen of Scots") was executed; with the defeat of the Armada in 1588, Elizabeth's policy was widely felt to receive its vindication, and her position was consolidated.

But a number of capable men who had lived as exiles on the Continent during Mary's reign returned to England on the accession of Elizabeth and were full of enthusiasm for Calvinism. In their view, the Elizabethan reform was not radical enough, and they endeavored to purify Anglicanism of all that still smacked of popery in its doctrine and usages. They contended that the surplice was a perpetuation of Romanist superstition, that kneeling at the eucharist implied a doctrine of Christ's physical presence, that the use of a ring in the marriage service entailed the notion of its sacramental character, and so on. By 1564 persons holding such opinions were commonly known as Puritans; members of the university at Cambridge were especially affected, and in 1570 Thomas Cartwright (1535–1603) was relieved of his professorship there because he advocated the substitution of presbyterianism for episcopacy in the Anglican establishment.

Most of the Puritans tried to reform the church from within, but a few considered that Anglicanism was beyond redemption and severed their relations with it. Among those who came to adopt separatist ideas was Robert Browne (*c.* 1550–1633), a graduate of Cambridge, who founded an independent church at Norwich in 1581; action was taken against him, and he fled to Holland, where he published a number of theological works (1582). He was apparently the first Christian thinker systematically to expound Congregationalist principles, but, as was the case with the Puritans generally, his fundamental ideas derived from Calvin. There were to be some influential representatives of his doctrines in the seventeenth century, notably, the Pilgrim Fathers, who sailed to America on the "Mayflower" in 1620, and Oliver Cromwell (1599–1658), the strange genius of the Commonwealth and Protectorate (1649–60).

Puritan criticism of the religious settlement came to expression in *The Admonition to Parliament* (1572), evidently written by a number of authors. Responsibility was fastened on two London clergymen, John Field and Thomas Wilcox, and they were imprisoned. The manifesto called for a presbyterian mode of constitution and the purification of accepted usages. The contentions were supported in a *Second Admonition* (1572), probably written by Thomas Cartwright, who was forced to flee the country. Both publications were prohibited in 1573, but the controversy continued, and it eventually led to the production of Richard Hooker's *Treatise on the Laws of Ecclesiastical Polity*, which came to be recognized as the classic defence of the Anglican position; Book 1 through Book 4 appeared in 1594, Book 5 in 1597, and Book 6 through Book 8 after the author's death, which took place in 1600.

Hooker maintained that the scriptures constitute the basis of all sound theological doctrine, but that in organizational and liturgical matters the church is free to prescribe such procedures as may be convenient, so long as biblical principles are not contradicted. If some form or rite is proved to be of popish origin, one cannot deduce that the form or rite in question is necessarily bad. And even if it is to some extent contaminated with evil, perhaps a greater evil would result from an attempt to remove it. The Bible itself offers no complete collection of regulations for conduct on all occasions, and some things that are good are not explicitly enjoined in scripture. Believers are members of a developing community, and in legislating for their collective constitution, tradition and reason, in addition to the Bible, have to be resorted to. Like any other earthly society, the church is dynamic, not static, and throughout the continuing process of its terrestial existence polity must be flexible enough to meet the ever-changing demands of historical circumstance.

In working out his thesis Hooker revived the Stoic concept of a universal and rational law of nature (Latin: *lex naturae*), to which, as he argued, all man-made laws, both civil and ecclesiastical, are subject. The law of nature remains permanently the same amid the multifarious vicissitudes of history, and yet particular legal forms, which are detailed expressions of the immutable *lex naturae,* are themselves modifiable. Hence no particular polity, not even one that may be sketched in the Bible, is to be regarded as always applicable. More specifically, with regard to the question of episcopacy, Hooker argued that it is not unbiblical, that it is deeply rooted in ecclesiastical tradition, and that it is in accordance with the dictates of reason.

Thus, in the elaboration of his apology, Hooker made much of the distinction between doctrine and polity, the former being more or less fixed in the scriptures, the latter subject to change and development. While such a distinction has only a limited validity—for there is always mutual interaction between thought and human organization—it does draw attention to two important aspects of the religious life, and it may be used in a brief characterization of the Anglican compromise. Under the new national dispensation episcopacy and other Catholic forms and usages were perpetuated, whereas the theological principles brought into prominence were largely taken over from the Continental Reformation. Luther, Zwingli, and Calvin greatly stressed certain biblical ideas (apparently to the relative neglect of others), and the same theological predilections come to expression in the Thirty-nine Articles.

This formulation of belief posits original sin and human bondage because of Adam's fall (Arts. 9–10), justification by faith through the merits of Christ alone (Art. 11), and the reality of divine predestination (Art. 17). But at some points the statement seems to be deliberately vague: for example, it is far from clear whether the dogma concerning Christ's physical presence at the Lord's supper is asserted or denied (Art. 28). Such ambiguity indeed illustrates the conciliatory nature of the Articles; evidently those responsible for them wished to give theological offense to as few people as possible. The doctrine of the universal priesthood of believers finds no mention, but this is not surprising since the traditional clerical orders of bishops, priests, and deacons were retained (Art. 36). It may further be noted that subscription to the Articles was required only of the clergy and (until 1871) of staff and students of the universities of Oxford and Cambridge.

During the reigns of James VI (1603–25) and Charles I (1625–49) Puritan opposition intensified. James had been king of Scotland from 1567, and he succeeded Elizabeth as ruler of Great Britain through the descent of his mother (Mary Stuart) from Henry VII. During his reign the "authorized" version of the Bible appeared (1611), but James, like his successor, had Catholic sympathies. Tactlessness and unreliability also contributed to the downfall of Charles.

The Puritans were in control from 1640. Civil war broke out in 1642, and in 1643 Parliament entered into "a solemn league and covenant" with Scotland. In 1645 the Royalists were defeated; the use of the Book of Common Prayer was proscribed, and Archbishop William Laud was executed. The Westminster Assembly, convened in 1643, eventually imposed a presbyterian form of church polity (1646).

The Westminster Confession, to become the classic statement of British and American Presbyterianism, was approved by Parliament in 1648, the Scottish General Assembly having accepted it in the previous year. The Confession was Calvinistic, and regarding predestination it posited infralapsarianism—that is, that God came to his predetermining decision *after* humanity's original disobedience. A covenant of works was distinguished from a covenant of grace, the former being concluded with Adam and his offspring, the latter with believers in Christ, who secure salvation freely through faith alone. The Christian Sunday was construed to be equivalent to the Jewish Sabbath, and the importance of observing it as a day of rest and worship received special emphasis.

The New Model Army contained many Independents (or Congregationalists, as they later came to be designated) and Baptists; Oliver Cromwell, himself an Independent, prevented the exclusive establishment of Presbyterianism. This action offended the Scots, and they allied themselves with Charles, who now promised that he would support Presbyterianism. Cromwell defeated the Scots in 1648, and Charles was beheaded in the following year. Under Cromwell's Protectorate there was some measure of toleration, and Episcopalians, Presbyterians, and Independents were permitted to hold clerical office within the established church.

When Cromwell died in 1658 an anti-Puritan reaction quickly developed, and the monarchy was restored under Charles II (1660–85). The Elizabethan Prayer Book, after some revision, again became mandatory, the Act of Uniformity (1662) enforcing its general use. About two thousand clergy were ejected for their refusal to conform, the result being that Puritanism became almost entirely secessionist. Various repressive measures were taken against all dissenting bodies, and considerable social turbulence ensued.

Both Charles and his successor, James II (1685–88), had Catholic inclinations, and at length revolution eventuated. William of Orange landed in England in 1688, and James fled to France. William and Mary became joint sovereigns, and those Anglican clergy (known as "Nonjurors") who refused to take the oath of allegiance to the new monarchy were deprived of their benefices. But they were able to form an unofficial ecclesiastical organization, which persisted through several decades, for, by the Toleration Act of 1689, a serious attempt was made to unite all Protestants (apart from Unitarians) under the new regime. Everyone who subscribed to the general doctrine of the Thirty-nine Articles, except those concerning polity and the sacraments, was granted freedom of worship; in the courts Quakers were allowed to make a simple affirmation instead of swearing an oath. Thus legalized Nonconformity came into being, and it was to persist as a significant feature of English life. By present-day standards the toleration permitted was not comprehensive. Unitarians and Catholics were excluded; Presbyterians, Independents, Baptists, and Quakers were barred from the civil service until 1828, and from the universities of Oxford and Cambridge until 1871.

Among the influential defenders of the principle of toleration during the seventeenth century were the poet John Milton (1608–74), whose *Areopagitica* was published in 1644, and the philosopher John Locke (1632–1704), whose *Letters Concerning Toleration* appeared in 1689–92. Neither advocated the toleration of Roman Catholics, and Locke explicitly excluded atheists also. Milton greatly admired Cromwell, but was disappointed by his failure to pursue a policy of complete disestablishment during his Protectorate. It would seem that, like Sir Isaac Newton (1642–1727) the physicist, both Milton and Locke clandestinely came to accept some form of theological Unitarianism.

BIBLIOGRAPHY

Clebsch, W. A. *England's Earliest Protestants, 1520–1535.* New Haven, Conn.: Yale University Press, 1964.

George, C. H., and K. George. *The Protestant Mind of the English Reformation.* Princeton, N.J.: Princeton University Press, 1961.

Marshall, J. S. *Hooker and the Anglican Tradition.* Sewanee, Tenn.: The University Press, 1963.

New, J. F. H. *Anglican and Puritan: The Basis of their Opposition, 1558–1640.* Palo Alto, Calif.: Stanford University Press, 1965.

Payne, E. A. *The Free Church Tradition in the Life of England.* 3rd ed. London: Student Christian Movement Press, 1951.

Powicke, F. M. *The Reformation in England.* New York: Oxford University Press, 1949.

Rupp, E. G. *The English Protestant Tradition.* New York: Cambridge University Press, 1949.

Simpson, A. *Puritanism in Old and New England.* Chicago: University of Chicago Press, 1955.

Torbet, R. G. *A History of the Baptists.* Philadelphia: Judson Press, 1950.

29 ‡ Radical Movements

The emergence of Protestantism brought into prominence such ideas as the authority of the word of God, justification by faith, and the priesthood of all believers, and a number of earnest people with Lutheran sympathies soon came to feel that doctrines of this kind were not being taken seriously enough by leading representatives of Reformation principles. They repudiated, among other things, infant baptism, arguing that the rite can be effective solely on the basis of faith: as a public testimony to a personal experience of God's saving grace, sacramental initiation must involve a voluntary act that is quite beyond the capacity of very young children. Hence the designation "Anabaptist" (*ana* in Greek means "again"), by which upholders of such a thesis came to be generally known, is not strictly correct. For they did not hold that baptism in the true sense can or should be repeated; in their view, infant baptism is sacramental in appearance only, and they made a public call for submission to the rite, because of their conviction that the vast majority of people had not yet really been baptized.

Owing to the harsh treatment they suffered at the hands of both Catholics and Protestants, the Anabaptists quickly became widely scattered. Catholics opposed them for obvious reasons, while main-line Protestants resented the criticism that they were not consistent enough in carrying out their own ideas, and they also wished to make it plain to the world that they had nothing whatsoever to do with the wild excesses of much Anabaptist extremism.

Thomas Münzer (*c.* 1490–1525), who ultimately led the peasants' revolt that was to be mercilessly crushed at Frankenhausen in 1525, appeared at the Saxon town of Zwickau in 1520 and demanded a radical application of Reformation doctrines. Fervently claiming direct inspiration by the Holy Spirit, he succeeded in founding a community of enthusiastic prophets. The authorities intervened, and after Münzer fled to Bohemia, the prophetic leadership was assumed by Nicholas Storch (*c.* 1480–1525), who in 1521 marched his followers into Wittenberg and announced that the entire ecclesiastical establishment stood under the terrible threat of God's imminent judgement. Luther's colleague, Andreas Bodenstein of Karlstadt, transferred his allegiance to Storch, and much commotion ensued. Luther himself was released from Wartburg Castle in 1522 to help the authorities restore order. Storch took flight to Strasbourg, and after Münzer's disastrous defeat at Frankenhausen, he lived as a refugee, first in Poland, then in Moravia, where he died. Karlstadt, who was violently denounced by Luther as a traitor to the cause of Christian truth, ultimately found refuge in Basel.

Similar trouble broke out at Zurich, where an Anabaptist sect, the Swiss Brethren, originated in 1525. Unlike the prophets of Zwickau, the Brethren exemplified a quietistic type of piety, maintaining a doctrine of nonviolence and refusing to participate in secular political life; some of them stressed the authority of the conscience or inner light as the testimony of the divine presence in the heart of the individual believer. The Zurich turmoil was in the first instance occasioned by Balthasar Hübmaier (*c.* 1485–1528), the parish priest at Waldshut and a former pupil of Johann Eck of Ignolstadt. Hübmaier had openly identified himself with the Zwinglian movement in 1523 but subsequently turned to Anabaptism; he sympathized with the aspirations of the insurgents in the Peasants' Revolt and undertook literary activity in their behalf. In 1525 he condemned infant baptism as unscriptural and took part in a public debate with Zwingli on the subject. Hübmaier and his associates were cautioned, but they continued to practice their beliefs in private, and one of their number was arrested and executed by drowning. Hübmaier fled to Moravia where, under the leadership of Jacob Hutter (*c.* 1490–1536), several communistic settlements of Anabaptists were established. These groups evidently sought to recapture the spirit of the primitive church, in which, according to Acts 4:32 ff., baptized Christians renounced their private possessions and held all property in common. Hübmaier himself continued to disseminate Anabaptist doctrines until his incarceration by the Austrian authorities; he was burned at the stake at Vienna in 1528.

Another denomination of Anabaptists were the Melchiorites, the followers of Melchior Hoffman (*c.* 1500–1543), a Lutheran preacher who moved into Scandinavia in 1526. He began to question the validity of the doctrine of consubstantiation and to proclaim the nearness of the end of the world. Eventually banished from Denmark, he joined a group of Anabaptists in Strasbourg. He went on to propagate extremist doctrines in the Netherlands and in Friesland, returning to Strasbourg fully convinced that the city was shortly to become the New Jerusalem prophesied in the scriptures. He was imprisoned and died in jail.

Large numbers of Anabaptist refugees gathered at Münster in the early thirties, and under the guidance of Jan Mathys (*c.* 1500–1534) and John of Leyden (1510–36), a militant effort was made to establish the divine Kingdom on earth. At length the city was besieged by Catholic and Protestant forces, and after the collapse of the defences in 1536 the population was dealt with ruthlessly. However, many of the refugees found a remarkable friend in Menno Simons (1496–1561), a priest recently converted to Anabaptism. He visited and encouraged the scattered companies in Holland and Friesland, and gradually they were reconstituted as Mennonites. The doctrines of Simons were nearer to those of Hübmaier than to the teaching of Mathys, and the Mennonites came to develop a form of quietistic piety, combining a strict discipline with a certain theological liberalism; during the seventeenth century some groups adopted the Unitarian doctrines of Socinus. But they all rejected infant baptism, besides refusing to participate in the affairs of secular politics; also, they advocated nonviolence and upheld the priesthood of all believers, a symbolic interpretation of the eucharist, and the right of each local congregation to elect its own officers.

Numerous Mennonites migrated to North America, and it is estimated that today there are over a quarter of a million in the United States and about fifty thousand in Canada; some of the Mennonite communities, like the Amish in parts of Pennsylvania, still show their independence of the world by tenaciously retaining the habits of the seventeenth century; they refuse to wear contemporary dress or to employ the mechanical contrivances produced by more recent technology.

Anabaptist refugees seem to have settled in England before 1540, and Robert Browne (*c.* 1550–1633), the first thinker systematically to expound a congregationalist theory of ecclesiastical polity, may have been influenced in 1580 by Anabaptists settled in the Norwich district. Browne had studied at Cambridge, where he was attracted by the Puritanism of Thomas Cartwright. But he later came to adopt separatist principles, and in 1580 he established an independent church at Norwich. He suffered imprisonment, and after his release he and certain members of his congregation took flight to Holland. In 1582 he published four short treatises which set forth his ideas concerning the true nature of the church. But he does not seem to have had much success in Holland, for he soon returned to England and taught in Southwark (London) for a while. He took Anglican orders in 1591 and became the rector of a parish in Northamptonshire, a position he retained to the end of his days. Browne was evidently an irascible person, and he died in jail after assaulting a policeman.

According to the treatises Browne published in 1582, a true church is essentially a voluntary organization of believers who have come together to form a covenant between God and them-

selves. Each local community thus constituted is completely autonomous and democratic, all officers being elected by the congregation; it is entirely independent of state control, and is
preserved from impurity by the self-enforcement of a strict
discipline. Browne apparently envisaged no program for the
transformation of secular society through the application of
Christian ethics. Rather, he thought of each believing congregation as an elect people, separated from an evil world for communal worship and mutual spiritual benefit.

Such a view has obvious affinities with certain Anabaptist
teachings, and it is remarkable that Browne should have continued to uphold infant baptism, a rite which he construed to
be of the nature of a promise or pledge made by parents to
bring up their children in the nurture and admonition of the
Lord. This meant that baptism is not a sacrament in the traditional Catholic sense of a means of grace, but a ceremony that,
from one point of view, could be likened to the marriage service, being the proclamation of a vow. It is not surprising that
some of Browne's followers should have felt that this interpretation ran counter to New Testament teaching; a group thus persuaded came to repudiate infant baptism altogether and founded
the first English Baptist church in 1612.

It is also important to note that most of Browne's early disciples did not subscribe to his purely negative view of the relations between church and state. For them, the civil authorities
were in duty bound to use their power in the service of the
faithful, suppressing false teachers and facilitating all worship
that accords with the word of God. So the pioneering Congregationalists in New England did not hesitate to utilize political
pressure to enforce stringent discipline upon the churches and
to exclude all exponents of deviationist teaching—and this despite their doctrine of the church as a "gathered" community,
organized on a voluntary basis.

A separatist congregation destined to be singularly influential
was founded on Brownist principles at Gainsborough in Lin-

colnshire around 1603, and an offshoot sprang up at Scrooby in Nottinghamshire, where a Puritan clergyman, John Robinson (*c.* 1575–1625), was appointed pastor in 1604. Another Puritan clergyman, John Smyth (*c.* 1554–1612), seems to have been instrumental in establishing the community at Gainsborough, but it was not until 1606 that he officially became its minister. Threatened by persecution, most of the Gainsborough congregation, led by Smyth, migrated to Amsterdam in 1608. There, perhaps through Mennonite influence, Smyth was led to question the validity of infant baptism and, after baptizing himself, reconstituted his congregation as a Baptist church. Certain members of this community, after returning to England, founded the first church of the so-called "General" Baptists at Pinners' Hall, London, in 1612.

The Scrooby congregation also resolved to move to Holland. They eventually settled at Leyden, where Robinson at length joined the university, despite the fact that, being a strict Calvinist, he objected to the Arminianism prevailing in that institution. After prolonged discussions a considerable portion of the congregation decided to establish a new society in America under the direction of John Carver (*c.* 1562–1621), a merchant from Doncaster in Yorkshire. Robinson had supported the project, but circumstances prevented him from sailing on the "Mayflower" in 1620, and he never crossed the Atlantic. He defended his theological position in an *Apologia*, published in 1619.

It may further be noted that Henry Jacob, who had been a member of the Leyden congregation, established an independent church at Southwark in 1616; a number seceded in 1633 and set up the parent church of the "Particular" Baptists, who were so named because of their insistence that Christ died, not for men generally, but only for those divinely elected to salvation.

The Friends of the Truth or Quakers (later known as the Society of Friends), founded by George Fox (1624–91), a shoemaker by trade, laid great emphasis upon the universal priesthood of sincere aspirants after religious truth; they vigorously

attacked Calvinistic predestinarianism, and showed some remarkable resemblances to the Anabaptist sect of the Swiss Brethren.
Fox was born in Leicestershire and, after a period of earnest
seeking, found religious assurance through the inner light of the
operative Christ (see John 1:9). In 1647 he undertook itinerant
preaching missions to proclaim the good news of his liberating
experience of the divine presence in his soul. He suffered imprisonment several times, but he persisted and won a following
that was by no means insignificant. He traveled abroad and
conducted missions in the West Indies and in North America
during the years 1671–72. Although drawn to mysticism, he was
a capable organizer and introduced a unique form of representative democracy into ecclesiastical polity.

Fox held that the supreme court of religious appeal is not
located in any external authority, such as the church or the
Bible, but in the divine illumination of the soul. God discloses
his will directly to those who wait in holy expectation before
him, and, since God is the Creator and Lord of all things, his
revelation can scarcely be restricted to a particular book or institution. Divine truth is inwardly apprehended, and intercommunication between man and God requires no external mediation via sacraments or priests. All human beings are equally
God's children, and so war and slavery must be contrary to
the practice of genuine religion. A true Christian, because he is
a man of his word, does not need to confirm his declarations
by taking oaths; and in virtue of his recognition that all men
are God's children, he is never servile in speech and shows great
restraint in his use of courtly titles that make for unnatural class
distinctions.

One of the most influential of the early upholders of Quakerism was William Penn (1644–1718), son of Admiral Sir William
Penn who had wrested Jamaica from the Dutch in 1655. In 1668
the younger Penn published his polemical work *The Sandy
Foundation Shaken*, a forthright critique of the traditional doctrine of the Trinity and of Calvinistic predestinarianism, for

which he suffered confinement in the Tower of London. After his release in 1680 he began to work for the establishment of a region in America where Quakers would be able to live in freedom, and in 1682 Charles II granted him East New Jersey and (as it came to be named) Pennsylvania; he promulgated a constitution that allowed complete freedom for all forms of worship of the one true God.

The classic statement of the doctrines of the early Quakers is *Theologiae Verae Christianae Apologia*, written by the Scottish disciple of Fox, Robert Barclay (1648–90); the first edition (in Latin) appeared at Amsterdam in 1676, and an English version came out two years later, bearing the title *Apology for the True Christian Religion, as the Same is Set Forth and Preached by the People Called in Scorn "Quakers."*

Strict Calvinism had earlier been attacked in Holland, under the leadership of Jacobus Arminius (1560–1609), a professor of theology at Leyden from 1603. The controversy was bitter and prolonged and came to include politics. In the year following Arminius' death his sympathizers briefly published their doctrines in a "Remonstrance": they posited the reality of human freedom without denying God's sovereignty, asserted that Christ died for all men and not for the elect only, and claimed that particular predestination (whether supralapsarian or infralapsarian) has no scriptural basis and that backsliding is a real possibility. The Arminians were condemned at the Synod of Dort (1618–19); repressive measures were taken, and though these were relaxed within a decade or so, the Remonstrants did not receive formal recognition until 1795.

The most famous of the early disciples of Arminius was Hugo Grotius (1583–1645), an expert in international law as well as in theology. He was imprisoned in 1618, but his wife arranged for his escape in a box of books, and he lived in Paris during the years 1621–31. It was there that in 1622 he published his most important theological work *De Veritate Religionis Christianae* ("On the Truth of the Christian Religion"), in which he set forth an ethical theism that is somewhat reminiscent of the teaching of Erasmus. Particular interest attaches to his thesis with regard to the atonement. According to Anselm, Christ's death was a satisfaction of God's outraged honor; according to the Protestant reformers, it was a penalty for sin suffered on man's behalf. Both these views had been criticized by the Socinians (Antitrinitarians), who argued that Christ's superlative obedience provided man with a moral example. Grotius, however, while agreeing with the Socinians that the Creator is a God of pardoning love, further contended that, if God forgave sinners without showing respect for his law, he would bring that law into contempt. The conclusion was therefore drawn that Christ's sacrifice must have been a tribute to the sanctity of the constitutive law entailed in God's providential government of the world.

Like Anabaptists, Antitrinitarians were subjected to harsh treatment by both Catholics and Protestants. They were less numerous, however; being of a more intellectual temper, they were affected by humanism. Especially notable was the case of Michael Servetus (1511–53), the Spanish physician who discovered the pulmonary circulation of the blood and who (in 1531) condemned the doctrine of the Trinity as unbiblical in his work *De Trinitatis Erroribus Libri VII* ("On the Errors of the Trinity, Seven Books"). After studying successively at Saragossa, Toulouse, and Paris, he practiced medicine at Vienne, and in 1553 he anonymously published his most substantial theological work *Christianismi Restitutio* ("The Restitution of Christianity"). A friend of Calvin, Guillaume Trie, disclosed, apparently at Calvin's instigation, the identity of the author to the Inquisition at Lyons. As a result Servetus was imprisoned, but he escaped from jail and made his way to Geneva, perhaps assuming that Calvin's opponents would rally to his support. This proved to be a grave miscalculation; he was arrested, tried, and burned at the stake in 1553.

Laelius Socinus (1525–62), a native of Siena, who took delight in theological speculation, seems to have been prompted by the Servetus affair to turn his attention to the dogma of the

Trinity; concentrated study induced him to question its validity. After his death, his unpublished writings fell into the hands
of his more famous nephew, Faustus Socinus (1539–1604), who
eventually came to deny the pre-existence of Christ and the congenital immortality of man. He was at Lyons in 1561, at Geneva
in 1562, and in Italy for the next twelve years or more, mainly
in the service of Isabella de Medici of Tuscany. In 1575 he
moved to Basel, where he made a frontal attack on certain doctrines of the Protestant Reformation. The situation became increasingly uncomfortable, and in 1578, at the suggestion of
George Biandrata (who had left Geneva in 1558 to become the
leader of a group of Antitrinitarians in Poland), he migrated to
Transylvania. He stayed there only a short time, and in 1579
he settled in Poland, where he died. In the year after his death
Socinian ideas were summarily set forth at Racow in the Racovian Catechism (1605). German and Latin translations were
published in 1608 and 1609 respectively. The statement is divided into eight main sections, each subdivided into chapters. A
ceremonial burning of a copy of the Latin version of the Catechism was staged at London in 1614 under the auspices of
James I.

The document affirms that reason needs to be supplemented
if man is to win salvation, and that such a supplementation is
exclusively provided in the divine revelation recorded in the
scriptures, the truth of which is demonstrated by the miracles
described therein, especially the resurrection of Christ. Biblical
literature contains nothing contrary to reason but much that is
beyond reason. Saving faith consists fundamentally in the conviction that the one Creator is the ultimate Judge who punishes
the wicked and who rewards the righteous by endowing them
with the transcendent capacity for a blessed immortality in
heaven. Thus the punishment of unrighteous people is necessarily confined to life in this world, whereas the reward that
attends obedience to the declared will of God extends to an
eternal existence *post mortem*.

Accordingly, man is a free and responsible individual, the

doctrines of Adam's fall, of human bondage, and of divine predestination being contrary both to the deliverances of reason
and to the implications of scriptural teaching. Moreover, Christ's
work was performed not for God's sake but for man's, since its
purpose must have been to reconcile the creature with the Creator, not the Creator with the creature. God can forgive sinners
unconditionally, without any atonement, and hence the notion
that Christ's death was a satisfaction or a substitution must be
founded upon a gross misconception of divine love, a mode of
grace that is in no way bound to the law of an eye for an eye.

Christ was not God who became man that man might become
God, but rather a paragon of virtue, an example to be imitated.
His existence did not antedate his birth, and the doctrine of the
Trinity is contrary both to reason and to scripture. Christ was
a human being who, because of his exemplary obedience to the
divine will, received from God the reward of a blessed immortality, as is proved by his resurrection. Individuals deeply concerned to follow his rule will be similarly rewarded, and the
church is made up of people thus devoted; they come together
for communal worship and mutual edification, and the rites of
baptism and the eucharist are outward signs of their loyalty to
Christ.

Thus the Socinians displayed striking independence of traditional ecclesiastical doctrine in the working out of their ethical
monotheism. On the other hand, in a characteristically Protestant fashion they adhered closely to the scriptures, and this led
to what seem to be inconsistencies in their teaching; for example, while asserting Christ's real humanity, they nonetheless subscribed to the doctrine of the virgin birth. It should also be
observed that, in thinking of Christianity primarily as an agency
for the attainment of immortality, the Socinians showed a notable resemblance to the kind of philosophical interpretation predominant in the ancient Greek church. But whereas the defenders of ancient orthodoxy (Irenaeus and Athanasius, for instance)
considered that victory over death was made possible through a

substantial union of the divine and the human in Jesus of Nazareth, the Socinians maintained that it was effected by obedience to the ethical principles he enunciated.

Socinianism did not long survive in Poland; largely through political pressure exerted by the Jesuits, all Unitarians were eventually banished from the country in 1658. Thenceforward antitrinitarian ideas were to be disseminated chiefly in the Netherlands, in England, and finally in the United States. During the seventeenth and eighteenth centuries the Dutch Remonstrants were affected by Socinian doctrines. In England John Biddle (1615–62) suffered much hardship in the service of Unitarianism and was assisted financially by the London philanthropist Thomas Firmin (1632–97). Among those who came to adopt theological positions of a Socinian character were John Milton (1608–74), John Locke (1632–1704), and Isaac Newton (1642–1727).

BIBLIOGRAPHY

Bainton, R. H. *Hunted Heretic* [Servetus]. Boston: Beacon Press, 1953.

Bolam, C. G., Jeremy Goring, H. L. Short, and Roger Thomas. *The English Presbyterians: From Elizabethan Puritanism to Modern Unitarianism*. London: Allen and Unwin, 1968.

Littell, Franklin. *The Anabaptist View of the Church*. 2nd ed. Boston: Star King Press, 1958.

Rupp, E. G. *Patterns of Reformation*. London: Epworth Press, 1969.

Russell, E. *The History of Quakerism*. New York: Macmillan, 1942.

Wilbur, E. M. *A History of Unitarianism*. 2 vols. Cambridge, Mass.: Harvard University Press, 1945–52.

Williams, G. H. *The Radical Reformation*. Philadelphia: Westminster Press, 1962.

30 ‡ *The Counter-Reformation*

The reformation of Spanish Catholicism under the guidance of Francisco Ximenes (1436–1517), had its admirers in the Italian hierarchy, even if they did not respect the absolutism of the Spanish monarchy. Among these was Giovanni Pietro Caraffa (1476–1559), elected a cardinal in 1536 and pope in 1555. Throughout his career he devoted himself to the cause of internal reform, seeking to improve the efficiency of the *curia* (papal court) and to eliminate current abuses. He endeavored to consolidate Latin Catholicism, weakened as it now was by grave disruption, and he stood firmly for the rigid repression of heresy. In this respect he differed from Gaspar Contarini (1483–1542), who became a cardinal in 1535 and subsequently took an active part in the deliberations of a committee that proposed a number of significant reforms with a view to the convocation of a general council. But Caraffa felt that the church should not make doctrinal concessions any more than it should relax its discipline, and he opposed Contarini's policy, which tended to be on the side of conciliation. For instance, at the Colloquy of Ratisbon in 1541 Contarini prepared a theological statement on the question of justification which, as he believed, might prove acceptable to Protestants; but Caraffa condemned the formulation as compromising the integrity of the Catholic faith.

In 1517 Caraffa had been a founding member of the Roman Oratory of Divine Love, an association dedicated to the furtherance of ecclesiastical reform. In 1524 he and a fellow Oratorian established the community of the Theatines, an order with a rigorous discipline intended generally to improve the moral standards of the clergy. More important, in 1540 he secured authorization from Pope Paul III (1524–49) to organize on the Spanish pattern a centralized Inquisition, and two years later the Congregation of the Universal Inquisition (or Holy Office) was established as the ultimate court of appeal in trials for heresy; it was originally composed of six cardinals presided over by the pope. Protestant congregations at Venice, Ferrara, Naples, and elsewhere were effectively dealt with.

In 1543 the printing or the possession of literature unsanctioned by the Inquisition became an offense, and in 1557 Caraffa, as Pope Paul IV, published a list of prohibited books, which included all the works from the presses of sixty-one printing houses that were cited by name. In 1571, under Pope Pius V (1566–72), the Congregation of the Index was constituted and formally charged with the responsibility of keeping the list up to date.

Besides providing the original idea behind the reorganized discipline, Spain furnished much of the military strength that enforced it. But during the reign of Philip II (1556–98) there was some tension between the papacy and the Spanish monarchy. For Philip, while supporting the ideals of the Counter-Reformation, also believed in the absolutism of royal power, and this led to a quarrel with Pope Paul IV. The defeat of the Armada in 1588 marked the beginning of the decline of Spain in European affairs, but Spanish influence continued to make its presence felt in hierarchical circles.

No less significant than the constitutional reforms was the revival of enthusiasm for disinterested service brought about by Ignatius Loyola (c. 1493–1556), the founder of the Jesuit order. A native of Spain, he originally embarked upon a military career. He was wounded in 1521 and during his convalescence he had a change of heart and resolved to enlist as a soldier for

Christ. Devoting a year to the practice of prayer and severe austerities, he enjoyed mystical experiences and apparently wrote the first draft of his influential *Spiritual Exercises*. After making pilgrimages to Rome and Jerusalem, he studied successively at Barcelona, Alcalá, and Salamanca. In 1528 he journeyed to Paris and there continued his education for seven years.

The Society of Jesus originated in the parish church at Montmartre, where in 1534 Loyola and six of his friends took the vows of poverty and chastity and solemnly promised to consecrate their lives to the service of Christ; among them was Francis Xavier, who later undertook pioneer missionary work in India and Japan. In 1537 all seven were ordained, and the group received official sanction from Pope Paul III in 1540. Rapid expansion ensued, and by 1550 a basic constitution had been worked out. The order was organized as a *militia Christi* under the absolute rule of an elected general, subject only to the pope. But no uniform dress and no fixed hours of worship were prescribed, so that appointed duties could be discharged with efficiency according to the demands of varying situations. Besides the vows of poverty, chastity, and obedience, all prospective Jesuits were called upon to declare their willingness to go wherever the pope might command for the purpose of saving souls. The training was both thorough and systematic, and scholarship came to be highly prized.

The new order quickly assumed the role of principal agent for the furtherance of the Counter-Reformation. Catholic orthodoxy was vigorously defended against heretics, and extraordinary enterprise found demonstration in the initiation of widespread missionary activities in the Far East, Africa, and the Americas, as well as in Europe. It was mainly through the Jesuits that Poland, South Germany, and the Rhineland were regained for Catholicism. In certain regions, however, circumstances were not so propitious. Jesuits entered England in 1558, and there they came to be commonly detested as servants of a foreign power and as unscrupulous persons who acted on the assumption that the end justifies the means. And in France during the seventeenth century their casuistry was severely criticized by Blaise Pascal (1623–62) in his important *Provincial Letters* (1657). Certain casuists of the order unquestionably took the ethical principle of probabilism too far, as when, for example, it was argued that any undesirable action would be rendered justifiable if an authoritative opinion of the slightest probability could be cited in its favor. Such laxity in fact was condemned by the Holy Office in 1659, and further official pronouncements of the same tenor were issued at Rome twenty years later by Pope Innocent XI in the bull *Sanctissimus Dominus*.

The ideals of the Counter-Reformation came to authoritative expression at the *Concilium Tridentinum* ("Council of Trent"— 1545–63), which defined Catholic doctrine in contradistinction to that of the Protestants and decreed a number of reforms, regulating the appointment of bishops, providing for the supervision of clerical morals, ordering the establishment of theological seminaries, and so on. For over a quarter of a century there had been demands for an ecumenical convocation. Luther had claimed the right to a hearing before a general council, and for years Emperor Charles V had hoped that such a gathering would finally resolve the Protestant problem. But successive popes opposed a move of this kind, doubtless to some extent fearing that it would mean a revival of the aspirations represented by Marsiglio of Padua and his followers, with a resulting subordination of papal authority. As things turned out, however, the Tridentine deliberations led to a triumph for the papacy and for the principles represented by Caraffa and his associates.

Proposals for an ecumenical convocation were repeatedly frustrated through political rivalries: one was made for a meeting at Mantua in 1537, another for a gathering at Vicenza in 1538, and yet another for a meeting at Trent in 1542. But it was not until 1545 that the Council of Trent began its deliberations. The voting was not by nations, as at Constance (1414–

18), but by bishops and heads of orders, a consequence being that there was a preponderance of Italian influence; all the decrees had to receive papal confirmation. The council covered three periods and had twenty-five sessions: the first term (1545–47) included eight sessions, the second (1551–52) six, and the third (1562–63) eleven.

During the first period it was ruled that the Niceno-Constantinopolitan Creed constitutes the foundation of all true doctrine, that tradition has an authority equal to that of the scriptures, that biblical exegesis is the prerogative of the church, that the Vulgate provides the authentic scriptural text, that justification involves meritorious works, and that Christ instituted seven sacraments. In the second period the validity of the doctrine of transubstantiation was affirmed and that of the supremacy of general councils denied. In the third period it was asserted that Christ is wholly present in each of the eucharistic elements, that the cup should be withheld from the laity, that the eucharist is a propitiatory sacrifice (effective for both quick and dead), and yet that Christ's sacrifice possessed inherent sufficiency.

The Counter-Reformation entailed something more than a concern for externals and formal definitions, however, a fact discernible not only in the religious enthusiasm of the Jesuits: missions in the Americas and other distant regions were founded by Dominicans, Franciscans, and others, and the Congregation of Propaganda (designed to supervise and coordinate the expanding missionary activity of the church) was established by Pope Gregory XV in 1622. Spain, the country that had contributed so much to the conduct of the Counter-Reformation, witnessed a renewal of spiritual life through the influence of Teresa of Avila (1515–82) and John of the Cross (1542–91), both of whom were Carmelites. The latter's works (*The Ascent of Mount Carmel, The Dark Night of the Soul, The Spiritual Canticle,* and *The Living Flame of Love*) have an honored place among the classics of mystical literature. Attention should also be drawn to Francis of Sales (1567–1622), who was titular bishop of Geneva from 1602. He combined missionary zeal and administrative ability with great generosity and deep spiritual discernment. His *Introduction to the Devout Life* is one of the most widely read of all devotional works; it was first published at Lyons in 1609, and the final revised edition appeared in 1619.

BIBLIOGRAPHY

Janelle, P. *The Catholic Reformation.* Milwaukee, Wis.: Bruce, 1949.
Jedin, H. *Ecumenical Councils in the Catholic Church: An Historical Survey.* New York: Herder, 1960.

VI ‡ RATIONALISM
‡ AND PIETISM

31 ‡ *Science and Philosophy*

The transition from the medieval to the modern period in the evolution of Christian thought was mediated by the Renaissance, the Reformation, and the rise of the empirical sciences. As we have seen, the Renaissance was already in progress before the fall of Constantinople in 1453, and Luther's dramatic protest in 1517 had been foreshadowed by Wycliffe and Huss in the fourteenth and fifteenth centuries. Perhaps we may date the birth of modern science in 1531, when Nicholas Copernicus, after a careful consideration of pertinent empirical probabilities, published his *Commentariolus*, setting forth the hypothesis of solar centrality in the planetary system. But it should not be forgotten that the empirical method had also been, or was being, more or less systematically applied in various fields by such thinkers as Lorenzo Valla (1405–57) in historical criticism, Leonardo da Vinci (1452–1519) in technological researches, Michael Servetus (1511–53) in physiological investigations, and so on.

In fact all three movements involved a questioning of commonly accepted ideas and standards, as well as a new appreciation of the importance of the individual's immediate experiences and valuations. In their condemnation of certain contemporary ecclesiastical practices, humanists scrutinized the church's basic documents, Luther relied on his own personal intimations of God's saving favor, and the pioneers of modern physics found their frame of reference in the evidence of the senses rather than in a priori principles and traditional doctrines. The early physicists exhibited much confidence in the order-liness of nature; although every actual situation is unique, they proceeded on the implicit assumption that events exemplify intelligible regularities.

A spirit of adventure was abroad. The sphericity of the earth had often been conjectured, and late in the fifteenth century men sought to find out for themselves what the truth might be. The Cape of Good Hope had been rounded by 1487, and five years later America was discovered. Of course, not all the gains in empirical knowledge were due solely to disinterested curi-osity; lust for wealth and power sometimes led to geographical discoveries, and Christian missionary activities in strange lands gradually awakened an interest in anthropological studies.

Despite the fact that geocentric cosmology was firmly es-tablished in the Christian tradition (it had the backing of bib-lical, Aristotelian, and Ptolemaic authority), Pope Clement VII (1523–34) congratulated Copernicus on the value of his re-searches. In all likelihood, however, the papal court had not realized the full significance of the new astronomy. Copernican theory entailed a relegation of man's habitat from a central to a peripheral location in the universe, and from this it could easily be inferred that humanity can scarcely be of primary interest to the Creator. Moreover, those who rejected the tra-ditional cosmology inclined to limit themselves to descriptions of the characteristic behavior of things in their patterned re-lations, answering questions of the *how* type and suspending judgment with regard to inquiries about the *why* and the *wherefore* of nature as a whole. And from this position, en-couraged by the repeated successes attending the application of the scientific method, one might be led to suppose that ul-timate questions are not of primary importance or that they are in principle unanswerable. It was not foreseen that excessive confidence in the adequacy of abstract mechanistic concepts for the explanation of concrete reality could possibly give rise to a narrow scientific dogmatism, claiming sacred rights in a secularized culture.

The scope and significance of the empirical procedure was first systematically examined by the English lawyer and man of letters Francis Bacon (1561–1626), in his *Novum Organum* ("New Instrument"), published in 1620. To gain sound knowledge of the workings of nature, he argued, thinking must be securely based upon the particular facts of experience, advancing inductively to the formulation of general truths. Knowledge is power. But if man is to reach the power that knowledge brings, he must learn how most efficiently to use the *novum organum* of inductive science; thereby he will come to master the forces of nature. Some years later a further methodological exposition was offered by the French mathematician and philosopher René Descartes (1596–1650), in his *Discourse on the Method of Rightly Conducting Reason* (1637). He greatly stressed the importance of the criteria of clearness and distinctness: no thinker should accept anything as true which he does not clearly know to be so; he should divide each of his problems into as many parts as possible and begin to work on those factors that are simplest and easiest to understand.

Descartes showed a deeper appreciation than Bacon of the importance of deduction in scientific research; theories cannot usually be directly verified, and so in most instances it is necessary to formulate a hypothesis tentatively, to deduce consequences from it, and to verify these by reference to experience. Descartes also showed a deeper appreciation of the importance of mathematics in the scientific investigation of nature. Himself an outstanding mathematician, he had made it possible to express the properties of curves in terms of algebraic equations; and it should further be noticed that the adoption of Arabic notation had greatly facilitated arithmetical operations since the thirteenth century. The mathematical work of such thinkers as Nicholas of Cusa (1400–1464) acquired an unexpected significance, for it came to be seen that nature's orderliness frequently admits of a mathematical representation. Thus the experiments with falling bodies, conducted by Galileo (1564–1642), brought into prominence the ideas of proportionality and of concomitant variation; and the same concepts were utilized by Blaise Pascal (1623–62) in his elucidation of the relation between altitude and barometric pressure, by Robert Boyle (1627–91) in his statement of the connection between pressure and the volume of gases, and by Isaac Newton (1642–1727) in his exposition of the law of gravitation.

Johann Kepler (1571–1630) furthered the heliocentric theory when he propounded his three laws of motion. And in 1610, using a new telescope, Galileo gave it striking experimental confirmation, publishing his findings in 1613; he was cautioned by the Holy Office in 1616, and Copernicus' enlarged statement of his theory, *De Revolutionibus Orbium Coelestium* ("On the Revolutions of the Heavenly Spheres"), which had appeared in 1543, was placed on the index of prohibited books (it was not to be removed until 1757). But Galileo did not hold his peace, and in 1632 he published his celebrated *Dialogues on the Two Systems of the World*. Brought for trial before the Inquisition (1633), he discreetly made a public recantation. Perhaps he recalled that thirty-three years earlier Giordano Bruno, a pantheist who defended Copernicanism, had been condemned by the Holy Office and burned at the stake on the Campo dei Fiori. Despite his recantation, however, Galileo was imprisoned; but he obtained his release after a few months.

The new physics found classic expression in Newton's famous work *Philosophiae Naturalis Principia Mathematica* ("Mathematical Principles of Natural Philosophy"), published in 1687, and the Copernican Revolution (as Kant was later to name it) issued in the concept of a vast cosmic mechanism: space and time are infinite and uniform containers of material bodies, whose activities exemplify universal laws capable of expression in mathematical terms; the Creator stands in an external relation to the world so conceived, although he occasionally interferes with its operations to effect minor adjustments; otherwise the world is an ongoing concern, functioning of its own accord.

The scientific movement profoundly affected philosophical thinking in the general field of natural theology. Some philosophers were particularly impressed by the empirical character of the new physics, its reliance on the evidences of sense experience, and in his *Essay Concerning Human Understanding* (1690) John Locke laid the foundations of the empirical school of philosophy. Others were more impressed by the mathematical character of the new physics, and Descartes in his *Meditationes de Prima Philosophia* ("Meditations on Primary Philosophy"), published in 1641, laid the foundations of the rationalist school of philosophy, which tended to prevail on the Continent. Because Descartes greatly influenced Locke and other English thinkers, as well as subsequent Continental philosophers, historians frequently refer to him as the father of modern philosophy.

Descartes (whose followers came to be known as Cartesians) was educated at the Jesuit college of La Flèche, and went to Paris in 1613. Six years later he determined to devote himself to philosophy. After a period spent in travel and a further sojourn in Paris, he went to Holland (1629), where he remained for twenty years. In 1649 he journeyed to Sweden on the invitation of Queen Christine, and he died there in the following year. Apart from the two works already mentioned, his publications include *Principia Philosophiae* ("Principles of Philosophy," 1644) and *Les passions de l'âme* ("The Passions of the Soul," 1649).

For Descartes, the primary philosophical task was to find some proposition that is clear and distinct, that refers to something actually existent, and that can be known with complete certainty. Hence, as he declares in his *Meditationes*, he decided to doubt whatever can be doubted, and he passed from one type of belief to another until at length he encountered a concept that resisted his most persistent attempts to doubt it. This was the idea of his own existence as a thinking being, and he expressed it in the form *cogito ergo sum*—"I think therefore I am."

This proposition, so the Frenchman argued, is indubitable. A doubting person cannot doubt that he doubts, nor can he doubt that in doubting he thinks. The *cogito* satisfies the three criteria already posited, and from it Descartes proceeded to effect a philosophical reconstruction in the grand manner. The subject of the *cogito* knows immediately by the light of natural reason that nothing cannot be the cause of anything, and that the more perfect cannot be produced by the less perfect. Hence all that is contained in an idea must actually exist in its principal cause; and from the idea of a completely perfect Being, which is present to the subject of the *cogito*, it must be concluded that there is in fact a Being of this kind, through whose causal agency the idea is produced.

Such is the argument for the existence of God presented in the Third Meditation, and in the Fifth he supplements it with a form of the ontological argument: by definition God is the most perfect Being conceivable, and so God cannot be without real existence, otherwise he would not be the most perfect Being conceivable. Thus, given the definition of God, the assertion of his existence could be denied only by committing a flagrant act of self-contradiction. *Deus est* ("God is") has therefore to be coupled with the *sum* ("I am") of the *cogito*.

Having established the existence of God, Descartes held that he could dispel the doubts that had led him to question the validity of the truths of reason, for one of the qualities belonging to God's perfection is veracity; and this implies that God could not will to deceive us. It is God's veracity, too, that ultimately guarantees the soundness of our belief in the independent existence of the physical world and of finite mental substances other than ourselves—but only, of course, as such objects are clearly and distinctly apprehended. Regarding the physical world, Descartes pointed out that a material entity (a piece of wax, for instance) undergoes numerous changes in varying conditions; certain qualities, such as hardness, are apt to disappear, whereas others, such as extendedness in space, remain throughout all modifications of size and shape. Thus sensible attributions (taste, smell, color) are secondary qualities contributed by the mind in the act of perception; but measurable attributions (extension, figure, mobility) are primary qualities objectively grounded in the independent nature of physical objects. It is such qualities as these that constitute the essence of materiality as this is clearly and distinctly apprehended.

Descartes further argued that figure and motion are related to extension as modes of a common attribute. Essentially, materiality is spatial extendedness, and physical things are particular determinations of extension. Empty space—that is, space devoid of matter—is impossible, and matter, being constituted by extension, must be infinitely divisible and infinitely spread out in all directions. Also, like extension, matter is necessarily inert or passive, motion being introduced into it *ab extra* by a fiat of God's omnipotent will. This interpretation, it may be noticed, is somewhat reminiscent of Aquinas' presentation of the cosmological argument for divine existence, God being thought of as the ultimate Cause of motion in the physical universe.

In endeavoring to determine the essence of mentality, Descartes employed the same kind of method as that which he used in his examination of the nature of materiality as clearly and distinctly understood. The mind possesses three cognitive faculties—thought, sense, and imagination—and these together constitute its general character. But since we have a clear and distinct conception of the mind apart from sense and imagination, neither of these two faculties can belong to its essence. Hence pure thought is the one attribute of mind, just as extension is the one attribute of matter. Sense and imagination, however, involve intellection, and they cannot be clearly apprehended apart from it. They are therefore related to thought as figure and motion are related to extension—that is, as modes of a common attribute.

The parallelism between the two spheres in such a presentation is not altogether satisfactory, and from the general drift of the argument one would have supposed that shapes or figures (as particular determinations of extension) have their proper counterpart in concepts (as particular determinations of thought); sense and imagination would then be external modifications of thought, as motion is an external modification of matter. Also, the doctrine of the isolated substantial ego of the *cogito* is a palpable abstraction, for in actual experience a person is deeply aware of himself as standing in vital historical continuity with the objective world from which he has emerged and by which his life is upheld. Furthermore, endless circularity is evidently entailed in the basic discussion of the being of God: divine existence is established by rational argumentation, and the reliability of such argumentation is guaranteed by reference to the veracity of God.

Nevertheless, the Cartesian system stands as a magnificent philosophical construction, broadly based and suffused with the intellectual spirit of a new age. Its general conception of physical nature, as amenable to interpretation in terms of geometry and kinetics, was engendered by the same kind of thinking as that which brought the Copernican Revolution to its triumphal vindication in Newton's *Principia*, while its insistence on the independence and freedom of finite, thinking substances, created and sustained by the Supreme Being, offered an intellectual framework for religious faith. Its noteworthy failure to refer to the doctrine of the total corruption of human nature (through original sin) was in accordance with the fundamental optimism that generally characterized the humanism that gave birth to scientific movement.

In view of the seeming cooperation between mind and matter in the human organism, the radicality of the Cartesian dualism, which precluded all psycho-physical interaction, gave rise to much philosophical discussion. The French Oratorian Nicolas Malebranche (1638–1715) sought an explanation in occasionalism: God always intervenes to cause a mental event when a corresponding material change occurs, and vice versa; for example, on the occasion of my willing to move my arm, God intervenes to bring about the required movement of the limb. The Jewish philosopher and biblical critic Benedict de Spinoza (1632–77), who elaborated a comprehensive monistic pantheism, argued that thought and extension are attributes of the one all-embracing Divine Substance, their common inherence in God being the ultimate ground of psychophysical correspondence. The German mathematician and philosopher Gottfried Wilhelm Leibniz (1646–1716) cut the gordian knot by arguing that matter is mere appearance; the world is ultimately composed of centers of psychic force, and these act concordantly because of a constitutional harmony pre-established by God. A materialist solution was suggested by the English philosopher Thomas Hobbes (1588–1679), who contended that mind has no independent reality: thoughts are internal motions, and in the last resort they are produced by the external motions of material bodies.

Cartesian influence is discernible in the doctrines of John Locke (1632–1704), the father of English liberalism and founder of the empiricist school of British philosophy. He was born near Bristol and educated at Oxford, later becoming secretary to Lord Ashley, the Earl of Shaftesbury. He lived in France from 1675 to 1679. After Shaftesbury's fall he migrated to Holland and did not return to the land of his birth until after the accession of William and Mary. From 1691 he was a guest of Lady Masham (daughter of Ralph Cudworth, 1617–88, one of the Cambridge Platonists) at Otes Manor near Ongar in Essex.

Locke's general philosophy, expounded in his *Essay Concerning Human Understanding* (1690), shows a marked subjectivist bias, doubtless due to Cartesianism. He argued that the mind is directly aware of itself but knows other things only by way of construction and inference through the mediation of ideas. Ideas of secondary qualities are purely subjective affections aroused by impacts from outside, whereas ideas of primary qualities are representative of external realities; that is, geometrical and kinetical attributions actually cohere in independent material substances. Thus in his cosmology Locke evinced a characteristically Cartesian predilection for the mathematical, but he was rather more sceptical than Descartes and denied that we are in a position to determine the essence of material substance, describing it as "an uncertain supposition of we know not what" —a mysterious something in which primary qualities find their support. On the other hand, he believed that the existence of God could be demonstrated, and in this connection he relied mainly on a form of the cosmological argument (*Essay*, 4:10).

In his work *The Reasonableness of Christianity as Delivered in the Scriptures* (1695) Locke contended that although biblically revealed truths surpass the possible findings of man's unaided reason, the miracles recorded in scripture by no means bear witness to anything that is finally irrational. Christianity consists essentially in the personal acceptance of the Messiahship of Jesus and in the practice of the moral principles he enunciated, which constitute an ethic that is generally in agreement with enlightened common sense. Such acceptance properly arises out of free decision, and genuine religion can never be imposed by force. Man's knowledge of God is always limited, and nobody has the right to force his theological idiosyncracies upon other people. Christianity can best be propagated in the world by exhibiting the reasonableness of adopting it as the rule of one's moral life.

An idealist form of theism was developed from Locke's empiricism by the Irish philosopher George Berkeley (1685–1753), the Anglican bishop of Cloyne from 1734 to 1752. He had hoped to found a Christian college in Bermuda and spent four years in America from 1728; but the failure of the government in London to grant him promised financial aid brought the scheme to nought. During his American sojourn he aroused much sympathetic interest in influential quarters, and his name was to find perpetuation in a divinity school at New Haven, Connecticut, and eventually in one of California's most celebrated university centers. He died in Holywell Street, Oxford, not many months after his retirement.

In his *Principles of Human Knowledge* (1710) Berkeley subjected Locke's theory of representative perception to severe criticism, contending that there is no justification for the view that some, but not all, ideas are copies of external archetypes. If we are acquainted with material things outside us only by way of ideas, we must be incapable of breaking the idea barrier to make the required comparison between external entities and the ideas that are alleged to represent them. He therefore concluded that the primary qualities have the same subjective status as the secondary qualities, and that there is no philosophical need for Locke's "uncertain supposition of we know not what." The idea *is* the object in all cases, not a *tertium quid* between the perceiving subject and a supposedly external and independent object, and so the existence of the object, like that of the idea, consists precisely in its being perceived (*esse ist percipi*—"to be is to be perceived").

But Berkeley refused to rest with a solipsistic doctrine which implied that things are being perpetually created and destroyed, and he went on to argue that when material objects are not being perceived by us they still continue to exist as objects of God's universal perception. Indeed it is ultimately the divine perception that arouses perceptions in us, and the world of nature is the language by which God communicates his will and character to his creatures. The discerning eye can read the continuing activity of the Creator in "all the choir of heaven and furniture of the earth" (*Principles*, 1:6).

Berkeley's critique of Locke's philosophical groundwork was taken a stage further by the Scottish philosopher and historian David Hume (1711–76). In his *Treatise of Human Nature*

(3 vols., 1739–40), he contended that the principle of causality, which is presupposed in the scientific investigation of the world, has no secure logical foundation. It is merely a creature of the association of ideas, "a gentle force which commonly prevails" (*Treatise*, 1:1:4), so that if an impression *A* is repeatedly given in conjunction with an impression *B*, the mind is eventually determined by custom to regard *A* as the necessary cause of *B*. Furthermore, Hume argued that while Berkeley had rightly rejected the objective validity of the idea of material substance, he failed to recognize that the notion of spiritual substance has no greater claim to objective validity. By introspection of the most careful kind it cannot be empirically discovered; all that can be found within us are discrete ideas and impressions "in a perpetual flux and movement" (*Treatise*, 1:4:6).

While Locke's rendering of the empiricist case collapsed under the force of Hume's attack, the latter's own conclusions were no less untenable. Thus, if there is no such thing as *de facto* causal compulsiveness, how can a mind (which is without actual existence in experience) be determined or causally induced to regard a constant conjunction as a causal relation? The fact that such a question is unanswerable on Hume's assumption really bears further testimony to the weakness of Locke's position, for Hume worked largely on the basis of principles derived from Locke, and a house is never more secure than its foundations.

As in his treatment of general epistemological themes, so in his discussions of specifically theological matters, Hume showed great acuteness as a critic. In the essay "Of Miracles," which forms part of *An Enquiry Concerning Human Understanding* (first published in 1748 as *Philosophical Essays Concerning Human Understanding*), he argued that experience witnesses much more powerfully to the uniformity of natural occurrences than to the infallibility of human testimony. Hence, when considering any account of a miracle, it should be recognized that there is much more likelihood of error or deception in the reporting than there is of a temporary suspension of nature's regular operations. Also, even if an unusual event is truly the subject of any report, it ought not to be assumed that a supernatural agency actually intervened to produce the irregularity concerned. In academic circles such criticism helped to weaken confidence in modes of religious apologetic that were based on the argument from miracle, and some defenders of the faith came to maintain that genuine revelation is ethically or spiritually self-authenticating for the discerning mind.

In his paper "The Natural History of Religion," one of the *Four Dissertations* (1757), Hume distinguished between the intellectual arguments for God's existence and the subjective processes through whose mediation religion actually arises, and he arrived at the conclusion that religion has its origin in the "melancholic" rather than in the "agreeable" emotions. This was a valuable contribution to the psychology of religion, while his further thesis that polytheism is older than monotheism came as a shock to Deists and others who believed in an original monotheism, rational and undefiled, from which humanity for some reason or other had fallen away.

His work *Dialogues Concerning Natural Religion* (published posthumously in 1779) presents a critical discussion of the traditional arguments for the existence of God: Kant's more celebrated treatment of the same general theme appeared soon afterwards in his *Kritik der reinen Vernunft* ("Critique of Pure Reason"—first edition, 1781; second edition, 1787).

BIBLIOGRAPHY

Burtt, E. A. *The Metaphysical Foundations of Modern Physical Science.* Rev. ed. Garden City, N.Y.: Doubleday, 1954.

Stace, W. T. *Religion and the Modern Mind.* Philadelphia: Lippincott, 1952.

Whitehead, A. N. *Science and the Modern World.* New York: Macmillan, 1925.

Wieman, H. N. *Religious Experience and Scientific Method.* New York: Macmillan, 1926.

32 ‡ Deism

Etymologically, the term "deism" (Latin: *deus*, "god")
should have the same significance as "theism" (Greek: *theos*,
"god") and should refer to beliefs or doctrines concerning the
existence and nature of the Divine Being. But in current usage
the expression has come to be employed in a more specialized
sense to denote a rationalistic kind of theism that developed in
England and elsewhere during the seventeenth and eighteenth
centuries. Representatives of such teaching commonly affirmed
the existence of a primordial religion, natural to all rational
beings, which stands behind the various positive or historical
religions, founded upon special revelations allegedly vouchsafed
to certain privileged individuals or groups.

However, the attitude of the Deists to positive religions in
general, and to Christianity in particular, varied considerably.
Some, like Lord Herbert of Cherbury, held that all historical
modes of revealed religion have done serious damage to humanity by defiling the pure religion of nature. A less extreme
position was taken by such thinkers as John Locke who, as we
have seen, considered that Christianity in its essential character,
if not in the form it had assumed under the papacy, fulfills a
valuable service by supplementing and vivifying the natural religion of enlightened common sense.

Sharing a fundamental conviction that in principle the one
true God can be discovered by man's unaided reason, the Deists
differed profoundly from prevailing orthodoxy, both Catholic
and Protestant. They were averse to the doctrines of original sin

and absolute divine predestination, contending that, although most people have become victims of superstition, man is congenitally quite capable of knowing and conforming with the will and purpose of his Maker. Such a relatively optimistic assessment of human nature already existed in the Italian Renaissance and in some of the radical Protestant sects, as well as in the humanism that gave rise to the empirical sciences. It may be recalled, for example, that Lorenzo Valla (1405–57) repudiated the monastic ideal and found supreme value in the sensuous life of the present world, that Faustus Socinus (1539–1604) asserted man's inherent freedom to obey the will of God, and that Francis Bacon (1561–1626) advocated the systematic employment of the inductive method as the one sure means for human advancement in knowledge and power. Doubtless, Galileo's striking confirmation of the Copernican hypothesis in 1610 encouraged the gradual diffusion of the notion that, given rational direction, man can work out his own salvation.

Besides being inclined to optimism, the Deists were perhaps to some extent motivated by a common desire to find a doctrinal basis on which the proliferating sects could agree. Perhaps they felt that theological differences cannot be settled by resorting to war, which brings only misery and devastation in its train. However this may be, Deism exemplified a tendency toward latitudinarianism. Thus Locke hoped for the establishment of a broadly based national church, in which men of various persuasions (except Catholic and atheistic) would have a place, a community allowing ample scope for diversity in doctrinal interpretation. In his view, Christianity essentially consists in a personal acceptance of the Messiahship of Jesus and the practice of his ethical precepts, the truth of the latter being immediately evident to man's natural moral consciousness. And, some seventy years earlier, in 1624, an even broader theological basis for human cooperation had been proposed by Lord Herbert of Cherbury; as we shall see, it consisted in five simple tenets of an allegedly natural and universal monotheism.

Furthermore, the Deists shared a common tendency to stress the transcendence of God. In this respect they typified the intellectualism of their time, although (as is usually the case) there were some notable exceptions, among them the immanentist mystics Giordano Bruno (1548–1600) and Jakob Boehme (1575–1624), and the monistic pantheist Benedict de Spinoza (1632–77). Two reasons may be cited for the characteristic emphasis of the Deists. Firstly, they were prone to think of religion primarily as an agency for the promotion of moral goodness, God being construed as the transcendent Lawgiver who rewards the virtuous and punishes the wicked, both in the present life and in the world to come. Of course, such a mode of interpretation goes back to the Hebraic origins of Christianity; and it came to New Testament expression in the synoptic traditions and elsewhere, and during the second century it found a distinguished exponent in Justin Martyr (*c.* 95–165). Secondly, the Deists were for the most part in touch with the expanding scientific movement, and the new physics sought to explain the material universe in mechanistic terms. Consequently, God was represented as the Maker of a vast cosmic machine, who, after he had finished his creative work, withdrew into himself and thenceforward was seldom called upon to interfere with the natural operations of what he had so marvelously constructed. Such is the kind of theological conception associated with Newton's *Principia* (1687).

Although Locke was sufficiently confident in human reason to believe in the demonstrability of God's existence, he considered that, for the achievement of a really satisfactory religion, man's intellectual faculty has to be supplemented by divine revelation. In the fourth book of his *Essay Concerning Human Understanding* (1690) and in his later work *The Reasonableness of Christianity* (1695) he argued that authentic disclosures of God never contain anything that is contrary to reason and virtue, and that, to win general recognition, revealed truth needs the external support of miraculous occurrences. Basic Christianity, which consists largely in personal allegiance to the moral authority of Jesus, satisfies all the fundamental requirements for genuine revelation: it conforms with the dictates of reason, promotes moral goodness, and was originally ratified by miraculous signs of its supernatural derivation. The gospels may include certain reports of suprarational events (as, for example, the resurrection of Jesus), but there was nothing involved that is definitely opposed to reason.

In its main features Locke's theological position bears striking resemblance to that of John Tillotson (1630–96), archbishop of Canterbury from 1691, and to that of Samuel Clarke (1675–1729), rector of the parish of St. James in Piccadilly, London, from 1709.

Clarke was influenced by Newton, whose doctrines on space and time he defended in his correspondence with Leibniz, published in 1717; and it might be noticed that in 1727 he declined an offer to become Newton's successor as Master of the Mint. He was also influenced by Descartes. In 1704 and 1705 he delivered two series of Boyle Lectures, entitled respectively *A Discourse Concerning the Being and Attributes of God* and *A Discourse Concerning the Unchangeable Obligations of Natural Religion, and the Truth and Certainty of the Christian Revelation*. In the first series he defended Cartesian rationalism, upholding the doctrine of innate ideas against the empiricism of Locke. In the second series, on the other hand, he put forward views on the relation of natural to revealed religion that are very similar to those of his compatriot; and this may serve as an indication that the latter's empiricism was not so thoroughgoing as he had supposed it to be.

Clarke agreed that man can arrive solely by natural reason at certain primary truths, namely, that God exists and rules the world on a moral basis, and that in a future life human beings are to be treated according to their deserts (for in the present world there scarcely obtains a just distribution of rewards and punishments, so adjustments will have to be made after death).

Such truths, being in principle discoverable by the light of nature, constitute the fundamental tenets of natural religion. But because of man's generally degenerate condition, few people can find their way to an appreciation of their validity without the additional light of revelation. The needed supplementation is supplied by Christianity, which alone among the positive religions makes justifiable claims to rationality in its manifestations of the Creator's character and purpose.

Clarke, then, like Locke, held that the content of biblical revelation surpasses the theology of natural religion without contradicting it. The truths disclosed in the scriptures are not irrational and are designed to promote the moral reformation of mankind; also, they found external confirmation in the miracles biblically recorded, as well as in Christ's fulfillment of Old Testament prophecies.

A very different assessment of the status of revealed religion was made by Lord Herbert of Cherbury; and, if Deism is taken to be normatively represented in his writings, then it was opposed in principle to all positive religions. For, in his view, the additions made by allegedly special revelations have, without exception, corrupted the purity of natural religion, introducing conflict and superstition where originally there was only agreement and truth. So far from furnishing additional illumination, they have cast great shadows over the minds of men.

Edward Herbert (1583–1648) was the elder brother of George Herbert, the well-known Anglican clergyman, poet, and hymn writer. He studied at Oxford (1595–1600), and not long after the accession of James I (1603) was made a Knight of the Order of the Bath. He had many adventures as a soldier of fortune on the Continent during 1608–18, and from 1619 was for five years British ambassador in Paris. He acceded to an Irish peerage in 1624 and was made an English baron in 1629; during the Civil War he prudently shifted his allegiance to the parliamentary side. His most important work *De Veritate* ("On the Truth") was published at Paris in 1624, after the manuscript had been read and commended by Hugo Grotius, a disciple of Arminius. In it Herbert maintained that certain common notions have their seat in natural instinct, are presupposed in all experience, and give rise to the basic principles of morality, science, and religion, In another treatise, *De Religione Gentilium* ("On the Religion of the Nations"), he made a spirited early contribution to the comparative study of religion, despite his central thesis that positive religions generally are degradations of the religion of nature.

In his *De Veritate* Herbert contended that there are five common notions at the root of all religion: (1) The existence of one supreme Being is an objective reality; (2) The Supreme Being ought to be worshiped; (3) The practice of virtue is the chief human factor in all true worship; (4) Men ought to repent of their sins; (5) Human beings are duly requited for their deeds both here and hereafter. Herbert held that, whenever human beings rely solely on their natural reason, they immediately recognize the validity of these five common notions, which together constitute the principle tenets of the pure religion of nature, adherence to which is sufficient guarantee of man's eternal blessedness. They sum up the teaching of the one truly catholic or universal church, which existed in its integrity before people allowed themselves to be misled by the covetous and crafty agents of sacerdotal superstition. In many times and places the multifarious rites and dogmas of institutional religions, besides obscuring the clarity of man's pristine vision of the Creator, have had the unwholesome effect of bringing the masses into subjection to individuals with an exaggerated sense of their own importance.

Thus Lord Herbert rejected the claims of the various positive religions to be founded upon special divine revelations, and his basic philosophical argument for such a position lay in an a priori deduction from the basic common notion of the divine supremacy. By definition God is all-surpassingly perfect, which implies that he must be just in the treatment of mankind; and justice would be flagrantly contravened if he chose to reveal himself to a particular people at a particular time. Divine favor cannot be consistently construed in terms of divine favoritism, whence it follows that authentic revelation must in principle be available to people of all periods and all locations. Accordingly, Herbert concluded that God originally endowed humanity with the capacity for true religion, and he opined that empirical support for such an inference was to be found in the testimony of the sages of diverse epochs and cultures.

In his work *Christianity not Mysterious* (1696), John Toland (1670–1720), an Irish Catholic converted to Protestantism in 1686, took up Locke's thesis that the scriptures, while containing much that is suprarational, teaches nothing that is contrary to reason. He subsumed truths beyond reason under the more general category of truths according to reason, and maintained that they simply amount to information received on the testimony of others, in contradistinction to what is discovered through direct personal experience; and he went on to contend that biblical assertions which are quite incomprehensible to the natural understanding must be due to baneful priestly or pagan influence. The book occasioned a veritable storm of protest, and Toland had to flee from Ireland to escape incarceration.

He continued to write, showing much versatility as a scholarly thinker. He became interested in early Christian apocryphal literature, and in his *Nazarenus* (1718) he differentiated primitive Jewish from primitive Gentile Christianity; in his contention that the former represented the new faith in its original mode he anticipated the teaching of the Tübingen School, which was to become of great importance in the field of New Testament criticism during the nineteenth century, Toland also became interested in the writings of Spinoza, and he coined the term "pantheism" (Greek: *pan*, "all" + *theos*, "God"), now commonly employed of extremist doctrines of the divine immanence. In his *Pantheisticon* (1720) he set forth a pantheistic liturgy, arranged after the fashion of a Christian service book; he thus repudiated the characteristically deistic conception of God as an external Creator who, having once set the cosmic machine in motion, allowed it for the most part to go on working of its own accord.

A theory of the essential identity of biblical and natural religion was elaborated by the Oxford thinker Matthew Tindal (1655–1733) in his book *Christianity as Old as Creation, or the Gospel as a Republication of the Religion of Nature* (1730). Tindal argues that the divine intention in Christianity was neither to add to nor to subtract from the perfect law of nature, but simply to confirm and reinstate it by delivering people from irrational fears and misdirected reverence. Like Lord Herbert, he maintained that, being what he is, God could never have withheld from certain sections of mankind the possibility of apprehending the ways of peace and eternal blessedness. Hence at the beginning of history he must have endowed the human race with the capacity for true religion, and the gospel was really meant to call men back to the pristine clarity of natural religion, which had been adulterated by the machinations of priestly agents of superstition. Unfortunately, however, such agents were allowed to get to work again, corrupting the pure religion of Jesus by producing the absurdities of ecclesiastical dogma. Basic Christianity can be recovered only by free and rational investigation.

Tindal was convinced that such inquiry showed, *inter alia,* that Samuel Clarke grievously erred when he contended that Christianity was intended to supersede natural religion by making valuable additions to it. True Christianity is nothing more than a particular reproduction of the universal religion of nature. God's purpose consists in the furtherance not of his own glory but of the welfare of his creatures, and the moral goal of all genuine religious devotion lies in the attainment of the divine spirit of disinterested benevolence. Such an ethical ideal requires no external miraculous confirmation, and, rightly understood, the gospel carries its own intrinsic authority within the self-authenticating content of its moral and spiritual teaching.

The proofs from prophecy and from miracle, which had been used by Locke and Clarke among others, were attacked by Anthony Collins (1676–1729) and David Hume (1711–76). In his *Discourse of the Grounds and Reasons of the Christian Religion* (1724) and *The Scheme of Literal Prophecy Considered* (1727) Collins denied the reality of the alleged cases of correspondence between Old Testament prophecy and New Testament fulfillment; and, as was observed in the previous chapter, Hume argued forcibly against the apologetic value of miracle stories. Of course, neither of these criticisms had any bearing upon Tindal's thesis, but the same cannot be said of the arguments contained in Hume's dissertation "The Natural History of Religion" (1757), where it is maintained that polytheism, besides being historically older than monotheism, may also have moral superiority, since belief in the existence of only one God is evidently liable to be accompanied by a baneful spirit of intolerance. Clearly, if such contentions are soundly based, Tindal's theory of the status and character of natural religion would require radical alteration.

The relatively unbridled rationalism of much deistic thinking was attacked from the side of mystical pietism by Nonjuror William Law (1686–1761); his book *The Case of Reason* (1732) to some extent anticipated the teaching of Immanuel Kant by maintaining that the transcendent truths of religion lie outside the sphere of man's intellectual competence. A more moderate position was adopted in what came to be respected as a standard work of Anglican philosophical theology, *The Analogy of Religion, Natural and Revealed, to the Constitution and Course of Nature* (1736), by Joseph Butler (1692–1752), who had seceded from Presbyterianism and was appointed bishop of Bristol in 1738 and bishop of Durham in 1750. According to his main thesis, natural religion involves as many intellectual perplexities as revealed religion, and if such difficulties do not hinder wise men from believing in God's creation and providential government of the world, they ought not to prevent credence in the validity of the more specific truths of biblical revelation.

A conservative rationalistic standpoint found representative expression in *A View of the Evidences of Christianity* (1794) and *Natural Theology* (1802) by William Paley (1743–1805), who was archdeacon of Carlisle from 1776. Both works are very lucid in style, and for several decades they were widely used as manuals in the theological colleges of the English-speaking world. But Paley's thought was marked by a certain rigidity, and he not infrequently resorted to arguments without showing any deep appreciation of the objections that had been brought against them. On the other hand, his rather mechanical conception of God and his ethical prudentialism ("Honesty is the best policy") betrayed an intellectual temper that prevailed at the time in many quarters. He made much of the teleological argument for God's existence, and his analogy of the watch became almost proverbial: as the mutual adaptation of the parts of a small timepiece bespeaks the intelligent activity of a watchmaker, so the purposiveness evident in the cosmos betrays the existence of a supreme Designer. Paley further contended that the divine revelation in Christ was confirmed by miraculous signs; and he was careful to point to the heavenly rewards that must eventually attend the practice of Christian charity.

The scientific concept of evolution being largely a creation of the nineteenth century, theological thought for the most part still showed little sense of historical development. Thus Hume's "Natural History of Religion" was a presage, in 1757, of things to come; and so it was with the monumental work *The Decline and Fall of the Roman Empire* (6 vols., 1776–88) by Edward Gibbon (1737–94). In the fifteenth and sixteenth chapters of the first volume he dealt with the history of the early church and argued that there were five main reasons for the rapid expansion of Christianity in the ancient world: A fanatical enthusiasm, derived from Jewish Messianism; a professed guarantee of victory over death; a superlative confidence in the power to work miracles; a strict ethical code; and a rigorous discipline coupled with an efficient ecclesiastical organization.

Gibbon's contentions gave rise to a bitter controversy, and the present-day reader may wonder why. In a large measure it was due to the failure of many of his critics, like most thinkers until fairly recent times, to enter into a sympathetic appreciation of the human past, and this in turn is partly to be attributed to a general lack of systematic training in objective historical research.

BIBLIOGRAPHY

Creed, J. M., and J. S. B. Smith, eds. *Religious Thought in the Eighteenth Century*. Cambridge: Cambridge University Press, 1934.

Stromberg, R. N. *Religious Liberalism in Eighteenth-Century England*. London: Oxford University Press, 1954.

Webb, C. C. J. *Studies in the History of Natural Theology*. Oxford: Clarendon Press, 1915.

33 ‡ Pietism and Methodism

During the Thirty Years' War, which culminated in the Treaty of Westphalia in 1648, Germany suffered appalling devastation, and the religious life of the country lost much of its vitality. Lutheranism had begun to develop into a stereotyped system with an emphasis on externals and doctrinal orthodoxy. It was into this hardening tradition that Pietism, under the inspiration of Philipp Jakob Spener (1635–1705), injected the dynamism of a renewed evangelical fervor.

Spener was born in Alsace and studied at Strasbourg. He subsequently spent some time in Switzerland, and there he came under Calvinistic and puritanical influence and was also deeply affected by the teaching of Jean de Labadie (1610–74), a mystic and erstwhile Jesuit, who came to embrace views reminiscent of certain Anabaptist doctrines, holding, for example, that only those inspired by the Holy Spirit can understand the scriptures. Appointed to a pastorate at Strasbourg in 1663, Spener began to give pulpit expression to a firm conviction that Christianity is essentially an affair of the heart and consists in a personal devotion to Christ rather than in an intellectual subscription to theological dogmas.

After his election to a ministerial charge at Frankfurt in 1666 he determined to put some of his newly acquired ideas into practice, and he eventually established what he called *collegia pietatis*—devotional groups which were regularly to meet at his residence for prayer and biblical study. In 1675 he published his basic and most influential work, *Pia Desideria* ("Pious Wants"), in which he made six main proposals for the renewal of the religious life of Christendom: (1) that personal religion be deepened by an ardent study of the scriptures; (2) that the doctrine of the priesthood of all believers be seriously applied, the laity being induced to play an active part in the work of the church; (3) that the practical character of Christianity be recognized, since religion is something much more than a mere subject for academic discussion; (4) that in all theological argumentation a spirit of charity be shown, the rightful aim being not to score debating points but to win men's hearts for allegiance to Christ; (5) that theological education at the universities be reformed, with special attention paid to ways of improving the moral and spiritual standards of both professors and students; (6) that there be a return to the mode of preaching that aims at the salvation and edification of souls. Despite the opposition he encountered from fellow ministers, Spener was optimistic; he believed that, given a wide acceptance of these proposals, the church would be vitalized, the Jews converted, and the power of the papacy finally broken.

Things became increasingly difficult at Frankfurt, however, and in 1686 Spener was happy to leave to take up an appointment as court preacher at Dresden, where he quickly found encouragement in the enthusiastic support he obtained from August Hermann Francke (1663–1727), a lecturer at the university in Leipzig. The latter, in accordance with Spener's teaching, proceeded to establish a *collegium philobiblicum* for the devotional study of the Bible, with a membership open to both staff and students. The *collegium* proved extremely popular among the students, and the local bookshops soon sold out all available copies of the Greek New Testament. But Francke's anti-intellectualism provoked hostility among the theological professors, and the opposition so intensified that Francke was finally compelled to leave the university, whereupon he accepted a pastoral charge at Erfurt (1690).

Meanwhile, things were not going well at Dresden. Elector John George III became more and more irritated by Spener's continual sermonic condemnations of drunkenness, and again the author of the *Pia Desideria* was glad to make a move. In 1691 he went to Berlin as rector of the Nikolaikirche, and there at last prosperity attended his efforts. This was mainly owing to the sympathetic interest of the elector of Brandenburg (who became King Frederick I of Prussia in 1701). Spener was invited to help in the devising of plans for a proposed university at Halle, an institution which Elector Frederick actually founded in 1694. Associated with him in the project was Christian Thomasius (1655–1728), a professor of law, who, despite his rationalism, had been dismissed from the university at Leipzig for defending Francke (1690). Like John Locke, he had a marked distaste for theological quibbling and strenuously advocated the principle of religious toleration. He was elected dean of the faculty of law at Halle, a position he held until his death. Besides making significant contributions to jurisprudence, he was the person first responsible for introducing German (in place of Latin) as the language of university instruction.

At Erfurt Francke involved himself in further difficulties, but Spener secured for him a pastorate at Glauchau (a village near Halle) along with a professorship at the new university. Thenceforward the tide of fortune ran in his favor. He established a school for children of the poor in 1695, and this was followed in quick succession by a counterpart for offspring of the nobility (the Adelspaedagogium), an orphange, a dispensary, a publishing house, and a Bible institute. King Frederick William I paid an official visit to the various foundations in 1713; he was greatly impressed and adopted some of Francke's ideas in his schemes for Prussian educational reform.

An interest in Christian service overseas was stimulated at Halle, and in the course of the eighteenth century about sixty people from the university and its associated institutions went abroad as missionaries. The most notable among these was Christian Frederick Schwarz, who worked in India without a break from 1750 to the time of his death in 1798.

Before Spener left Dresden, Pietism had become widely diffused in Germany, and doubtless the popularity of the hymns of Paul Gerhardt (*c.* 1607–76) helped to disseminate the basic sentiments and concerns of the movement. Spener, however, continued to meet with opposition from the orthodox clergy, and in 1695, at a university convocation in Wittenberg, 283 of his theses were condemned as heretical. Nevertheless, he pressed on with his work undismayed.

The most influential Pietist of the eighteenth century was Count Nikolaus Ludwig von Zinzendorf (1700–1760). A native of Dresden and a godson of Spener, he was a pupil at Francke's Adelspaedagogium before going on to read law at the university in Wittenberg. After his graduation he took a post in the civil service at Dresden in 1721, but his main interest had become the promotion of pietistic Protestantism. At this time scattered remnants of the old Hussite church, the Moravian Brethren, happened to be seeking refuge in Saxony, for in Austrian territories they were still exposed to persecution. Zinzendorf began to welcome them as settlers on his estate at Berthelsdorf (east of Dresden), and in 1727 he resigned from the civil service so that he could devote all his time to promoting the religious life of the growing settlement, which had now been named Herrnhut ("Watch of the Lord").

The colony was ruled by elected elders, and the general character of the organization was monastic, although there was no vow of celibacy. The unmarried were separated on a sexual basis, and the children were brought up much as they would have been in an orphanage. Thus the community was self-contained, and the immigrants aspired after a reconstitution of the old Moravian church. This ran counter to Zinzendorf's desire to keep the society within the Lutheran communion as a *collegium pietatis* on a grand scale. But it was the separatist aspiration that finally prevailed.

In 1730 Zinzendorf attended the coronation of King Christian VI of Denmark, where he met natives of Greenland and the West Indies, and he returned to Herrnhut full of enthusiasm for foreign missions. His zeal proved infectious. Missionaries were dispatched to the West Indies in 1732, to Greenland in 1733, to Georgia in 1735, and in 1738 a religious society was founded in Fetter Lane, London, by one Peter Boehler, who was vitally to influence John Wesley.

The Lutheran authorities were alerted to Zinzendorf's activities, and representatives of orthodoxy accused him of heresy; his doctrines were investigated in 1734, but they escaped formal condemnation by the examining tribunal. Two years later he encountered political difficulties; the Austrian government made an official complaint that Zinzendorf was enticing Austrian subjects from their homeland, and the Saxon authorities took action by banishing him. His enforced exile lasted for eleven years (1736–47), and during this period he traveled extensively, disseminating his pietistic doctrines wherever he went. He received episcopal consecration in 1737 at the hands of the Moravian royal chaplain in Berlin, and he went on to establish Moravian societies in the Baltic areas, the Netherlands, England, the West Indies, and the North American colonies.

During Zinzendorf's enforced absence from Germany the Moravian Brethren were officially recognized as a separate religious community by the Prussian government, and in 1745 the revived church was formally reconstituted with the three traditional orders (bishops, elders, deacons), but the polity was in fact more presbyterian than episcopal in the generally accepted sense. In England, by an act of Parliament in 1749, the Moravian Unitas Fratrum ("Unity of Brethren") received official recognition as an ancient Protestant Episcopal church.

The Saxon ban on Zinzendorf was lifted in 1747, and he worked at Herrnhut in 1747–49 and again from 1755 until the time of his death in 1760. During the years 1749–55 he worked as a missionary in England.

Zinzendorf was definitely averse to theological intellectualism, and the whole tenor of his teaching was opposed alike to the scholastic orthodoxy of Protestantism and to the rationalism of the Cartesians. For him, religion was fundamentally an affair of the heart, and his dominant concern was to promote a personal sense of fellowship with Christ as the Creator and Redeemer of the world. His intense emotionalism at times inclined to morbidity, and for a while he actually resorted to childish modes of expression in literal conformity with the gospel injunction that followers of Jesus should become as little children (Matt. 18:3). On the other hand, Zinzendorf undoubtedly strengthened a movement that did much to revitalize a rather arid Protestantism; and, paradoxically enough, through the mediation of the romanticism of Kant and Schleiermacher, he was destined to affect the subsequent course of academic thinking, both Catholic and Protestant.

It is often said, not without truth, that religious life in England during the early decades of the eighteenth century was at a very low ebb. But it would be a mistake to suppose that Christian piety there had lost all its animation. John Bunyan (1628–88), the Bedford brazier who, after the Restoration, suffered prolonged imprisonment for his nonconformist Congregationalism, issued his literary classic *The Pilgrim's Progress* in 1678; and this work, with its direct and homely expression of the doctrine of salvation by faith through divine grace, must have been exercising a strong influence in certain quarters. Isaac Watts (1674–1748), who served as a Congregational minister at Stoke Newington in London, published his celebrated *Hymns and Spiritual Songs* in 1707 and his *Psalms of David* in 1719; and these compositions, which quickly won widespread popularity, must have done much to diffuse the joy of personal faith in the grace and providence of God. William Law (1686–1761), who became a Nonjuror after refusing the oath of allegiance to King George I, issued his *Serious Call to a Devout and Holy Life* in 1728, and certain sections of the Anglican clergy were deeply affected by it; the work, which reflects the influence of Johannes Tauler and Thomas à Kempis, stresses the importance of meditation and ascetical habits in the cultivation of true piety.

Moreover, devotional groups for biblical study were spreading in the Anglican churches of London during the later years of the seventeenth century. To some extent the regular meetings of such voluntary societies carried on the tradition of the Calvinistic conventicles, and they bore a striking resemblance to Spener's *collegia pietatis*. The clergy generally frowned upon them as fanatical, but the fact that they continued to proliferate indicates that they were fulfilling a felt religious need. Besides seeking to deepen the spiritual life of the people, they helped to promote missionary enthusiasm, and it may be noted that Thomas Bray (1656–1730), who strengthened Anglicanism in Maryland, founded the Society for Promoting Christian Knowledge (the S.P.C.K.) in 1698 and the Society for the Propagation of the Gospel in Foreign Parts (the S.P.G.) in 1701.

John Wesley (1703–91) was the fifteenth child of Samuel Wesley, rector of the Lincolnshire parish of Epworth, and studied at Charterhouse and Christ Church. He was elected to a fellowship at Lincoln College, Oxford, in 1726 and acted as curate to his father during the years 1727–29. In 1729, much under the influence of Law's *Serious Call*, he became the leader of a society of earnest students, among whom was his younger brother Charles (1707–88), the Epworth rector's eighteenth child, who had gone up to Oxford in 1726. The society habitually met for group study of the scriptures, and besides practicing frequent communion and observing regular fasts, its members paid pastoral visits to prisoners in the local jail. The strictness of their piety aroused resentment, and such taunts as "Bible Moths," "Methodists," and "the Holy Club" became current among the academic population.

The group membership acquired a notable addition in George Whitefield (1714–70), a native of Gloucester and a servitor at Pembroke College, who was to become the most impressive orator in the country. After his ordination he went to America in 1736, under the auspices of the S.P.G. He founded an orphanage in Georgia and made effective use of his eloquence in the raising of funds for its upkeep. In all, he visited America seven times, and his electrifying evangelical zeal was mainly responsible for the so-called Great Awakening there. He died at Newburyport, Massachusetts, worn out by his arduous labors. His theology was rigorously Calvinistic.

The Wesleys had already made the crossing to Georgia in 1735, also as ordained missionaries sent out by the S.P.G. A number of Moravians were traveling by the same boat, and John was struck by the courage they showed during a storm, lamenting his own personal lack of a faith which they evidently enjoyed. Charles was not happy in the colony, and he returned to England in 1736. John stayed on, but his open condemnation of traffic in slaves and intoxicating liquor, as well as his rigidity and tactlessness, set the colonists against him, and he returned to England in 1737.

Back in London both brothers associated themselves with various devotional societies, and they made the acquaintance of Peter Boehler, the Moravian who had established a religious group in Fetter Lane. On May 24, 1738, John attended the meeting of an Anglican society at St. Botolph's church in Aldersgate Street, and while Luther's preface to his commentary on Paul's Epistle to the Romans was being read, his heart was (to use his own words) "strangely warmed," and he suddenly felt assured that through his faith in Christ, God had saved him from "the law of sin and death." Thus the Lutheran doctrines of justifying faith and personal certitude of divine forgiveness, so greatly stressed by the Pietists, became Wesley's own, and thenceforward his consuming passion was "to promote vital practical religion" among the people. In his subsequent evangelistic work he was ably assisted by his brother Charles, who had a remarkable talent as a hymn writer. It has often been said that Methodism was born in song; Charles alone produced over fifty-five hundred hymns, and a number of these (for example, "Love divine, all loves excelling" and "Hark! the herald angels sing") are still among the most popular in the English language.

John Wesley went to the Continent in the summer of 1738. He met Zinzendorf at Marienborn and visited Herrnhut. He admired the Moravian practice of meeting in groups for regular confession and mutual edification, and such gatherings became integral to the life of the Methodist societies he soon began to establish.

In 1739 Whitefield was engaged in a preaching mission to coal miners at Kingswood, near Bristol, giving proof of his extraordinary oratorical power. Wesley accepted, not without trepidation, an invitation to join him in the campaign. But his preaching met with a response that amazed him, and not long afterward the first Methodist society was founded at Bristol. He went on to become a field preacher unique in English history. During the next fifty years he traveled more than a quarter of a million miles on horseback and preached more than forty thousand sermons. He crossed the Irish Channel forty-two times and paid twenty-two visits to Scotland. He wrote thousands of letters, a voluminous journal, numerous tracts, and several books. Among the latter were the Hebrew, Greek, and Latin grammars he prepared for use at the school he founded at Kingswood in the interest of the sons of Methodist preachers. In his *Notes on the New Testament* (1754), officially recognized as a Methodist doctrinal standard in 1763, Wesley shows the influence of the *Gnomon Novi Testamenti* (1742) by J. A. Bengel (1687–1752), a Lutheran with pietistic sympathies. Bengel was an outstanding scholar, and his critical edition of the Greek New Testament (1734) helped to further the scientific study of the biblical text.

Wesley had considerable talent for organization. Every Methodist society was divided into classes of about twelve members, and each class leader was responsible for those who belonged to his group. The classes met weekly for prayer and discussion, and each member paid a penny a week. Thus authority was

distributed throughout the whole structure. The societies themselves were arranged in circuits, and these came to be represented in the supreme legislative organ of the movement. Two
orders of preachers were established: those who were itinerant
and paid, devoting all their time to the work and moving from
circuit to circuit, and those who were local and voluntary, serving in a part-time capacity. In 1744 Wesley conferred with his
preachers at a meeting in London; such a conference was to
become an annual gathering and Methodism's highest organ of
government. Although Wesley himself was autocratic, the movement was organized in the form of a representative democracy;
in principle the polity was of the presbyterian form.

Fundamentally, Wesley's theological thought reflects Lutheran and Calvinistic influence. He held that the personal experience of justification by faith in Christ is followed by a
process of sanctification under the inspiration of the Holy Spirit,
so that the Christian is gradually brought to a state of perfect
love for God and man. Unlike some of his followers, however,
he did not believe that the state of entire sanctification is in fact
frequently reached in the present life. On the question of predestination, Wesley was Arminian, and in this respect he differed from Whitefield, who subscribed to the rigorous Calvinistic belief in God's election of some to salvation and others to
damnation. Whitefield found an influential supporter in Selina,
Countess of Huntingdon (1709–91), a convert of Wesley's, who
eventually founded a distinct organization known as the Countess of Huntingdon's Connexion. The Calvinistic Methodists in
Wales also owed their origin to Whitefield rather than to
Wesley.

Methodism began to spread in North America in 1766. The
first Methodist preaching house in New York was opened in
1768, and the first American conference took place five years
later at Philadelphia. Wesley had long been pressed to allow the
itinerant preachers (few of whom were in Anglican orders) to
administer the sacrament of the Lord's supper. Such a move

would have meant an open break with the establishment, and this he never desired. But he came to feel that the needs of the American field called for special treatment, and in 1764 he ordained two preachers as presbyters and "set apart" Thomas Coke (1747–1814) as a bishop or superintendent for service on that fast-developing continent. In performing these actions Wesley was opposed by his brother Charles, among others, and he replied by arguing that in the New Testament "priest" (Greek: *presbyteros*) has the same meaning as "bishop" (Greek: *episkopos*). In American Methodism the term "superintendent" dropped out of use in favor of "bishop" as a designation of the holders of higher ministerial office; nevertheless, as in Britain, the movement was essentially presbyterian in polity, not episcopal in the traditional Catholic sense. Doctrinally, the emphasis was (and remains) upon personal faith and the believer's own experience of God's saving grace.

Wesley's appeal to the New Testament to justify his assumption of the right to conduct ordinations betrays a tendency to think of the scriptures as the final authority in religious matters. Actually there was also a different tendency at work in Wesley's thinking, just as there was in Luther's. On the one hand, he regarded the personal experience of God's saving favor as the sufficient basis of true Christianity, and, on the other hand, he regarded the scriptures as the written word of God, conformity with which constituted the essence of Christianity. According to the first view, all forms of rationalistic argumentation can do nothing more than skim the surface, failing to touch the profundities of the religious life, whereas, according to the second view, they are to be condemned as irreligious expressions of sinful pride, products of a refusal to accept with childlike trust what God has revealed in his word.

Hence it is not surprising that there existed a certain ambivalence in Wesley's moral and spiritual outlook. In some respects he was liberal, rejecting the doctrine of absolute predestination and repudiating slavery; and yet in other respects he was conservative, believing in witchcraft and in special providence, rejecting the Copernican astronomy, and opposing the critical approach to the Bible. Moreover, like Calvin, he was otherworldly in his general orientation, holding that "friendship with the world is spiritual adultery"; he maintained that, since a Christian must pursue his vocation in secular society with diligence and deep earnestness, activities such as dancing, gaming, and theater-going, should be shunned as devilish distractions from the serious business of living life as God meant it to be lived.

The evangelical revival of the eighteenth century greatly stimulated the practice of religion in the English-speaking world. Soon after Wesley's death in 1791 Methodism separated from the Anglican church, but the evangelical or low-church party that remained within the establishment continued to be influential. Among its outstanding members was William Wilberforce (1759–1833), who successfully advocated the abolition of slavery in the British Empire in 1833. Also, missionary enthusiasm spread in most of the Protestant denominations. The Baptist Society for Propagating the Gospel among the Heathen was founded in 1792, the London Missionary Society in 1795, the Church Missionary Society in 1799, the British and Foreign Bible Society in 1804, the American Board of Commissioners for Foreign Missions in 1810, the American Bible Society in 1816, and so on. In England during the early nineteenth century the power and influence of Methodism continued to increase, especially in areas much affected by the industrial revolution; and a number of the early leaders of the cooperative and trade-union movements were drawn from Methodist circles. In the United States, Methodism, with its approximately twelve million adult adherents, is today some sixteen times larger than the parent body in Britain.

BIBLIOGRAPHY

Cameron, R. M. *The Rise of Methodism.* New York: Philosophical Library, 1954.

Gelfand, M. *Livingstone the Doctor: His Life and Travels.* Oxford: Blackwell, 1957.

Harrison, E. *Son to Susannah.* Harmondsworth, Middlesex: Penguin Books, 1944.

Hildebrandt, F. *Christianity According to the Wesleys.* London: Epworth Press, 1956.

Monk, R. C. *A Study of the Christian Life: John Wesley, His Puritan Heritage.* London: Epworth Press, 1966.

Stoeffler, E. *The Rise of Evangelical Pietism.* Leiden: E. J. Brill, 1965.

Weinlick, J. R. *Count Zinzendorf.* New York: Abingdon Press, 1956.

Zabriskie, A., ed. *Anglican Evangelicalism.* Philadelphia: Church Historical Society, 1943.

34 ‡ Continental Rationalism

The term "Enlightenment" is often applied to the rationalism that developed on the Continent during the eighteenth century. Besides exemplifying something of the spirit that informed the Renaissance and the rise of the empirical sciences, it had connections with Cartesianism as well as with English Deism. Generally, stress was laid on the unity of mankind and on the perfectibility of human nature; the concept of special revelation was felt to be incompatible with the common notion of God's justice, while the orthodox doctrine of original sin was construed as an affront upon man's dignity as a free and rational being, endowed with the capacity to achieve a full and satisfying life for himself in the present world.

Thus, like many examples of English Deism, the Enlightenment was characterized by cosmopolitan and optimistic tendencies: if only man could be freed from the shackles of ignorance and superstition, then the light of reason would be sufficient to guide humanity along the road that leads to happiness and fulfillment. A primary requisite was education, and efforts were made to implement the diffusion of recently acquired knowledge. Pierre Bayle's *Dictionaire historique et critique* had appeared in 1697, but especially important in this connection was the *Encyclopédie* (35 vols., 1751–80) published under the general editorship of Denis Diderot (1713–84). Among the contributors were Voltaire and Rousseau. Many of them, like Diderot himself, were opposed to organized Christianity, both Catholic and Protestant. They came to be known as *les philosophes*, and they did much to disseminate the rationalistic and humanitarian ideals that to a considerable extent inspired the French Revolution, which broke out in 1789.

As with Deism in England, so with the rationalism on the Continent, the broad humanistic assumptions admitted of a wide variety of interpretation on specifically theological matters. Voltaire (1694–1778) was a Deist more or less after the fashion of Lord Herbert of Cherbury; Georges-Louis Leclerc, Comte de Buffon (1707–88), and Jean-Baptiste Robinet (1735–1820) were —perhaps under Spinoza's influence—pantheistic; Heinrich Dietrich, Baron von Holbach (1723–89) was a materialist, and his main work *Le système de la nature* (1770) gained a singular reputation as the atheist's bible; Jean-Jacques Rousseau (1712–78), who stressed the importance of feeling in religion, was a forerunner of nineteenth-century romanticism.

Voltaire (his real name was François-Marie Arouet), outstanding as a critic, dramatist, and poet, perhaps did more than any of his contemporaries in France to further the cause of the Enlightenment. He had a keen wit and poured ridicule on orthodox Christianity, especially Catholicism. Although he greatly admired Locke's empiricism and Newton's natural philosophy, his own theological position was more extreme vis-à-vis revealed religion. He did not wish for a purified form of Christianity, but rather for its total elimination, and so in this respect his attitude was analogous to that of Lord Herbert of Cherbury. In his view, Christianity had helped to corrupt the religion of nature and to bring man into the bondage of superstition and fanaticism. His attacks on Catholicism were vehement, and in his denunciations he frequently betrayed a sincere assurance that he was conducting a campaign for truth against deceit and falsity. He hated war, tyranny, and oppression, and he tirelessly advocated social reforms that would lighten the burden of the toiling masses and defended men who (like the Huguenot Jean Callas) were victims of the persecuting measures applied by the French government against Protestantism.

Voltaire was born in Paris and educated at a Jesuit college. Early in life he came into conflict with authority. In 1717 he was imprisoned in the Bastille for deriding the regent, but soon afterward he demonstrated his remarkable literary talent by the publication of the tragedy *Oedipe.* After a second period of incarceration in the Bastille he spent the years 1726–29 in England, where he made the acquaintance of some of the leading representatives of Deism. In 1734 he issued his *Philosophical Letters on the English,* extolling the toleration he had found in London and contrasting it with the bigotry prevailing in his own country. He commended the enlightened culture of Deism and made a spirited attack on Blaise Pascal (1623–62), the mathematician and man of letters who had defended a morally rigorous form of Augustinian quietism against the relative laxity of Jesuit casuistry. However, Voltaire was far from being a friend of the Jesuits; on the contrary, he is to be counted among their bitterest enemies.

The French authorities took prompt action. The *Philosophical Letters* were publicly burned; their author found refuge in Lorraine at the country house of Madame de Châtelet, where he stayed for several years, and his literary activity continued. He expounded and defended Deism in his *Treatise on Metaphysics* (1734) and wrote an impious narrative poem on Joan of Arc, *La pucelle,* in 1739, but it was not published until 1755. During this period he also completed a number of plays, notably *Alzire* (1736) and *Mahomet* (1741). From 1750 to 1752 he lived in Berlin at the court of Frederick the Great, an enthusiastic patron of the Enlightenment. In 1758 he acquired the estate of Ferney on the Franco-Swiss frontier, near Geneva, and took up residence there.

While holding that orthodox Christianity, both Catholic and Protestant, was wholly nefarious, Voltaire firmly believed in the existence of God and in the validity of natural religion. His justifications of theism relied mainly on the teleological argument from cosmic orderliness. He also maintained that the beliefs in God and immortality are common requirements for the practice of moral goodness, being convinced that social turmoil and immorality would ensue if atheism became widespread. On the other hand, he was of the opinion that it is better to be devoid of religious belief than to pay homage to a God of cruelty and injustice: atheism is preferable to intolerant theism (see the article "Atheism" in his *Philosophical Dictionary*).

Accordingly, he took belief in a just Creator to be more reasonable than disbelief, and he went so far as to declare that confidence in the existence of a wise Creator, eternal and supreme, had its derivation, not in faith, but in reason ("Faith," *Philosophical Dictionary*). If theism has its intellectual difficulties, atheism has its absurdities (see the early sections in his *Treatise on Metaphysics*). The one religion needful simply includes the worship of God and the practice of the good life; the sole necessary gospel is the book of nature written and sealed by the hand of the Creator. Such reasonable religion, enduring and morally fortifying, is incapable of producing evil, but Christian enthusiasm has produced little else; it brings peace, whereas Jesus brought not peace but the sword (see the concluding passages of his work on Bolingbroke, *Examen important de Milord Bolingbroke*, 1767).

The disastrous Lisbon earthquake of 1755 (which Wesley regarded as an act of divine retribution) profoundly shocked Voltaire, and he tended to become more pessimistic. "Lisbonne est abimée, et l'on danse à Paris" ("Lisbon is ruined, and they are dancing in Paris"), he wrote in his poem on the catastrophe; and in his novel *Candide* (1757) he dealt scornfully with the easy optimism born of the Leibnizian doctrine that this is the best of all possible worlds. Nevertheless, he continued to hold that man by nature has a sense of right and wrong, and that God intended justice and harmony to reign in human society. So in his work *The Ignorant Philosopher* (1767) it is argued that the cosmos testifies to the existence of a supreme designing Intelligence: God is the ultimate ground of the outer world of physical things and of the inner world of human thought (sec. 21). The *sine qua non* of true religion is the worship of the Creator; and the abstruse speculations of theological orthodoxy, which are quite unintelligible to common sense, cannot serve any useful purpose in the furtherance of human welfare (sec. 23).

Thus Voltaire was a Deist in the tradition established by Lord Herbert of Cherbury; but it should be borne in mind that, unlike the majority of the English Deists, he did not stress the notion of the divine transcendence so as to make the Creator external to the physical universe. In the work just cited, for example, he wavered between a pantheistic and a more orthodox theistic interpretation, maintaining that we cannot be sure whether God is distinct from nature, or permeates it, as the soul permeates the body it animates (secs. 16–17).

A still more potent philosophical influence than Voltaire was Jean-Jacques Rousseau (1712–78), a very different personality, who although associated with the Enlightenment, exalted feeling above the intellect and thereby prepared the way for the romanticism of the nineteenth century. Of Franco-Swiss descent, he was born into a French refugee family at Geneva. His career was a checkered one; he experienced the misery of direst poverty and knew what it was to ride on the crest of literary fame. Of a mercurial temperament, he was extremely sensitive and inclined to moods of deepest melancholy, and near the end of his life he went mad. Despite his emotionalism, his argumentation, if not always consistent, was generally marked by great lucidity. Like Voltaire, he denounced the injustices of his time and deeply influenced the French Revolution, but he did so in the name, not the reason, but of sentiment, for he revelled in the ecstasies of emotion and brooded incessantly over his own inner reactions to outer events.

Rousseau was brought up in the Reformed church, but in 1728, largely through Madame de Warens, who assisted him financially and educationally and subsequently became his mistress, he turned to Catholicism; the lady herself was a convert from pietistic Lutheranism, and she had quietistic and Deistic sympathies. Rousseau lived with her for about nine years (until 1740). He moved to Paris in 1741, and there he fell in love with a domestic servant who later bore him five children, these being successively consigned to an institution for foundlings. He also made the acquaintance of Denis Diderot, who induced him to write a number of articles for the *Encyclopédie*. But he eventually broke with the circle of the *philosophes*, becoming a bitter opponent of Voltaire and Diderot, among others.

In 1750 appeared his celebrated *Discourse on the Arts and Sciences*, a dissertation that won him a prize from the university at Dijon; in it he argued that the development of cultural disciplines is responsible for man's moral degeneration. After his return to Geneva about four years later, the same kind of thesis was further elaborated in his *Discourse on the Origin and the Foundations of Inequality among Men*, which, like the earlier work, adumbrates a widespread mythological motif in its supposition of a golden age of unspoiled innocence in the distant past, when primitive man lived joyously in the freedom of his immediate instinctive responses. In Rousseau's judgment, it is the pursuit of the arts and sciences that has made man false to his true nature, whence it follows that paradise can be regained only by repudiating intellectualism and returning to the pristine freshness of instinctive living. Ratiocination, which has brought about the division of labor, the segregation of class from class, and the lust for the accumulation of private property, is to be held responsible for the inordinate acquisitiveness that constitutes the bane of modern civilized society.

In 1756 Rousseau moved to Montmorency, and there he produced his most influential works. In the novel *Julia, or the New Heloise* (1760) he denounced the common practice of separating love from marriage and upheld a natural religion, founded upon feeling and rendered consonant with his own interpretation of the gospels. In a second novel *Emile, or on Education*

(1762) he defended a tutorial method of education conducted privately, in isolation from the corrupting influences of society; therein a well-known chapter, "The Confession of Faith of the Savoyard Vicar" sets forth his theological views.

Rousseau's romanticist theology, which stressed personal sentiment and the importance of being true to one's self, pleased neither the ecclesiastical authorities nor the representatives of the Enlightenment. *Emile* was consigned to the flames at the order of the government, and its teachings were repudiated by the *philosophes*. The vicar of Savoyard declares: "The more I strive to prove the infinite being of God, the less I understand it. But I feel he does exist, and that is enough for me. The less I comprehend, the more devoutly I pray. . . . Respect in silence what you can neither reject nor comprehend, and humble yourself before the great Being, who alone knows the truth." Rousseau maintained that natural religion, correctly understood, is not utterly opposed to religions claiming to be founded upon revelation. Thus, with regard to Christianity, he argued (rather after the fashion of Matthew Tindal) that the gospel is in essence a form of natural religion. So the vicar can assert: "There is no religion that exempts one from the duties of morality. . . . In every country and every denomination to love God above all else and one's neighbor as oneself is the first of these duties. . . . A just heart is the veritable temple of divinity."

Accordingly, Rousseau was not opposed to the religion of Jesus as such, but rather to what he considered to be perversions of it, and in this respect he differed from Voltaire. And some scholars have felt that in this connection he was committing the fallacy of the looking-glass, which was to become all too frequent in more recent times, namely, the fallacy of seeing one's own views reflected in a supposedly historical Jesus, and of rejecting as secondary accretions all those features of the gospel portrayals that fail to harmonize with one's own particular standpoint. At any rate, whether or not he was being narcissistic, Rousseau obviously admired the Jesus he found in the gospels. As the vicar is allowed to put it: "Shall we say that the gospel history was freely invented? . . . The gospel contains marks of truth so great . . . the inventor of them would be more extraordinary than the hero. . . . Yes, if the life and death of Socrates were those of a man of wisdom, the life and death of Jesus were those of a god."

Despite his own instability and weakness of will, Rousseau extolled personal responsibility, and so the vicar can confess: "Has not he [God] endowed me with a conscience to love the right, reason to know it, liberty to choose it? If I do wrong I am without excuse; I do it because I desire it. To ask him to change my will is to ask of him what he asks of me—is to wish that he could do my work and that I might get the reward; . . . the supreme wish of my heart is, Thy will be done."

In his work *On the Social Contract* (1763) Rousseau argued that in a well-ordered community, where justice reigns, religious intolerance and dogmatic exclusivism can have no place. His fundamental contention was that, since organized society is ultimately founded upon the consent of the people, government is properly the organ of the general will of the *moi commun*, or communal self of the collective whole. Hence a government has justifiable existence only in so far as it serves the rightful demands of the individual citizens.

Emile was placed on the index in 1762, and the *Social Contract* was denounced both in France and in Geneva. Rousseau found refuge in Neuchâtel and then fled to Strasbourg. In 1766 he was befriended by David Hume, who secured for him a cottage in Derbyshire. But in 1767, obsessed with the fixed idea that he was being persecuted, Rousseau left England, and in the following year he married "according to nature" Thérèse Levasseur, the domestic servant by whom he had previously begotten five children. His voluminous *Confessions* were brought to a conclusion in 1772.

Rousseau's influence was widespread and powerful. In the Revolution his notions concerning the rights of the common man were taken up and applied with passionate ruthlessness, and they came to succinct and dramatic expression in the paradoxical pronouncement of Robespierre to the Jacobins: "Our will is the general will. The government of the revolution is the despotism of liberty against tyranny." In the philosophical domain Rousseau's influence is discernible in Kant's doctrine of the limitations of the understanding, as well as in his thesis that intrinsic value belongs to the good will alone, which, like a jewel, shines by its own light. In his emphasis on feeling Rousseau also foreshadowed the romanticist theology of Schleiermacher and his successors, while his idealization of the collective whole, endowed with an inscrutable faculty for right judgment, is reflected in the Hegelian concept of the ethos of a people as the truthful embodiment of its developing national consciousness.

As early as the mid-seventeenth century Cartesianism was studied in Germany, but it was largely through the mediation of Gottfried Wilhelm Leibniz (1646–1716), philosopher and mathematician, that rationalism came to prevail in academic circles there. Leibniz worked out his ideas within the cadre of Cartesianism, but he transformed the metaphysical dualism into a panpsychist pluralism, according to which the universe constitutes a system of spiritual entities (monads) in various stages of development. He also formulated an important epistemological distinction between the necessary truths of reason and the contingent truths of fact.

Leibnizianism found a competent apologist and exponent in Christian Wolff (1679–1754), who became a professor of mathematics and natural science at Halle in 1706. He was something of a syncretist, and he systematized the doctrines of Leibniz, seeking to apply them to all departments of life, practical as well as theoretical. He wrote prolifically, and his numerous works rapidly became popular; but his rationalism was disliked by the Pietists at Halle, and they engineered his ejection from the university in 1723. He secured a post at Marburg; however, in 1740, soon after the accession of Frederick the Great, he was recalled to Halle, where he remained for the rest of his career. His writings were now being eagerly studied in the German universities, and Kant, who inaugurated a new era in Western philosophy, was deeply affected by them in his earlier years.

According to Wolff, the criteria of truth are clearness, distinctness, and reasonableness. The realm of possibility includes all that is not self-contradictory, while the realm of actuality includes everything for whose existence there is a clear and sufficient reason. Wolff's work on natural theology (*Theologia Naturalis*, 2 vols.) was published in 1736–37. He maintained that God is the totality of compossibles (that is, of all realities that can exist together), relying on the argument that, being superlatively perfect, the unconditioned Ground of finite existence can lack nothing. The traditional notion of miracle did not harmonize very well with Wolff's form of rationalism, but he refrained from explicitly denying that divine interventions in the natural order can actually take place. On the other hand, he repudiated the doctrine of eternal damnation and maintained that the scriptures could not disclose anything contrary to reason. He thought of divine revelation as being general rather than special, and held that man was originally endowed with intellectual capacities so that reason might guide him along the way of individual and social progress. The advance to human fulfillment, not miraculous deliverance from a supposed original sin, is the true concern of all enlightened religion.

A German rendering of Tindal's work *Christianity as Old as Creation* appeared in 1741, and this was followed by other published translations of English philosophical treatises; also, of course, French influence was widely felt. The result was that representatives of the *Aufklärung* (as the Enlightenment was styled in Germany) tended to combine deistic doctrines in one way or another with the principles of Wolffian rationalism. As already observed, the movement was promoted through the generous patronage of Frederick the Great; and to some extent rationalism affected Catholicism, partly through the support of

Joseph II. Among the outstanding exponents of German Deism were Hermann Samuel Reimarus (1694–1768) and Gotthold Ephraim Lessing (1729–81).

Reimarus was born at Hamburg and studied under Johannes Albertus Fabricius (1668–1736), a Lutheran classical scholar and bibliographer, whose daughter he eventually married. He went on to the university at Jena, and subsequently taught at Wittenberg and Wismar. From 1727 he was professor of Hebrew and oriental languages at Hamburg. He had traveled in England as a young man, adopting Deism during his stay there. His published works included *Abhandlungen von den vornehmsten Wahrheiten der natürlichen Religion* ("Studies of the Supreme Truths of Natural Religion," 1754) and *Die Vernunftlehre* ("The Doctrine of Reason," 1756). In these works he defended natural religion against atheism and materialism, holding that there is but one miracle and one revelation, namely, the world of nature itself, of which humanity is an integral part.

Reimarus addressed himself to vigorous polemic against revealed religion, especially Christianity, in his *Apologie oder Schutzschrift für die vernünftigen Verehrer Gottes* ("Apology or Defense for the Reasonable Worshipers of God"). His general thesis was really a variation on the deistic theme that, in particular revealed religions, universal natural religion has been corrupted through the machinations of evil-minded priests. Reimarus contended that the writers of the books of the Bible were fanatics who deliberately sought to deceive their readers. But he prudently withheld the manuscript from publication, and after his death it went to the library of Wolfenbüttel, near Brunswick. Lessing examined the work, and in 1774–78 he edited and published seven extracts from it as *Wolfenbüttel Fragments*. In the seventh extract, concerning the purpose of Jesus, Reimarus argued that the birth of Christianity is to be understood in terms of eschatology, the mission of Jesus being governed by the conviction that the end of the world was perilously imminent.

The manuscript—a long one, which occupied Reimarus for many years—has never been published in its entirety. David Friedrich Strauss gave an account of the whole argument in his book on Reimarus (1862), and Albert Schweitzer devoted a chapter to it in his widely-read work *Von Reimarus zu Wrede: Eine Geschichte der Leben-Jesu-Forschung* (1906)—the English translation, *The Quest of the Historical Jesus,* appeared in 1910—in which a modified eschatological interpretation of the mission of Jesus is presented.

Lessing, the son of a Lutheran minister, was born in 1729 at Kamenz, Oberlausitz, and studied at the university in Leipzig. His father hoped that he would pursue theology and enter the ministry, but he turned with remarkable success to art and dramatic criticism and distinguished himself in the writing of plays. His *Laocöon,* an important contribution to aesthetics, appeared in 1769, and his *Hamburgische Dramaturgie* in 1767–69, while he was holding a position in connection with the theater at Hamburg.

In 1770 he was appointed librarian at Wolfenbüttel, and his main interest switched to theologico-philosophical questions. During his first year of office he discovered an incomplete manuscript of Berengar's work on the eucharist, *De Sacra Coena,* which was not published until 1834. In a treatise on gospel criticism, *A New Hypothesis on the Evangelists, Considered as Purely Human Writers of History,* he argued that St. Matthew's gospel is based on an Aramaic original that was known to the other synoptists; this work was published posthumously. As we have seen, in 1774–78 he edited and issued the *Wolfenbüttel Fragments.*

The publication of the *Fragments* caused a great stir, and Lessing was at the center of the ensuing controversy. His ideas developed, and in 1779 appeared his influential dramatic poem *Nathan the Wise,* in which a Jew, a Christian, and a Moslem are assigned the principal roles. The hero of the drama is Nathan, a benevolent Jew who embodies Lessing's religious ideal, and it is instructive to compare him with the Savoyard vicar of Rousseau's *Emile*. Nathan exemplifies a spirit of tolerance and good will, which puts him on a higher plane than the Christian and the Moslem. He is taken to represent the true essence of Christianity, and indeed of all religion, in the enlightened magnanimity of his generous heart.

In 1780 appeared Lessing's most significant theologico-philosophical treatise, *Die Erziehung des Menschengeschlechts* ("The Education of the Human Race"), which had a determining effect upon the subsequent course of Protestant liberalism in Germany and elsewhere. He distinguished the eternal and ideal essense of religion from its manifestations in the actual religions of history. While agreeing with Reimarus that the latter are limited and imperfect, he did not condemn them outright, regarding them as necessary stages in the evolution of humanity. So far as they go, they have performed valuable services in the areas where they originated and developed. There is a perfection in the bud and a perfection in the flower. The truths contained in positive religions may be entangled with elements of immorality and superstition, and yet the fact remains that they do, to a greater or lesser extent, contain elements of truth.

Thus Lessing disagreed with all who hold that their particular mode of traditional faith is the final religion and thereby incorporates the absolute truth; he contended that theological dogmas have always been limited and conditioned by the historical circumstances in which they were enunciated. From one point of view, what really matters is not dogmas and credal formulations but the exemplification of love and generosity in thought and conduct. From another point of view, there is always a rift between the ideal, which is universal, and the actual, which is particular; the latter can never adequately embody the former.

Nevertheless, the actual can represent the ideal in varying degrees; hence Lessing was led to introduce the concept of evolution into religious philosophy, and he assigned perfection to the end of history. For him, salvation does not consist in the regaining of a paradise that has been lost; it consists in the attainment of an ideal which has so far never been actualized. The perfect is not at both the termini of the world-process, but only at the prospective end, after which human beings are aspiring. In this respect Lessing broke with traditional Christian doctrine and with deistic orthodoxy. History has had no original Eden of bliss; primitive man was really a savage, uncouth and unenlightened, and perfected nobility belongs to the human future.

It was in the light of such ideas that Lessing interpreted human history in terms of education, arguing that the development of the human race is analogous to the development of the individual from childhood through adolescence to adulthood. To condemn biblical religion for its failure to reflect all the ideas and standards of a later age is rather like condemning children because of their incapacity to grasp the principles of the infinitesimal calculus. It betrays a lack of historical sense, an inability to appreciate that different factors are appropriate to different ages and epochs. On the other hand, to argue that an earlier religious mode is identical with a later one, or to claim that finality has been achieved in the past, is to refuse to face reality. Historical circumstances are subject to continuous change, and revelation is properly progressive, each generation benefiting by its predecessors. If Jesus had lived in modern times, he would not have been the Jesus who lived in the first century.

Lessing therefore represented God as the divine Educator, the universal Pedagogue who is ever revealing truths suitable to the developing capacities of man. A child is educated through promises of immediate rewards or threats of immediate punishments; in the same way the Hebrews of the Old Testament were trained in elementary ethics and theology through promises of earthly prosperity or threats of earthly adversity. Again, a youth will sacrifice immediate pleasures for the sake of rewards in a relatively distant future, as when he engages in ardu-

ous studies to qualify for a profession; in the same way the
Christians of the New Testament were taught to practice virtue, even to the extent of surrendering all worldly goods,
through promises of treasures in heaven or threats of torments
in Gehenna. Furthermore, a mature scholar pursues his studies
not because he hopes for some external benefit from them, but
because he finds intrinsic value in his scholarly activities; in the
same way men generally may one day be able to dispense with
the notion of external sanctions in their religion, recognizing,
as Spinoza did, that virtue is its own reward.

Accordingly, in Lessing's view, the beliefs of any particular
age can never be final, but rather they represent a stage in the
education of the human race. Man is essentially *homo viator*,
ever on the way; he is so constituted as to strive for the ideal,
not to possess it wholly. So Lessing could make the dramatic
confession that if God were to offer him complete truth with
one hand and the pursuit of it with the other, he would choose
the latter.

BIBLIOGRAPHY

Berlin, Isaiah, ed. *The Age of Enlightenment.* Boston: Houghton
Mifflin, 1956.
Cassirer, E. *The Philosophy of the Enlightenment.* Princeton, N.J.:
Princeton University Press, 1951.
Clive, Geoffrey. *The Romantic Enlightenment.* New York: Mer-
idian Books, 1960.
Cragg, G. R. *Reason and Authority in the Eighteenth Century.*
Cambridge: Cambridge University Press, 1964.
Lacroix, Jean. *Spinoza et le problème du salut.* Paris: Presses Uni-
versitaires de France, 1970.
Manuel, F. E. *The Eighteenth Century Confronts the Gods.* Cam-
bridge, Mass.: Harvard University Press, 1959.

35 ‡ Catholic Trends

Under Henry IV, by the Edict of Nantes (1598), the Huguenots were allowed rights of worship and were made eligible for public office, though with certain restrictions. During the seventeenth century, however, their situation deteriorated, and they encountered increasing opposition from the Jesuits, the most effective arm of the Counter-Reformation. After his marriage to Madame de Maintenon (1684), Louis XIV (1643–1715) revoked the Edict of Nantes in 1685, and severe persecuting measures were applied against Protestantism. Thousands of Huguenots fled to Holland, Prussia, England, North America, and elsewhere. It was not until 1787, under Louis XVI (1774–89), that toleration was restored, and two years later the Revolution began. During the reign of Louis XV (1715–74) the Jesuits rose to the height of their power and influence, but they suffered dramatic reversals of fortune between 1759 and 1773.

Louis XIV believed in absolute monarchy and sought to bring French Catholicism under his direct control. In 1682 he persuaded the clergy to subscribe to the four so-called Gallican Articles, which were drawn up by Jacques Bénigne Bossuet (1627–1704), one of the greatest pulpit orators in history and the bishop of Meaux from 1681. The first of the Articles repudiated the temporal authority of the papacy and affirmed the autonomy of kings in all civil affairs; the second endorsed the ruling of the Council of Constance (1414–18) that ecumenical councils are superior to the papacy; the third asserted that ancient Gallic ecclesiastical usages limit the scope of papal jurisdiction; and the fourth affirmed that no papal judgment can be regarded as unrevisable. Thus the Gallican Articles reflected the basic ideology of the conciliar movement, and although they were nullified in 1693, they exemplified a certain independence of spirit that has continued to characterize French Catholicism up to the present day.

Two further developments of the seventeenth century that militated against the orthodoxy of the Counter-Reformation were Quietism and Jansenism. Quietism, which stresses the importance of passivity in the attainment of union with God, is frequently a feature of mystical disciplines, but the prominent Spanish confessor and spiritual director Miguel de Molinos (*c.* 1640–97) made it central in his teaching. Molinos was born near Saragossa, and after his theological education he went to Rome (1663), where he won respect in high places. His *Spiritual Guide* appeared in 1675, and certain Jesuits and Dominicans soon accused him of heresy, but without effect. In his subsequent correspondence the method of passivity came to receive increasing emphasis, and he maintained that, to reach a religious state of complete perfection, all specific ideas and projects must be eliminated. External observances were adjudged to be distractions, and even the exercise of volition in efforts to resist temptation was frowned upon. Those who are perfected in mystical union with God cannot commit sin, although it may sometimes seem to the ordinary believer that they do so; for in the continuous ecstasy of oneness with the Divine, the finite capacity for decision no longer exists.

It is not surprising that people under the spiritual direction of Molinos became neglectful in their outward religious life: monastics ceased to recite their office, refused to report for confession, and so on. Feelings against him grew, and in 1685 he was arrested. Two years later Pope Innocent XI (1676–89) condemned sixty-eight of his theses. Molinos recanted but was nevertheless sentenced to life imprisonment on charges of immorality; he maintained remarkable composure to the end of his days, and it is not easy to deny his personal sincerity.

Quietism became a subject of controversy in France through the activities of Madame Guyon (1648–1717). Her marriage was an unhappy one, and after her husband's death (1676) she devoted herself entirely to the mystical life and came under the spell of Molinos' teaching. In 1681, together with her confessor, Francois Lacombe (1643–1715), she undertook a missionary journey to disseminate her ideas throughout the country. Six years later they were both charged with heresy and immorality and were incarcerated, but through Madame de Maintenon's intervention Guyon was liberated, and she went on to achieve prominence at the royal court. Lacombe, on the other hand, did not obtain his release until 1699.

François Fénelon (1651–1715), appointed tutor of the Duke of Burgundy in 1689 and archbishop of Cambrai in 1695, became sympathetically disposed to Madame Guyon's quietistic mysticism and entered into correspondence with her. Bossuet, however, considered her doctrines dangerous, and in 1694 he served her with a dogmatic epistle. Intensely annoyed by such an action, she promptly demanded that her case be officially examined. A theological commission duly met in 1695 and, contrary to the plaintiff's confident expectation, found her guilty of heresy; she was imprisoned and was not released until 1702, when she recanted. Despite his subscription to the verdict of condemnation, Fénelon (who had been assigned a seat on the examining board) continued to give Quietism his qualified support, and the publication of his *Explication des maximes des saints* ("Explanation of the Maxims of the Saints," 1697) marked the beginning of an acrimonious controversy with Bossuet, which culminated in the censoring of the book in 1699.

The originator of the Jansenist movement was Cornelius Otto Jansen (1585–1638), who studied at Louvain, Paris, and Bayonne. He became the director of a college at Louvain in 1617, and the bishop of Ypres in 1636. He was strongly opposed to the new scholasticism of the Counter-Reformation and found a strong supporter of his views in Abbé de Saint-Cyran, Jean Duvergier (1581–1643), a friend of his student years. He began to write *Augustinus*, his magnum opus, in 1628, but its publication did not take place until 1640. This treatise, which was based on the anti-Pelagian writings of Augustine, came to constitute the doctrinal manual of Jansenism. It was condemned as heretical in 1642 by Urban VIII (1623–44), the pope who had assailed the astronomy of Galileo in 1633.

Through Saint-Cyran's activity, however, Jansen's doctrines continued to spread, and what proved especially eventful was the winning over of the Cistercian convent of Port-Royal. After Saint-Cyran's death the leadership was assumed by Antoine Arnauld (1612–94), who in four publications defended Augustine's conception of irresistible grace, stressed the importance of rigorous ecclesiastical discipline, and denounced the laxity of Jesuit moral probabilism. He was censured by the Sorbonne in 1656, and this prompted Blaise Pascal's attack on the Jesuits in his famous *Provincial Letters* (1656–57), which numbered eighteen in all.

In 1653 Pope Innocent X had declared five Jansenist theses to be heretical, an action resulting in the lodging of a complaint that the propositions in question were *de facto* not Jansenist. The plea was disallowed in 1656 by Pope Alexander VII, and in 1668 an uneasy compromise was concluded. The movement persisted, showing a singular resilience, and in 1693 Pasquier Quesnel (1634–1719) published his *Moral Reflections on the New Testament*, a work that quickly aroused a fresh outburst of Jesuit hostility. At length in 1713 Pope Clement XI formally repudiated a hundred and one of Quesnel's theses in the bull *Unigenitus* (1713). A number of Jansenists, who were inclined to Gallicanism, vainly made an appeal against the papal verdict to a prospective ecumenical council.

In France the Jansenists had now become a persecuted body,

and many found refuge in Holland. In 1723 the Dutch Jansenists nominated a schismatic bishop, and this led to the foundation of the Jansenist Catholic church, with an archbishop at Utrecht and episcopal sees at Haarlem and Deventer.

The most distinguished thinker associated with Jansenism was Blaise Pascal (1623–62), a physicist and mathematician as well as a theologian. He first became acquainted with Jansenism in 1646, and he entered into communication with Port-Royal. But an inner struggle soon began to torment him: he was drawn to the movement, and yet the idea of joining it repelled him. In 1651 his father died, whereupon his sister, Jacqueline, decided that she ought to take the veil and enter Port-Royal. Pascal, who did his utmost to prevent her from making such a move, went on with his scientific research and continued to enjoy the pleasures of polite society. In 1654, however, his resistance broke down, and the inner conflict was resolved. He passed through a transforming religious experience, in which, as he put it, he personally discovered the God of Abraham, Isaac, and Jacob, as opposed to the God of philosophers and scientists—a distinction that was destined to play a significant role in the formation of the existentialism of Søren Kierkegaard (1813–55).

In the following year Pascal withdrew from the world and lived as a solitary in the vicinity of Port-Royal, about twenty miles southwest of Paris. He practiced severe austerities, and in 1658 his health began to be seriously impaired. As we have seen, Arnauld's condemnation by the Sorbonne prompted Pascal's polemic against the Jesuits in his *Provincial Letters*, which, besides revealing their author as a master of the French language, exercised an important influence on the subsequent course of Jansenism; they were placed on the index in 1667.

Pascal's *Pensées* ("Thoughts"), occasional reflections on the meaning of human existence, constitute a literary and philosophical classic. Their author may have started to write them immediately after his liberating experience of conversion; the first edition, very incomplete, was published in 1670. Although unsystematic, the *Pensées* are not without a governing purpose: they were evidently meant to justify the theism of Christianity against materialism and rationalistic scepticism.

Pascal was deeply aware of the tragic paradox of human existence. On the one hand, man is of dust, earthy, and his life is precariously poised between the hazards of birth and death; on the other hand, man is endowed with mental and spiritual qualities that render him capable of transcendent nobility. Confronted by the pathos of such a situation, Pascal maintained that one should take the risk of trusting in God, a gamble that alone could save human beings from despondency and strengthen them for the fulfillment of their spiritual destiny. He further maintained that, as an object of faith, God cannot be comprehended by the intellect. He is known in the intimacy of feeling, for "the heart has its reasons, of which reason knows nothing." Thus Pascal foreshadowed the theological romanticism of Rousseau and his successors in Germany and elsewhere.

So far as the Jesuits are concerned, by the middle of the eighteenth century they were encountering increasing opposition from representatives of the Enlightenment. Their first major reverse came in Portugal. The Marquis de Pombal (1699–1782), the influential minister of King Joseph, had rationalistic sympathies and, in 1759, when the Jesuits (who wanted free trade) resisted his policy in Paraguay, he promptly ordered their deportation. French hostility was aroused by Jesuit commercial activity in Martinique, and the Order was banished from French territories in 1764. Three years later the Jesuits were expelled from Spain and Naples. After hesitating for a time Pope Clement XIV (1769–74) surrendered to French and Spanish pressure, and he formally suppressed the Order in 1773; but Jesuits continued to operate in certain non-Catholic countries—in Prussia (until 1780), for example, as well as in Russia.

With the storming of the Bastille in 1789 the French Revolution began, and the church was quickly deprived of its lands.

The civil constitution of the clergy, established in the following year, was intended to exclude papal interference in French affairs, and it was ruled that the appointment of bishops and parish priests be subject to the approval of the civil electorate. The majority of the clergy, following the instructions of Pope Pius VI (1775–99), refused to swear to the new constitution, and their position remained precarious for the next five years.

The concordat of 1801, concluded between Napoleon and Pope Pius VII (1800–1823), substituted the nonjuring exiles for the constitutionalists, the government recognizing that most of the French people were Catholic. The church surrendered all confiscated properties that had been assigned to private owners, while those confiscated properties still in the hands of the government were to be restored. The state agreed to supply adequate maintenance to bishops and parish priests; the former were to be appointed by the pope on state nomination, and the latter by bishops, though the state had the right to veto.

Gallicanism came to yet more powerful expression in the Organic Articles, promulgated by Napoleon in 1802. These asserted the state's control over the meeting of synods and the publication of papal decrees, and *inter alia* they required that a study of the Gallican Articles be included in the curricula of the Catholic seminaries. The papacy objected, and in fact the ordinances were not strictly enforced for long; but they remained on the statute book until 1905, when the separation of church and state in France finally took place.

The excesses of the Revolution and the imperious conduct of Napoleon had the effect of bringing Gallicanism into much discredit, and after the French defeat at Waterloo in 1815 a powerful reaction in favor of Ultramontanism quickly developed. The medieval Latin term *ultramontanus*, which was used of dwellers "beyond the mountains"—more specifically, "beyond the Alps"—had, in northern Europe, come to refer to those who advocated a pro-Italian ecclesiastical policy, favoring the centralization of administrative competence in the papacy.

And much more was involved than matters of church government pure and simple. In accordance with the spirit of the Counter-Reformation, reinforced by the climate of Catholic opinion after Napoleon's downfall, the Ultramontanists of the nineteenth century contended that only an absolute papal authority could provide a sure bulwark of integral Christianity amid the encroaching liberal and disruptive forces of modern secularized society.

The first significant expression of the resurgent spirit of Ultramontanism lay in the reconstitution of the Jesuits in 1814, and this was followed in succeeding decades by several papal declarations assailing various tendencies and movements of the time. These were summed up in the *Syllabus Errorum* ("The Syllabus of Errors"), issued in 1864 by Pope Pius IX (1846–78). The *Syllabus* took cognizance of eighty theses held to be erroneous or incompatible with true religion. The matters condemned included: the separation of church and state, secret associations, nonsectarian educational institutions, Bible societies, the toleration of varieties of religion, pantheism, naturalism, latitudinarianism, socialism, and communism. The tenor of the whole document may be discerned in the last of the theses to be denounced, namely, that the papacy ought to be reconciled with, and adjusted to, progress, liberalism, and modern civilization.

The *Syllabus* rapidly became the doctrinal basis of Ultramontanism, and at the Vatican Council of 1870 its main principles were largely embodied in the dogmatic statement *Dei Filius*. At the same council the Ultramontanes gained a further victory in the approval (by a vote of 533 to 2) of a declaration of the pope's infallibility when he speaks *ex cathedra* on matters touching faith and morals. However, since the declaration did not include an assertion of the infallibility of the central *curia* (the papal offices of administration), it can hardly be said to have represented a complete triumph for Ultramontanism. Also, a logical difficulty was involved, for if ecumenical councils are not themselves infallible, how can any such council issue a necessarily true statement concerning the inerrancy either of itself or of any other agency?

The opposition to the declaration of papal infallibility, which was stronger than the voting would suggest, led to the foundation of the Old Catholic churches in Germany, Austria and Switzerland, episcopal ordination being eventually obtained from the Jansenist church in Holland.

Despite the dominance of Ultramontanism in the later decades of the nineteenth century, liberal tendencies continued to operate within Catholicism, and severe repressive measures against so-called modernist teaching were taken during the years 1907–10.

BIBLIOGRAPHY

Adam, K. *The Spirit of Catholicism*. New York: Sheed and Ward, 1929.

Chadwick, W. O. *From Bossuet to Newman*. Cambridge: Cambridge University Press, 1957.

Phillips, C. S. *The Church in France, 1789–1848*. London: Mowbray, 1929.

———. *The Church in France, 1848–1907*. London: Society for Promoting Christian Knowledge, 1936.

Stewart, H. F. *The Secret of Pascal*. Cambridge: Cambridge University Press, 1941.

Webb, C. C. J. *Pascal's Philosophy of Religion*. Oxford: Clarendon Press, 1929.

36 ‡ American Developments

Christianity in North America is predominantly Protestant, but it is marked by great diversity. There are more than 250 denominations in the United States alone, and while the vast majority are small, the variety betrays something of the vitality involved in the country's religious life and the heterogeneous character of the immigration. On the other hand, in Central and South America Christianity is characterized by a basic uniformity of type. In these regions immigration from Iberia predominated, and evangelization took place almost exclusively through the activities of the great mendicant orders, frequently with the support of the Spanish government. Franciscans were in Venezuela by 1508, Dominicans in Mexico by 1526, Jesuits in Brazil by 1549. There was also Catholic activity in the North. The same three orders had appeared in Florida by 1568; Franciscans were in New Mexico by 1597, in Texas by 1700, and in California from 1769; Jesuits moved into Canada in 1611.

Of the English colonies only Maryland had a Catholic foundation, being chartered to Lord Baltimore in 1632. But it became a royal colony in 1691, and Anglicanism was legally established eleven years later. Catholicism within the colony lay under the general supervision of a vicar apostolic in London, and it was not until 1790 that a bishopric was founded, at Baltimore; this became an archbishopric in 1808. It is estimated that around this time there were scarcely a hundred priests working in the United States, but in the course of the nineteenth century Catholicism grew at a remarkable rate, partly through Irish, Italian, and south German immigration, and partly through the incorporation into the Union of Latinized areas, like Louisiana, New Mexico, and California.

Anglicanism existed in Virginia from 1607; many of the clergy, not always of the best caliber, were drawn from England up to 1776. Southern colonies also generally had Anglican establishments, but Nonconformists were allowed, and among these Baptists and Methodists were to figure prominently. New York (then New Amsterdam) became a Dutch trading colony in 1624, and a Reformed (Calvinistic) church was founded there. However, the English captured the colony in 1664, and introduced Anglicanism; Trinity Church, on Broadway at Wall Street, was founded in 1697. Pennsylvania was granted to William Penn in 1681 as a sanctuary for Quakers. The influence of the Quakers has always far exceeded their numbers, and since they repudiated coercion in religion, people of various other persuasions—Presbyterians, Mennonites, Moravians, Lutherans, and so on—found refuge in the territory.

The New England colonies were destined to make the most enduring impression on the American tradition. In this region the colonies were founded by English Puritans and Separatists, and on the whole the leadership was competent. Many of the clergy were Cambridge graduates who had crossed the ocean because of their dissatisfaction with the religious status quo in England. Harvard College was established in 1636 to ensure the perpetuation of an educated ministry, and Yale College opened its doors in 1701. The motives behind the creation of the institution that was to become Harvard University are thus described in *New England's First Fruits*, a work published in London (1643) on behalf of the colonists, to promote a positive interest in their achievements:

After God had carried us safe to New England, and we had builded our houses, provided necessaries for our livelihood, reared convenient places for God's worship, and settled the civil government, one of the next things we longed for and looked after was to advance learning and perpetuate it to posterity, dreading to leave an illiterate ministry to our churches, when our present ministers shall lie in the dust.

A foundation (in the form of a library) had been bequeathed by John Harvard, minister of the settlement at Charlestown.

The Pilgrim Fathers, who settled at Plymouth in 1620, were Calvinist in general theology but Independent (Congregationalist) in ecclesiastical polity; that is, they were Brownists. But those who settled in the Boston area were Anglicans of the Puritan party and had not actually broken with the establishment in England. Nevertheless, they began to ordain their own ministers in 1629, and they quickly came to adopt the Congregationalist polity of the settlers at Plymouth. However, the Independency of the New England settlements did not involve the separation of church and state, and in this respect it was not so thoroughgoing in its Brownism as the Congregationalism that developed in the home country. All civic rights were derived from church membership, and until near the end of the seventeenth century no other form of Christianity was tolerated; in Massachusetts, for example, freedom for Protestants generally was first permitted in 1691. In three of the states Congregationalism remained legally established, the ministers being paid out of general taxation, until the early nineteenth century.

The situation was different in the colony of Rhode Island. This was owing to the work of Roger Williams (*c.* 1604–83), a Cambridge graduate in Anglican orders, who in 1630 sailed for Boston in a search for religious liberty. He was dismayed at the intolerance he found there, for after opening a nonconformist church in the area, he received official instructions to leave Massachusetts forthwith (1635). He made friends with the neighboring Indians and in the following year founded the Rhode Island settlement of Providence; in 1639 he established what was evidently the first Baptist church on the American continent. While visiting England to obtain a charter for the new colony, he published anonymously a booklet entitled *The Bloody Tenent of Persecution* (1644), which argues strongly for religious freedom. In 1656 the immigration of Quakers began, and by 1661 four of them had been hanged in Boston. Williams, however, permitted Quakers to settle in Rhode Island, although he personally disapproved of their teaching.

The eighteenth century was marked by the Great Awakening, a significant religious revival, and by the diffusion, in the later decades, of rationalism, which manifested itself in the Deism of the fathers of the federal constitution and in the rise of Unitarianism. The Awakening was brought about largely through the preaching of George Whitefield (1714–70), the associate of the Wesleys who visited America on seven occasions, and Jonathan Edwards (1703–58). Emotional excitement spread, and those who could not claim to have passed through a cataclysmic experience of sudden conversion were liable to be condemned as heathens. So much commotion was engendered that in 1742 the General Court of Massachusetts put a ban on traveling preachers, save where they operated with the permission of the local clergy. Fervor was at its height during the years 1740–43.

Like Whitefield, Edwards was a strict Calvinist who believed in double election but was opposed to excessive emotional excitement in religion—as is shown in his *Treatise Concerning Religious Affections* (1746). In his adolescence he had shown a keen interest in philosophy, reading Locke's *Essay* when he was fourteen. He graduated from Yale in 1720 and, after an experience of conversion, he was ordained as minister of the congregation at Northampton, Massachusetts, in 1727. He resisted Arminian tendencies, defending stringent Calvinism with much acuteness. Religious revival attended his preaching in 1734, and on a grander scale (through the reinforcement of Whitefield's mission) in 1740.

Edwards' rigorism came to expression in his proposal to

exclude "unconverted" Christians from celebrations of the Lord's supper; the plan met with strong opposition, however, and this led to his leaving the pastorate at Northampton in 1749. He moved to Stockbridge, where he engaged in missionary work among the Indians and wrote a number of treatises which greatly enhanced his reputation as a philosopher and theologian. In his *Inquiry into the Modern Prevailing Notions Respecting that Feedom of the Will which is Supposed to be Essential to Moral Agency* (1754) he upheld the theory of divine election in its extreme form, contending that the moral freedom to turn to God is a divine gift. During the last year of his life he was president of Princeton College, an institution that had been founded in 1746, mainly by Presbyterians sympathetically disposed toward the Great Awakening. Harvard and Yale had both come to regard revivalism with a certain disfavor.

Edwards' mode of Calvinism (in which there was a Platonic strain) continued to be defended in New England by several of his followers, among whom was his son and namesake, Jonathan (1745–1801). But the latter's work *The Necessity of the Atonement and its Consistency with Free Grace in Forgiveness* (1785) showed some willingness to make limited concessions to Arminianism and to Universalism, He argued that Christ died for all men, not for the elect only, adopting a form of Grotius' governmental theory of the atonement: Christ's death was a sacrificial tribute to justice rather than a penal satisfaction for human sins. This version of Grotianism came to be known as "The New England Theory of the Atonement" and was widely accepted in theological circles of the northeastern United States for the next fifty years or more.

In the later decades of the eighteenth century many political leaders—Thomas Jefferson, for example—were deeply influenced by the rationalism of the European Enlightenment. As pointed out in earlier chapters, rationalist exponents of Deism were frequently opposed to the notion of special revelation, an idea historically associated with so-called positive faiths, and advocated the cultivation of a supposedly simple religion of nature, which they took to be universal in principle and perfectly rational. Such pure religion consisted fundamentally in the worship of God, the just and wise Creator, and in the practice of virtue. Thinkers like Voltaire wished to transcend sectarianism and to bring men back to the one religion of all enlightened responsible beings, a form of devotion purged of sacerdotal superstition and destructive bigotry, which would put an end to interreligious strife and restore peace and harmony among all peoples.

The same kind of cosmopolitanism, with its emphasis on the basic oneness of humanity, came to political expression in the Declaration of Independence (1776) and in the Constitution of the new Federal Republic (1789). The existence of God, the just and benevolent Creator, was taken for granted, and men were assumed to be so constituted that if justice were realized, peace and happiness would be attained in the present life. From the higher standpoint of the theology of the Enlightenment, the Constitution looked with a certain disdain on the vulgar rivalries of religious particularism, and it formally enjoined the separation of church and state: no subscription to any specific creed was to be required of candidates for federal office, and no specific form of religion was to be officially sponsored. Evidently, the framers of the Constitution failed to see that they themselves were commending a particular historical or man-made religion, namely, a recognizable form of the rationalistic Deism of the Enlightenment.

Although avowedly antisectarian, the rationalism in question led to the formation of groups in sympathy with it; and since human associations do not function efficiently without organization, the way was prepared, paradoxically enough, for the creation of more denominations, namely, Universalism and Unitarianism. A similar kind of development took place in England, where Joseph Priestley (1733–1804), a Presbyterian minister, did much to promote the cause of latitudinarian or liberal theology. Besides being learned in divinity, he showed singular competence in the field of natural science, becoming renowned for his discovery of oxygen in 1774. Early in his career he adopted an Arian christology, but he later renounced it in favor of Socinianism and was eventually appointed to the teaching staff of Manchester College, a Nonconformist liberal institution, founded in 1786 (and transferred to Oxford in 1889). He rejected the doctrine of original sin along with satisfaction theories of the atonement, and his Unitarianism found signal expression in his *Appeal to the Serious and Candid Professors of Christianity* (1770).

Priestley supported the American struggle for independence, and in his *Letters to Burke* (1791) he defended the ideals behind the French Revolution. In 1794 he settled in Pennsylvania, where he began to expound a revised version of Origen's universalist theory that all men will finally attain salvation. Richard Price (1723–91), a Nonconformist minister and a close friend of Priestley, also moved to a Unitarian position and vigorously supported the French and American revolutions. In 1791, together with Priestley and others, he became a founding member of the Unitarian Society. Some years earlier Theophilus Lindsey (1723–1808) had seceded from Anglicanism and opened a Unitarian church in the Strand, London (1774). Unitarianism in England, then, was organized as a separate denomination, and this development doubtless had its effect on the course of events which led to the formation of the American Unitarian Association in 1825.

The separate organization of American Universalists had occurred earlier—mainly through the efforts of John Murray (1741–1815), who strongly opposed George Whitefield for his defense of the Calvinistic doctrine of double election. Murray traveled to New England in 1770 (the year of Whitefield's death at Newburyport), and on his preaching campaigns he proclaimed that Christ had died for the sins of human beings and that all would eventually win salvation. Independently of Murray, Elhanan Winchester (1751–97), a Baptist minister, promoted similar ideas in Philadelphia, and in 1790 a Universalist convention was held there. Three years later another convention met in New Hampshire, and a creed was accepted which became the doctrinal basis of organized Universalism. Through the influence of Hosea Ballou (1771–1855), an Arian who defended a moral-influence interpretation of the atonement, the theology of the Universalists tended to move towards Unitarianism.

After the Declaration of Independence in 1776, deistic liberalism gathered strength, especially in the Boston area, and nine years later all references to the Trinity in the Prayer Book were eliminated at King's Chapel, the Anglican congregation there becoming the first Unitarian Church in America. Latitudinarian theology continued to spread, and the election of Henry Ware (1764–1845) to the Hollis Chair of Divinity at Harvard in 1805 represented a notable liberal victory. Two years earlier William Ellery Channing (1780–1842) had begun his influential ministry in Boston.

Channing graduated from Harvard in 1798, and in 1803 he became minister of the Congregational Church in Federal Street. His christology was Arian, and he severely criticized the traditional doctrines of original sin, the Trinity, and the atonement as a satisfaction for sin. A sermon he preached during an induction service at Baltimore in 1819 came to be regarded among American Unitarians as a classic statement of the basic principles of liberal Christianity. In the spirit of the Enlightenment, Channing condemned sectarianism and thought of himself as belonging to a community of emancipated minds.

Antitrinitarianism won over majorities in many of the oldest Congregational churches of New England, and it was these communities that came together to form the American Unitarian Association in 1825. During the nineteenth century several men of much eminence were Antitrinitarians, mostly connected with Harvard University. Among these was Ralph

Waldo Emerson (1803–82), minister, philosopher, essayist, and poet, whose so-called Transcendentalism, and, more specifically, whose address to the Harvard Divinity School in 1838, with its generous sympathies and haunting mysticism, made a deep impression on the liberal churches.

Despite its stress on simplicity and cosmopolitanism, however, deistic teaching evidently had a limited appeal, and during 1790–1800 there were fresh outbreaks of evangelical fervor in New England and the middle states, as well as in the South; and revivalism continued to figure with fluctuating effectiveness in the religious life of the country throughout the nineteenth century. Baptists and Methodists especially were involved in the revivals, and their numbers grew enormously as the frontier was pushed westward.

Anglicanism alone among the denominations in North America sustained serious damage through the revolutionary war; this was due partly to its organic connection with the government in London and partly to the loyalism of many of its clergy. Nevertheless, the movement proved strong enough to reorganize itself as the Protestant Episcopal church, a designation adopted in 1780; and by 1789 an independent constitution, allowing greater scope for lay representation, had been established. Thus American Anglicanism survived the strain of the revolutionary turmoil, and was destined to make a remarkable recovery.

Immigration from Ireland and elsewhere made for a great increase in Catholicism, while Protestant immigration from Continental Europe led to the multiplication of Lutheran and Reformed denominations, organized within different ethnic groups (German, Swedish, and so on). Several national churches of the Eastern Orthodox persuasion were also founded.

The cultural and religious ferment, with its tensions, rivalries, and continuous expansion, produced various separatist movements of a more or less original character. The Disciples of

Christ emerged as a new denomination in 1827 through the work of Thomas Campbell (1763–1854) and his son Alexander (1788–1866). The senior Campbell was a minister of the Secession Presbyterian church (founded by John Glas, who broke away from the Church of Scotland in 1728), and in 1807 he settled in western Pennsylvania. He welcomed Presbyterians of all types into his congregation, and this offended the ecclesiastical authorities, who took action against him. Campbell was dismayed at this expression of narrow sectarianism, and he determined thenceforth to work for the union of all Christians on a biblical basis.

Having migrated from Glasgow in 1809, Alexander joined his father and together they founded a church at Bush Run, Pennsylvania, in 1811. All credal supplementations to the scriptures were rejected, adult baptism by immersion was practiced, and celebration of the Lord's supper took place every Sunday. The church was affiliated to the Redstone Baptist Association, but at length theological disputes developed. The Campbells were averse to the stringent Calvinism of the Baptists, as well as to their belief in uniform biblical inspiration, contending that the New Testament represented a higher authority than the Old. The consequence was that in 1827 their church severed all connection with the Baptists, and this meant the birth of a new denomination organized on congregationalist lines. Today it has a membership of about two million, and the Disciples have continued to stress the need for Christian unity on the simple credal foundation of a common acceptance of biblical authority.

The Church of Jesus Christ of Latter-Day Saints—the Mormons, as they are popularly called—was founded by Joseph Smith (1805–44), who had Methodist and Presbyterian connections, and who became dissatisfied with the rivalries among the various denominations. In 1820 he declared that by divine revelation he was led to unearth the Book of Mormon on a wooded hill at Palmyra, New York. This work, written in a strange language, purported to record the history of Christianity in America long before the trans-Atlantic crossing of Columbus in 1492; and perhaps part of the appeal of Smith's philosophy derived from its professed non-European foundation.

According to Mormon's alleged account (which Smith, as he claimed, was miraculously enabled to read), a prophet in the sixth century B.C. migrated from Jerusalem via the Pacific to America, where he foretold the coming of Christ with such clarity that those who responded to his teaching virtually became Christian. The church thus established survived for several centuries, but because of widespread and persistent sinfulness ancient American civilization was wiped out. But Mormon had received divine instruction to bury his historical records and the promise that hundreds of years later a prophet would arise and discover them by supernatural means.

Smith established the first Mormon Church at Fayette, New York, in 1830. Eight years later the leaders moved westward, and in 1840 settled at Nauvoo, Illinois. In 1843 Smith made claim to a further revelation permitting the practice of polygamy, despite the monogamy enjoined in the Book of Mormon. Popular hostility was eventually aroused, and Smith suffered a violent death in 1844.

Brigham Young (1801–77), a man of great organizing ability, succeeded Smith, and in 1847 he led the believers on the arduous trek to the Great Salt Lake in Utah, whither, as was held, he had been divinely guided, so that he could establish there the headquarters of the Latter-Day Saints. That a thriving community should have been built up in that geographically most inhospitable region is a striking testimony to the Mormons' faith and industry, as well as to the competence of their leadership.

After a lengthy dispute with the federal government on the marriage question, Wilford Woodruff (1807–98), who had become the head of the sect, finally ruled in 1890 that the practice of polygamy should be relinquished. Six years later Utah was incorporated into the United States.

The Mormons hold that salvation is achieved by faith and repentance (sealed by baptism) through the atoning sacrifice of Christ, and that baptism by proxy is available for the dead. They have consistently shown great enthusiasm for missionary activity, and it is estimated that today the membership of the church throughout the world exceeds two million.

In the course of the nineteenth century several Adventist movements developed, recapturing something of the eschatological excitement of primitive Christianity and its negative attitude to worldly institutions. Among these perhaps the best known is the International Bible Students Association (Jehovah's Witnesses), a sect founded by Charles Taze Russell (1852–1916), a draper from Pittsburgh, Pennsylvania, who revolted against the Calvinistic predestinarianism of his Congregationalist background. He could not bring himself to accept the view that God arbitrarily elects some for eternal torments in hell, and, believing in the verbal inspiration of the scriptures, he sought and found biblical warrant for the conviction that God offers men a chance to repent of their sins.

So Russell began to proclaim that the last judgment was near, and that all who failed to repent and join the elect of Jehovah would be permanently excluded from the joys of the millennial kingdom to be established on earth after the great assize. He elaborated his doctrines by indulging in unscholarly exegesis, especially of the books of Daniel and Revelation. On the other hand, he rightly asserted that modern forms of Christianity lack a fundamental factor operative in the life of the apostolic church, namely, a lively belief in the imminence of the end of the present world-order.

Russell became the pastor of a congregation at Pittsburgh in 1878, and in the following year he began to issue *Zion's Watch Tower and Herald of Christ's Presence* (called *The Watch-*

tower since 1909), a periodical which attracted a large number of readers and later appeared in various foreign language editions. In 1884 he founded a publishing agency, the Watch Tower Bible and Tract Society of Pennsylvania, and soon books and pamphlets were pouring from its presses in great abundance. Around this time Russell planned to set forth his philosophy of history in an ambitious series of books under the general title *Millennial Dawn*. In the second volume of the series, *The Time Is at Hand*, he argued that the return of Christ had secretly occurred in October 1874, establishing the Age of Restitution, and he predicted that all the governments of this world would be overthrown before the end of 1914. He identified the pope with the Antichrist.

After Russell's death in 1916 the leadership was assumed by Joseph Franklin Rutherford (1869–1941), popularly known as Judge Rutherford, an attorney with a Baptist background who had not infrequently defended Russell in legal processes. Rutherford was an energetic person and had a flair for writing; of his numerous works perhaps *The Harp of God* has had as wide a circulation as any. He held that after the Battle of Armageddon, the final conflict between the forces of good and evil, Christ would set up his own government, thereby inaugurating the millennium; and that, as citizens-designate of the Messianic Kingdom, Jehovah's Witnesses could owe no real allegiance to political authorities of the present world, which is dominated by satanic powers.

Christian Science is another legacy of the late nineteenth century which found much of its inspiration in a feature of the New Testament that had long since ceased to figure prominently in the life of Christians generally. The apostolic church was an eschatological community, offering health to the body as well as salvation (victory over sin and death) to the soul; and if Russell sought to restore the adventist enthusiasm of primitive Christianity, Mary Baker Eddy (1821–1910), the founder of Christian Science, sought to reinstate its practice of the art of healing. In the Churches of Christ Scientist her main work, *Science and Health* (1875), is respected as an authoritative supplement to the scriptures—and this despite the fact that its idealist metaphysics, according to which the spiritual alone is real, seems to be at variance with biblical presuppositions. The principal thesis of the book posits that disease, like matter and death, is an illusory product of erroneous thinking, and hence that health is to be restored, not by medical or surgical treatment, but by inducing a right attitude in the mind of the patient. The First Church of Christ Scientist was established at Boston in 1879, and the movement is now widely represented.

In the mid-nineteenth century extensive controversies took place on the question of the abolition of slavery, and most of the larger Protestant denominations were divided. The southern section of the Methodist church, for example, seceded in 1845, and reunion was not effected until 1939. Some of the divisions still persist; on the other hand, the breach in the Protestant Episcopal church was healed shortly after the conclusion of the Civil War.

The Universalist and Unitarian denominations remained relatively small, and yet from about 1850 liberal tendencies inceasingly affected Protestant thought, especially in the northeastern regions. Horace Bushnell (1802–76), who graduated from Yale and subsequently served as a Congregational minister at Hartford, Connecticut, was of importance in this general connection. His book *Christian Nurture* (1847) showed a preference for the gradualism of enlightened religious education, as opposed to the highly-charged emotionalism usually associated with cataclysmic conversion; and in his later work, *The Vicarious Sacrifice* (1866), he expounded a form of the moral-influence theory of the atonement. Significant, too, was the reorganization of Harvard Divinity School under the presidency of Charles W. Eliot (1869–1909), who, like his older English contemporary and fellow Unitarian, James Martineau

(1805–1900), was much concerned to promote a broad and nondogmatic approach in theological education.

Following in the wake of the *Aufklärung*, liberal Protestantism in post-Kantian Germany was making creative contributions to theology, and its influence spread. Modern biblical criticism, mainly a product of German scholarship, was taken up and seriously pursued at Harvard, Yale, and elsewhere. Also, the theory of biological evolution, propounded in *The Origin of Species* (1859) and *The Descent of Man* (1871) by Charles Darwin (1809–82), tended to combine with a quasi-Hegelian belief in progress, the kingdom of God being construed (if we may use the words of Alfred, Lord Tennyson, 1809–92, the celebrated Poet Laureate of Victorian England) in terms of a "far-off divine event, / To which the whole creation moves." Thus, as in the case of the rationalism of immediately preceding centuries, the notion of a fallen world was deemed unworthy of serious attention. There had occurred no primordial lapse from paradise, and the ills of society were taken to indicate that man has to struggle against hardships and imperfections in order to transcend the limitations of his animal origins and to realize a satisfying fulfillment of his spiritual capacities. Clearly, in such an assessment the supreme aim of Christian service can scarcely be to rescue men and women from a corrupt nature by pointing heavenward to a supernatural source of saving grace; rather, the dominant practical interest must be to improve economic conditions and educational opportunities through the application of the ethic of peace and good will. Man is potentially little lower than the angels, and he is called to be a fellow worker with the immanent God of all creation in the realization of justice and peace in the world.

As in Europe, so in America, theological reaction set in after the First World War. The American assault on alleged liberal optimism came somewhat later, after the economic recession of 1929, and it rapidly gained in strength in the years following the accession to power of the National Socialists in Germany

(1933). In the vanguard of the attack was Reinhold Niebuhr (b. 1892), a professor at Union Theological Seminary, New York, who in a number of publications set forth what has been termed an integral prophetic Christianity, a formulation in which (as will be made clearer at a later stage) the reality of original sin received great emphasis.

During the present century the American theological scene has also been marked by an increasing concern for interdenominational cooperation. The Federal Council of the Churches of Christ in North America was established in 1908, and there have been several reunions and mergers. The ecumenical movement (see Chapter 41) has owed much of its success to the sustained support of American Protestantism.

BIBLIOGRAPHY

Brauer, J. C. *Protestantism in America: A Narrative History*. Philadelphia: Westminster Press, 1966.

Ellis, J. T. *American Catholicism*. Chicago: University of Chicago Press, 1956.

Kurtz, P. W., ed. *American Thought before 1900: A Sourcebook from Puritanism to Darwinism*. New York: Macmillan, 1966.

Miller, Perry. *Jonathan Edwards*. New York: W. Sloane Associates, 1949.

Niebuhr, H. Richard. *The Social Sources of Denominationalism*. Hamden, Conn.: Shoestring Press, 1954.

Olmstead, C. E. *History of Religion in the United States*. Englewood Cliffs, N.J.: Prentice-Hall, 1960.

Schneider, H. W. *The Puritan Mind*. New York: Holt, Rinehart and Winston, 1930.

Smith, Shelton H., Robert T. Handy, and Lefferts A. Loetscher. *American Christianity: An Historical Interpretation with Representative Documents*. 2 vols. New York: Scribner's, 1960–63.

Walsh, H. H. *The Christian Church in Canada*. Toronto: Ryerson Press, 1956.

Wieman, H. N., and B. E. Meland. *American Philosophies of Religion*. Chicago: Willett, Clark, 1936.

VII ‡ RECENT TENDENCIES

37 ‡ Kant and His Successors

Immanuel Kant (1724–1804) was born at Königsberg, and he remained within the borders of East Prussia throughout his life. From an early age he was keenly interested in mathematics and physics. Philosophically, he was educated in the tradition of Cartesian rationalism, as modified and developed by Leibniz and Wolff. He taught at the University of Königsberg from 1755, being appointed to the chair of logic in 1770. His dissertation *De Mundi Sensibilis et Intelligibilis Forma et Principiis* ("On the Form and Principles of the Sensible and Intelligible World," 1770) indicated that he was moving away from Wolffian rationalism and searching for a more satisfying philosophical position.

Kant's new system of doctrine was eventually expounded in a series of three Critiques (whence the designation "critical" philosophy): in *Die Kritik der reinen Vernunft* ("The Critique of Pure Reason," 1781; revised second edition, 1787) he argued that the mind organizes the raw data of sense to make the intelligible world of phenomena and that the understanding can operate fruitfully only within the phenomenal sphere of space and time; in *Die Kritik der praktischen Vernunft* ("The Critique of Practical Reason," 1788) he presented his ethical doctrines; and in *Die Kritik der Urtheilskraft* ("The Critique of Judgment," 1790) he considered purposive action (teleology) and the experience of beauty (aesthetics).

In 1792 it was officially noticed that Kant's critical philosophy conflicted with some of the tenets of Lutheran theology, but the ecclesiastical authorities took no suppressive measures against him, and in 1793 appeared his *Religion innerhalb der Grenzen der blossen Vernunft* ("Religion within the Bounds of Mere Reason"), a treatise which interprets religion on traditional deistic lines and evinces something of Spener's characteristic aversion to the subtleties of speculative theology (Kant was brought up under pietistic influences). Among his later works, mention should also be made of his essay on perpetual peace, *Zum ewigen Frieden* (1795). Certain literary remains, which were not published until long after his death (see E. Adickes, ed., *Kant's Opus Postutum*, 1920), would seem to indicate that near the end of his life his general philosophical outlook was becoming more like that of Spinoza.

It is somewhat surprising that Kant's *Religion innerhalb der Grenzen der blossen Vernunft* was so little affected by the doctrines of the three Critiques; evidently the rationalism of the *Aufklärung* had made an indelible impression upon his mind, for genuine piety is taken to be largely a matter of theistic ethics. Religious faith consists essentially in the recognition of duties as divine commands: to know a rule of conduct as God's injunction, before apprehending it as a duty, is distinctive of revealed religion, whereas to know such a rule as a duty, before apprehending it as God's injunction, is distinctive of natural religion.

In Kant's view, Christianity is both revealed and natural, and in certain respects his attitude in this connection resembled that of Matthew Tindal. As a natural religion, Christianity is self-authenticating, requiring neither the fulfillment of prophecy nor the performance of miracles to guarantee its validity. The supreme commandments of love for God and love for man signify, respectively, duty for duty's sake and distinterested service for human welfare, and their effective truth is self-evident to all rational beings. They found vivid exemplification in the life of Jesus—the paragon of virtue, the example to be followed.

As a revealed religion, Christianity entails numerous precepts, but these are valid only in so far as they clarify and reinforce the moral duties recognized in the natural religion of pure reason. Man can be pleasing in God's sight only when he does his duty, living a life of righteousness. Hence injunctions which imply that man can please God in other ways—as, for example, by observing some form of religious ritual—are nothing but superstition. Valid religious maxims always subserve the ethic of natural religion, and they never presume that the human understanding can grasp what is beyond the natural order of the world. Notions of miracle and of physical means of supernatural grace are quite irrational.

It was in his critical philosophy that Kant made his great contribution to Christian thought, and inaugurated a new epoch in Western philosophy. He sought a comprehensive world view that would do justice to the conflicting claims of diverse schools. Besides being to a considerable extent the converging point of the main philosophical streams that took their rise in the period of the Renaissance, Kantianism is the source to which subsequent trends of thought may largely be traced. As we have seen, Kant's earlier theorizing was in the rationalistic tradition of Leibniz and Wolff, but, partly through the influence of David Hume, he came to doubt the truth of some of its fundamental notions, eventually denying the possibility of a rational demonstration of God's existence and repudiating the doctrine that causality can be understood in terms of the logical relation of ground and consequence. But he did not go so far as to embrace empiricism in the sense of Locke and his successors; *inter alia* he felt that Hume oversimplified the situation and finally involved himself in an impasse through presupposing what he claimed to reject. Accordingly, Kant sought to synthesize what he held to be the valid theses of both rationalism and empiricism, as well as to provide a philosophical basis for Newtonian physics and for the deliverances of man's "deep hidden nature"—a realm which Rousseau had explored.

The comprehensive character of the critical philosophy is

illustrated in the distinction made therein between the understanding and the sensibility. Thus, for Leibniz, all knowledge is a construction originating within the knowing subject, its validity being guaranteed by a pre-established harmony among all actual entities. On the other hand, for Locke, the mind is fundamentally passive in perception, knowledge consisting in the apprehension of the relations between ideas that have been impressed on the mind by the active agency of external things. And Kant endeavored to make room for these opposed theories by arguing that the mind is basically passive as sensibility, and organizationally active as understanding. Knowledge arises when these two faculties operate together, and in considering the functioning of each a distinction has to be made between form and content. All objects are presented to us through space and time, the pure forms of sensibility, or a priori conditions of experience generally. Everything in the sensible world has a spatial configuration and a location, and everything in that world also endures in time with its passage from the past via the present to the future.

Kant further contended that the apprehension of objects in the realm of sense experience entails other forms than those of space and time, namely, the categories of the understanding, by which the manifold data of experience are organized into an intelligible world. He identified three categories of quantity (unity, plurality, totality), three of quality (reality, negation, limitation), three of relation (substantiality, causality, reciprocity), and three of modality (possibility, existence, necessity). The form of this classification was founded upon a somewhat obscure analogy between the synthetic activity involved in the making of judgments and the more basic synthetic activity that produces the knowable world, and there is a certain artificiality about the whole scheme. Nevertheless, the main thesis is clear: the categories, in active partnership with the sensible forms of space and time, make possible the ordered world of common experience; they are among its indispensable conditions.

Moreover, in Kant's view, our recognition of order and succession in phenomena presupposes an abiding self-consciousness, a continuing point of reference that unifies and conditions all awareness of the fleeting concatenations of objects in the sphere of space and time. This so-called transcendental unity of apperception is the ultimate subjective ground of our knowledge of objects, so that in the last resort the world we know is a mental creation. Hence the objects of common sense, whose characters and interrelations are elucidated by the laws of natural science, are not noumenal (or intelligible) things-in-themselves, but empirical phenomena—that is, they are realities as they appear to the apprehending mind. Things-in-themselves act upon the sensibility, providing the raw materials of organized knowledge, but things-in-themselves (reality as such) must ever be transphenomenal, a problematical unknown beyond the ken of human understanding.

Nevertheless, inherent in man's cognitive constitution is a persistent demand to know absolute reality, and this arises from reason, a mental organ which, in the first *Critique,* is sharply distinguished from the sensibility and the understanding. Reason is an extremely dangerous faculty, for while it performs an important service in urging the mind forward in its search for an intelligible unity in the world, it tends to advance beyond sensible data and to apply its ideas to the unconditioned which lies outside the bounds of experience. When such application is made, regulative concepts become constitutive principles, and the mind begins to grope in the domain of transcendental illusion, where, for example, it can be argued with equal force that the will is free and that the will is not free. Antinomies of this kind arise from an illegitimate employment of the categories (their use in an illusory world of tempting phantoms), and this is why the arguments of speculative rationalism never lead to definite conclusions. In any strictly metaphysical argument "both parties to the dispute beat the air," since they have allowed themselves to drift beyond the phenomenal to "a region where their dogmatic grips find nothing to lay hold of." Accordingly, the human mind operates effectively only in the phenomenal sphere of space, time, and causality—the world explored by the natural sciences, in which physical entities behave in ways capable of statement in terms of uniform laws.

But Kant did not let the matter rest there, for he was convinced that man can act freely as a noumenal being and rise superior to the phenomenal domain. Such is the fundamental thesis of the second *Critique*. Unlike other creatures, human individuals are endowed with practical reason or rational volition, and this comes into play whenever a person acts from a sense of duty. Moral conduct is action according to the dictates of a law that is at once self-imposed and unconditional (or categorical) in its demands, and so in the performance of a duty the human will is self-legislative.

The autonomy of the will, however, is not open to theoretical demonstration but is something of which we are practically assured whenever we fulfill a moral obligation. In the depths of our moral consciousness we are aware that *ought* volitionally entails *can*, and since all phenomena are subject to the category of causality, being determined from outside, it is to man in his noumenal capacity that the ethical imperative is addressed. In other words, the freedom of the will is a postulate of the moral life, and the same holds of the beliefs in immortality and the existence of God. For, in addition to enjoying the law of duty, practical reason in its normal functioning really assumes as the ultimate goal of ethical endeavor the *summum bonum*, in which virtue is crowned with happiness. There are obviously grave moral maladjustments in the present world, but practical reason postulates the soul's continuing existence after death, a perpetuation enabling God finally to bring about a just distribution of happiness in due proportion to the amounts of virtue achieved.

Thus Kant confined all genuine theoretical knowledge to the universe of matter and motion, the phenomenal system organized by the categories of the understanding. But this only served to make room for faith—the ethical assurance of the reality of God, freedom, and immortality. Although this assurance has a practical epistemological status, the doctrine should scarcely be equated with pragmatism as ordinarily understood. For example, Kant was not arguing that the belief in God's existence is valid because its widespread repudiation would have deleterious effects on human welfare; rather, the belief in question consists in an activating postulate or practical entailment of our nature as moral and rational beings. In this case, however, it might be legitimately asked whether the postulate in question must not represent a philosophical claim whose truth is to be adjudged by scientific or theoretical criteria. If it makes no such representation, logical discussion of ethical questions would seem to be futile, and Kant may be really admitting a mode of nonsensuous cognition, independent of the forms of space and time and the categories of the understanding.

Indeed, it sometimes seems that Kant was in fact halting between opposing possibilities: evidently he did not wish to encourage superstition by admitting a species of mystical intuition, and he refrained from giving full place to the scientific understanding lest this should sap human confidence in the objective validity of moral values. So one could infer that his position was an uneasy compromise between conflicting philosophical attitudes, which foisted an unresolved dualism upon the one world of common experience, with the causality of physical events and the causality of moral freedom being ascribed to entirely different orders of existence. But if man is a part of nature, not a visiting angel, perhaps the autonomy of the will is anticipated in the subhuman biological sphere; and could not the relation between moral freedom and natural causality be elucidated by reference to modes of determinacy already present at the physical level? Kant did suggest the possibility of an interpretation along these lines in the third *Critique*, but, as the *Opus Postutum* seems to indicate, a serious attempt to foliow up any such suggestion would involve a repudiation of the central theses of the critical philosophy.

In consequence of the dualistic tradition to whose establishment Kant greatly contributed, Western philosophy since his time has to a considerable extent exemplified three principal tendencies, namely, positivism, romanticism, and absolute idealism. Representatives of the first of these tendencies more or less accept Kant's doctrine of the limitations of the human understanding while rejecting as sheer nebulosity his proposed way out, as it were, from mere appearance to veritable reality via the autonomy of the will. After all, so it is thought, the tremendous advances of empirical science can only be due to the fact that man has at last discovered a sound method of investigating nature, a method purified of all metaphysical obscurantism. The experimental method holds the future; by its continuing application the progress of humanity is assured, and the paradise of the optimistic rationalist will at length come to be in a world freed from ignorance and superstition.

Such is the spirit that informed the teaching of Auguste Comte (1798–1857), who held that there are three main stages in man's cultural development, the scientific era being in process of superseding the metaphysical, just as the theological or mythological era had earlier given way to the comparative enlightenment of metaphysics. Comte was born at Montpellier and studied mathematics and physics at the Ecole Polytechnique in Paris. While still quite young he also displayed an interest in sociology and political philosophy, and in 1822 appeared his *Système de politique positive* ("System of Positivist Politics"). His main work, *Cours de la philosophie positive* ("Course of Positivist Philosophy") appeared in six volumes between 1830 and 1842. The views he defended were officially taken to be subversive, and in 1844 he was relieved of his post in mathematics at the Ecole Polytechnique. He devoted the rest of his life to promoting the cause of positivism, and his influence spread; among his distinguished admirers in the English-speaking world were John Stuart Mill (1806–73), empiricist and utilitarian; Herbert Spencer (1820–1903), agnostic and evolutionary naturalist; and Marian Evans, alias George Eliot (1820–80), the novelist.

Like Lessing, Comte argued that collective human evolution is paralleled in the development of the individual. In the first stage the mind is dominated by theologico-mythological notions, interpreting external events as productions of supernatural agents; feeling effectively asserts itself, and imagination resorts to fetishism or polytheism, and eventually to monotheism, in the prevailing explanations of occurrences; at this stage society is organized on a military basis. In the second stage reason comes into prominence, and in the resulting metaphysical explanations divine agencies are set aside in favor of impersonal forces and first causes, the regularity of whose operations induces the mind to conclude that they are inherent in nature, and not the results of spasmodic interventions on the part of a supposed external Creator; at this stage society is organized on a legal basis. In the third stage the positivism of the scientific mentality holds sway, and explanations offer answers to questions of the *how* type, not to questions of the *why* type; it being seen that all enquiry into causes and essences is uncivilized vanity, intellectual activity is confined to the classification of things and to the formulation of natural laws as schematic descriptions of the characteristic ways in which entities behave. The method employed is the inductive method of systematic observation and experiment, and at this stage society is organized as an industrial state on a scientific basis.

Positivist polity was not democratic. In Comte's view, egalitarianism is quite irrational, for all men are *not* equal. Scientific sociology calls for the establishment in society of two main authorities, one temporal, the other spiritual. The temporal authority is to be composed of industrial leaders and experts in economics, and the spiritual authority is to be composed of philosophers or sociologists. The latter are responsible for the maintenance of a cooperative spirit among the various social classes, principally by the promotion of true religion. For the supersession of theological myth does not mean the elimination of positivist piety, which, through the veneration of mankind, *le grand être* ("the Great Being"), guarantees the ultimate harmony of human existence. Only the worship of the Great Being of Humanity is able to bring about the subordination of egoism to altruistic interests and to evoke in modern man the virtues of faith and charity. Positivist religion is purified of all theological and metaphysical superstition and has "love for its principle, order as its basis, and progress for its goal."

Comte worked out an elaborate liturgical system, drawing chiefly on Catholic sources. Immortality amounts to perpetuation in the memory of the race, and noble achievements are celebrated in sacraments and festivals along with the saving grace of natural forces. In the revised sacred calendar the heroes of the past (scientists, scholars, and pioneers) figure as examples to be followed, the supreme ethical ideal being the promotion of neighborly love and disinterested service for the common good.

The second philosophical tendency to which attention has been drawn is the contrary of positivism in that representatives of romanticism share a certain epistemological disdain for the empirical sciences. Kant himself, despite his enduring interest in physics, discovered noumenal reality in man's moral consciousness, not in scientific intellection. Thus, although his romanticism was severely tempered by his rationalist treatment of philosophical questions, he undoubtedly possessed romanticist affiliations. Pascal had declared that the heart has its reasons of which reason knows nothing, and Kant could have declared that the moral consciousness has its reasons of which the scientific or categorial understanding knows nothing. Such an attitude came to uninhibited expression in the doctrine of Friedrich Daniel Ernst Schleiermacher (1768–1834), who in his *Reden über die Religion* ("Addresses on Religion," 1799) argued that religion has its basis in feeling, an inner sense of Eternal or Infinite Being.

Schleiermacher, the son of an army chaplain, was born at Breslau. He was educated in Moravian schools, and the effect of Pietism is doubtless to be seen in his emphasis on the importance of feeling in religion. He entered the university at Halle in 1787 and was ordained in 1794. Two years later he took up a hospital chaplaincy at the Charité in Berlin. His *Reden*, which show the influence of Spinoza and Leibniz, as well as of Kant, were directed specifically to the cultured despisers of religion, many of whom had been alienated from the church by the regnant rationalism of the Enlightenment; they were the outcome of an effort to persuade such people of the truth and relevance of Christianity.

From 1804 to 1807 Schleiermacher was professor of theology at Halle, and in 1809 he became minister of the influential Trinity Church in Berlin; when a university was founded there (1810) he was elected dean of the faculty of theology. While the country was engaged in the struggle against Napoleon, Schleiermacher became renowned for his inspiring sermons. His mature doctrinal views were set forth in *Der christliche Glaube* ("The Christian Faith," 1821–22), a more systematic work than the *Reden;* in it religion is identified with a feeling of absolute dependence, a sentiment alleged to be most adequately articulated in monotheism, and in Christianity especially.

Schleiermacher revolted against both the credal formalism of ecclesiastical orthodoxy and the rationalism of the Enlightenment, each of which, he felt, construed religion exclusively in intellectual or ethical terms. In his view, religion primarily consists neither in the acceptance of certain theological propositions (whether truths of revelation or of reason) nor in the adherence to a set of moral regulations (whether derived from divine inspiration or discovered by the light of nature). On the contrary, religion has its roots in the intimacies of feeling. It arises in the depths of the finite consciousness from an intuition of what is changeless amid change, a sense of union with the dynamic principle of the one absolute Totality that transcends and yet sustains the shifting parts of the world in which we participate. Such an experience of oneness with the Infinite has a liberating effect on the soul, overcoming disruptive feelings of fragmentariness and alienation.

Basic religious intuition comes to different modes of intellectual and ethical expression in different individuals, and this accounts for the great diversity of historical faiths. Religions should not be divided into two mutually exclusive classes, the true and the false, but rather should be graded according to the adequacy of their forms for the articulation of the creative sense of the Infinite. All religions to some extent adumbrate such a sense, and it may be said that monotheism is theologically superior to polytheism, and that universalism is ethically superior to tribalism, for the Absolute is an all-embracing unity. The supremacy of Christianity is due largely to the fact that its founder most effectively demonstrated the reconciliation of the finite with the Infinite, thereby becoming the mediator between the Divine and the human.

Schleiermacher's doctrines greatly affected the subsequent development of Christian thought, and he is sometimes referred to, not without justice, as the father of liberal Protestantism.

The third philosophical tendency that has figured prominently in recent thought is absolute idealism. Kant stressed the creative activity of the cognizing mind, and this idealist trend in his teaching was taken up and developed by Johann Gottlieb Fichte (1762–1814), Friedrich Wilhelm Joseph von Schelling (1775–1854), and Georg Wilhelm Friedrich Hegel (1770–1831), the classical exponent of modern absolute idealism. These philosophers directed attention to certain fundamental difficulties involved in Kant's critical philosophy and attempted to overcome them. Kant, while representing things-in-themselves as transphenomenal, and therefore unknowable, had argued that they were known to provide the raw material of knowledge by acting on the sensibility *ab extra*. Also, while asserting that the mind in cognition produces its own intelligible world, he had assumed, apparently without sufficient grounds, not an indefinite number of private universes but a common objective world of experience as the basis of rational intercommunication. Facing up to such difficulties, Hegel contended that things-in-themselves cannot lie beyond the range of experience. They are knowable in principle and hence they must be included in experience, not my experience or your experience as such, but the universal experience of creative thought. Finite minds and the objects they know are both modal organs for the self-expression of the Absolute Mind, which constitutes the ultimate basis of the common objective world of finite experience.

Hegel was born at Stuttgart. He studied at Tübingen (1788–93) before holding tutorships with wealthy families in Switzerland and at Frankfurt (1793–1801). While in Switzerland he wrote a biography of Jesus, which he never completed and which was not published until 1906; in it he argued that truth is to be discovered in the actualities of historical development rather than in formal speculation, and that the notion of eternal life signifies the transcendence of moral distinctions through the absorption of the finite into the Infinite. From 1801 to 1806 he was a lecturer in philosophy at the University of Jena, where he came under the influence of Schelling for a while, but after the latter's appointment to Würzburg, he began to work out his own ideas more independently, and his *Phänomenologie des Geistes* ("Phenomenology of the Spirit") appeared in 1807.

After the battle of Jena in 1806 he edited a newspaper at Bamberg (1807–8), and then taught at a grammar school in Bavaria for eight years (1808–16); his *Wissenschaft der Logik* ("Science of Logic") was published in three volumes during 1812–16. He became a professor at Heidelberg in 1816 and two years later was appointed to the chair of philosophy at Berlin, which had previously been occupied by Fichte. He strongly opposed Schleiermacher's romanticism. His *Encyclopädie der philosophischen Wissenschaften im Grundrisse* ("Encyclopedia of the Philosophical Sciences in Outline") appeared in 1817 (enlarged edition, 1827), and his *Grundlinien der Philosophie des Rechts* ("Outlines of the Philosophy of Right") in 1821. At Berlin his reputation increased enormously, and he was elected rector of the university in 1830; but he died of cholera during the following year. His lectures on aesthetics, the philosophy of religion, and other subjects, were included in the publication of his complete works (19 vols.) in 1832.

As we have seen, according to Kant's critical philosophy, the mind as the subject of knowledge imposes form or order upon the indeterminate material of sense. It plays an artistic role and could perhaps be described as the poet of the intelligible world of nature; viewed in this light, Kant's idealism is subjectivist in tendency. But certain passages of his writings betray a more radical form of idealism. Thus in the section on the Dialectic in the *Critique of Pure Reason* there are suggestions that it is solely by virtue of the distinction between the understanding, as the source of the categories, and reason, as the source of the idea of the Unconditioned (Absolute Being), that the real significance of the opposition between appearance and reality can be properly appreciated. In this kind of interpretation our consciousness of the contingent character of the empirical world presupposes some awareness of the Unconditioned, and so the distinction in question is no longer between what is experienced and a problematical unknown beyond experience, but between contingent particulars and the conditioning Universal within rational experience. Clearly, the transcendental subject of knowledge is here more or less equivalent to the Absolute Consciousness, of which any finite individual's experience is merely a transitory expression; and such is the sort of philosophical position which Hegel eventually came to adopt.

He maintained that the Absolute externalizes itself in cosmic history and comes to self-consciousness in finite minds. There is no awareness apart from self-consciousness, and self-consciousness ever bodies itself forth in the subject-object relation, with its opposition between the self and the nonself. Neither subject nor object exists independently of knowing, and it is ultimately in the Absolute's self-consciousness that all subjects and objects are included. As universal in its scope, the Absolute is *Ens Realissimum* ("the Most Real Being"), and its experience is one of active self-fulfillment, effected dialectically through the overcoming of internal contradictions.

Thus interpreted, the universe exists as a process of continuous advancement through struggle. The Absolute is active thought, and its development occurs in accordance with the laws of logic (the knowable must be rational), a logic which, however, unlike traditional Aristotelian logic, is dynamic, not static. In the beginning was thought, and this idea operates creatively in passages that always exemplify a triadic scheme: first there is the thesis, which persists until it encounters a limiting opposition, the antithesis; and the conflict between thesis and antithesis eventually issues in a third phase, wherein the contraries are taken up and transcended in a supervening synthesis.

Das Sein ("being") as such is emptiness of any assignable determination; it is not this, or that, or anything else. Pure being is nothingness; *what is* amounts to *what is not*. Such a contradiction is not to be dismissed as sheer fantasy, as it would be on the static principles of traditional logic, for it applies to every instance of becoming, and the universe itself is an infinite process of creative development. What becomes continuously projects itself into the future, so that at any specific moment of the shifting present *what it is* must be *what it is not*, the evolving essence being already on the way into the *not yet* of the future. *Das Wesen ist was gewesen ist* ("The essence is what has been"); fixed essences belong only to the past, for the actualities of the present constitute an uninterrupted advancement into the future.

Absolute thought is realized in creative activity and comes to self-consciousness in finite minds, and in so far as man recognizes his status in the dialectics of infinite Being, the Absolute becomes divine, the highest Object of venerating cognition. As Hegel himself put it: "God is divine only to the extent that he knows himself; his self-awareness is his self-consciousness in man, is the awareness man has *of* God, which progresses to man's self-awareness *in* God" (*Die Encyclopädie*, sec. 565). Human development, then, is at once the history of God's becoming and the history of divine revelation. The Absolute discloses itself in the free arrangement of percepts in art, in the imaginative liturgies and credal formulations of religion, and supremely in the dialectical schematizations of conceptual philosophy. Each of these disciplines has a dialectical history of its own, and Hegel held that if Schleiermacher had really understood the character of cultural evolution, he would not have interpreted man's response to the sacred in terms of feeling, which is the lowest form of knowledge. Animals may have feelings of dependence, but they are devoid of religion.

Accordingly, in Hegel's view, theological dogmas are imaginative constructions which, with greater or less success, shadow forth metaphysical truths. They call for elucidation by being translated into philosophical terms; despite the useful services they may have performed in the evolution of the human spirit, it remains that they are products of an inferior mode of consciousness and need to be clarified and rectified in the light of dialectical criteria. In other words, the so-called truths of revelation are not self-authenticating; they have to be submitted for examination at the bar of intellection.

Hegel held that Christianity is the highest of the positive religions because its central tenets are the easiest to render into what he held to be valid philosophical concepts. Thus, in the doctrine of the Trinity, the Father stands for the thesis, the divine unity of Absolute Thought; the Son is the antithesis, the finite mind in which the Absolute objectifies itself; and the Holy

Spirit signifies the synthesis, the mutual participation by which the Infinite and the finite come to self-fulfillment. The dogma of the incarnation of the Logos is a parabolic representation of the dialectical truth that, in the flux and reflux of cosmic existence, the Absolute finds its life by losing it in the objectification of humanity.

Thus Hegel made the notion of history central in metaphysics, and in this respect his work was characteristic of the thought of the nineteenth century. As we have seen, Lessing had outlined a philosophy of man's religious development in his treatise *The Education of the Human Race* (1780), but in Hegelianism the historical permeates the entire metaphysical structure. His work stimulated, among other things, the study of the rise of Christianity, and Ferdinand Christian Baur (1792–1860), who founded the influential Tübingen School of higher criticism, applied Hegel's dialectical method to early ecclesiastical history. Within three decades of Hegel's death Charles Darwin set forth his theory of biological evolution in *The Origin of Species* (1859), and this gave added force to the awakened interest in history. It came to be widely felt that, to know a thing, one must discover how it has come to be what it is. The English thinker Herbert Spencer (1820–1903) elaborated a philosophy of evolutionary naturalism in his *First Principles* (1862) and in numerous other works; he held that progress is a fundamental feature of the world we know, and he defined evolution as "the continuous change from incoherent indefinite homogeneity to coherent definite heterogeneity in structure and function by progressive integrations and differentiations."

While upholders of theism generally approved of Hegel's assertion of the primacy of mind or spirit, representatives of orthodox Christian theology were averse to his pantheistic depersonalization of God, as well as to his predilection for optimistically construing evil as a necessary stage in the realization of good. Moreover, among professed disciples of Hegel there was considerable reaction against the monism of the master, exception being taken to his tendency to reduce the finite individual to the dependent status of a mere instrument of Absolute Thought.

Disputation of a similar character developed within the Hegelian movement in the English-speaking world, which perhaps may be dated from 1865, the year that saw the publication of John Hutchison Stirling's work *The Secret of Hegel*. Monistic idealism was represented by such thinkers as Francis Herbert Bradley (1846–1924), an Oxford philosopher, in his treatise *Appearance and Reality* (1893), and less rigorously perhaps by Josiah Royce (1855–1916), a Harvard professor, in his two volumes published under the general title *The World and the Individual* (1900–1901). On the other hand, forms of personalistic Hegelianism, which stressed the autonomy of finite moral beings, are exemplified in such works as *The Realm of Ends* (1911) by James Ward (1843–1925) of Cambridge, *The Idea of God in the Light of Recent Philosophy* (1917) by Andrew Seth Pringle-Pattison (1856–1931) of Edinburgh, and *God and Personality* (1918) by Clement C. J. Webb (1865–1954), an Anglican philosopher who taught at Oxford for many years.

Hegel's doctrines were adapted to and combined with positivist principles in the materialist philosophies of Ludwig Andreas Feuerbach (1804–72) and Karl Marx (1818–83). Feuerbach contended that the Hegelian Absolute represents nothing more than an illusory objectification of certain universal features of human nature, and that the deification of the fantasy-construction results from the projection of a comforting desire. Feuerbach's teaching influenced Nietzsche and Marx, among others, and anticipated the psychoanalytic interpretation of religious faith as a wish-fulfillment, a thesis that received classic defence in Sigmund Freud's work *Die Zukunft einer Illusion* ("The Future of an Illusion," 1927), first made available to English readers in 1928.

While agreeing with Feuerbach that Hegelianism must be

freed of its idealistic mystifications, Marx followed Hegel in making the concept of development philosophically fundamental, and in interpreting it dialectically. He thus elaborated a system of so-called dialectical materialism, which united a patient economic analysis of contemporary industrialized society in England with a passionate desire for a just distribution of material wealth. He considered that Christianity is a baneful illusion, an opiate of the people, promoted by the holders of political power to keep the toiling masses in a state of quiet subjection. Wholly nefarious is its myth that social ills result from original sin, and quite unfounded is its promise that those content with their miserable lot in the present life will receive a reward of eternal bliss in heaven. The real situation requires not pious acquiescence but informed action for the world's reformation.

Like Plato and Benedict, Marx thought ill of private property. He argued that capitalism, which emerged dialectically out of medieval feudalism, is in the process of engendering its own antithesis. This was taken to be revealed in the subversive activities of enlightened members of the working class, who, as the vanguard of the proletariat in the coming revolution, are destined to seize political authority. They will fulfill their historic role as agents of the supervening synthesis by socializing the major means of industrial production, thereby putting an end to the class struggle between rich and poor, and inaugurating the new era of the classless society.

Marx, whose parents were Jewish and turned Protestant, was as violently opposed to Judaism as he was Christianity. Nevertheless, his leading philosophical themes may to a great extent be understood as a reshaping of biblical doctrines through the dual influence of positivism and the Hegelian concept of dialectical development. Thus his concern for a fair distribution of surplus value reflects the prophetic proclamation that Yahweh is the God of righteousness who requires the practice of justice in the world; his historical determinism adumbrates the biblical

view that the processes of history are the medium for the working out of a divine purpose; his concept of the vanguard of the
proletariat recalls the Jewish and early Christian doctrine of an
elect people as the special instrument of God's will; and his belief in the ultimate emergence of a classless society is reminiscent
of scriptural eschatology.

Despite the mounting prestige of empirical science, romanticism persisted and came to new forms of expression. In one way
or another its representatives would limit the empire of reason,
arguing that life is more than intellection and that God is larger
than life. Pascal had declared that the heart has its reasons, of
which reason knows nothing; Rousseau (like D. H. Lawrence
more recently) extolled the instinctive intuitive reasonings of ingenuous and unsophisticated humanity; Schleiermacher discovered the core of religion in a deep personal sense of the Infinite;
and in his *Faust*, Part I, Goethe celebrated a naturalistic type of
religion in the Doctor's eloquent speech which ends with the
words:

> Feeling is all that matters;
> Names are naught but noise
> And smoke
> That enshrouds the heavenly light.

Such a version of romanticist anti-intellectualism comes nearer
to Pascal's assessment than does the transcategorical moralism of
Kant, who feared the extravagances of mysticism. In Kantianism
it is volition, not feeling, that receives pride of place; instead of
the sublime intimations of the heart we are confronted with the
practical logic of the three moral postulates (God, freedom, and
immortality). But romanticist opposition to reason in the name
of will or volition need not be so far removed from Pascalian-
ism, a truth amply illustrated in the existentialism of Søren Aaby
Kierkegaard (1813–55), the Danish thinker who contended that
any rationalist system, such as Hegelianism, fails to shed light on
personal reality in the uniqueness of its freedom; the subjective

life of self-commitment has its reasons, of which the generalizing and objectifying intellect knows nothing.

Kierkegaard, a native of Copenhagen and the son of a prosperous merchant, was brought up in a gloomy atmosphere of earnest Lutheran piety. His father, whose personality dominated the household, suffered from the obsession that he had committed unforgivable sin. Evidently, while still quite young he had blasphemed in a moment of direst misery, actually cursing the Creator; and much later, to make matters worse, he was forced to marry his domestic servant within a year of the death of his first wife. In consequence he lived under the constant fear that God was about to bring him to destruction, and his melancholy proved infectious.

Kierkegaard must have been relieved when he left home to take up his studies at the local university (1830). He did well in the first examination, but thereafter his life was for several years largely divided between sessions of gay distraction, sometimes to the extent of dissipation, and heavy moods of deepest depression. In 1838, however, his father (perhaps aware that death was near) boldly acknowledged the religious crimes he had perpetrated, and this led to a radical change in Kierkegaard's mode of conduct. He repented and eventually completed the university course in theology, but after his graduation he refrained from proceeding to a pastoral charge. In 1841 he decided on marriage, and then, after some hesitation, he broke off the engagement. An ensuing despondency gave way to feelings of regret and to a grim self-questioning which led him to a new realization of the creative significance of personal decisions that issue from the depths of an anguished heart; he revolted violently against rationalist systematization, particularly in its regnant Hegelian form, fearing that it would destroy human freedom by reducing individuals to mere instances of general principles. From 1843 he therefore devoted himself almost exclusively to literary activity, expounding his existentialist doctrines and distinguishing true Christianity from the superficiality of the conventionalism prevailing in the established church of his day.

Among his important works (to give the titles in English) are: *Either-Or* (1843), an exposition of the fateful significance of personal choice, which betrays an ascetical tendency in the contrast it draws between aestheticism and ethical seriousness; *Philosophical Fragments* (1844) and *Concluding Unscientific Postscript* (1846), which set existential individualism in opposition to Hegelian universalism, besides stressing the discontinuity of religious faith with reasonable belief; *The Concept of Dread* (1844) and *Sickness unto Death* (1849), psychological studies of sin and faith, wherein dread is represented as an agonizing premonition of nothingness, an anguish that becomes despair (sickness unto death), when it is realized more specifically as an incapacity to make the leap of religious faith.

Thus, according to Kierkegaard, the human individual is not merely a sample or an instance of humanity. No man comes into the world with a ready-made universal essence, on the basis of which his life can be mechanically built up. This is because a human being is not an object but a subject of self-conscious freedom. With an artificial thing, such as a house, the essence or architectural plan is there prior to the work of actual construction. But with a human individual the reverse obtains; each person has to realize his own essence or character through the mediation of his creative decisions. Such decisions may be born out of agonizing struggles, for a choice always involves the exclusion of various possibilities, and a recognition of this may bring the soul to the sickness of despair. In any case human existence always precedes its essence.

Because of each individual's uniqueness, an integral personality can never be subsumed under a general principle, and in virtue of its subjectivity it cannot be understood as one element among others in an objective system. The highest metaphysical form of truth is always subjective, and every human individual is subjective in his freedom, which is unamenable to external rational tratement. A scientist is quite incapable of standing outside his freedom and investigating it as he might examine the structure of a machine, for the act of scrutiny would at once treat volitional liberty as an objective fact, and this is precisely what freedom is not.

In certain respects Kierkegaard's interpretation was much like Luther's: God is known by faith, and faith supervenes upon the travail of the soul's lonely struggles with guilt, fear, and despair. Moreover, faith is opposed to reason; it is the outcome of a personal decision, and its experiential meaning vanishes when it is rendered in terms of abstract principles. Similarly, God himself suffers impoverishment at the hands of rationalistic theologians, so that in metaphysical manuals he commonly stands as but one lifeless object among others, a pale reflection of the living God encountered existentially. A thesis of this kind found vivid expression in Kierkegaard's so-called dialectical lyric, *Fear and Trembling* (1843): the typical philosophical concept of the Divine is an ineffective relic of the imperious Authority that may command even a teleological suspension of the ethical; only in the personal fulfillment of God's unconditional requirements in dreadful prostration (such as is portrayed in the biblical story of Abraham's willingness to sacrifice his son) can a creaturely being come to know God for what he truly is: Infinite Subjectivity.

It was not until after the First World War that Kierkegaard's doctrines became a powerful influence in the development of Western thought. Antiliberal dialectical theology owes much to him, and this was introduced by the Swiss theologian Karl Barth (1886–1968) in his commentary on the Pauline Epistle to the Romans, *Der Römerbrief*, in 1919. During the same year the German thinker Karl Jaspers (b. 1883) issued his treatise on possible world views, *Die Psychologie der Weltanschauungen* ("The Psychology of World Views"), in which he contended that the decisions an individual makes in *Grenzsituationen* ("extreme situations") represent a determining factor in the formation of his philosophical outlook. Subsequent decades saw the emergence of more systematic forms of existentialism, notably, in *Sein und Zeit* ("Being and Time," 1927) by Martin Heidegger (b. 1889) of the university at Freiburg-im-Breisgau, and in *L'être et le néant* ("Being and Nothingness," 1943) by Jean-Paul Sartre, the French writer and philosopher (b. 1906). Sartre's later work *Critique de la raison dialectique* (vol. I, 1960) was partly motivated by a desire to integrate existentialism with basic Marxist principles. Gabriel Marcel (b. 1889), French playwright and philosopher who became a Roman Catholic in 1929, moved from an idealistic position to existentialism, as is shown in his *Journal métaphysique* ("Metaphysical Diary," 1930); and Etienne Gilson (b. 1884), Neo-Thomist and renowned authority on medieval philosophy, maintained in his work *Le thomisme* (3rd ed., 1941), that Aquinas was basically existentialist in his philosophical orientation. On the other hand, in the encyclical *Humani Generis* (1950) Pope Pius XII officially denounced existentialism.

Another highly individualistic species of romanticism was expounded in a number of vigorous works by Friedrich Wilhelm Nietzsche (1844–1900), who contended that, since life is larger than reason, any effective philosophy must spring from a thinker's total personal response to the world. The son of a Lutheran minister, Nietzsche studied at Bonn (1864–65) and Leipzig (1865–69) and was then appointed professor of classical philology at Basel in Switzerland. He served as a medical orderly during the Franco-Prussian War of 1870, and his health was affected. While at Basel he formed a short-lived friendship with Richard Wagner, the composer. Because of sickness he resigned his professorship in 1879, and during the next ten years he engaged in feverish literary activity. He suffered a complete mental breakdown in 1889 and thereafter was cared for successively by his mother and his widowed sister until his death near the beginning of the present century.

Nietzsche has been widely influential and widely misrepresented. He was a prophetic writer, prone to making exaggerated statements, and often deliberately provocative. His aphoristic pronouncements, his strongly worded contrasts, his metaphorical assertions, all tended to make misinterpretation easy, especially when passages were taken out of context. Also his sister's redaction of his notes to make up his posthumous *Der Wille zur Macht* ("The Will to Power," 1901) was far from satisfactory by scholarly standards. Indeed, she helped, in all likelihood more than anyone else, to give rise to the erroneous idea that Nietzsche supported the Germanic doctrine of the *Herrenvolk*, the racialistic theory of nordic superiority. His best-known work is *Also sprach Zarathustra* ("Thus Spake Zarathustra," 4 parts, 1883–91).

While a student at Leipzig, Nietzsche came under the influence of the doctrines of Arthur Schopenhauer (1788–1860), who had elaborated a pessimistic philosophy in his treatise *Die Welt als Wille und Vorstellung* ("The World as Will and Idea," 1818), wherein the Kantian thing-in-itself had become the nonrational urge or will to live. Nietzsche adopted the concept of a basic animating impulsion, but transformed its significance. He noticed, for example, that certain male insects sacrifice their lives for the sake of sexual intercourse, and he went on to uphold the thesis that the fundamental biological impulse must be, not the will to survival, but the will to power.

So far as human life is concerned, the will to power comes to satisfactory fulfillment neither in the vulgar expressionism of the voluptuary nor in the ascetical emasculatedness of traditional Christianity, but in the integrated personality of the *Übermensch*, the Superman, who by self-discipline has sublimated his passions and perfected himself in mental and physical strength. The Superman knows what suffering is, but he triumphs over it and rejoices in the constructive affirmation of his forceful being.

Those who are too mean to adopt an integrating project for their lives need a God to supply their deficiency—particularly to provide a heaven of endless pleasure for themselves and a hell of endless torments for the men they envy. Also, the established ecclesiastical ethic of charity really amounts to a practical expression of the same inner inadequacy that constitutes the basis of the Christian's cherished hopes of heaven and hell. Current religious beliefs and morals are therefore bound up with the resentment characteristic of the slave mentality; and, Nietzsche argued, this is not surprising in view of the fact that Christianity was first widely diffused among the slaves of Roman imperial society. A slave cannot strike his master, so he seeks to ingratiate himself with the man he hates by acting as if he were meek and kind; but the fire of revenge burns in his heart, and he comes to find solace in a comforting religion of the imagination, the irrational faith in a transcendent power that will bring the mighty to naught and the weak to ultimate triumph.

Like a slave, then, the Christian suffers from a disturbing inhibition of the will to power and compensates for his traumatic sense of impotence by resorting to the belief in a God who conveniently metes out rewards and punishments; and he escapes from himself by seeking to help his neighbor, for it is always easier to do good to others than it is to improve oneself. Hence what is supremely required is a transvaluation of all values in the light of the ideal of the Superman. Mediocrity must give way to individuality, pity to stimulating competition, and mawkish commiseration to the open avowal that pain and suffering are necessary elements in all forms of creative achievement.

Despite the one-sidedness of much of Nietzsche's teaching, a number of Christian thinkers now recognize that it contains important segments of truth; and it is noteworthy that, perhaps mainly through the mediation of the psychoanalysis of Sigmund Freud (1856–1939), such concepts as those of compensation and sublimation have become part of common knowledge.

BIBLIOGRAPHY

Burkill, T. A. *God and Reality in Modern Thought.* Englewood Cliffs, N.J.: Prentice-Hall, 1963.

Desan, W. *The Marxism of Jean-Paul Sartre.* Garden City, N.Y.: Doubleday, 1965.

Kaufmann, W. *Nietzsche: Philosopher, Psychologist, Antichrist.* Princeton, N.J.: Princeton University Press, 1950.

Löwith, K. *From Hegel to Nietzsche: The Revolution in Nineteenth-Century Thought.* New York: Holt, Rinehart and Winston, 1964.

Mackintosh, H. R. *Types of Modern Theology: Schleiermacher to Barth.* New York: Scribner's, 1937.

Moore, E. C. *An Outline of the History of Christian Thought since Kant.* New York: Scribner's, 1912.

Price, G. *The Narrow Pass: A Study of Kierkegaard's Concept of Man.* London: Hutchinson, 1963.

Stace, W. T. *Religion and the Modern Mind.* Philadelphia: Lippincott, 1960.

Webb, C. C. J. *Kant's Philosophy of Religion.* Oxford: Clarendon Press, 1926.

——. *A Study of Religious Thought in England from 1850.* Oxford: Clarendon Press, 1933.

Wieman, H. N. *The Wrestle of Religion with Truth.* New York: Macmillan, 1927.

38 ‡ Biblical Criticism

The expression "higher criticism" (which apparently owes its origin to the German scholar Johann Gottfried Eichhorn, 1752–1827) seems to have gained currency in the English language through W. Robertson Smith (1846–94), Scottish theologian and semitist, who in his *Old Testament in the Jewish Church* (1881) referred to higher (or historical) criticism in contradistinction to lower (or textual) criticism. Higher criticism concerns itself with questions appertaining to the authorship, date, circumstances, and intentions of the books of the Bible and involves comparative literary study, source analysis, investigations of oral tradition, and so on. Lower criticism is required because of the numerous variant readings in the biblical manuscripts, its aim being to reconstruct the text nearest to the autograph.

The main types of manuscript evidence for the Old Testament are: (1) The Hebrew documents that witness to the so-called masoretic form of text, which was established as authoritative in the rabbinical schools during the centuries after the fall of Jerusalem in A.D. 70 (the earliest of these manuscripts date from the ninth and tenth centuries); (2) Hebrew manuscripts of certain parts of the Old Testament found among the Dead Sea Scrolls, which were discovered in the region of Qumran in 1947 and subsequent years (these manuscripts are about a thousand years older than the earliest extant documentary witnesses to the masoretic text, but not necessarily more trustworthy);

398

(3) Greek versions, including the Septuagint (LXX); (4) Targums or Aramaic versions; (5) Latin versions, including the Vulgate, a revised translation prepared by Jerome (*c.* 400), which received general acceptance in the West.

The main types of manuscript evidence for the New Testament are: (1) Nearly five thousand Greek manuscripts, of which the most valuable (for example, the Codex Sinaiticus and the Codex Vaticanus) originated in the fourth century; (2) About seventy-five Greek papyri discovered in Egypt during recent decades, the earliest of which (now in John Ryland's Library, Manchester, and published by C. H. Roberts in 1935) reproduces a fragment of the Fourth Gospel and is considered to have originated in the first half of the second century; (3) Ancient versions, especially the Old Latin (pre-Vulgate), the Sahidic, and the Old Syriac; (4) Patristic quotations.

Biblical criticism first began to be pursued scientifically during the nineteenth century, and in the field of the textual study of the New Testament an important contribution was made by the German professor Karl Lachmann (1793–1851), whose studies helped to inspire research on the part of other scholars. Among these were B. F. Westcott (bishop of Durham from 1890 until his death in 1901) and F. J. A. Hort (of Cambridge) who in 1881 issued their significant work *The New Testament in the Original Greek* (2 vols.). They maintained that there are four principal families of text: the Syrian, marked by attempted clarifications of obscurities, conflate readings, and harmonizations of parallel passages (this was the type of text used in the preparation of the King James or Authorized Version of 1611); the Western, found chiefly in the Codex Bezae and Old Latin authorities; the Neutral, represented almost solely by the Codex Sinaiticus and the Codex Vaticanus; and the Alexandrian, a production of literary purists who wished to bring the text into greater conformity with classical standards. Westcott and Hort relied mainly on the so-called Neutral Text in their own redaction of the New Testament.

Much work has been done in the textual field since 1881, and new evidence has come to light, principally through the discovery of Greek papyri. The genealogical scheme (with its four families) has been revised and developed in certain directions, but scholars now generally recognize that no one family should be slavishly adhered to, and perhaps Westcott and Hort failed to attach sufficient importance to Western readings. This means that, in the last resort, each particular case must be decided on the basis of internal evidence, and the critic should be guided by such canons as these: the hardest reading is preferable; the reading most in accord with the author's tendencies (stylistic or other) should be accepted; the shortest reading is to be favored; the reading that best explains the other variants should be given the greatest weight. Unfortunately, these canons not seldom come into conflict with each other; for instance, the shortest reading may not be the most difficult one.

Like Judaism, Christianity has its roots in the religion of Israel, and from apostolic times the church has revered the Hebrew scriptures as the authentic word of God. It must not be overlooked, however, that early Christian respect for the Old Testament had certain qualifications. Thus the Jesus portrayed in the synoptic gospels does not regard the scriptures as being uniformly binding; in a general way they constitute the word of God, and yet not all biblical rulings are taken to be of equal standing. For example, in Mark 10:1 ff. he regards the provisions for divorce in Deut. 24:1 ff. merely as an accommodation to human weakness, and, relying on such passages as Gen. 2:24 and 5:2, he declares that, in God's real intention, man and wife are to become "one flesh" in a lifelong union. Moreover, the Pauline thesis that the Christ's advent somehow entailed the supersession of the Mosaic Law quickly came to prevail; and this meant that the authority of the Hebrew scriptures had certain limitations.

Nevertheless, the Old Testament was venerated as the authentic record of God's declared purpose; the church took it for granted that its prophecies were divinely inspired, and the contention that Jesus fulfilled those prophecies was a fundamental feature of early Christian apologetics. In the middle decades of the second century, as we saw in an earlier chapter, Marcion sought to eliminate the Old Testament, as well as to restrict the New Testament to a revised edition of the Third Gospel and ten Pauline epistles. But Marcion's views were rejected, and thereafter the Old and the New Testament (the contents of the latter had been substantially determined by the end of the second century) were, with virtual unanimity, accepted as trustworthy records of God's revealed will. Inconsistencies were explained largely by the employment of allegorical methods of exegesis.

As the centuries passed the conviction seems to have become increasingly strong that the scriptures, more or less literally interpreted, imparted reliable information in all fields—scientific and historical as well as moral and theological. A view of this kind was regnant during the sixteenth century, and it came to be popularly held that the Reformation had simply involved the substitution of scriptural for papal authority. Protestants tended to argue that biblical literature provides the one supreme court of appeal on all matters, and representatives of the Counter-Reformation really inclined to adopt much the same position. Defenders of traditional Latin Christianity did not assert that Protestants were wrong in upholding the authority of scripture, but contended that they erred in their exegesis, particularly in supposing that biblical affirmations were at variance with established Catholic belief and practice.

Hence a number of the well-known cases of so-called conflict between science and religion in the modern period have really been conflicts between certain cosmological ideas prevalent in the ancient world (which came to expression in the Bible) and certain hypotheses held to have been confirmed through sustained application of the empirical method of verification. In 1633 Galileo was condemned for repudiating the geocentric astronomy evinced in scripture; in 1860 the English thinker, T. H. Huxley (1825–95), was denounced by Samuel Wilberforce (1805–73), the bishop of Oxford, for repudiating the biblical idea of creation and defending the biological theory of evolution; and in 1925, the famous "fundamentalist" legal case began, when J. T. Scopes, a school teacher in Dayton, Tennessee, was charged with contravening the state law by giving public instruction in the unbiblical doctrines of Darwinian theory.

But it was inevitable that the scientific method of free empirical inquiry, which was being applied with such singular success in the physical and biological spheres, should eventually be applied to the study of the scriptures. As early as the seventeenth century there were presages of things to come. Thomas Hobbes in his *Leviathan* (1651) contended that the Bible is not so much God's revelation as the human and fallible record of that revelation. Benedict de Spinoza in his *Tractatus Theologico-politicus* ("Theologico-political Tractate," 1670) argued that the Pentateuch (the first five biblical books) is a composite literary production and denied that Moses could have been its sole author. About eighty years later Jean Astruc (1684–1766), professor of medicine at the University of Paris, in his *Conjectures* (1753) drew attention to various awkward features of the book of Genesis, notably, the curious distribution of the divine names *Elohim* ("God") and *Jehovah* (more correctly, *Yahweh* —"the Lord" in the English version of 1611), the repetitions, and the chronological confusions; and he deduced that the work must have been composed (albeit by Moses) through the piecing together of earlier documents.

Pentateuchal criticism advanced rapidly in Germany during the nineteenth century. Wilhelm de Wette in his *Dissertatio Critica* ("Critical Dissertation," 1805) was the first to connect Deuteronomy with the reign of King Josiah (*c.* 640–609 B.C.). Wilhelm Vatke in his *Biblische Theologie* ("Biblical Theology," 1835) showed that the lengthy document which uses

Elohim of God and begins with the first creation story (Gen. 1:1–2:3), constitutes the basic constituent of the Pentateuch and the latest to be written. Karl H. Graf in his *Geschichtliche Bücher des Alten Testaments* ("Historical Books of the Old Testament," 1866) supported Vatke's thesis, maintaining that the priestly laws of the said Elohistic document (designated *P*) were later than Deuteronomy (*D*) and probably post-exilic (the exile began with the fall of Jerusalem in 586 and was formally terminated by Cyrus, the Persian king, soon after his defeat of the Babylonians in 539 B.C.). Significant results of previous scholarship were taken up and adapted in a comprehensive theory propounded by Julius Wellhausen (1844–1918), professor successively at Greifswald, Marburg, and Göttingen, in his works *Die Komposition des Hexateuchs* ("The Composition of the Hexateuch," 1876–77) and *Prolegomena zur Geschichte Israelis* ("Prolegomena to the History of Israel," 1883).

Wellhausen interpreted Israel's cultural history in evolutionist terms. Hebrew religion developed (partly through contact with the more advanced Canaanite civilization) from the simple tribalism of the nomadic period, via the moralistic monolatry of the great writing prophets (Amos, the first of the line, flourished around 750 B.C.) and the prophet-influenced Deuteronomic legislation of the seventh century, to the explicit ethical monotheism of the anonymous prophet of the exile, whose writings are preserved in the fortieth through the fifty-fifth chapters of Isaiah, and so to the priestly rigorism of the restored community in the post-exilic period. The successive stages in this development are reflected in the various strands of the Pentateuch, which, so far from being the product of a single individual (Moses), as traditionally supposed, represents the complex result of several centuries of cultural growth.

According to the Wellhausian school of criticism, the principal documentary sources of the Hexateuch (the first six biblical books) are:

1. *J*, the Jehovistic (or Yahwistic) document which begins

at Gen. 2:4 with stories of Adam and Eve and their nearer descendants; it goes on to recount the doings of the patriarchs, the marvels of the exodus, and so on. Its accounts frequently run parallel to those of *E*, but God is referred to as Yahweh. The document was probably drawn up in the ninth century.

2. *E*, the Elohistic strand, which uses *Elohim* to designate God, and like *J*, is largely composed of narrative. Its redaction probably took place in the eighth century.

3. *D*, the source represented mainly in Deuteronomy. Its style is hortatory, and its seeks to further the ethical monotheism implied in the teaching of Amos and his prophetic successors, besides making a demand for the centralization of the sacrificial cultus. It has a close connection with the Book of the Law found in the temple at Jerusalem in 621 B.C., during Josiah's reign (II Kings 22–23), a discovery that induced the king to destroy the provincial sanctuaries and to restrict sacrificial worship to the capital. Thus *D* originated in the seventh century.

4. *P*, the Priestly Code, promulgated in the community restored to Jerusalem after the exile, when Israel determined to preserve its holiness in a pagan world. The laws in the twenty-fifth through the fortieth chapters of Exodus and in the whole of Leviticus belong to *P*. The *P* legislation is part of a total history, commencing with the world's creation which is recounted in Gen. 1:1–2:3, a passage that characteristically culminates in a theological justification of the institution of the Sabbath. Anthropomorphisms such as are found in *J* and *E* are absent, and the style (as in Gen. 1:1 ff.) is usually dignified. Not all Levites are priests (as in *D*), the priesthood being confined to the Aaronite segment. God (Hebrew: *Elohim*) is first revealed as Yahweh to Moses (Exod. 3). Although containing traditional material, it was not edited until the fifth century.

5. *H*, the Holiness Code (so named by A. Klostermann in 1877), found in the seventeenth through the twenty-sixth chapters of Leviticus. The document is apparently based on the

teaching of the exilic prophet Ezekiel. Perhaps the codification was carried out around 550 B.C., the incorporation into *P* taking place in due course.

J and *E* were probably combined in the early decades of the seventh century, the purpose of the editors being to win over the loyalty of the surviving population of the Northern Kingdom (which had collapsed in 721 B.C.) to the cultus of the temple at Jerusalem, for the combination seems to represent a merging of southern traditions (*J*) with northern (*E*). The final redaction of the Hexateuch, with its union of *JE*, *D*, and *PH*, had been completed before 250 B.C.

There is now less unanimity among Old Testament scholars regarding the validity of the Wellhausian position than there was a generation ago, and the theory has been subjected to attacks from various standpoints. But no alternative solution has won predominant support, and a knowledge of the Wellhausian hypothesis remains an essential requisite for the full understanding of more recent research in the fields of form-critical analysis and traditio-historical investigation.

Higher criticism of the New Testament, as with that of the Old, advanced rapidly during the nineteenth century. G. E. Lessing prepared the way when he published the last of the seven so-called Wolfenbüttel fragments in 1778. As previously observed, these fragments were extracts from a work by H. S. Reimarus (1694–1768), and the seventh, which concerned the purpose of Jesus and his disciples, drew attention to certain remarkable incongruities in the gospel records. It noted that Jesus, despite his alleged divine status, must have been mistaken in his eschatological expectations; that the disciples would not have been surprised by news of the Lord's resurrection if the reported predictions of it had actually been made; that a curious mixture of secrecy and publicity attaches to the accounts of the Master's Messiahship; and that the discrepancies between the synoptics and the fourth gospel betray a will to deceive credulous readers. The publication at once gave rise to stormy disputations, most unprofitable; nevertheless, serious historical research was stimulated in some quarters.

Lessing's *New Hypothesis about the Evangelists Considered as Merely Human Historians* appeared posthumously in 1784 and set forth the view that an Aramaic protogospel lay behind the three synoptics; the hypothesis was further developed by J. G. Eichhorn (1752–1827), who was also (following Schleiermacher's lead) induced to deny Pauline authorship of the pastoral epistles.

More significant was the work of Ferdinand Christian Baur (1792–1860), professor of theology at Tübingen from 1826, who, using Hegelian principles in his study of the church's origins, brought about a radical reorientation in the field, besides making notable contributions to the history of Christian ideas. His most striking contention was that ancient Catholicism, established by the end of the second century, was a synthesis, the reconciling outcome of a vehement conflict between two opposing interpretations. For the primitive church at Jerusalem, originally represented by the Apostle Peter, Jesus was the promised messianic prophet who called men to repent and reform their lives in view of the impending advent of the Kingdom of God; this constituted the thesis, a form of messianic Judaism. For the Christianity of the Greek-speaking churches, at first largely represented by the Apostle Paul, Jesus had become a supernatural Christ whose Spirit was the saving mystery that informed a redeemed community; this was the antithesis, a form of Hellenistic religion.

The struggle between the Petrine (or Judaistic) thesis and the Pauline (or pagan) antithesis persisted into the second century. But in the superseding Catholic synthesis the differences were taken up and absorbed, so that by A.D. 200 the violence of the conflict had slipped into oblivion, and the Apostles Peter and Paul, *de facto* the bitterest of enemies, came to enjoy a cherished life of peaceful coexistence in the golden haze of the church's memory.

Baur, who dated the books of the New Testament in the light of his over-all theory, expounded his views on the early church in three principal works. In his *Untersuchungen über die sogennanten Pastoralbriefe des Apostels Paulus* ("Investigations Concerning the So-called Pastoral Epistles of the Apostle Paul," 1835) he set forth his theory of the creative tension between Jewish and Hellenistic Christianity and repudiated the traditional belief in the Pauline authorship of the pastorals. In his *Paulus, der Apostel Jesu Christi* (1845) he contended that Paul was the archenemy of Peter and the other disciples who had known Jesus in the flesh, and that the epistles to the Galatians, the Corinthians (both), and the Romans are the only extant writings of Paul, the other allegedly Pauline letters being, like the Acts of the Apostles, irenic or conciliatory expressions of the synthetic Christianity which supervened during the later decades of the second century. In his *Kritische Untersuchungen über die kanonischen Evangelien* ("Critical Investigations Concerning the Canonical Gospels," 1847) he argued that Matthew's gospel, which is eminently Jewish in tenor, must be the earliest, and that the latest member of the canonical quartet must be the one ascribed to John, a document which shows Gnostic and Montanist tendencies and can scarcely be said to supply trustworthy biographical information regarding the Jesus of actual history.

Baur's works aroused considerable acrimonious debate, especially his *Paulus* of 1845, but even more violent controversy had been occasioned about ten years earlier by one of his former pupils, David Friedrich Strauss (1808–74), who had issued a provocative two-volume work *Das Leben Jesu* ("The Life of Jesus") in 1835–36. Strauss was a native of Ludwigsburg and in 1821 entered the church school at Blaubeuren, where Baur taught history and philology (1817–26). Four years later he continued his studies at Tübingen and, after a period at Berlin, he returned to Tübingen as lecturer in Hegelian philosophy.

Strauss was greatly influenced by Baur's teaching and also

by the work of B. G. Niebuhr (1776–1831), who had interpreted early Roman history in terms of myth. So in his *Leben
Jesu* Strauss argued that the history of primitive Christianity
could best be understood on dialectical principles and that the
Christ of the church's faith was mainly an artifact of ingenuous
mythologization. The miracles of the gospels resulted neither
from misinterpretations of natural happenings (a not uncommon rationalist view) nor from deliberate intentions to deceive
the public (as Reimarus supposed). The truth is rather that in
the period between the crucifixion and the writing of the gospels in the second century, supernatural elements were gradually imported into the historical traditions concerning Jesus,
whose person thus became a savior figure, a satisfying embodiment of contemporary religious hopes and aspirations.

In the Jewish world of the first century many people were
eagerly awaiting the advent of a miracle-working Messiah who
would fulfill certain scriptural prophecies; and in the Hellenistic
world it was widely held that man is so constituted that by
mystical union with the Divine he can win victory over death.
Such mythical motifs gathered around the primary object of
the church's memory, transforming a Galilean prophet into the
supernatural Christ of the emerging Catholic faith.

Strauss' book pleased neither the traditionalists nor the ra-
tionalists, and the hostility it provoked led to his ejection from
the university. He found himself in the unfortunate position
of not being able to secure another academic appointment, and,
not unnaturally, he became embittered against organized Christianity. But his work proved extremely influential, and *La vie
de Jésus* ("The Life of Jesus," 1863) by the French scholar
Joseph Ernest Renan (1823–92) owed much to Strauss. This
book has become something of a literary classic, although to
some extent its portrayal of the Galilean prophet as a man of
superb charm may be sentimental romanticization. Its publication led to angry protestations, a consequence being that in
1864 Renan was suspended from the professorial staff at the
Collège de France.

Just as important, if not so exciting, was a painstaking article on the orders of narration in the synoptic gospels by the Berlin philologist and textual critic Karl Lachmann; it was published in 1835 under the title "De Ordine Narrationum in Evangeliis Synopticis" in the periodical *Theologische Studien und Kritiken* (vol. VIII). This was the first piece of detailed criticism to bring forward strong evidence for the view that Mark's gospel (not Matthew's, as usually supposed) must have been the basis of the other two synoptics. The argument commended itself to others and, through the work of such scholars as Heinrich Julius Holtzmann (1832–1910) and Bernhard Weiss (1827–1918), the two-document solution of the synoptic problem came to prevail. Briefly stated, the theory meant that Mark was used by Matthew and Luke, that non-Markan material common to Matthew and Luke derived from a lost sayings-source (designated *Q*—the initial letter of the German word *Quelle:* "source"), and that Matthew and Luke made liberal use of additional tradition in the composition of the sections peculiar to each of their works (often designated *M* and *L* respectively).

At the beginning of the present century it was commonly held among independent critics that Mark, the earliest gospel, was more or less a transcript from life, relatively free from dogmatic interests, and therefore at the opposite extreme to the fourth gospel, which was supposed to be an essay in dramatic theological interpretation. This sort of assumption was vigorously attacked by Wilhelm Wrede (1859–1906), professor of New Testament at Breslau, in a treatise on the messianic secret in the gospels (*Das Messiasgeheimnis in den Evangelien*, 1901). He maintained that Mark was fundamentally concerned with doctrinal matters, not with questions of biographical accuracy, and, more specifically, that the motif of secrecy, a dominant feature of the gospel, was the outcome of an attempt to explain why Jesus was not recognized as the Messiah during his lifetime. According to Wrede, Jesus did not claim to be the Messiah, and Mark's notion of the messianic secret was intended to account for the difference between the church's christological assessment and the factual situation that obtained prior to the crucifixion.

Wrede's book was subjected to much adverse criticism—for example by Albert Schweitzer (1875–1965) in his work *Von Reimarus zu Wrede: Die Geschichte der Leben-Jesu-Forschung* (1906; published in English as *The Quest of the Historical Jesus*, 1910). But Wrede's thesis that Mark's gospel was doctrinally motivated soon gained effective support, especially among so-called form critics. Also influential in this connection was Julius Wellhausen, who, in a series of short but acute commentaries on the gospels (for example, *Das Evangelium Marci*, 1903), showed that the synoptics were to a great extent composed of isolated units of a tradition that had originally been transmitted by word of mouth.

The investigation of such elements was pursued by representatives of the school of form criticism. The units were classified according to the character of their formal structure, and their possible histories and functions in the oral tradition of the apostolic churches were closely examined. Among the numerous studies issuing from the school may be mentioned *Die Formgeschichte des Evangeliums* (1919; English translation of the second edition, 1933, published as *From Tradition to Gospel*, 1934) by Martin Dibelius (1883–1947), professor of New Testament at Heidelberg from 1915; and *Die Geschichte der synoptischen Tradition* (1921; enlarged edition, 1931; English translation, *The History of the Synoptic Tradition*, 1963) by Rudolf Bultmann (b. 1884), professor of New Testament at Marburg (1921–51). Because of the emphasis laid upon the creative character of the gospel tradition, the charge has been frequently made that form criticism led to biographical negativity. The unwarrantedness of such a view received demonstration in the work *On the Trial of Jesus* (1961) by the London scholar Paul Winter (1904–69), who, besides making notable contributions to form-critical studies, especially with regard to the controversy stories and the birth and passion narratives, came to certain positive conclusions about the historical course of events which led to the tragic termination of Jesus' earthly career.

So far as Pauline criticism is concerned, Wrede in his *Paulus* (1905) argued that Christianity, in the form it assumed in the Roman world, was to a large extent the creation of Paul, who radically transformed the religion of Jesus. This kind of thesis was subsequently upheld in numerous studies representing various schools of thought; for example, *The Earlier Epistles of St. Paul* (1911) by Kirsopp Lake, professor of New Testament at Leyden and subsequently at Harvard; *Paulus* (1911; second edition, 1925; English translation, *St. Paul: A Study in Social and Religious History*, 1926) by Adolf Deissmann, professor of New Testament at Berlin; and *From Jesus to Paul* (1944) by Joseph Klausner, who eventually settled in Jerusalem. The thesis was opposed in such works as *St. Paul and the Mystery Religions* (1913) by H. A. A. Kennedy, the Scottish scholar; *Christianity according to St. Paul* (1927) by C. A. A. Scott of Westminster College, Cambridge; and *Paul and Rabbinic Judaism* (1948) by W. D. Davies of Duke University. A grand attempt at a balanced assessment was made by Maurice Goguel of Paris in his comprehensive, *Jésus et les origines du christianisme* ("Jesus and the Origins of Christianity," 3 vols., 1932–50).

After the First World War certain Protestant scholars began to react violently against higher criticism of the Wellhausian type and to stress the need for an informed exegesis that focused, not upon the original meaning of biblical texts, but upon their significance for life in the twentieth century. This kind of attitude came to forceful expression in Karl Barth's commentary on the Pauline Epistle to the Romans, *Der Römerbrief* (1919), which made a deep impression in certain quarters. Biblical theology, as distinct from the historical study of the evolution of Israelite religion, was endowed with crucial importance: the theological unity of the Bible was greatly emphasized, sometimes at the expense of scriptural variety; and the Wellhausian tendency to regard the prophetic (not the priestly) factor as the higher creative element in biblical religion was seriously questioned. Certain exponents of this type of hermeneutics thought of a reunion of divided Christendom on the basis of the essential integrity of God's spoken word.

Catholic resistance to biblical criticism continued throughout the nineteenth century and tended to intensify in the course of the modernist controversy (see Chapter 39). The Biblical Commission was instituted by Pope Leo XIII in 1902 to further biblical scholarship in accordance with traditional Catholic doctrine. Four years later the Commission asserted the Mosaic origin of the Pentateuch, and in 1907 it upheld the apostolic authorship of the Fourth Gospel; in 1912 it rejected the two-document solution of the synoptic problem and posited the temporal priority of Matthew's gospel. In 1950 Pope Pius XII (in his encyclical *Humani Generis*) denounced the denial of the historical existence of Adam. On the other hand, Catholic scholars (especially French and German) have made solid contributions to biblical scholarship; the *Revue biblique*, for example, which is published in Paris by the Dominicans of St. Etienne's monastery at Jerusalem, is a periodical maintaining the highest scientific standards, particularly in the sphere of archeology; it was founded in 1892 by M. J. Lagrange (1855–1938), whose commentaries on the gospels (1911–25) constituted a considerable scholarly achievement.

BIBLIOGRAPHY

Burtchaell, J. T. *Catholic Theories of Inspiration since 1810.* Cambridge: Cambridge University Press, 1969.

Conzelmann, H. *An Outline of the Theology of the New Testament.* London: Student Christian Movement Press, 1969.

Eissfeldt, O. *The Old Testament: An Introduction.* Oxford: Basil Blackwell, 1965.

Finegan, J. *The Archeology of the New Testament*. Princeton, N.J.: Princeton University Press, 1969.

Fuller, R. H. *The New Testament in Current Study*. New York: Scribner's, 1962.

Gray, E. D. M. *Old Testament Criticism, Its Rise and Progress*. New York: Harper, 1923.

Hahn, H. F. *The Old Testament in Modern Research*. Philadelphia: Muhlenberg Press, 1954.

Howard, W. F. *The Romance of New Testament Scholarship*. London: Epworth Press, 1949.

Hunter, A. M. *Interpreting the New Testament, 1900–1950*. London: Student Christian Movement Press, 1951.

Hyatt, J. P., ed. *The Bible in Modern Scholarship*. Nashville, Tenn.: Abingdon Press, 1966.

Kenyon, F. G. *Our Bible and the Ancient Manuscripts*. Rev. ed. New York: Harper, 1958.

McCown, C. C. *The Search for the Real Jesus: A Century of Historical Study*. New York: Scribner's, 1940.

Metzger, B. M. *The New Testament: Its Background, Growth, and Content*. Nashville, Tenn.: Abingdon Press, 1965.

Minette de Tillesse, G. *Le secret messianique dans l'évangile de Marc*. Paris: du Cerf, 1968.

Rowley, H. H. *The Old Testament and Modern Study*. Oxford: Clarendon Press, 1951.

Thompson, R. J. *Moses and the Law in a Century of Criticism since Graf*. Leiden: Brill, 1970.

Vielhauer, P. *Aufsätze zum Neuen Testament*. Munich: Christian Kaiser Verlag, 1965.

Wikenhauser, A. *New Testament Introduction*. New York: Herder, 1958.

Willoughby, H. R., ed. *The Study of the Bible Today and Tomorrow*. Chicago: University of Chicago Press, 1947.

39 ‡ Catholic Modernism

Ultramontanism tightened its hold on the church during the nineteenth century. Under Pope Pius IX (1846–78) the *Syllabus Errorum* ("Syllabus of Errors"), condemning numerous current ideas and tendencies, was published in 1864; and the same kind of attitude received further exemplification in the dogmatic constitution ratified at Vatican Council I (1870), a gathering that also approved a declaration of papal infallibility. Under Pope Leo XIII (1878–1903), the bull *Aeterni Patris*, enjoining Thomist studies in theological education, was promulgated in 1879; and the establishment of a Biblical Commission, for the regulation of the critical investigation of the scriptures, took place in 1902. Under Pope Pius X (1903–14), the decree *Lamentabili* and the encyclical *Pascendi Gregis*, denouncing the modernist movement, were issued in 1907; and three years later it was ruled that all clerics suspected of having liberal sympathies must take an antimodernist oath.

Both in 1907 and 1910 the official pronouncements ordained that scholastic philosophy in its Thomistic form be made the basis of the sacred sciences. *Pascendi Gregis* ruled that those who displayed a partiality for novelty in history, archeology, or biblical exegesis, or who furthered the modernist cause by carping at scholasticism, be excluded from directorships and other offices in Catholic educational institutions.

Modernism (a term which does not seem to have been used of the movement before 1900) developed rapidly in certain

414

intellectual groups during the nineties, and its principal aim (to use the phraseology of the last of the eighty errors condemned in the *Syllabus* of 1864) was to bring about a reconciliation or adjustment between Catholicism and the progressive liberalism of modern civilization. The movement was strongest in France but had representatives in various countries. Among them were: in Britain, Friedrich von Hügel (1852–1925), philosopher and mystical writer; and George Tyrrell (1861–1909), ordained in 1891, who contrasted living faith with dead theology and eventually questioned the finality of Christianity; in Italy, Antonio Fogazzaro (1842–1911), novelist, poet, and philosopher; in France, A. F. Loisy (1857–1940), priest and biblical critic; Lucien Laberthonnière (1860–1932), ordained in 1886, who interpreted religious doctrines pragmatically; Maurice Blondel (1861–1941), who formulated a philosophy of action; and Edouard Le Roy (1870–1954), mathematician and philosopher, who succeeded Henri Bergson at the Collège de France when the latter took up an appointment with the League of Nations. For the most part, the clerical (if not the lay) representatives suffered excommunication in 1907 or soon afterward.

Although there was much diversity of view among the Modernists, they were united in their basic orientation, subscribing to some form of evolutionist philosophy and stressing the importance of the scientific study of history. They thus reflected the spirit of the time, with its eager search for origins. Hegel had maintained that the Absolute Spirit is continously developing, and a generation later Darwin had propounded the theory of biological evolution. It was commonly argued that *what is* consists in a *becoming* which needs to be interpreted in terms of *what has been*, and that the full significance of *what has been* cannot be determined without taking into account its outcome in *what has become*. Any philosophy that fails to take history seriously is doomed from the outset.

As applied to Christianity, this meant that the apostolic origins of the church must be laid open to scientific scrutiny, as must its roots in Hebraic culture. So the Modernists inclined to accept the principles of biblical criticism as it was being conducted at Tübingen and other German universities. God did not reveal himself all at once, and the Bible is a record of God's progressive revelation to a particular people. Being subject to common human limitations, the writers responsible for the sacred record were not infallible; and being conditioned by circumstances, what they wrote can be understood only in the light of history.

Also, God is immanent, and his revelation constitutes a continuing process that has persisted throughout the centuries of the Christian era. Hence there may be justifiable elements in the life of the modern church that were absent at its beginning. Christianity has developed under the guidance of God's indwelling Spirit, and to justify the Christianity of the present day one does not always have to demonstrate that what obtains in our own time was also true of the apostolic period. There is no such thing as a closed epoch of revelation.

Moreover, the evolutionist philosophy tended to engender strong reaction against the alleged aridity of scholastic intellectualism; and in this respect, despite their inclination to defend scientific exegesis, the Modernists displayed romanticist affiliations. To some extent they were haunted by the ghost of Schleiermacher, and this may have been partly due to the influence of Auguste Sabatier (1839–1901), professor and dean of the Free Faculty of Protestant Theology in Paris, who advocated what was aptly designated "symbolo-fideism" in his widely read *Esquisse d'une philosophie de la religion* ("Outline of a Philosophy of Religion," 1897) and earlier works, arguing that dogmas are to be construed as outward signs of inner religious feelings rather than as theoretical propositions.

But doubtless it was the basic philosophy of the movement that proved decisive in this as in other connections. For evolutionism teaches not only that everything has a history which calls for systematic scrutiny, but also that the intellect itself has developed out of the pressures of practical exigencies. Like the sense organs, reason evolved pragmatically as an instrument in the biological struggle for existence. Therefore, so it was contended, the intellect can only mislead if it is taken to supply the sole criterion of truth. Intellection is subservient to life, and when thinkers make it an ultimate end in itself and suppose that its conceptual productions can adequately represent vital reality in its concrete integrity, they grossly misunderstand its nature and function. Such was the cardinal error of Auguste Comte and his positivist successors; and the same kind of false assessment vitiated the thinking of those who formulated the classical creeds, and of those scholastic theologians who devised grandiose intellectualistic systems.

Alfred Firmin Loisy (1857–1940) was the outstanding biblical critic associated with the modernist movement, and is sometimes said to have been its founder. After seminary training at Châlons-sur-Marne he was ordained in 1879. Two years later he proceeded to the Catholic Institute in Paris and came under the influence of Louis Duchesne (1843–1922), the professor of church history who was rejecting as legendary accretions many of the commonly accepted early Christian traditions; he also attended the public lectures that were being delivered by Joseph Ernest Renan, the celebrated author of the controversial *Vie de Jésus* of 1863. Although angered and dismayed by the dismissal of Duchesne (1885), Loisy accepted the professorship of sacred scripture at the Institute in 1889. But eventually he had to resign because of his deviationist teaching. From 1894 to 1899 he was attached as chaplain to the Dominican convent at Neuilly, and from 1900 to 1904 he taught in the Ecole des Hautes Etudes at the Sorbonne.

In 1902 appeared his *L'évangile et l'église* ("The Gospel and the Church"), an attack on Adolf von Harnack's much-discussed exposition of liberal Protestantism, *Das Wesen des Christentums* (1900; published in English as *What is Christianity?*, 1901). Loisy countered Harnack's thesis that the essence of

Christianity can be discovered in the unhellenised religion of Jesus, and contended that the church is continuously developing under the inspiration of the Holy Spirit, ever adapting itself to changing conditions and producing new syntheses. Growth is creative. Jesus himself may not have envisaged the sacrifice of the mass, but logically this can scarcely be taken to imply that the mass has no integral connection with genuine Christianity. Such a judgment would be rather like frowning upon the skills of maturity on the ground that they are not achieved in childhood.

The book was denounced by the archbishop of Paris, and Loisy was thenceforward a marked man; the three works he issued in 1903 were at once placed on the index. His masterly two-volume study *Les évangiles synoptiques* ("The Synoptic Gospels," 1908), directly contravened the orders of the papal decree *Lamentabili* and the encyclical *Pascendi Gregis* (both of which were published in the previous year), and he suffered excommunication. From 1909 to 1930 he was professor of the history of religions at the Collège de France. He wrote profusely; his thought continued to develop, and toward the end of his life he came to adopt a form of positivistic humanism.

Important philosophically was the activist teaching of Maurice Blondel, which received its earliest systematic exposition in his book *L'action* ("Action," 1893). Still more influential, however, was the work of Henri Bergson (1859–1941), who, although not directly connected with the movement, was giving lively expression to doctrines congenial to the modernist spirit.

A native of Paris and of Jewish descent, Bergson studied at the Ecole Normale Supérieure, and in 1900 he became professor of philosophy at the Collège de France. After the First World War he served in an official capacity with the League of Nations for some years, working for the promotion of world-wide intellectual cooperation. A man of rare academic versatility and brilliance, he was equally at home in the classics and the natural sciences; and, like Plato and Schopenhauer, is to be assigned a place among that lamentably small company of philosophers who are masters in the art of writing elegant and lucid prose. He was also an accomplished public speaker and, as if an Abelard redivivus, he attracted crowds of people to his public lectures at the Collège de France in the early years of the present century.

Bergson's works included: *Un essai sur les données immediates de la conscience* (1889; published in English as *Time and Free Will*, 1910), *Matière et memoire* (1896; *Matter and Memory*, 1911), *L'évolution créatrice* (1907; *Creative Evolution*, 1911), *Les deux sources de la morale et de la religion* (1932; *The Two Sources of Morality and Religion*, 1935). Like Kant, he was devoted to empirical science, while holding that life contains more than can be grasped by discursive intellection.

According to Bergson's central thesis, the essence of the universe is creative change, operating under the direct inspiration of the *élan vital*, the dynamic thrust behind the evolutionary process. Men do not normally apprehend the world as creative change because the activity of the intelligence is cinematographical, ever reflecting its primitive office as the servant of practice in the struggle for existence. Even in science human intellection is not freed from its subservience to practical purposes, and so the world tends to be represented in physicochemical theory as a composition of separate elements spatially interrelated in a mechanical fashion. Discursive reason substitutes succession for the continuity of real duration, spatializing time and fixating its perpetual flow in sequences of static snapshots.

On the other hand, metaphysical intuition, which is instinct become self-conscious, imparts a knowledge of real time as opposed to discrete points in motion and isolated moments in an artificial clock-time. The immediacy of intuition is not the clear-cut focus of the attentive consciousness, but coextends with the wide range of subliminal experience and includes the total historical past that swells with the duration it accumulates

as it gnaws into the future. Intuition is thus a mode of intellectual sympathy whereby the mind is led into an unmediated apprehension of the *élan vital* at the heart of the evolving nature
of things.

Profoundly influenced by Bergsonian teaching was Edouard
Le Roy (1870–1954), mathematician, philosopher, and theologian, who entered the vanguard in modernism's philosophical
attack on traditional Catholicism. He studied the mathematical
sciences at the Ecole Normale Supérieure, and in 1898 his thesis
on the integration of the thermodynamical equations was the
subject of a paper presented to the French Academy of Science by Henri Poincaré (1854–1912), who was perhaps the
first physicist to think in terms of relativity theory. Le Roy
subsequently became professor of mathematics at the Sorbonne,
and he continued to function in that capacity even after his
appointment as Bergson's successor at the Collège de France.
The formation of his thought was affected by Poincaré in the
field of mathematics and physics, by Bergson in general philosophy, by Lucien Laberthonnière in theological interpretation,
and later by Pierre Teilhard de Chardin (1881–1955) in the
domain of evolutionary anthropology, as well as by Samuel
Alexander (1859–1938) of the University of Manchester.

Of Le Roy's works may be mentioned: *Dogme et critique*
("Dogma and Criticism," 1907), *Une philosophie nouvelle*
(1912; published in English as *A New Philosophy*, 1913),
L'exigence idéaliste et le fait de l'évolution ("The Idealist
Exigency and the Fact of Evolution," 1927), *Les origines hu-
maines et l'évolution de l'intelligence* ("Human Origins and the
Evolution of the Intelligence," 1928); *La pensée intuitive* ("Intuitive Thought," 1930), *Le problème de Dieu* ("The Problem
of God," 1930), *Une introduction à l'étude du problème re-
ligieux* ("An Introduction to the Study of the Religious Problem," 1944), and *La pensée mathématique pure* ("Pure Mathematical Thought," posthumous).

Le Roy elaborated Poincaré's doctrine of the conventional

character of the laws of physics, extending its application to include science in its empirical aspect. Scientific facts, as well as scientific concepts and laws, owe their existence to definition. Intellection carves out convenient data from the continuum of experience, thereby making reality more amenable to rational treatment. But the world in its vital actuality is known only by intuition, especially in deep religious experience. And so far as theological dogmas are concerned, they are properly rules for action, not demonstrable theoretical statements.

In 1905 Le Roy published an article "Qu'est que c'est un dogme?" ("What is a Dogma?") in the fortnightly review *La quinzaine*, and it gave concise expression to a leading modernist point of view. The text of the article, and numerous clarifications and replies to objections, appeared two years later in the volume *Dogme et critique*.

Le Roy argued that the traditional dogmas of the church are presentations in terms of outmoded philosophical doctrines which bear no effective relation to the intellectual life of the twentieth century. Such concepts as that of the Logos, or such distinctions as that between substance and accidents, which figure so prominently in traditional dogmatics, fail to shed the slightest ray of light on questions that concern the modern mind, such as the philosophical problems arising from the laws of thermodynamics. Also, traditional ecclesiastical doctrine contains many metaphors that resist direct conceptual interpretation, since literalism in this connection can only give rise to impossible anthropomorphisms; for instance, it would take the dogma of the fatherhood of God to imply that the Creator has sex, a notion that is quite absurd.

Nevertheless, considerations of this kind do not mean that Catholic doctrine must be discarded. A dogma has at least an understandable *negative* significance, for it excludes certain possible errors. Thus the assertion *God is personal*, while not defining the nature of the Supreme Being, does affirm the negative proposition *God is not impersonal;* it signifies that God is not a law or an ideal principle or a universal substance. In other words, theological statements possess prohibitive meaning, and the classical creeds derive their intellectual meaningfulness from the positions they were devised to reject.

Moreover, there is a sense in which dogmas actually contain positive affirmations, namely, in the sense of practice as distinct from theory. Thus the dogma *God is personal* means *Comport yourself in relation to God as you do in relation to human persons*. Similarly, the doctrine of the eucharistic Presence signifies that, confronted by the consecrated host, one should adopt an attitude analogous to that which one would adopt if actually confronted with the Christ incarnate.

Hence, according to Le Roy's thesis, Christianity is not a system of speculative theology, but a way of life, a discipline for moral and spiritual renewal. Dogmas are practical prescriptions, and therefore the charge made by positivists and others that Catholic dogmas are intellectually unacceptable completely misses the mark. Being rules for action, dogmas possess effective significance for people with little education, and they can be retained through centuries of cultural change. In its essence religion is something lived through, not a product of metaphysical dialectics, and theological directives are devoid of value unless they find an echoing responsiveness in the deep intimacies of personal spiritual experience.

In the decree *Lamentabili* and the encyclical *Pascendi Gregis* the new teaching was condemned in no uncertain terms (1907). The decree listed sixty-five modernist errors, while the encyclical went so far as to describe Modernism as "a synthesis of all heresies." *Inter alia* the leaders of the movement were accused: of agnosticism in denying that the human intellect can know ultimate reality; of substituting subjective intuitions for the authentic deliverances of revelation; of preferring symbolofideism to the objective rationalism of natural theology; of relativizing religious truth in such a way as to put all religions on the same basis; of reducing the stabilities of faith to the transient status of mere instruments in a pragmatist philosophy; of seeking to rescue religion from scientific attacks by making it unscientific.

Thus in 1907 Pope Pius X proscribed Modernism. At the same time he commended a form of scholasticism; in *Pascendi Gregis* (Part III) he cited Leo XIII's bull *Aeterni Patris* (1879), which had ruled that Thomistic studies be made the foundation of theological education. Under official encouragement Neo-Thomism quickly gained in power and influence, and within a generation of the suppression of Modernism, it had become the dominant doctrinal trend in Catholicism. Among its outstanding representatives have been: Désiré Joseph Mercier (1851–1926), Belgian philosopher and cardinal; Martin Grabmann (1875–1949), successively professor of medieval philosophy at Vienna and Munich; Jacques Maritain (b. 1882), professor at the Catholic Institute in Paris; and Etienne Gilson, (b. 1884), professor of medieval philosophy at the Collège de France and director of the Pontifical Institute of Medieval Studies at Toronto.

BIBLIOGRAPHY

Ranchetti, M. *The Catholic Modernists.* London: Oxford University Press, 1969.

Tyrrell, George. *Christianity at the Crossroads.* London: Longmans, Green, 1910.

Vidler, A. R. *The Modernist Movement in the Roman Church: Its Origins and Outcome.* Cambridge: Cambridge University Press, 1934.

——. *A Variety of Catholic Modernists.* New York: Cambridge University Press, 1970.

40 ‡ Tractarianism and Liberalism

Although embodying contrary tendencies, both Tractarianism (the Oxford Movement or Anglo-Catholicism) and liberal Protestantism arose to some extent in reaction against forms of evangelical Pietism. As pointed out in an earlier chapter, the Pietism of Spener, Francke, and Zinzendorf profoundly affected the religious life of Germany in the late seventeenth and the early eighteenth century. Then, largely through the combined influence of the modified Cartesianism of Leibniz and Wolff, and of the Deism of Lord Herbert of Cherbury and his successors, the rationalism of the Enlightenment came into prominence, opposing the emotionalism of the Pietists, as well as the narrowness of Protestant orthodoxy. It is true that in the ensuing romanticism of Kant and Schleiermacher an autonomous status was conferred upon the moral or religious life. But the Pietism there taken up was radically transformed by being subjected to a process of philosophical refining; and such exponents of the new romanticism as Goethe welcomed the continuing expansion of scientific culture, demanding only that a worthy place be found in it for the deliverances of the moral and spiritual consciousness.

In England during the eighteenth century the Deistic rationalism that had found so much favor among the country's intellectual leaders tended to give way to the evangelicalism associated with the Methodist revival. John Wesley was impressed by the earnest Pietism of the Moravians, and it is sig-

nificant that his conversion occurred when a passage from a
Lutheran commentary was being read. After his death Methodism seceded from the Anglican church, and yet, in spite of this,
a relatively strong evangelical party remained within the establishment. Nonconformity received invigoration, and Methodism maintained its rapid growth during the early decades of the
nineteenth century, meeting with particular success in the
newly industralized areas.

The changed situation was bound to manifest itself in a
political way; the Test and Corporation Acts were repealed in
1828–29, while the parliamentary reform of 1832 gave new
power to the middle classes. A number of Anglicans at Oxford
and elsewhere felt that the glory of the established church was
fast departing, and they cast wistful glances at the Caroline
divines of the post-Cromwellian period. It was feared that the
gains of the Restoration had been lost, and that (in view of the
Catholic Relief Act of 1829 and the rising tide of evangelicalism
with its liturgical poverty) many sensitive souls would transfer
their allegiance to Rome. Such anxiety was involved in a sermon
bearing the title "National Apostasy"—a declaration preached
at Oxford in 1833 by John Keble (1792–1866) and commonly
taken to mark the beginning of the Tractarian movement. Two
of its leaders, John Henry Newman (1801–90) and Henry
Edward Manning (1808–92), reacted against evangelical back-
grounds in their passage via Tractarianism to Roman Catholicism.

In the spirit of Spener and his followers, the Evangelicals
stressed the importance of an emotional experience of conversion, effected by personal trust in the atoning death of
Christ. They posited the supreme authority of scripture, holding that its saving significance is revealed to attentive readers
and that the church is composed of those who are saved by
grace through faith. They subordinated sacramental observances to the preaching of the word of God, inclined to believe
in the proximity of the second advent, and, subscribing to the

doctrine of verbal inspiration, were averse to the critical investigation of the scriptures.

The Tractarians, on the other hand, exalted the ancient ecumenical creeds, and increasingly emphasized that salvation is sacerdotally mediated through the ministrations of priests who owe their authority to valid episcopal ordination. More specifically, they maintained that the Anglican communion stands in vital historical continuity with medieval Catholicism, and that in its essential content the Book of Common Prayer is not a product of the Protestant Reformation but a derivative from the orthodox faith of the early Christian centuries.

Richard Hurrell Froude (1803–36), a tutor at Oriel College, who identified himself with the Oxford Movement from its inception, advocated the practice of fasting, clerical celibacy, and the veneration of the saints. In 1833 he supported Newman and others when they ventured to launch so-called *Tracts for the Times*, periodical publications designed to disseminate high church doctrines (whence the designation "Tractarianism"). Newman had come to regard Anglicanism as the golden mean between Roman Catholicism, with its excessive subservience to papal authority, and Protestantism, with its anarchic individualism and unrefined temper. In all, Newman wrote twenty-four of the *Tracts*, and they helped to gain many supporters for the movement. Edward Bouverie Pusey (1800–1882), regius professor of Hebrew at Oxford from 1828, was won over in 1835; and Manning, who was destined to become the Roman Catholic archbishop of Westminster and the founder of the cathedral there, wrote the seventy-eighth *Tract*.

Newman grew more and more favorably disposed to the doctrines characteristic of the Counter-Reformation, and in the ninetieth *Tract*, published in 1841, he went so far as to argue that the Thirty-nine Articles should be understood in the sense of the decrees of the Council of Trent (1545–63), not in accordance with the intention of those who actually drew them up. The document had a stormy reception, and the Anglican bishop at Oxford ordered that the *Tracts* thenceforth cease to be published. From that time Newman began to withdraw from active participation in the life of Oxford, but he did not resign from his office as vicar of St. Mary's, the university church (to which he had been appointed in 1828), until 1843. He submitted to Roman Catholic rites of initation two years later; others followed, including Manning, who conformed in 1851 and was made a cardinal in 1875, four years before Newman attained that dignity.

The works of Newman, a vigorous and brilliant writer, include: *An Essay on the Development of Christian Doctrine* (1845), which argues that post-Tridentine Catholicism represents the legitimate outcome of the church's continuous evolution under the guidance of the divine Spirit; *Apologia pro Vita Sua* (1864), presenting an autobiographical account of the author's theological ideas up to the time of his reception into Roman Catholicism; *The Grammar of Assent* (1870), which contends that man possesses an "illative" faculty whereby, independently of logical procedures, he can arrive at an assurance of the validity of religious truths.

Despite the numerous secessions to Rome, Anglo-Catholicism succeeded in maintaining itself. It owed much to the capable leadership of Pusey, who sought to enrich the Anglican liturgy by introducing elements that the reformers of the sixteenth century had cast aside; he also encouraged the establishment of institutions of a monastic character, holding that the sense of religious vocation is deepened when an individual lives under corporate discipline as a member of a dedicated Christian community.

Largely through the influence of Charles Gore (1853–1932), the first principal at Pusey House in Oxford, Anglo-Catholics became more or less reconciled to the critical approach to the Bible (which Pusey himself had resisted) and developed a deep concern for the application of Christian ethical standards in endeavors to solve social problems. Gore subsequently became the first bishop of Birmingham (1905–11) and the bishop of Oxford (1911–19). Among his works may be mentioned: *The Anglo-Catholic Movement Today* (1925), *The Reconstruction of Belief* (1926), and *The Philosophy of the Good Life* (1930). Gore was mainly responsible for the foundation of the Community of the Resurrection, which moved from Oxford to Radley, Berkshire, in 1893, and to Mirfield, Yorkshire, five years later.

In nineteenth-century Germany the influence of Kant and Schleiermacher persisted, along with that of Hegel. This is amply illustrated in the thought of Albrecht Ritschl (1822–89), the most influential Protestant theologian of the late nineteenth century, whose work subjected Lutheran Pietism to further critical refinement. The son of a minister, he studied at Bonn, Halle, Heidelberg, and Tübingen, and was later professor of theology, first at Bonn (1851–64) and then at Göttingen (1864–89).

In Ritschl's two earlier studies—one on the gospel of Marcion and its relation to the canonical gospel of Luke (1846) and the other on the rise of ancient Catholicism (1850)—he wrote as a member of the Tübingen School, supporting Baur's thesis that orthodoxy originally emerged as a supervening synthesis out of the conflict between Petrinism and Paulinism. But by 1857, when a revised edition of his second book appeared, he had come to feel that Baur had oversimplified the concrete actualities of apostolic Christianity; the primitive church, he argued, embraced multifarious shades of belief, and its development involved much more than the adaptation of an expanding form of Jewish Messianism to a Hellenistic cultural environment.

Ritschl's main interest gradually shifted from historical to systematic theology, a subject on which he regularly lectured from the early fifties. Following Schleiermacher, he postulated that religion is *sui generis,* an irreducible factor in human existence; and, following Kant, he held that God is known not intellectually but practically in the valuing activity of the moral and spiritual life. On the other hand, unlike Kant, and in the spirit of Hegel, he stressed the corporate character of religion, maintaining that the divine revelation in Jesus was mediated through an adoring fellowship of disciples who together constituted the nucleus of the primitive church. Thus was developed a form of theological positivism, which combined an aversion to speculative metaphysics with a keen sense of the social dynamics of historical situations.

In his endeavor to elucidate the precise nature of religious knowledge Ritschl turned neither to ethical imperatives as such nor to mystical feelings, but to acts of valuation. He argued that theoretical understanding and religious conviction derive from radically different modes of mental activity. The mind relates itself to the external world in two distinct ways: either it makes theoretical judgments, directing its attention outwardly and connecting things as parts of an objective causal system, or it makes value judgments, estimating things according to their worth in relation to subjective needs. These two attitudes, the theoretical and the axiological, are quite independent of each other, and only confused thinking can lead us to suppose that conflict ever arises between them. And since religion arises as a social phenomenon from value judgments, it does not matter to what metaphysical school a person belongs. The divinity of Jesus, for instance, is not an objective determination of his essence but rather the result of an assessment made by his votaries; he enjoys worshipfulness, not intrinsically, but extrinsically, in his relationship with the communities that profess religious allegiance to his person.

Accordingly, the intellectual subtleties of the ancient creeds were, in Ritschl's view, largely irrelevant, and one of the principal tasks of the theologian is to clarify the axiological significance of Jesus for the primitive church. A recognition of such significance can still arouse a positive spiritual response in the modern mind, and this, as in the first century, brings about the renewing experience of justification and reconciliation.

Ritschl's main ideas were embodied in his great treatise *Die christliche Lehre von der Rechtfertigung und Versöhnung* (3 vols., 1870–74; English translation of vols. I and II, *The Christian Doctrine of Justification and Reconciliation,* 1872, 1900). Among his other works are *Theologie und Metaphysik* ("Theology and Metaphysics," 1881) and *Die Geschichte des Pietismus* ("The History of Pietism," 3 vols., 1880–86).

Among Ritschl's followers was Adolf von Harnack (1851–1930), whose work on the essence of Christianity, *Das Wesen des Christentums* (1900; published in English as *What is Christianity?,* 1901) is frequently regarded as the classic exposition of liberal Protestantism. The son of a minister, he studied at Dorpat and Leipzig, and became professor successively at Leipzig, Giessen, Marburg, and Berlin. In 1910 he was elected president of the Kaiser Wilhelm Gesellschaft ("Society") for the promotion of science and learning.

In his massive *Lehrbuch der Dogmengeschichte* (3 vols., 1886–89; English translation, *History of Dogma,* 7 vols., 1894–99) Harnack expounded in detail the development of Christian doctrine up to the Reformation of the sixteenth century. His central thesis (in line with Ritschlianism) was that the metaphysical concepts appropriated by ancient Catholicism from its Hellenistic environment corrupted the pure essence of the original Aramaic gospel. Christianity, thanks to Paul and others, spread in the Gentile culture of the Eastern empire, but it was paganized in the process. Hence when defenders of the orthodox faith contrast the sacred with the secular, they really do so in the name of a tradition that has itself been subjected to centuries of secularization.

Of his other works on Christian history may be mentioned *Die Geschichte der altchristlichen Literatur bis Eusebius* ("The History of Ancient Christian Literature up to Eusebius," 4 vols., 1893–1904) and *Die Mission und Ausbreitung des Christentums in den ersten drei Jahrhunderten* (1902; enlarged fourth edition, 1924; published in English as *The Expansion of Christianity in the First Three Centuries,* 2 vols., 1904–5). In his *Beiträge zur Einleitung in das Neue Testament* (4 parts, 1906–11; English translations: *Luke the Physician,* 1907; *The Sayings of Jesus,* 1908; *The Acts of the Apostles,* 1909; *The Date of the Acts and of the Synoptic Gospels,* 1911) he argued that the Acts of the Apostles, the sequel of the Third Gospel, was written while Paul was still in jail at Rome (the imprisonment described in the twenty-eighth chapter of Acts). This led him to assign Luke's gospel to an earlier date than is usually supposed, for it is generally held among scholars that since Mark's gospel was written around A.D. 70 (the year of the fall of Jerusalem), Luke-Acts must have been composed some ten to twenty-five years later.

In *Das Wesen des Christentums* Harnack turned to the synoptic gospels to elucidate the essence of Christianity, holding that they bear witness to the faith in its pristine purity and conserve its most precious traditions. In certain respects, admittedly, these ancient writings are liable to alienate the modern reader. They are disjointed in their narration of events, lacking the continuity characteristic of systematic biography; also, they exemplify outmoded cosmological beliefs, take it for granted that demons may cause diseases, and betray a predilection for the miraculous. Such features as these, however, only go to show that the documents in question are products of a prescientific culture, and they should not be allowed to give offense; once recognized as belonging to the husk of the faith, they can scarcely affect the value of the moral and spiritual kernel they enshrine.

In various ways the gospels draw the reader's attention to the life and teaching of a superb master in the art of living. They reproduce some of his sayings and delineate some of his actions, besides revealing the tremendous impression he made upon his disciples. They disclose that Jesus of Nazareth stood in the great prophetic tradition of his people, that he was moved by a burning moral conviction, and that he prayed and struggled for the establishment of justice. Nevertheless, despite the depth of his ethical perspicacity and the passionateness of his endeavor to bring men to repentance, the personality that shines through the synoptic reports was far from being unbalanced or pathological. An equable breadth of attitude pervaded his words and deeds. The disciplinarian who advocated the amputation of obstreperous limbs was in the habit of attending sumptuous dinner parties, so that in certain quarters he acquired the reputation of being a glutton and a winebibber.

According to Harnack, the transcendent concern of Jesus entailed three principal motifs: the Kingdom of God and its coming, or the rule of God in the soul; the fatherhood of God and the infinite value of each human individual; the higher righteousness and the commandment of love. Deficient though they are by modern standards, the synoptics indicate how devotion to such ideals issued in the master's fulfillment of his religious vocation. It was Jesus' conviction that God is the ultimate ruler, the heavenly King, who governs the world with justice; but he also had the assurance that God is the heavenly Father who clothes the flowers of the field and cares for the meanest sparrow that falls in the street. God's justice is tempered with mercy, for he causes his sun to rise on the evil and on the good, and sends his rain on the just and on the unjust. And as love motivates the Creator's presiding providence, so love should motivate the conduct of his most gifted creatures. By parable and vivid word, by forthright statement and paradox, by precept and example, Jesus tried to awaken his contemporaries to their high responsibilities as children of the heavenly Father. And despite the archaic character of the gospels, his words dart across the centuries with the freshness of the present, communicating the essential significance of Christianity.

For Harnack, then, the fundamental religion of Jesus, bereft of outworn philosophical concepts, is no less acceptable to the educated mind of today than it was to men of discernment two thousand years ago, and it should still be promoted for the health of contemporary scientific culture. The metaphysics of the ancient orthodox creeds, like disputes concerning ecclesiastical polity, belong to the periphery of the genuinely religious life and are therefore without vital pertinence. Thus, although Jesus lived in a world long since passed and his ideas on cosmology and history have been superseded, the spiritual essence of his religion is as relevant today as it was in the first century.

Liberalism spread in the Protestant denominations of Europe, America, and elsewhere during the later decades of the nineteenth and the early decades of the twentieth century, and not infrequently it came to be coupled with the so-called social gospel; that is, liberal theology tended to ally itself with a concern to improve society by removing economic inequalities and other injustices. In certain quarters patriotism was condemned as a major cause of the scourge of international war, and pacifist minority movements often had connections with forms of Protestant liberalism. But perhaps the most signal triumph for liberal theology is to be found in the widespread acceptance of the principles of biblical criticism.

Several Protestant countries saw the emergence of various modernist movements that cut across denominational barriers. For example, in England the Modern Churchman's Union was founded in 1898 by a group of Anglicans who were anxious to promote liberal theology. Among those involved in its earlier years was Hastings Rashdall (1858–1924), dean of Carlisle from 1917, who made a name for himself in the field of historical scholarship with his work *Universities in Europe in the Middle Ages* (3 vols., 1895), and who subsequently defended a moral-influence theory in his book *The Idea of Atonement in Christian Theology* (1919). Also important was William Ralph Inge (1860–1954), dean at St. Paul's Cathedral, London (1911–34), whose works included *The Philosophy of Plotinus* (2 vols., 1918), *Christian Ethics and Modern Problems* (1930), and *God and the Astronomers* (1933).

The Union of Modern Free Churchmen, established at Blackheath Congregational Church, London, in 1933, eventually incorporated Presbyterians, Baptists, Unitarians, Quakers, and Methodists, as well as Congregationalists. The leaders—among whom was Thomas Wigley (1891–1961), the minister at Black-heath—formulated a new creed or statement of faith, which emphasized the inherent spiritual capacities of human nature and maintained quite simply that God's purpose for the world (as revealed by Jesus) is to express the divine love and holiness in both individual and corporate life. The statement was not intended to be imposed upon the members of the Union after the fashion of an immutable decree; it was devised merely as a convenient schematization of the tenor of liberal theological thinking in English Nonconformity during the thirties of the present century.

BIBLIOGRAPHY

Barth, Karl. *Protestant Thought from Rousseau to Ritschl.* New York: Harper, 1959.

Cadoux, C. J. *Catholicism and Christianity: A Vindication of Progressive Protestantism.* New York: Dial Press, 1929.

Cauthon, Kenneth. *The Impact of American Religious Liberalism.* New York: Harper and Row, 1962.

Chadwick, W. O., ed. *The Mind of the Oxford Movement.* London: Black, 1960.

Ollard, S. L. *A Short History of the Oxford Movement.* Milwaukee, Wis.: Young Churchman, 1915.

Reardon, B. M. G., ed. *Liberal Protestantism.* London: Black, 1968.

Reville, Jean. *Liberal Christianity: Its Origin, Nature and Mission.* New York: Putnam's, 1903.

Stewart, H. L. *A Century of Anglo-Catholicism.* London: Dent, 1929.

Webb, C. C. J. *Religious Thought in the Oxford Movement.* London: Society for Promoting Christian Knowledge, 1928.

41 ‡ *Ecumenism*

A remarkable feature of recent Christian history is that more and more people, belonging to diverse denominations and representing different theological traditions, have shown a growing concern for coming together to consider questions of common interest. After the Reformation in the sixteenth century, Christendom was subjected to increasing partition; separatism and mutual alienation ensued because of varying religious convictions and patriotic sentiments. The dismembering process continued until well into the nineteenth century, but eventually a new spirit became evident in certain circles. Foreign missionaries, for instance, began to realize that their sectarian peculiarities had not the significance in Africa or India or China that they had in Europe or America, while some became more convinced that a missionary should have an understanding of the culture of the people among whom he had gone to minister, and this was partly responsible for the development of the comparative study of religion. In 1910 an important international missionary conference took place at Edinburgh, and this gathering is often taken to mark the birth of contemporary ecumenism (Greek: *oikoumenē*, "inhabited earth"). Today, the World Council of Churches is an institution of global significance, representing as it does more than two hundred non-Catholic denominations.

The ecumenical movement owes much to initiative from the United States, where, despite a certain detachment from tradi-

435

tional European sectarianism, there had been an extraordinary proliferation of denominations, with an attendant emergence of new rivalries. And presumably it is in the light of such a situation that the American initiative in question is to be explained. However this may be, as early as 1853 the Protestant Episcopal church appointed a commission to confer with other American churches that recognized the desirability of promoting Christian unity; and since that time numerous ecclesiastical fusions have taken place in various parts of the world.

Thus in Scotland in 1900 the United Presbyterians and the Free Presbyterians merged to form the United Free Presbyterian church, and in 1929 this communion was absorbed into the Church of Scotland. In Canada in 1925 Presbyterians, Congregationalists, and Methodists came together to constitute the United Church of Canada. In England in 1907 the New Connexionalists, the Bible Christians, and the United Methodist Free church coalesced into the United Methodist church, and in 1932 this body combined with the Wesleyan Methodists and the Primitive Methodists to form the Methodist Church of Great Britain. In France in 1939 the larger Protestant denominations united to constitute the Reformed church. In the United States in 1939 three Methodist communions combined to form the Methodist church, and in 1960 the Association of Congregational Christian Churches and the Evangelical and Reformed church came together to establish the United Church of Christ.

The formation of the Church of South India in 1947 is a matter of special interest because it involved a merging of episcopal with nonepiscopal bodies. Entailed in this union were : (1) Four dioceses of the Anglican church of India, Burma, and Ceylon; (2) The South India Province of the Indian Methodist church; (3) The South India United church (a body resulting from a fusion of Presbyterian, Congregationalist, and Dutch Reformed denominations in 1908), which had incorporated the Malabar District of the Basel Mission (Lutheran and Reformed) in 1919. The prolonged negotiations that preceded the union showed a serious concern that the new church should be so constituted as to preserve essential features of the congregationalist, presbyterian, and episcopalian polities; nevertheless, as things now stand, it is envisaged that by 1978 almost all the active clergy will have received episcopal ordination. Limited intercommunion with the Church of England was authorized by the convocations of Canterbury and York in 1955.

Although most of the Protestant missionary societies were founded in the wake of the Methodist revival, there was no united missionary conference until 1888. The meeting took place in London, to be followed twelve years later by a similar gathering in New York. And in 1910 at the Edinburgh World Missionary Conference the ecumenical movement showed sufficient momentum to organize itself on a permanent basis; before the delegates dispersed, they established a continuation committee under the secretaryship of John Raleigh Mott (1865–1958). An American Methodist and an alumnus of Upper Iowa and Cornell universities, Mott had been general secretary of the World Student Christian Federation and was a dynamic personality whose enthusiasm for integrated ecclesiastical action proved extremely infectious.

Interest in missionary cooperation was stimulated on a global scale. *The International Review of Missions* first appeared in 1910, and in 1920 the continuation committee was consolidated as the International Missionary Council. At Jerusalem in 1928 a further World Missionary Conference took place, and younger Eastern and African churches were well represented. The next World Missionary Conference met at Madras in 1938, and missionary cooperation was carried a stage further.

After the Edinburgh Conference of 1910 Charles Henry Brent (1862–1929) returned to America abounding with zeal for the ecumenical idea, and he stirred the General Convention of the Protestant Episcopal church to promote a World Conference on Faith and Order. Born at Newcastle, Ontario, Brent studied at Trinity College, Toronto, and was consecrated bishop of the Philippines in 1901. Preliminary work on the scheme suffered delay because of the First World War, and it was not until 1920 that Brent presided over a preparatory conference at Geneva, with delegates from seventy denominations and forty countries. A continuation committee was formed, and this prepared for the first World Conference on Faith and Order, over which Brent presided, at Lausanne in 1927. A continuation committee was again established, and it prepared for the second World Conference on Faith and Order, which took place at Edinburgh in 1937, representing over one hundred denominations. The main purpose was to report to the constituent churches on the progress made in joint studies concerning the obstacles that would have to be overcome before organic union on a grand scale could be achieved.

During the First World War it had come to be widely felt that the tragic confusions of the time called for organized cooperation among the churches for the application of their ethical ideals to special problems, and a preliminary conference on Life and Work was held at Geneva in 1920—a gathering that included consultative representatives of certain Eastern Orthodox churches. The leadership was assumed by Nathan Söderblom (1866–1931), the Lutheran archbishop of Upsala, whose own theological position had been profoundly influenced by the writings of Albrecht Ritschl, Auguste Sabatier, and Alfred Loisy, as is made abundantly clear in his treatises *The Nature of Revelation* (1903) and *The Living God* (1933). His suggestion at Geneva that the prospective World Conference should be held in Sweden found ready acceptance.

Preparation continued in various countries, and especially noteworthy was the Conference on Politics, Economics, and Citizenship (usually known as COPEC) held at Birmingham, England, in 1924, for the reports of its commissions provide valuable statements on social questions. It was in 1925 that the first World Conference on Life and Work met at Stockholm, and by 1929 its continuation committee had become sufficiently permanent to be designated the Universal Christian Council for Life and Work. The research department of the Council assumed responsibility for the production of several series of scholarly reports on Church, Community, and State. These eventually received authorization from the second World Conference on Life and Work, which met at Oxford in 1937, and thereupon they were published in seven volumes.

At the Oxford and Edinburgh Conferences of 1937 it was decided that the business of Life and Work (Stockholm and Oxford) and that of Faith and Order (Lausanne and Edinburgh) should be integrated under the auspices of a single institution—the World Council of Churches. The full formation of the Council was delayed by the Second World War, but a draft constitution was drawn up by a provisional committee under the chairmanship of William Temple (1881–1944), successively archbishop of York (1929–42) and of Canterbury (1942–44).

The first Assembly of the World Council met at Amsterdam in 1948, and the definition of the new institution as "a fellowship of churches which accept our Lord Jesus Christ as God and Savior" received formal sanction. Representatives of some one hundred and fifty denominations were present; the main bodies not involved were the Roman Catholic church, the Patriarchate of Moscow (and certain other Orthodox churches within the Soviet sphere of influence), and the Southern Baptist church of the United States, as well as Unitarians and Quakers (who could not accept a creed that identifies Christ with God). The Assembly appointed a central committee to meet annually for the purpose of carrying out the Assembly's decisions, and this committee elected a smaller executive body to supervise the operations of the Council's permanent offices at Geneva. Six presidents were duly installed, and W. A. Visser't Hooft (of Holland) was placed in charge of the secretariat.

The Assembly ratified a constitution and formulated the aims of the World Council's activities somewhat in the following terms: (1) To perpetuate and coordinate the ecumenical concerns of Faith and Order and Life and Work; (2) To facilitate common action by the represented ecclesiastical bodies; (3) To promote mutual consultation in the study of pertinent questions; (4) To encourage the growth of an ecumenical consciousness within the member churches; (5) To establish active relations with denominational federations of world-wide scope; (6) To convoke world conferences periodically for the discussion of matters of special interest; (7) To support the churches in the work of world evangelization. Also, provisions were made for communication with the constituent denominations, for action through national councils of churches, and for cooperation with the International Missionary Council. *The Ecumenical Review,* a quarterly periodical published at Geneva, made its first appearance in 1948.

The second Assembly of the World Council of Churches met at Evanston, Illinois, in 1954, and the third at New Delhi in 1961. The work of the International Missionary Council was integrated with that of the World Council, and the Russian Patriarchate successfully negotiated with the relevant political authority in Moscow to secure due representation at the New Delhi assembly. Early in 1966 Eugene Carson Blake, chief executive official of the United Presbyterian church in America, was appointed to succeed Visser't Hooft as director of the World Council's secretariat in Geneva.

Until 1958 Roman Catholicism remained officially aloof from the ecumenical movement, and any representatives it may have authorized to attend gatherings sponsored by the World Council functioned largely as detached spectators. It maintained its defensive stance as the church of the Tridentine Reformation (1545–63), the body that promulgated the Syllabus of Errors (1864) and denounced modernism as a synthesis of all heresies (1907). However, after the accession of Pope Pius XII (1939–58) and the outbreak of the Second World War there appeared various signs of liberalizing tendencies, and these became more pronounced as the years passed. On the whole, Pius XII upheld the status quo, but it is noteworthy that his confessor was Cardinal Augustine Béa (1881–1968), a scholarly German Jesuit with progressive inclinations. The tendencies in question came to open expression in 1958, soon after the accession of Pope John XXIII (the Pope John XXIII deposed by the Council of Constance in 1415 is not officially recognized). This led to a great surge of fresh vitality within Latin Christendom, involving a stronger desire for closer fellowship with non-Catholic churches and for more active participation in the cooperative work of the ecumenical movement, which had come to acquire great importance.

Evidently disturbed by Christianity's growing irrelevance to practical life in the modern world, Pope John was prompted to convene a council of bishops to consider ways and means of redefining and updating the thought and action of Catholicism in the contemporary global situation with its pressing social and international problems. His concern for broader ecclesiastical sympathies was more widely shared than may have seemed likely at first.

Apparently, various ideological developments during and after the First World War, with their flagrant repudiation of elementary biblical ethics, had convinced many influential persons that the church had an urgent obligation to make unequivocal demands for the recognition of certain basic human rights in the common conduct of secular affairs. Communism, based on Marxist principles, spread rapidly after the Bolshevik Revolution (1917), and, while its ideal of justice for the common man was not unbiblical, its practical adherence to the view that the end justifies the means often resulted in savagery and inordinate suffering. Other totalitarian quasi-religions emerged, notably, Fascism and National Socialism, which, although patriotic and racist and therefore in principle opposed to Marxism, had *de facto* affiliation with Communism in the ruthlessness of their methods. Fascism established itself in Italy, and National Social-

ism in Germany, and the latter, which stressed a racialistic doctrine of Nordic superiority, carried its teaching to such lengths
that during the period of its ascendancy (1933–45) some six
million Jews were exterminated. And while such atrocities were
being committed by diverse secular authorities, the church had
seemed to stand by quite helplessly.

Moreover, even in countries where the democratic principle
had managed to survive, it had become quite obvious that the
masses were largely alienated from the church. In France, for
example, it was increasingly felt that there should be greater
clerical involvement in the secular affairs of the people and
greater lay participation in ecclesiastical activities, so as to
strengthen the rapport between organized Christianity and the
population at large. After the Second World War, signs of such
a modified orientation included the widespread concern for liturgical reform, the institution of so-called worker-priests (that
is, priests with full-time secular employment who continued to
fulfill their sacerdotal functions during their leisure time), and
the insistent demand for educational curricula that would take
into sympathetic account the achievements of twentieth-century
science and scholarship.

Remarkable in this last connection was the encyclical *Divino
Afflante Spiritu* ("By the Divine Inspiration of the Spirit"),
published by Pius XII in 1943, which dealt specifically with
biblical scholarship and allowed a range of freedom that would
have appalled such popes as Pius IX (1846–78), Leo XIII (1878–
1903) and Pius X (1903–14), under whose suzerainty, as we
have seen, all modernizing tendencies within the church were
vigorously suppressed. The encyclical inaugurated a new era in
Catholic biblical studies; to cite but one example, the treatise
*Das Wahre Israel: Studien zur Theologie des Matthäus-Evan-
geliums* ("The True Israel: Studies on the Theology of Matthew's Gospel," 1959), by Wolfgang Trilling, a Roman Catholic scholar of Leipzig, not only belonged to the front rank in
the field of New Testament erudition, but displayed a liberalism

of outlook that could scarcely be matched by many Protestant experts on the same subject.

In January 1959 Pope John announced his intention to convene a general council of bishops to examine the position of the church in the contemporary world and thereby to supplement the work of the first Vatican Council (1869–70), whose deliberations had been cut short through the outbreak of the Franco-Prussian war. But John's attitude was quite different from that of his nineteenth-century predecessor, Pius IX. If the latter had wished to close windows, the former was anxious to open them, that fresh air might blow in and reinvigorate the church. The council eventually met at Rome in the autumn of 1962 for its first series of meetings, and there were three further autumnal sessions in 1963–65. More than two thousand bishops attended from most parts of the world, and some sixty Eastern Orthodox and Protestant observers accepted invitations; the latter witnessed all the council's deliberations, were allowed to see the draft texts of the enactments, and had regular consultations with the members of the various commissions that produced them.

Pope John died in 1963 before the second session took place and was succeeded by Pope Paul VI, who, if in a less forthright and more diplomatic way, continued to serve the ideals to which John had given such direct expression. The spirit behind the council received dramatic recognition in two of its closing events: at a simple service of worship, with prayers and scriptural readings, the pope shared its conduct with Orthodox and Protestant clergymen; and some days afterward Paul and Patriarch Athenagoras I of Constantinople simultaneously rescinded the mutual sentences of excommunication that had characterized the great schism between Greek and Latin Christianity in 1054.

Altogether, four constitutions, nine decrees, and three declarations were approved by large majorities at the four sessions of the council. In constitutions, it may be noted, the stress is upon doctrine and in decrees upon discipline or practice, while in declarations theory and practice tend to share the emphasis.

The first of the four constitutions, *De Sacra Liturgia* ("On the Sacred Liturgy," session 2), allows the celebration of the mass in vernacular languages (except for the canonical words of consecration, which must remain in Latin) and permits the simplification of certain ceremonies. *De Ecclesia* ("On the Church," the second constitution, session 3) places a new emphasis on the solidarity of the church. The layman enjoys an inherent apostolic dignity, and the clergy are to respect that dignity and the legitimate freedom it involves. Likewise, the bishops are to respect the rights of the priest, and they themselves, in virtue of their episcopal collegiality, share with the bishop of Rome responsibility for the government of the church as a whole. *De Divina Revelatione* ("On Divine Revelation," the third constitution, session 4) rules that the divine revelation in Christ comes primarily through the biblical records, and that the church, with its continuing tradition, is called upon to interpret and apply the meaning of scripture. The fourth constitution, *De Ecclesia in Mundo huius Temporis* ("On the Church in the World of this Time"—officially published in English as "On the Church in the Modern World"—session 4), was promulgated on the last day of the council and deals somewhat sketchily with such questions as war and the nuclear menace, marriage and the population explosion, economic poverty and racial discrimination. It notices that the invention of nuclear weapons weakened the persuasiveness of the kind of argument traditionally used by the church since the time of Augustine to validate Christian participation in a just war. One might compare with this a statement approved at the 1948 Assembly of the World Council of Churches, which reads: "Law may require the sanction of force, but when war breaks out force is used on a scale which tends to destroy the basis on which law exists."

Of the nine decrees, *Inter Mirificas* ("Among the Marvels," session 2) offers a very brief consideration of the use of contemporary media of mass communication. *De Oecumenismo*

("On Ecumenism," session 3) envisages increased Catholic participation in the movement that led to the establishment of the World Council of Churches, and members of non-Catholic Christian communions are referred to as "separated brethren" (not as "heretics"). *De Ecclesiis Orientalibus* ("On the Oriental Churches," session 3) primarily relates to Uniat communities— that is, to Eastern churches that acknowledge the pope's supremacy but retain their own peculiar liturgies and other forms —but indirectly it has a bearing on Greek Orthodoxy. The validity of the distinctive Eastern rites is acknowledged, and suggestions are made for increasing mutual understanding. *De Activitate Missionali Ecclesiae* ("On the Missionary Activity of the Church," session 4) allows to bishops in the mission fields greater independence of the *curia*. Forced conversion is condemned, and greater cooperation between Catholic and non-Catholic Christian missionaries is commended in various connections. *De Pastorali Episcoporum Munere in Ecclesia* ("On the Pastoral Office of Bishops in the Church," session 4) makes a number of inferences from the concept of episcopal collegiality (the active participation of the bishops in the church's government). *De Ministerio et Vita Presbyterorum* ("On the Ministry and Life of Priests," session 4) proposes certain modifications in the traditional priestly attitude, an implication being that satisfactory communication always involves a two-way traffic of ideas. If the bishops should listen to the priest, the priest should listen to the layman. *De Apostolatu Laicorum* ("On the Apostolate of the Laity," session 4) takes account of possible ways in which the laity may make a positive contribution to the furtherance of Christianity in the contemporary world. *De Accommodata Renovatione Vitae Religiosae* ("On the Adaptive Renewal of Religious Life," session 4) makes various suggestions regarding the renovation of the monastic orders. The ninth decree, *De Institutione Sacerdotali* ("On the Sacerdotal Institution," session 4) contemplates possible reforms in seminary education with a view to broadening typical priestly training, recommending, among other things that the curricula might show more interest in such subjects as biblical criticism, psychology, and the history of separated churches.

The first of the three declarations, *De Libertate Religiosa* ("On Religious Liberty," session 4), is sensitive to the not-infrequent charge that Roman Catholics demand religious liberty where they are in a minority, while denying it in such countries as Spain, where they are in the majority. Conservative delegates strongly opposed the draft text, and in the course of the discussions certain concessions were made to their position—a circumstance which helps to account for the ambivalence in the document as finally approved. On the one hand, it is assumed that the Latin hierarchy transmits what is essential for the regeneration of a humanity corrupted by original sin, whence it follows that, in the interest of human welfare, the saving truth must be disseminated at whatever cost. On the other hand, perhaps partly in the light of twentieth-century experience of various forms of political totalitarianism, it is acknowledged that the human individual enjoys an inalienable dignity as a child of God, and that truth cannot really be promoted by coercion, whence it follows that every person in the last resort must judge for himself what is good, following the will of God as mediated by his own conscience. Accordingly, although the philosophico-theological tendencies (evolutionism and relativism, coupled with an advocacy of unhampered historical and biblical criticism), which so disturbed the nineteenth-century papacy, are by no means entirely cleared of earlier imputations, the declaration definitely recognizes the dignity of man as a free being whose conscience has to be respected.

The second declaration, *De Ecclesiae Habitudine ad Religiones non-Christianas* ("On the Relation of the Church to Non-Christian Religions," session 4), was partly designed to promote a more open attitude towards Hinduism, Buddhism, Judaism, and Islam. The passages dealing with the Jewish question were the subject of much debate at the council, and some delegates felt that, even in the form they eventually assumed, insufficient penitence is shown for the church's prolonged involvement in the crimes of anti-Semitism and insufficient attention is paid to Christianity's native connection with Judaism through their common ancestry in the religion of ancient Israel. However, the statement plainly repudiates the view (whose roots can be traced back to the New Testament period) that the Jewish people are to be held corporately responsible for the crucifixion of Jesus. The third and last declaration, *De Educatione Christiana* ("On Christian Education," session 4), asserts that a Christian education should be made available to everyone and has a significant bearing on the problem of state assistance for church-related schools.

This brief review may serve to show that the four Vatican sessions of 1962–65 supplied considerable reinforcement to ecumenical aspirations for more effective Christian cooperation. They prepared for new developments in the way of increased religious openness; and, soon after the closure of the final session, the Congregation of the Index (instituted in 1571 as part of the Universal Inquisition to keep the list of prohibited books up to date) was abolished in response to a widespread feeling that the *curia* should undergo radical reformation. Hence liberal elements greeted with dismay the papal encyclical of 1968, *Humanae Vitae* ("Of Human Life"), a declaration which, despite the so-called population explosion and the increased independence of women in contemporary civilization, condemned artificial contraception as intrinsically evil.

Actually, the question of birth control was removed from the agenda of Vatican II by Pope John XXIII and was referred to a pontifical commission, the membership of which was progressively enlarged (from an original six to a final seventy-nine) under his successor Paul VI. The latter, having received its divided findings in 1965, proceeded to reserve judgment to himself. In *Humanae Vitae* he countered the commission's majority report and substantially reaffirmed the pronouncements of Pope

John's immediate predecessors. In 1930 Pius XI had stated that the conjugal act is primarily designed for the begetting of children and that those who deliberately frustrate its proper effect commit a sin against nature; nonetheless, with qualifications, the safe-period or rhythm method of birth control was expressly allowed by Pius XII. And such was the complex kind of position upheld in the encyclical under consideration.

It is not surprising, therefore, that the *magisterium* ("teaching authority") of the Latin Church was subjected to considerable strain, for in relying fundamentally upon a particular interpretation of natural law Pope Paul apparently made the implicit claim that the whole matter was amenable to reason as distinct from revelation (or from infallible pronouncements *ex cathedra*). Broadly, the queries raised and keenly debated fell into two categories, namely, those that concerned papal authority and those that bore more or less directly upon the argument from natural law. Questions of the first kind included: What had become of the principal of collegiate authority, a principle so prominent at Vatican II? Why should a pontifical commission have been appointed when its majority report was summarily overruled by an exercise of papal prerogative? And what had become of the concept of lay participation in the government of the church? To the second category belonged such questions as: While in general erotic passion may have its biological basis in the perpetuation of the species, could this be logically particularized into the assertion that humanity has no right to separate the unitive from the procreative aspect of marital intimacy? Did not the endorsement of the rhythm method imply that sexual intercourse could be licitly practiced otherwise than for the production of offspring? And, while there may be social and even political dangers involved in a general practice of contraception, did not these potential evils derive from the misuse of techniques which in themselves are morally neutral?

Rome had spoken, but as recent history has come to show, in this instance the case was not closed.

BIBLIOGRAPHY

Abbott, W. M., ed. *The Documents of Vatican II.* New York: Guild Press, 1966.

Barth, Karl. *Ad Limina Apostolorum: An Appraisal of Vatican II.* Richmond, Va.: John Knox Press, 1968.

Bird, T. E., ed. *Modern Theologians, Christians and Jews.* New York: Association Press, 1968.

Boney, W. J., and L. E. Molumby, eds. *The New Day: Catholic Theologians of the Renewal.* Richmond, Va.: John Knox Press, 1968.

Brandon, S. G. F., ed. *A Dictionary of Comparative Religion.* London: Weidenfeld and Nicolson, 1970.

Brown, R. McAffee. *The Ecumenical Revolution: An Interpretation of the Catholic-Protestant Dialogue.* Garden City, N.Y.: Doubleday, 1967.

Grant, F. C. *Rome and Reunion.* New York: Oxford University Press, 1965.

Horton, W. M. *Christian Theology: An Ecumenical Approach.* 2nd ed. New York: Harper, 1955.

Küng, H. *The Changing Church.* London: Sheed and Ward, 1965.

Neill, S. C. *Christian Faith and Other Faiths: The Christian Dialogue with Other Religions.* 2nd ed. New York: Oxford University Press, 1970.

Rouse, Ruth, and S. C. Neill, eds. *A History of the Ecumenical Movement, 1517–1948.* 2nd ed. Philadelphia: Westminster Press, 1967.

Vorgrimler, H., ed. *Commentary on the Documents of Vatican II.* 5 vols. New York: Herder, 1969.

42 ‡ Quests for Clarity

During the modern period Christianity became increasingly complicated through the proliferation of denominations and the multiplication of diverse schools of theological thought. In the eyes of many people the complexification had the unfortunate effect of obscuring the basic significance of the faith, and the question has frequently been raised: What precisely is the vital religious essence that has assumed such a great variety of forms? Or, otherwise expressed: How exactly may the true nature of Christianity be clarified? As we have seen, one celebrated answer was offered by Adolf von Harnack near the beginning of the present century, and since then numerous other proposals have been made.

As pointed out in an earlier chapter, during the late nineteenth century the Roman Catholic hierarchy, confronted by growing doctrinal diversity, sought a clear and uniform theological foundation in the teaching of Thomas Aquinas; and the ensuing efflorescence of modernism, by way of reaction, strengthened the official reversion to constructive scholasticism, the result being that the principles of a modified Aristotelianism soon became the normative basis of Catholic thought. Among the outstanding exponents and defenders of Neo-Thomism was Jacques Maritain (b. 1882), who, as a young man, revolted against the evolutionism of Henri Bergson. In his small book *An Introduction to Philosophy* (1920; English translation, 1930) and in a number of other treatises, the most systematic of which being *The Degrees of Knowledge* (1932; English translation, 1937), Maritain, operating on the foundation of Thomist principles, worked out a philosophico-theological world view that took into account post-medieval intellectual achievements.

However, most thinkers outside Catholicism (and a minority within) saw a certain inappropriateness in the constant appeal to Aquinas. It was commonly argued that his fundamentally Aristotelian concepts provided quite inadequate equipment for minds grappling with the problems of a scientific age (what light could Aristotle shed on the thermodynamical equations and the doctrine of the survival of the fittest?); and that the biblical exegesis of Aquinas, excogitated as it was before the era of systematic textual and historical criticism, must be rejected as ill-informed (what light could Thomism shed on the questions faced by Wellhausen and his successors?)

More specifically, so far as Protestantism is concerned, the gathering strength of the ecumenical movement after the First World War encouraged numerous attempts to justify efforts for Christian unity by elucidating the reality of a common theological basis in the scriptures. All ecclesiastical and intellectual developments within Christendom, despite their apparent heterogeneity, have their ultimate source in biblical literature; hence, so it was contended, the pure and common essence of Christianity is to be found in the canonical records of God's self-disclosures to humanity. Important in this general connection was the influence of Karl Barth (1886–1968), the Swiss thinker who in his book *Der Römerbrief* (1919; an exposition of the Apostle Paul's Epistle to the Romans) violently attacked the allegedly facile assumptions entailed in the so-called liberal theology of Harnack and his followers, maintaining that, since man is enslaved by original sin, he can be saved only by attending in faith to the word of God revealed in the scriptures. After the manner of Luther and Calvin in the sixteenth century, Barth posited a complete discontinuity between reason and religious faith; natural theology is a counterfeit discipline, and the vaunted accomplishments of modern culture, having sprung from humanity's corrupted condition, stand under God's threatening condemnation; and Barth could point to the mass carnage of 1914–18 in proof of his central thesis. Noteworthy in the systemization of the new orthodoxy was the Zurich professor Heinrich Emil Brunner (1899–1966), whose works *Der Mittler* (1927; English translation, *The Mediator*, 1934) and *Das Gebot und die Ordnungen* (1932; published in English as *The Divine Imperative*, 1937) were particularly influential; however, more rigorous representatives of Barthianism condemned him for allowing of a certain validity to natural theology.

Following in the wake of Barth and Brunner, Reinhold Niebuhr (b. 1892), an American theologian with a deep ethical concern, reacted strongly against what he considered to be the inordinate optimism of the liberal movement and, during the thirties, became the most influential exponent of Protestant neoorthodoxy in the English-speaking world. Since theological liberalism had made considerable gains during the nineteenth century and the early years of the twentieth, perpetuating the spirit of the Enlightenment in an age that had come to believe in the evolutionary progress of humanity, it was being ever more widely held among Protestant intellectuals that man, equipped with the instruments of an industrialized economy, enjoys an inherent capacity to work out his own salvation: given the democratization of education and a just ordering of society, the Kingdom of God, characterized by broad sympathies and harmonious cooperation, could be established in the world. In the United States this manner of thinking found lucid and vigorous expression in such works as *Christianizing the Social Order* (1912) and *A Theology for the Social Gospel* (1917) by Walter Rauschenbusch (1861–1918), who was eventually elected to a professorship at Rochester Theological Seminary; earlier he served as minister of a church in Hell's Kitchen on the west side of Manhattan, and his conscience was stirred by the appalling economic conditions then prevailing in that neighborhood.

Niebuhr, however, like Barth (and like the reformers of the sixteenth century), turned to the Paulino-Augustinian doctrines of original sin and divine grace, contending that man can attain salvation only by faith in God's redemptive mercy. Among his more substantial works may be mentioned *The Nature and Destiny of Man* (1941–43) and *Faith and History* (1949). He studied at Yale Divinity School, and after occupying a pastorate in Detroit where he took an active part in movements for social reform, in 1928 he became a professor at Union Theological Seminary in New York.

According to Niebuhr, man's evident ability to question the worth of his own existence points to the uniqueness of his status among the created works of God. The human individual is a part of nature, and yet in a significant sense is preternatural. World-negating and life-denying philosophies, entailing ascetical disciplines of one sort or another, bear witness to the truth that he is something more than a biological specimen. Standing outside himself, he can act as his own inquisitor, and by resorting to a nonempirical axis of reference, he can condemn as valueless all that is involved in the evolutionary struggle for existence. Thus, subject though he is to the rigorous decrees of the natural order, man is nonetheless a transcendent being; and in any valid general interpretation of existence the paradox of human bondage and freedom must needs be the focal point of attention. Naturalism plays down man's distinctiveness, whereas an absolutist mystical idealism may too easily equate the human essence with the one eternal Ground of Being behind the chances and changes of historical time.

The biblical doctrine of God as the sole Creator of the universe precludes the possibility of an ultimate dualism between mind and matter. The world is of God, and as such it must be good. Man himself is integral to the created scheme of things; but, having been constituted in the divine image, he inevitably became the beloved object of the Creator's redemptive purpose. Such a purpose was necessitated by the fact of sin, an eventuality that always owes its origin to man's unique endowment: moral freedom. All men have fallen short of the glory of God. Essentially human sinfulness is bound up with the will, and more specifically, with the will to be what one is not. In their pride people make false pretensions, refusing to recognize their creaturely status and acting as if they actually enjoyed the standing of their Maker. This is the point of the myth of Adam's fall (Gen. 3:1 ff.) and of the Pauline doctrine that men became degenerate in the vanity of their imaginings, representing the incorruptibility of God in finite terms, and thereby confounding the creature with the one and only Creator (Rom. 1:18 ff.).

Although the ethical ambiguity inherent in man's dignity as a free being should have become clearer through recent advances in the technologies of destruction, modern culture has continued to stress the creative possibilities of humanity to an extent that is apt to make Christianity seem morbidly pessimistic. The truth is that it is healthier in its realism than the typical optimism of contemporary scientific civilization. Dignity of status is no guarantee of virtue. The gift of freedom, which makes for man's distinctive excellence, is the latent source of nefarious deeds that make him inferior to the beast. All this receives due emphasis in the Christian assessment that human beings generally stand under God's condemnation and are in need of the redemptive mercy exemplified in the self-giving love of a Messiah who died on a cross. And in so far as men surrender themselves in faith and contriteness to their Creator's lovingkindness, pride and egocentricity can be overcome.

But, as Niebuhr goes on to admit, such surrender does not eliminate *ipso facto* the maladjustments and moral incoherencies of the world. Natural evils, which are indications of the failure of cosmic processes to attain perfect conformity with human purposes, belong to the very structure of temporal existence.

Also, religious faith does not rectify the inequalities of circumstance and congenital endowment, nor does it remove the possibility of undeserved suffering. While recognizing the perfection of justice in self-abnegating love, the true Christian has no illusions. Being fully aware of the pervasive pathology of original sin, he recognizes that faith affords no justification whatsoever for a Utopianism that fondly seeks to establish an economic and moral paradise under the temporal exigencies of earthly history.

During the early twenties most Protestant thinkers were of the opinion that the new orthodoxy was unduly one-sided in its interpretations. But as the years passed (and particularly after the rise of Hitlerism in the troubled Germany of 1933), an increasing number of theologians in both Europe and North America were persuaded that Barth was perhaps a modern prophet who had been called to confront the twentieth-century church with the scriptural realities of Christianity; and this, combined with the influence of the ecumenical movement, led to the production of many expositions of biblical theology with a view to clarifying the common scriptural source of the multiple forms of Christian thought and action. One may discern something of this temper (to cite a few English examples) in such works as *The Authority of the Bible* (1952) by Charles Harold Dodd of Cambridge, *The Unity of the Bible* (1954) by Harold Henry Rowley of Manchester, and *The Bible Today* (1955), a symposium edited by Thomas Walter Manson, also of the University of Manchester.

On the other hand, it was the diversity of outlook exemplified in the scriptures that continued to impress certain outstanding scholars, a point well displayed in the Swarthmore Lecture *Quakerism and Early Christianity*, delivered at Friends' House, London, in 1957 by Henry Joel Cadbury of Harvard. So it could be argued that the canonical writings, taken at their face value, are incapable of yielding a clear and definite theological basis for Christianity in the modern world. In any case, the various books of the Bible need to be understood in the light of the circumstances in which they were originally written, and this would seem to imply that a sound hermeneutics (or general interpretation) requires a solid foundation in historical and literary criticism. In a scientific age there can be no short cut to Christianity's supposed biblical essence or common root.

To take an example, a discussion concerning the nature of Christianity could easily raise the question as to what precisely the word "Christian" signified in the primitive church. Acts 11:26 states that the disciples were first called Christians at Antioch in Syria. Apparently this meant that members of the church in question affirmed that Jesus was the promised messianic king (Greek: *Christos*). But were further implications involved? Did it mean that disciples elsewhere refrained from making such an affirmation? Also, did *Christos* mean in the Hellenistic churches what "Messiah" meant in the Aramaic-speaking churches of Palestine? And is it likely that Jesus actually thought of himself either as Israel's hoped-for political ruler or as the Son of Man, appointed finally to judge the world in righteousness? Philipp Vielhauer of the university at Bonn, in his incisive contribution to the *Festschrift für Günther Dehn* (1957), taking it for granted that Jesus entertained no political (messianic) aspirations, further maintained that the synoptic sayings concerning the advent of the Son of Man are secondary to those concerning the advent of the Kingdom of God; and he was induced to conclude that the historical Jesus must have been an eschatological prophet whose teaching was conditioned by his belief that the present world would shortly give way to a transcendent order of existence. This is not the place to enter upon a detailed discussion of Vielhauer's thesis; it is mentioned here merely to illustrate that the exegesis of scriptural passages cannot be satisfactorily executed without gaining admission into the field of critical scholarship.

Moreover, long before the rise of biblical criticism, Martin Luther openly asserted that the Bible was not uniformly inspired and he personally attached far greater importance to the Pauline writings than, say, to the Epistle of James. Other readers of the sacred documents have shown different preferences, and this suggests that the variety of teaching within scripture itself should be counted among the causes of the diversified character of Christianity as it exists in the world of today.

Eastern Orthodoxy, during the first half of the present century, found notable theological representatives in Sergius Bulgakov (1870–1944), dean at the Orthodox Theological Academy in Paris from 1923 up to the time of his death, and Nicholas Berdyaev (1874–1948), a layman who late in life accepted a lectureship at the Sorbonne. The careers of the two thinkers took a remarkably similar course: both were born in Russia and subscribed to Marxism in their early years; both experienced some disillusion after the revolution of 1905 and gradually came to embrace Eastern Christianity, Bulgakov eventually deciding on ordination; and, after the Bolshevik Revolution (1917), both finally settled in Paris, where they died on attaining the same age.

However, Bulgakov's thought was theologically less speculative and more in line with the popular tradition of Eastern Orthodoxy, and his endeavors to clarify the nature of Christianity for the modern mind revolved around the notions of the divine *sophia* (the Greek word for "wisdom") and of *sobornost* (from the Russian term *sobor*, "assembly"). He maintained that the true temper of Christianity, signified by *sobornost*, lies in a certain conciliatoriness, a character that comes to its most vital modern expression in Eastern Orthodoxy as properly practiced. *Sobornost* represents the ethos of the church's corporate life; and, being the Body of Christ, the fellowship of the faithful is informed and sustained by the *sophia* of God. He further argued that the distinctive dynamism of the *sobornost* spirit or principle stands in remarkable contrast both to the centralized bureaucracy of the Latin church and to the anarchic sectarianism typical of Protestant Christianity. Two of Bulgakov's books were published in English—*The Orthodox Church* (1935) and *The Wisdom of God* (1937). During his later years he gave strong support to the ecumenical movement.

After the Bolshevik revolution Berdyaev was still sufficiently in sympathy with Lenin and his associates to be appointed professor of philosophy at the university in Moscow. However, his deviationism became increasingly obvious, and in 1922 he was forced to leave the Soviet Union. For two years he resided in Berlin, and in 1924 he moved to Paris, where he remained for the rest of his life, teaching and writing. Throughout the French period of his career he continued to attack middle-class morality, severely criticizing the Christianity of the modern West on the ground that it had largely adapted itself to the bourgeois values of industrialized capitalism. He also persisted in his opposition to the official Marxism of the Comintern, which he took to be a secularized form of Jewish Messianism that was all too prone to treat everything as a means to an ideal and, located in a morrow that is always coming but never is. No less than under the competing pressures of capitalist society, the human individual who lives under the aegis of Bolshevism is subject to a process of reification that would reduce him to the status of a commodity or instrument for manipulation. Hence, since the twentieth-century situation in both East and West is marked by spiritual degeneracy, the church generally must be radically revitalized if it is to discharge its proper vocation in the modern world.

Berdyaev held that Christianity essentially consists of creative freedom, and in the elaboration of his central contention he was influenced by Kant and the Russian novelist Dostoievsky, as well as by the existentialism that stemmed from Søren Kierkegaard. His thought was also affected by gnostic speculations and by the theosophical adventures of Jakob Boehme (1575–1624), the so-called *Philosophus Teutonicus*. As one would expect, Berdyaev greatly admired both Marx's passionate concern for economic justice and Nietzsche's stubborn defiance as exemplified in his proclamation of the death of God and in his refusal to become a mere article of trade within the expanding bourgeois civilization of the nineteenth century.

In such works as *Freedom and the Spirit* (1935), *The Meaning of History* (1936), and *The Destiny of Man* (1937) Berdyaev denied that the goal of human endeavors is the terminal event in a series of happenings. The end of history, which contains its final meaning, is immanent throughout the entire course of cosmic occurrences, and so the right attitude to adopt cannot be one of pure prospectiveness—a thesis, incidentally, that to some extent inspired Aldous Huxley to write his celebrated *Brave New World* (1932). Correctly understood, the immediacies of the present are not, as ardent Utopianists so easily assume, to be used and discarded as mere instruments on the way to a supposedly desirable future, but are endowed with an intrinsic value of their own, the enduring reality of God's kingdom being discernible in creative moments of the here and the now. Such moments are productions of freedom, and freedom itself is uncreated.

Of course such doctrines were opposed not only to the Marxist orthodoxy of the Soviet Union but also to the views of Auguste Comte (1798–1857) and his positivist successors. The latter boldly sought to clarify the whole theological situation by arguing that its confusions were due to the speculative nature of its fundamental affirmations. The continued existence of religious thought in the modern world merely testified to the survival of a mental habit that had really lost its efficacy in the new era dominated by the empirical method. But with the passage of time, as man became adapted to the requirements of scientific culture, both theology and metaphysics would surely die a natural death.

It was in accordance with Comte's leading idea that, soon after World War I, certain academics formed the Vienna Circle (*Wienerkreis*), established on the philosophical basis of what came to be known as logical positivism; and during the thirties, the main doctrines of the group found singularly lucid general expression in a small book *Language, Truth and Logic* by Alfred Jules Ayer (b. 1910) of Oxford. He alleged that all genuine or meaningful statements fall into two principal categories, namely, the tautological, comprising formal logic and pure mathematics, and the factual, comprising the content of the various branches of scientific knowledge. As for the value judgments of morals and aesthetics, they belonged to the quite distinct category of emotive pronouncements and had fundamentally the same kind of status as ejaculations, merely giving expression to subjective moods or to the likes and dislikes of the people who made them. Metaphysical and theological propositions were condemned as spurious and excluded from the threefold classification on the ground that, although they pretended to characterize existence, no assignable experience could be adduced that was unambiguously relevant to the determination of their truth or falsity; they were meaningless in the sense that they could not be empirically verified (or falsified).

Reactions were varied, and in many quarters it was argued that, as in its French so in its Austrian form, positivism unduly simplified the cultural situation and was finally untenable. Among other things, its critics pointed out that the natural sciences entail certain presuppositions (such as the legitimacy of sampling) that admit of no direct empirical demonstration; that the verification principle itself is a presumption that always eludes proof in a scientific laboratory; and that, if all value judgments are without determinable significance, the natural sciences themselves must be either valueless or nonsensical.

In view of these and other difficulties, certain thinkers who were in general sympathy with the positivist movement maintained that philosophy's proper task in the modern world lay in the clarification of the cardinal forms of linguistic usage. Remarkable in this regard was the influence of the Austrian engineer and philosopher Ludwig Wittgenstein (1889–1951), who belonged to the Vienna Circle for a while and who in 1939 became a professor at Cambridge. During his career he shifted his philosophical position, moving away from a relatively stringent version of logical positivism. In his early work *Tractatus Logico-Philosophicus* (1922) he defended the thesis that meaningful or factually informative language is monopolized by the propositions of the natural sciences, all other classes of statement being either tautological deductions from definitions (as in logic and mathematics) or nonsensical sentences (as in theology and metaphysics). Nonetheless, allowance was made for what he termed a "mystical" factor in experience, a mode of empirical awareness which cannot be rendered into coherent language after the manner of an ordinary scientific hypothesis. Thus the bare datum *that* nature exists in contradistinction to *how* it exists, eludes all attempts at scientific description. Otherwise put, the sheer givenness of the world as existent is something about which we ought to remain silent, for such givenness is a deliverance of ineffable feeling in the intimacy of immediate experience.

According to some interpreters, such an admission considerably weakened the logical positivist case, implying that scientific language has a metaphysical basis, mystical or inexpressible though that basis allegedly is. However this may be, Wittgenstein's posthumous work *Philosophical Investigations* shows that in his later years he came to advocate what might be termed a multilateral approach to linguistic analysis, recognizing that the exigencies of living assign many roles besides those of the logician and mathematician on the one hand, and of the empirical scientist on the other. We commonly employ language in a great diversity of ways, and these severally call for careful scrutiny. So Wittgenstein drew attention to our day-to-day engagement in multifarious "language-games" of varying seriousness—as when we command or request, bless or curse, thank or pray, exhort or tell funny stories. The philosopher's task is to analyze these different games and to elucidate their governing rules.

Apparently, therefore, informative meaning might be determined by nonscientific uses; and such was the sort of attitude adopted, for instance, in the work *An Empiricist's View of the Nature of Religious Belief* (1955) by the Cambridge philosopher Richard Bevan Braithwaite (b. 1900), who sought to broaden the verification principle by arguing that the meaning of a statement is conditioned by its mode of employment in a context with a *Sitz im Leben* or setting in life. He agreed that ethical assertions were neither tautologous (like mathematical propositions) nor empirically verifiable (like scientific hypotheses), but he refused to regard them as nonsensical since they yielded rules that could be used for guidance in the eminently empirical business of practical morality. Somewhat after the fashion of Edouard Le Roy about fifty years earlier, he further contended that the vital import of religious doctrines could be translated into ethical terms. Thus the pronouncement that God is love, which belongs to the heart of Christianity, was construed to be a declaration of the speaker's intention to pursue the agapeistic (Greek: *agapē*, "love") way of life. The language of religious assertions differs from the bare legalism of pure ethical rules largely in the force and liveliness of its parabolic imagery, familiarity with which reinforces the will of the devout in their determination to live in accordance with the moral ideals commended by their religion.

Thus Braithwaite's thesis amounted to a radical species of ethical reductionism. On the other hand, Le Roy (whose thought received attention in an earlier chapter) came increasingly to recognize that more is involved in religion than moral policies, and that an ethical pragmatism, while valid up to a point, lacks the adequacy required of a general philosophical assessment. He discerned a certain metaphysical world view within the primary affirmations of religion—a somewhat vague cosmological presumption that the universe is so constituted as to provide an environment graciously disposed to human aspirations after nobler forms of finite existence. So it was not unnatural that the devotional life should be frequently characterized by a deep feeling of harmony with underlying reality, and that it should occasionally issue in an ecstatic experience of mystical union with the productive Source of all things.

The positivist tendency to assert scientific omnicompetence was vigorously repudiated by the French Catholic playwright and philosopher Gabriel Marcel (b. 1889) in such works as *Being and Having* (1935; English translation, 1949), *The Mystery of Being* (2 vols., 1950–51), and other publications. Moving away from the absolute idealism of his earlier years, because of its excessive abstractness, he came to defend an existentialist position, though not without lamenting his loss of faith in the possibility of constructing a satisfying rational system of comprehensive philosophy. Deeply affected by his repeated studies of human beings in particular dramatic situations, he was eventually persuaded that any individual person, as a free and choosing subject, constituted a mystery that ever eluded the net of generalized intellectual explanation: not only was the choosing subject the creative personal condition of all scientific endeavors, but also rationalistic enterprise could never treat of the choosing subject without externalizing it, and thereby transforming its nature into that of an object. As for religion, despite the universality of Deity in theistic theories, divine grace has to be appropriated by each individual in his own unique way, for in the deep transactions of piety men and women always exist as free beings. Hence, while necessarily expressing itself in communicable forms by means of intellectual activity, religion is essentially bound up with the intimate fidelities of personal commitment, an existential engagement whose constraining truth is made manifest to those who lay themselves open to the mystery of Transcendent Being by making themselves available to others, thereby breaking the bounds of narrow egocentricity.

Of course the personal and subjective character of religion, so ably considered in Marcel's brand of existentialism, had been differently interpreted by various thinkers with psychological interests. The Harvard psychologist and philosopher William James (1842–1910), in his significant work *The Varieties of Religious Experience* (1902), examined *inter alia* temperamental differences in their relation to the religious life; his studies induced him to infer that supersensible Reality makes contact with human beings at the level of subliminal consciousness, and that in a general way belief in God, of whose existence we could have no scientific assurance, had a salutary effect on the personality. Hence in his books *The Will to Believe* (1897) and *Pragmatism* (1907) he proposed that we should judge by fruits not by roots, thus advocating the application of a pragmatic criterion in attempts to assess the truth value of the religious element in our modern scientific culture.

On the other hand, the Viennese founder of psychoanalysis, Sigmund Freud (1856–1939), came to a very different conclusion, holding that religion is essentially pathological, its perpetuation in modern civilization being nothing else than a mass neurosis. And in his work *Die Zukunft einer Illusion* (1925; English translation, *The Future of an Illusion*, 1928), and in various other publications, he expressed the view (in the spirit of naturalistic positivism) that, with the expansion of scientific education, human beings would perhaps eventually learn to stand on their own feet; that is, the repressed complex of unpleasant experiences causing the malady of religion would be finally eradicated. A persistent feature of Freud's diagnosis lay in his notion that men shy away from the demands involved in the process of growing up; and religion was taken to afford confirmation for such a judgment, its continued practice being understood as amounting to the retention of infantile attitudes in adult life. Passing through adolescence, the individual feels alien and painfully alone in a world of appalling vastness, and he compensates for his disconcerting sense of isolation and inferiority by resorting to childhood memories of his earthly father, evaluated and secretly cherished as the archetypal symbol of creation, protection, and the security of law. Progressively magnified, the paternal figure is projected upon the universe to become the heavenly Father of a macrocosmic nursery, a God to whom adults may turn and find comfort, much as a frightened child finds consolation in the protective arms of its parent. Thus religious faith is based on the fabrications of a mythology which, despite its public character, literally performs a dream-like and escapist function in the life of the psyche; and its inducements are therefore to be explained in terms of the so-called pleasure principle, since it fulfills certain repressed wishes in gratifying fantasy—a fulfillment they were denied in the imperious world of reality.

One line of adverse criticism made of Freud's diagnosis stressed the one-sidedness of his understanding of the religious consciousness. Although it contained elements of truth, his interpretation, besides being unduly affected by a particular aspect of patriarchal Judaism, tended to discount the activist and psychologically unpleasant components of religious commitment, factors that are not so easy to explain on the basis of the concept of fantasy-compensation. Critics stressed that, even if religion as a whole were shown to be wish fulfillment, the deduction therefrom that it is entirely devoid of objective truth would have to be rejected as a *non sequitur;* human creations in general are subjectively motivated and, from a psychological standpoint, all the constructions of science, including Freud's own theories, constitute a massive case of wish fulfillment, and the same could be said of the multitudinous productions of art and technology.

A remarkable contribution in the sphere of religion from the field of phenomenology was made in the treatise *Das Heilige* (1917; published in English as *The Idea of the Holy,* 1923) by Rudolf Otto (1869–1937), successively professor of theology at Breslau and Marburg. (Phenomenology was a term coined by the German thinker Edmund Husserl, 1859–1938, to denote a method of purely descriptive analysis that would exhibit the basic structures of conscious attitudes.) Following

Schleiermacher, Otto maintained that man's reaction to the divine element in the world is unique and irreducible, something *sui generis* that ever eludes adequate translation into conceptual and ethical terms. An awareness of *das Heilige* (German for "the holy") has centrality in the religious attitude, and it is mediated by a special faculty of divination.

Because such words as "holy" and "divine" had acquired moral and theoretical associations, Otto preferred to employ the term "numinous" as a designation of the sacred in its elemental character. This appellation came from the Latin *numen*, an expression that could refer to any manifestation of occult and incalculable power operating spasmodically in nature for good or ill. Man is inspired with fear and trembling in the presence of numinous Being. But Otto considered that more was involved, and, to bring out the bipolarity in the structure of the religious consciousness, he used the Latin formula *mysterium tremendum et fascinans*—"tremendous and fascinating mystery." Confronted by the Wholly Other (the *mysterium* in its transcendent aspect), the finite individual undergoes a process of self-devaluation: he is abased in his creatureliness and feels himself to be but dust and ashes. On the other hand, being captivated and entranced by the dynamic energy of the numinous Reality, he apprehends a certain affinity between himself and the surpassing *mysterium*, thereby entering upon a supervening moment of exaltation.

In Otto's view, therefore, fundamental theological concepts, like sin and salvation, really derive from one of the two contrasted moments of numinous experience, and all the doctrines of institutionalized religion are to be understood as interpretative ideograms of what is disclosed by the *senus numinis* or faculty of divination. They are imperfect attempts to render in rational language the experiential immediacies of the worshiper's encounter with the *mysterium*, and their efficaciousness, even as means of communication, is severely limited, for verbal schematizations can never reproduce a numinous actuality which, by its very nature, defies complete intellectual penetration. Hence, since the intimations of the numinous consciousness are by nature incapable of complete rational systematization, theological assertions are to be taken symbolically, and are not to be construed in a strictly logical sense.

Otto's striking analyses, besides directing attention to the transcendent factor in religious experience, confirmed many thinkers in the view that religion has a distinctive character of its own which resists radical reduction either to purely ethical or to purely theoretical categories. On the other hand, his postulation of a special faculty of divination, his doctrine of the nonrationality of the numinous, and his assignment of a secondary role to intellection occasioned much critical comment. And some thinkers, while freely acknowledging the uniqueness of the *sensus numinis,* argued that religion arises from a total response of the natural man to the daunting presence of the strange or unfamiliar, and that, even in its most primitive forms, religious experience involves some measure of intellectual interpretation, which connects an awareness of overwhelming cosmic forces with the private and public concerns of moral aspiration.

The concept of ethical concern played an important part in the philosophical theology of Paulus Johannes Tillich (1886–1965), who, after occupying university posts at Marburg, Dresden, and Frankfurt, migrated to the United States on the accession to power of the National Socialists, and subsequently served as professor at Union Theological Seminary, New York (1933–55), Harvard University (1955–62), and the University of Chicago (1962–65). He sought to do justice to the subjective and objective aspects of religion, and to both revealed and natural theology. His numerous publications include: *The Protestant Era* (1948), *The Shaking of the Foundations* (1949), *Systematic Theology* (3 vols., 1951–63), *The Courage to Be* (1952), *Dynamics of Faith* (1957), and *Theology of Culture* (1959). From one point of view, he may be said to have represented a form of existentialist Neo-Kantianism, for he upheld the thesis of a dualism between religious faith and the claims of empirical science: faith can conflict only with faith, and science only with science, these two dimensions of human activity being so divergent as to exclude the possibility of a real clash between them.

Hence Tillich's argumentations were often reminiscent, not only of Kierkegaard, but also of Albrecht Ritschl, who tried to make Kant's distinction between faith and knowledge more acceptable by arguing that, whereas religion is based on value judgments, science relies upon theoretical judgments of fact. From this Ritschl had inferred, for example, that the religious value attached to the Jesus of the gospels was quite independent of biographical questions regarding his career as a historical personage. And Tillich, in accordance with his emphasis on the subjective or existential character of faith, was able to affirm that humanists, in so far as they are unconditionally serious or ultimately concerned about the welfare of humanity, have to be assigned a place in the company of the faithful.

It might be objected that such an interpretation is exposed to much the same difficulties as the doctrines of Ritschl and Kierkegaard. Religion normally postulates a certain metaphysical world view (naïve though it often may be), some sort of implicit theistic theory of the universe; and the sciences themselves, despite their empirical basis, are inseparable both from faith and from human valuations. Who would engage in prayer if he did not hold that the Being to whom he addresses himself had a life of its own apart from the worshiping activities of certain finite individuals? And who would devote himself to scientific pursuits if he possessed no faith in the constancy of the natural order, or if he did not attribute value to his laborious researches? So one could contend that any human concern necessarily entails theoretical presumptions of factual truth; that these are always liable to conflict with the findings of science and scholarship; and that the more vague and general among them, because of the various parts they play in the conscious life of different persons, serve to distinguish theistic from nontheistic attitudes. Thus the progressive humanist, by concentrating on certain particular techniques for individual and social betterment, may be inclined to disregard all intimations of the precariousness of human existence with its cherished values; and, in contradistinction to the practicing theist, perhaps he deems it pointless to busy one's mind with man's ultimate dependence on the propitiousness of forces that infinitely surpass those at his own command.

Moreover, in many biblical passages the implication would seem to be that God is fulfilling a purpose in human history, and purpose is essentially a category of time, entailing as it does the distinction between a present need and the possibility of a future satisfying of that need. On Tillich's principles, this means that typical Jewish and Christian preoccupation with a purposeful Creator has to be condemned either as inadequate symbolism or as idolatrous, since genuinely religious concern finds its center and focus in the one sufficient Absolute that lacks nothing and includes everything. Such a consideration betrays the fact that Tillich was influenced not only by Ritschl and Kierkegaard, but also by the Neoplatonic tradition as mediated by Schelling and Hegel, although, unlike Hegel he did not take time so seriously as to assert that the Absolute fulfills itself in the affairs of the spatiotemporal world. Rather, he felt that the Divine is recognizable in the depths of personal experience as the inexhaustible and potent Ground of Being, and that, while conditioning historical existence, God himself eternally transcends the processes of history.

In this connection Tillich's line of reasoning was in accord with the spirit of the ontological argument for God's existence. The starting point is the self, with its consciousness of its own limited being, and with its inkling of final truth—a notion that Tillich held was involved in all self-questioning. An awareness of the finitude and contingency of subjective experience implies some prior cognizance of the necessary Ground of Being, which saves finite entities from dissolution and provides the point of identity beyond the rift between the knower and the known, supplying the unseen light by which historical existence is seen. In its all-comprehensiveness the Ground of Being cannot be one object among others, not even the highest of objects, for its productive essence is such as to transcend any assignable subject-object relation, and yet its presence lies in the depths of religious concern properly so called. It is the one true God as distinct from the false gods of spurious religion, and idolatry arises whenever anything less than the ultimate Ground of Being is made subjectively ultimate in personal concerns. Whence it follows, for example, that a man who makes the welfare of his own nation the god of his basic quest must be no less an idolator than the pygmies of equatorial Africa.

Having affirmed that God is the inexhaustible and eternal Ground of Being, Tillich went on to argue that whatever else is said about God needs to be treated symbolically. Since all finite entities are rooted in the Infinite, they may point to God, but they are devoid of the capacity to represent the Divine with complete adequacy; and whenever any particular things are taken to possess such a capacity, they become idols and possible sources of demonic mischief. Mythologies figure prominently in traditional religious symbolism, and despite their wealth of imagery, they can never contain the one true God, whose Being is wholly transcendent in its infinitude. Like other products of man's constructive genius, religious modes of expression have their necessary limitations, and the human mind is so constituted that mythical language can never be entirely discarded in human transactions with God. On the other hand, interpretative literalism can and ought to be discarded, for it is a habit of mind that leads to idolatry, taking the less for the more, the finite for the infinite, and the proximate for the ultimate.

While Otto's theory of the numinous and Tillich's doctrine of ultimate concern may shed light on religion in its general aspect, some scholars have argued that neither did justice to the distinctive character of Christianity. In certain circles, for example, it has been maintained that Tillich's concept of the changeless Ground of Being had more in common with Neoplatonic ideas of the eternal Reality than with the God who clothes the lilies and finds spiritual refreshment in the responsive love of the human heart. So one might proceed to defend Harnack's thesis that, for the clarification of Christianity, the theologian should turn to the synoptic gospels, the documents that evidently preserve the oldest extant traditions concerning the historical Jesus. Although Harnack did not deny that Jesus believed in the imminence of a cosmic catastrophe that would terminate the existing world order, he deemed that such an expectation had no value for the spiritual life of scientifically-minded persons of the twentieth century. The *telos* or *eschaton* (Greek words for "end") anticipated by Jesus did not in fact occur; nevertheless, although he erred in his cosmology, the moral and spiritual kernel of his teaching was endowed with abiding value and significance.

Albert Schweitzer (1875–1965), scholar, musician, and medical missionary, in his treatise *Von Reimarus zu Wrede: Die Geschichte der Leben-Jesu-Forschung* (1906; published in English as *The Quest of the Historical Jesus*, 1910), contended, in accordance with the thesis of *Die Predigt Jesu vom Reich Gottes* ("The Preaching of Jesus Concerning the Kingdom of God," 1892) by Johannes Weiss (1863–1914), that the eschatological expectation of Jesus was an essential factor in his consciousness of mission; and from this Schweitzer went on to infer that such a factor could not be relegated to the periphery of the original gospel without doing violence to the actualities of history.

After reviewing certain important earlier attempts (made for the most part in the nineteenth century) to reconstruct the life of Jesus on a sound historical basis—all of which were found to be more or less unsatisfactory—Schweitzer proceeded to argue that, when the world did not come to an end, Jesus decided to take upon himself the birth pangs of the age to come, suffering as a ransom for his subjugated people and thereby forcing God to intervene on their behalf. Because of his ardent eschatological expectation, Jesus attached little value to material possessions. His moral teaching generally amounted in fact to an interim-ethic, valid just for the period between the time of its enunciation and the awaited *eschaton*. And, in view of the delay in the advent of the final judgement, he came to devise a plan for radical action, only to be destroyed in a desperate yet heroic endeavor to compel the forces of destiny to conspire dramatically in favor of the righteous cause he had made his own.

While there may be general agreement that Schweitzer rightly insisted on the importance of eschatology in the foundation of Christianity, a considerable number of present-day experts in the New Testament field are much less disposed to dogmatize about the detailed course of Jesus' career and about the precise nature of his motives and personal reactions to specific historical situations. Thanks largely to form-critical research, it is now widely recognized that the varying ways in which traditional materials are presented in the gospels bear primary witness, not to the intentions of Jesus himself, but rather to the literary and theological aims of the evangelists.

Despite the differences in their historical assessments, Schweitzer concurred with Harnack regarding the unacceptability of an eschatological outlook in the twentieth century; and in his autobiographical work *Aus meinem Leben und Denken* (1931; published in English as *My Life and Thought*, 1933) he re-affirmed that the ethical religion of Jesus had to be taken out of the context of his outmoded world view and placed into the context of a philosophy adapted to the demands of modern scientific culture. And although Christianity, in Schweitzer's own interpretation, remained a religion of redemption, its essential concern was no longer to save men from a doomed cosmic order but to redeem civilization itself by injecting it with the vital spirit of sacrificial service. In their general purport, then, Schweitzer's final proposals were not unlike those of Harnack: in both cases the basic attitude was world-affirming, not world-negating, and in both cases an ethic of disinterested benevolence was commended. But Schweitzer was less of a Ritschlian than Harnack and held that value judgments stood in need of theoretical support. So he did not claim that the ethical religion he had discovered in the gospels was self-authenticating; since it was more than the outcome of a personal taste or subjective preference, Schweitzer's ethical religion required rational corroboration from the sphere of natural theology. There was thus an intellectual obligation to demonstrate that the ethical religion of Jesus cohered with the deliverances of an acceptable general philosophy, and Schweitzer sought to fulfill the obligation in his *Kulturphilosophie*, (English translation, 1923: vol. I, *The Decay and Restoration of Civilisation*, vol. II, *Civilization and Ethics*).

In working out his philosophy of culture Schweitzer substituted for the Cartesian *cogito ergo sum* ("I think therefore I am") the proposition (which he took to be equally self-evident, besides being more significant) *I am a life that wills to live in the midst of life that wills to live;* and he deduced from the system of thought built on this foundation an ethic of reverence for life. Fundamentally, man must passively accept what nature offers, and yet, since he is afforded limited scope for creative participation in the cosmic process, he can to some extent determine the shape of things to come. From such considerations Schweitzer proceeded to argue that the passivity of a basic attitude of resignation (which engenders peace of mind) should come to fruition in the positive action of a supervening stance of world-affirmation; the human individual can find his true vocation only when he shows to all life the same kind of respect as that which he normally feels for his own. Moreover, sustained moral action, motivated by a deep sympathy with all that lives, echoes the dynamism of active love exemplified in the synoptic gospels, and so it may be legitimately concluded that there is no real discord between the ethical religion of the historical Jesus and the practical implications of a philosophy adapted to the requirements of contemporary scientific culture.

A somewhat positivist approach to gospel history was combined with a form of existentialism in a paper "Neues Testament und Mythologie" (one of several published in *Offenbarung und Heilsgeschehen*—"Revelation and Salvation-Happening"—1941) by Rudolf Bultmann (b. 1884) of Marburg, a scholar whose researches in form criticism were mentioned in an earlier chapter. His contention was that, since the essential contents of the primitive gospel were couched in a mythological framework, the true significance of Christianity could be made plain and acceptable to men of the twentieth century only if the New Testament were subjected to a demythologizing treatment. The proposal occasioned much discussion, as is amply illustrated in the symposium (which included Bultmann's original essay), edited by Hans Werner Bartsch, *Kerygma und Mythos* (3 vols., 1948–52; English translation, selections, *Kerygma and Myth*, 1953). Bultmann observed that Jesus' evident belief in the proximity of the cosmic *eschaton* was refuted by the subsequent course of history, and that in recent centuries the natural sciences had invalidated his general cosmological outlook. From a modern standpoint, the idea of a last judgment, like that of a three-storied universe, with heaven above and hell beneath, belongs to the outmoded forms of prescientific thought and is quite unacceptable: the biblical world view is obsolete, and so the New Testament stands in need of demythologizing.

According to Bultmann, therefore, so far from debilitating the word of God, demythologizing, when properly conducted, adds effective power to the gospel by divesting it of circumstantial ideas that have become encumbrances with the passage of the centuries. The vital meaning of divine revelation is clarified by being brought into direct relation with the *existentialia* of man's actual situation, and modern minds are made aware afresh of God's insistent call that we should abandon the over-riding pursuit of man-made security and the baneful ways of selfishness. We are far too prone to turn a blind eye upon the finitude of our world and to make decisions without considering the possible imminence of the personal *eschaton* that awaits us all. We would shut ourselves off from God's future, a future that may come as a thief in the night; we would become masters of our fate and possess all things as instruments of our personal power.

So we build up our schemes without due care. We forget that life is transient and terminates in death, that every human security is ultimately vain, and that to turn all things into tools is to make mere instruments of ourselves. Jesus had the per-spicacity to see through common illusions, and so he invited men to opt for repentance. He confronted them with the sur-passing mystery of God, which, like the authentic decisions of existential faith, ever eludes incarceration in the objective and tool-making world of the scientific understanding.

Reactions to Bultmann's proposal were varied, and three types of criticism may be mentioned here. In the first place, there were those who argued that he was not radical enough. Thus Dietrich Bonhoeffer (1906–45), a Lutheran minister, whose thought moved beyond the Barthianism of his earlier years and who, after protracted imprisonment, eventually suf-fered martyrdom under the Nazi regime, maintained that Bult-mann did not go far enough in his program for the demy-thologizing of the gospel (see his *Widerstand und Ergebung*— "Resistance and Surrender"—ed. Eberhard Bethge, 1951; pub-lished in England as *Letters and Papers from Prison* and in the United States as *Prisoner for God*, 1953). Unfortunately, Bon-hoeffer was put to death before his later ideas could come to full maturity; they remained somewhat confused, and this is not surprising when one considers the stress under which he lived during his last years. Nevertheless, his literary remains make it clear that he detected in Bultmann's revised version of Christianity an effete survival of the archaic *Deus ex machina*, the concept of an external God who spasmodically intervenes to deliver whom he elects from disaster or to supply explanations whenever science is at a loss. Bonhoeffer regarded such a notion as a mythical image to be discarded, along with other childish things, as men come of age; also, he employed the term "religion" to denote devotion to that image, a somewhat curious usage that would seem to imply an absence of religiousness in all defenders of immanentist and absolutist forms of theism. In any case, Bonhoeffer claimed that the typical representatives of modern scientific culture were irreligious since they did not feel the need for a deity of miraculous interventions in either the practical or the theoretical sphere. He further argued that in true piety God is always at the center of life, not at (or beyond) its periphery; and that personal dedication to such a God of irreligion could be promoted among the secularized masses of a technological epoch only in a worldly way—by giving oneself, as Jesus did, to the service of others.

In the second place, there were those who thought Bultmann's program doomed from the outset on the ground that mythical motifs, so far from being expressions of an infantilism to be outgrown, derived from permanent elements in the dynamics of the psyche and provided enduring models for thought and practice. They pointed out that the Zurich psychiatrist Carl Gustav Jung (1875–1961) in his *Wandlungen und Symbole der Libido* (1912; the revised edition of 1952 was published in English as *Symbols of Transformation*, 1962) and various other writings, had been led to account for the remarkable similarities between dreams and timeworn myths by postulating the existence of certain mental archetypes. Beneath the personal unconscious lies the subliminal region of the collective unconscious, the repository of general racial experience, which each person brings with him into the world at his birth. Within it the manifold deposits of ancestral experience crystallize around certain archetypal images or structures that embody vital truths

which come to light in the persistent themes of universal mythology and serve to assist mankind in its struggle to adapt to the
stern demands of its environment. Evidently, therefore, while
remythologization is doubtless continually taking place, there is
no possibility of any complete demythologization; and, since
the image of God holds a prominent place among the archetypes, there must be an innate religious predisposition that leads
to personal unbalance and incipient neurosis when denied adequate expression in the conscious life of the individual. Critics
also noticed that perhaps Jung's general thesis found limited
confirmation in the somewhat similar conclusions of other thinkers, working in quite different fields. The Oxford professor
Henry Habberley Price (b. 1899), for example, in *Some Aspects of the Conflict between Science and Religion* (1953)
proposed that such psychical phenomena as telepathy and clair-
voyance might well occur through the mediation of a common
unconscious in which all human minds participate at the depths
of their being. And the historian and phenomenologist of religion Mircea Eliade (b. 1907), successively professor at Bucha-
rest, Paris, and Chicago, in his book *Le mythe de l'éternel re-
tour: Archétypes et répétition* (1949; English translation, *The
Myth of the Eternal Return*, 1954; American paperback edition,
Cosmos and History, 1959), propounded a theory which might
be taken to imply that, the human constitution being what it is,
mythological habits of mind cannot be entirely supplanted. He
argued that primitive myths provided archetypal models for
sacred rituals that reactualized the creative events supposed to
have occurred at the world's initiation, when the confusion of
chaos gave way to the differentiations of a cosmic order; and
that contemporary secularity still shows signs of the persistence
of underlying mythical motifs such as the nostalgia for paradise
—a fact apparently evinced, for example, in popular advertise-
ments for luxury cruises to southern waters and in the widespread appeal of the Marxist promise of a classless society.

In the third place, there were those who objected to Bultmann's postulation, not only of an undue discontinuity between man and nature, but also of an inadmissible dualism between faith and knowledge—oppositions that could be traced, via the refinements of Kant's critical philosophy, to the elemental teaching of Paul, Augustine, and Martin Luther. More immediately, the form of the antinomies in this case was largely determined by the influence of Kierkegaard and Barth, and particularly by that of Martin Heidegger (b. 1889), who in his *Sein und Zeit* (1927; English translation, *Being and Time*, 1962) interpreted the personal life of the human individual as *Sein zum Tode* ("being unto death"), and who a few years later lent his support (as rector of the University of Freiburg-im-Breisgau) to the National Socialists when they gained accession to political power at Berlin in 1933. Hence the conviction, frequently expressed by critics of existentialism, that Bultmann's version of a demythologized gospel had its foundation on shifting sands. Among other things it was maintained that man is a child of nature and stands in vital historical connection with it; that, within the sphere of biological evolution, continuity of process is quite compatible with the emergence of real differences; and that scientific intellection, so far from being exclusively a depersonalizing agency, is a requisite in the formation of sound judgment and the valid exercise of freedom. This last point was related to a line of argument directed against Bultmann's evident inclination to endow the existential decisions of religious faith with an unimpeachable authority of their own, as though they inhabited some romanticist holy of holies, securely protected from intellectual criticism. Such a philosophical tendency, so it was contended, should be recognized as fraught with grave danger, exposing civilization to the wildest enthusiasms of barbaric fanaticism. For one may believe in things evil, as well as in things desirable; whence it was deduced that, to be acceptable for reasonable people, assurances that stem from the privacy of personal conviction, however luminous they might appear to those who make claim to them, must have some external corroboration supplied after a rational scrutiny of the deliverances of general human experience. The Manchester philosopher Samuel Alexander had once been moved to ask: What if the inner light should turn out to be a wandering fire? (in Julian Huxley and others, *Science and Religion*, 1931); to which it might have been added: What if the intimations of faith (Luther) or *Existenz* (Kierkegaard), of the heart (Pascal) or the blood (D. H. Lawrence, the English novelist) betray traces of the cloven hoof?

Accordingly, despite the persistence of romanticist and positivist trends, and despite the revival of biblical dogmatics in the writings of certain influential Protestant theologians, natural theology with a scientifico-cosmological approach continued to have its distinguished representatives during the decades that followed World War I. In a general way it was deemed that romanticism and existentialism were dangerously subjective; that the positivist dismissal of all theological argumentation as meaningless was founded upon a normative claim that could not be directly substantiated in experience; and that the dichotomy between faith and reason in dogmatic biblicism was scarcely satisfactory since it utilized natural knowledge in the formulation of its doctrines, incorporating concepts derived from common experience and philosophical discourse, besides betraying personal predilections in its stress on certain scriptural passages to the neglect of others. In this connection, the contributions of such Neo-Thomists as Jacques Maritain should be borne in mind. Bergson's treatise *The Two Sources of Morality and Religion* (1932; English translation, 1935) has already received mention; and while there was a romanticist strain in his teaching, it should be noticed that in his mature judgment intuition was no short cut to ultimate truth but rather a mode of insight that supervened upon rigorous intellectual discipline. Reference may also be appropriately made here to *Philosophical Theology* (2 vols., 1928–30) by the Cambridge thinker Frederick Robert Tennant (1866–1957), who sought to adapt the traditional teleological argument for God's existence to the exigencies of contemporary scientific theory; to *Nature, Man and God* (1934) by William Temple (1881–1944), who maintained that the distinction between natural and revealed theology should be understood as one of method rather than as one of subject matter; and to *The Purpose of God* (1935) by Walter Robert Matthews (b. 1881), dean of St. Paul's Cathedral in London (1934–67), who took time seriously enough to stress the temporality of the Creator, arguing that the notion of God's static self-sufficiency was a legacy of Neoplatonism, not of the biblical tradition from which Christianity originally sprang.

So far as the present writer is aware, the most systematic and comprehensive essay in radically naturalistic philosophical theology that appeared in the early decades of the present century was *Space, Time and Deity* (2 vols., 1920) by Samuel Alexander (1859–1938), who left Oxford in 1893 to take up a professorship at the university in Manchester. A seminal thinker who affected the philosophies of such diverse individuals as William Temple, Alfred North Whitehead, and Pierre Teilhard de Chardin, Alexander elaborated an all-embracing scheme of emergent evolution and defined God as the entire universe of space-time with its nisus to diety—that is, with its tendency to produce ever more complicated modes of patterned existence. In general accordance with post-Newtonian physics (but by independent philosophical argument), he submitted that space apart from time is an abstraction, and vice versa, what we inhabit being a four-dimensional continuum (three dimensions for space and one for time, with its irreversible direction from past to future). He went on to deduce that space-time, as the creatively restless matrix of all particular things, is originally dispersed in what he termed point-instants and provides the basic stuff out of which finite entities are composed. Given certain conditions, matter (electrons, atoms, molecules, etc.) emerges from point-instants, which are the simplest modes of spatiotemporal individuation; and, given certain more specific conditions (such as have obtained on the Earth), life emerges from matter, and mind from life. At each crucial stage of emergent transition, complexity of organization takes on a distinctive and unpredictable character, the emergent quality summing up in a new totality the manifold elements of the patterned components. Hence humanity has to be recognized as *sui generis,* and psychology can no more be entirely reduced to biology than biology can be reduced to physico-chemical principles. Furthermore, Alexander considered it sheer dogmatism to assume that evolutionary development must come to a stop with the emergence of mind, and he used the word "deity" to denote the next higher quality that lies ahead as the object of reasonable religious anticipation. The precise nature of deity cannot be known in advance of its actual appearance, but one may legitimately presume that it will include the qualities of mind, life, and matter in the internal structure of its new being. Like other creatures, man reflects the formal constitution of the spatio-temporal source of all finite entities, his mind serving as the time of his body, which itself serves as the space of his life; he exemplifies something of the creative restlessness of primordial space-time, and amid the ferment of his multifarious strivings may be discerned the ground of hope and the rational basis of religious confidence in a nobler future.

Also important in the same naturalistic and antidualist tradition were such works as *Process and Reality* (1929) by Alfred North Whitehead (1861–1947), mathematician and philosopher successively holding positions at Cambridge, London, and Harvard, who argued that both God and the world are in the grip of the ultimate metaphysical ground, the creative advance into novelty; *Man's Vision of God* (1941) by Charles Hartshorne (b. 1897), successively professor in Chicago, Georgia, and Texas, who rejected the static God of orthodox theism, maintaining that the Creator actually completes himself through involvement with his creatures; and *Realms of Value*

(1954) by Ralph Barton Perry (1876–1957), professor of philosophy at Harvard and biographer of William James, who considered that religion arises when man apprehends the transcendent forces that encompass him in their bearing upon his moral concerns and aspirations. Moreover, in his much-discussed treatise *The Phenomenon of Man* (1955; English translation, 1959) Pierre Teilhard de Chardin (1881–1955), French Jesuit and paleontologist (and closely associated philosophically with Edouard Le Roy), sought to combine dynamic naturalism with certain fundamental concepts of traditional christology, going so far as to assert that evolution is the general condition to which all theories must conform and a light that clarifies all facts. And it is fitting that a recounting of the evolution of two thousand years of philosophico-theological doctrines should be brought to a conclusion with the citation of such a thesis, particularly when the final chapter itself concerns quests for clarity.

BIBLIOGRAPHY

Baillie, John. *The Idea of Revelation in Recent Thought.* New York: Columbia University Press, 1956.

Bainton, R. H. *Christian Attitudes toward War and Peace: A Historical Survey and Critical Re-evaluation.* New York: Abingdon Press, 1960.

Burkill, T. A. *God and Reality in Modern Thought.* Englewood Cliffs, N.J.: Prentice-Hall, 1963.

Craig, R. *Social Concern in the Thought of William Temple.* London: Gollancz, 1963.

Desan, W. *The Planetary Man.* Vol. I, *A Noetic Prelude to a United World.* Washington, D.C.: Georgetown University Press, 1961.

Garrigou-Lagrange, Reginald. *Reality: A Synthesis of Thomistic Thought.* St. Louis, Mo.: B. Herder, 1953.

Gollwitzer, H. *The Christian Faith and the Marxist Criticism of Religion.* Edinburgh: St. Andrew Press, 1970.

Hardy, A. C. *The Divine Flame: An Essay towards a Natural History of Religion.* London: Collins, 1966.

Hartwell, H. *The Theology of Karl Barth: an Introduction.* London: Duckworth, 1964.

Lacroix, Jean. *La crise intellectuelle du catholicisme français.* Paris: Fayard, 1970.

Macquarrie, John. *Twentieth Century Religious Thought.* New York: Harper and Row, 1963.

Neill, S. C., ed. *Twentieth Century Christianity: A Survey of Modern Religious Trends by Leading Churchmen.* London: Collins, 1961.

Page, R. J. *New Directions in Anglican Theology.* London: Mowbray, 1967.

Peacock, A. *Fellowship through Religion.* London: World Congress of Faiths, 1958.

Philp, H. *Freud and Religious Belief.* London: Rockliff, 1956.

Pittenger, N. *Process Thought and Christian Faith.* London: Nisbet, 1968.

Rahner, K. *Studies in Modern Theology.* London: Burns and Oates, 1965.

Ramsey, Paul. *Deeds and Rules in Christian Ethics.* New York: Scribner's, 1967.

Raven, C. E. *Teilhard de Chardin: Scientist and Seer.* New York: Harper and Row, 1963.

Roberts, D. E. *Existentialism and Religious Belief.* New York: Oxford University Press, 1957.

Schmemann, A., ed. *Ultimate Questions: An Anthology of Modern Russian Religious Thought.* New York: Holt, Rinehart and Winston, 1965.

Smith, J. E. *Reason and God.* New Haven: Yale University Press, 1961.

Weatherhead, L. D. *Psychology, Religion and Healing.* London: Hodder and Stoughton, 1952.

Zahrnt, H. *The Question of God: Protestant Theology in the Twentieth Century.* London: Collins, 1969.

GENERAL BIBLIOGRAPHY AND INDEX

General Bibliography

(Books marked with an asterisk contain comprehensive guidance for further reading which may be found particularly useful)

Baillie, John, J. T. McNeill, and H. P. van Dusen, gen. eds. *The Library of Christian Classics.* 26 vols. planned. Philadelphia: Westminster Press, 1953——.

Berthold, Fred, Jr., Alan W. Carlsten, Klaus Penzel, and James F. Ross, eds. *Basic Sources of the Judaeo-Christian Tradition.* Englewood Cliffs, N.J.: Prentice-Hall, 1962.

Bréhier, Emile. *The History of Philosophy.* 7 vols. Chicago: University of Chicago Press, 1963–69.

* Chadwick, W. O. *The History of the Church: A Select Bibliography.* London: Historical Association, 1962.

Congar, Yves M.-J. *A History of Theology.* Garden City, N.Y.: Doubleday, 1968.

* Cross F. L., ed. *The Oxford Dictionary of the Christian Church* New York: Oxford University Press, 1957.

Franks, R. S. *The Work of Christ: A Historical Study of Christian Doctrine.* London: Nelson, 1962.

Gerrish, B. A., ed. *The Faith of Christendom: A Source Book of Creeds and Confessions.* Cleveland, O.: World, 1963.

Harnack, Adolf von. *A History of Dogma.* 7 vols. London: Williams and Norgate, 1894–1903, and (reprint) New York: Russell and Russell, 1958.

Latourette, K. S. *A History of Christianity.* New York: Harper, 1953.

* McGiffert, A. C. *A History of Christian Thought* [to Erasmus]. 2 vols. New York: Scribner's, 1931.

Nichols, J. H. *History of Christianity, 1650–1950: Secularization of the West.* New York: Ronald Press, 1956.

Spinka, Matthew. *Christian Thought from Erasmus to Berdyaev.* Englewood Cliffs, N.J.: Prentice-Hall, 1962.

Troeltsch, Ernst. *The Social Teachings of the Christian Churches.* 2 vols. New York: Macmillan, 1949.

* Walker, Williston. *A History of the Christian Church.* Rev. ed. New York: Scribner's, 1959.

Index

Aachen, Synod of, 152
Abbott, W. M., 449
Abelard, 160, 174 ff., 179 ff., 191, 419
Absolute Idealism, 378, 382 ff., 463; *see also* Neoplatonism
Absolution, 62; *see also* Penance
Absurdity, 60
Act of Uniformity (1662), 267
Adam, K., 351
Adeney, W. F., 113
Adickes, E., 372
Adoptionism, 12, 39, 81; *see also* Dynamic Monarchianism
Adventists, *see* Eschatology
Aeterni Patris, papal bull, 192, 414, 423
Agatho, Pope, 106
Ailly, Pierre d', 202
Albertus Magnus, 184
Albrecht of Brandenburg, 235
Alcuin, 148
Alexander, Bp. of Alexandria, 88, 90
Alexander IV, Pope, 180
Alexander V, Pope, 203, 209
Alexander VII, Pope, 346
Alexander, P. J., 113
Alexander, Samuel, 420, 479, 480 ff.
Allegorization, 68 f., 401
Alogi, 82
Altaner, B., 33
Ambrose of Milan, 118, 131
American Declaration of Independence, 357
American developments, 352 ff.
Ammonius Saccas, 67
Anabaptism, *see* Baptists
Ancyra, Council of, 48
Androgyny, 17 f., 143; *see also* Marriage *and* Sex

Anglicanism, 257, 259 ff., 262 f., 264 ff., 267 f., 353, 360, 426
Anglican Orders, 262
Anglo-Catholicism, 424 ff.
Anicetus, Pope, 27
Anomeans, 91
Anselm, Abp. of Canterbury, 154, 170 ff., 189, 191
Anselm of Laon, 174
Antichrist, 18, 28, 240, 364
Antinomies, 375
Anti-Semitism, 18, 28, 41 ff., 183, 229, 442, 446 f.
Antitrinitarianism, 278 ff.; *see also* Dynamic Monarchianism, Modalist Monarchianism, Monotheism, Socinianism, *and* Unitarianism
Antony of Egypt, 136
Apocalypticism, *see* Eschatology
Apocrypha, 141; *see also* Septuagint
Apollinarianism, 96, 112
Apologists, 34 ff.
Apostasy, 61 f., 77
Apostles' Creed, 52
Apostolic Fathers, 25 ff.
Apostolicity, 25, 47, 51; *see also* Reason and revelation
Apostolic succession, 26, 44, 47, 52 f.; *see also* Episcopacy
Apostolos, 25
Aquinas, Thomas, 112, 131, 181 f., 184 ff., 197, 216, 220, 297, 450
Archeology, 413
Arianism, 78, 87 ff., 94, 110, 358
Aristides of Athens, 34
Aristotelianism, 164, 170, 182, 184, 187, 216, 385, 451
Arminianism, 277, 324, 355
Armstrong, A. H., 71

Arnaud, A., 346
Artemon, 83
Asceticism, 6, 43 f., 46, 48, 66 f., 136 ff., 160
Astruc, Jean, 402
Athanasius, 88 ff., 96, 137
Atheism, 331, 338, 476
Athenagoras of Athens, 35
Athenagoras I, Ptr. of Constantinople, 443
Atonement, 15, 31 f., 58, 61, 64, 68, 112, 124, 134, 165, 174, 177, 191 f., 243, 255, 278, 280, 356, 358 f., 363, 433
Aufklärung, see Enlightenment
Augsburg, Peace of, 241
Augsburg Confession, 239, 261
Augustine of Canterbury, 132
Augustine of Hippo, 117 ff., 131, 152, 165, 169, 172, 191, 208, 235, 242, 346, 444, 453
Augustus, Emp., 9
Aurelian, Emp., 83
Authority in religion, 276, 286, 325, 361, 400 f., 448, 451, 455; *see also* Episcopacy
Autonomy of the will, 376
Averroism, 182, 184, 193
Avicenna, 182
Ayer, A. J., 460

Bacon, Francis, 293, 305
Bailey, D. S., 145
Baillie, J., 21, 482, 487
Bainton, R. H., 244, 281, 482
Ballou, Hosea, 359
Baltimore, Lord, 352
Baptism, 5, 28, 60 ff., 92, 127, 133, 140, 166, 192, 214, 237, 244, 261, 271, 273 f., 361, 363
Baptists, 238, 247, 257, 267, 270 ff., 274 f., 354
Barclay, Robert, 277
Bardas, 153
Bardy, G., 86
Bar-Kokba, 12
Barnabas, Epistle of, 27
Barnard, L. W., 33, 40
Bar-nasha, 5
Barth, Karl, 393, 411, 434, 449, 451
Bartsch, H. W., 474
Basel, Council of, 203, 210
Basil of Caesarea, 91, 137
Battenhouse, R. W., 125

Baur, F. C., 387, 406 ff., 428
Bayle, Pierre, 328
Béa, A., Cardinal, 441
Beare, F. W., 20
Benedict of Nursia, 138, 159, 389; *see also* Monasticism
Benedict XI, Pope, 200
Bengel, J. A., 323
Ben Sira, *see* Ecclesiasticus
Berdyaev, Nicholas, 457 ff.
Bergson, Henri, 415, 418 ff., 450, 479
Berkeley, George, 300 ff.
Berlin, I., 342
Bernard of Clairvaux, 159, 175
Berthold, F., Jr., 487
Bessarion, 227
Bethge, E., 475
Bethune-Baker, J. F., 49, 101
Bettenson, H. S., 21
Biandrata, G., 279
Bible, translations of, 206, 238, 261, 266; *see also* Septuagint, Targums, *and* Vulgate
Biblical Commission, 412, 414
Biblical criticism, 229 ff., 247, 259, 338 f., 366, 398 ff., 416, 433, 442, 456
Biblical theology, 455, 479
Bibliolatry, 244, 402
Biddle, J., 281
Bindley, T. H., 95
Birch, T. B., 207
Bird, T. E., 449
Birth control, 447 ff.
Black, M., 20
Blackman, E. C., 49
Blake, E. C., 440
Blondel, M., 415, 418
Boccaccio, 227
Bodenstein of Karlstadt, 236, 238, 271
Body of Christ, 16, 214 f.; *see also* Church, nature of the
Boehler, Peter, 319, 322
Boehme, Jakob, 306, 458
Boethius, 164
Bogomiles, 160
Bohemian Brethren, 211
Bolam, C. G., 281
Boleyn, Anne, 259 ff.
Bolshevism, 441, 457 f.; *see also* Communism
Bonansea, B. M., 196
Bonaventura, 162, 193, 220, 229
Boney, W. J., 449
Bonhoeffer, Dietrich, 475 f.

Boniface of Mainz, 146
Boniface II, Pope, 128
Boniface VIII, Pope, 199
Book of Common Prayer, 261 f.,
266 f., 426
Bora, Katherine von, 239
Bornkamm, H., 244
Bossuet, J.-B., 343, 345
Bourgeois values, 458
Bousset, W., 56
Boyle, Robert, 294
Bradley, F. H., 388
Braithwaite, R. B., 462
Brandon, S. G. F., 20, 449
Brauer, J. C., 367
Bray, Thomas, 321
Brent, Charles H., 437
Brethren of the Common Life, 221,
230
Brown, P., 125
Brown, R. McAffee, 449
Browne, Robert, 263 ff., 273 ff., 354
Brunner, H. E., 452
Bruno, Giordano, 294, 306
Bucer, M., 236, 252, 254, 261
Buffon, Comte de, 329
Bulgakov, Sergius, 457 ff.
Bullinger, J. H., 256
Bultmann, Rudolf, 410, 474 ff.
Bunyan, John, 320
Burkill, T. A., 20, 397, 482
Burnaby, John, 95
Burtchaell, J. T., 412
Burtt, E. A., 303
Bushnell, Horace, 365
Butler, Joseph, 312
Butzer, Martin, see Bucer, M.

Cabala, 229
Cadbury, H. J., 455
Cadoux, C. J., 49, 434
Caecilian, Bp. of Carthage, 77
Cajetan, 236
Calixtenes, 210, 211
Callas, J., 329
Callistus I, Pope, 46, 48, 84 f.
Callistus II, Pope, 151, 198
Calvinism, 250 ff., 263 f., 278, 324, 355,
361, 451
Cameron, R. M., 327
Campbell, A., 361
Campbell, T., 361
Campenhausen, H. E. von, 64, 71
Canon of the New Testament, 43, 51

Capitalism, 257, 458
Caraffa, G. P., see Paul IV, Pope
Carlsten, A. W., 487
Carolingian Renaissance, 148
Cartesianism, 293, 295 ff., 328 ff., 371,
424, 473
Cartwright, Thomas, 263 f.
Carver, John, 275
Cassian of Marseilles, 128, 138
Cassirer, E., 233, 342
Castration, 67
Casuistry, 285, 346
Cathari, 160 f., 199
Catherine of Aragon, 260
Causation, 188, 302; see also Proofs of
God's existence
Cauthon, K., 434
Celestine I, Pope, 98
Celestius, associate of Pelagius, 126
Celibacy, 6, 8, 17, 36, 42, 48, 122 f.,
139, 141 ff., 149, 237, 261, 400, 426,
447
Celsus, 68
Cerinthus, 13, 82
Chadwick, H., 71
Chadwick, W. O., 145, 351, 434, 487
Chalcedon, Council of (451), 100
Chalcedonian Creed, 100, 215
Channing, W. E., 359
Charlemagne, 79, 109, 147 ff., 152
Charles the Bald, Emp., 166
Charles I, King, 266
Charles V, Emp., 237, 239, 260, 285
Châtelet, Madame de, 330
Chitty, D. J., 145
Christian Science, 364 f.
Christos, 3 ff., 456
Church, nature of the, 15 ff., 44, 214,
252 ff., 256, 264, 266, 273, 280, 444,
446, 457
Church and State, 18 ff., 28 f., 34,
75 ff., 102, 108 ff., 117, 124, 143,
146 ff., 150, 197 ff., 205, 253 ff., 273 ff.,
349 ff.
Church of England, see Anglicanism
Church of South India, 436 f.
Cistercians, 159
Clarke, Samuel, 307 ff.
Claudius, Emp., 10
Clebsch, W. A., 268
Clement of Alexandria, 65 ff.
Clement of Rome, 26
Clement V., Pope, 200, 202
Clement VII, Pope, 202, 239, 292

Clement XI, Pope, 346
Clive, G., 342
Cluniac Monasticism, 150, 159, 175, 198
Cochrane, A. C., 245
Cochrane, A. N., 125
Codex Bezae, 399
Codex Sinaiticus, 28, 399
Codex Vaticanus, 399
Coercion, *see* Toleration
Cogito ergo sum, 296
Coincidentia oppositorum, 229
Coke, Thomas, 325
Colet, John, 230 f., 259
Collective unconscious, 476
Collegia pietatis, see Pietism
Collins, Anthony, 312
Columbus, Christopher, 226, 292
Communicatio idiomatum, 37
Communism, 16, 142, 206, 272, 389, 441
Comparative religion, 176, 339, 382, 435, 446, 449
Complutensian Polyglot, 226
Comte, A., 378 ff., 417, 459
Conciliarism, 196 ff., 344
Concupiscence, *see* Sex
Confirmation, 63; *see also* Sacramentalism
Congregationalism, 257, 263 ff., 267, 273 ff., 354
Constance, Council of, 203, 208, 210, 343
Constantine I, Emp., 19, 75 ff., 87 ff., 102
Constantine IV, Emp., 105
Constantine V, Emp., 108
Constantinople, Council of (381), 87
Constantinople, Council of (553), 87
Constantinople, Council of (680), 87
Constitutum of Vigilius, 103
Consubstantiation, 244, 248, 256
Contarini, G., 282
Contraception, *see* Birth control
Conzelmann, H., 412
Cop, Nicholas, 251
COPEC, 438
Copernicus, 291 f., 298
Coptic Church, 101
Cornelius, Pope, 48
Cosmological proof, 172 f., 190, 297, 300 f., 462, 468
Cossa, B., *see* John XXIII (1410–15), Pope

Counsels of Perfection, 145, 231; *see also* Monasticism *and* Double standard
Counter-Reformation, 282 ff., 426, 440
Cox, A. C., 21
Cragg, G. R., 342
Craig, Robert, 482
Cranmer, Thomas, 260 f.
Creativity, 69, 168, 385, 418 ff., 480 ff.
Creed, J. M., 314
Cromwell, Oliver, 264
Cross, F. L., 487
Cross, F. M., 20
Crusades, 154, 160, 227
Cuis regio, eius religio, 241
Cullmann, O., 20
Curia, 282, 445
Cyprian, 48, 61 ff., 117, 124, 256
Cyril, Bp. of Alexandria, 97 ff., 105, 152
Cyril, Bp. of Jerusalem, 94

Daniélou, J., 71
Dante, 200 f.
D'Arcy, M. C., 125
Darwin, Charles, 366, 387, 415
Davies, W. D., 411
Dead Sea Scrolls, 140, 398
Decius, Emp., 19, 67
Defensor Fidei, 259
Defensor Pacis, 201
Deification, 33, 54, 124, 215, 218 f.; *see also* Immortalization
Deism, 304 ff., 328 ff., 356, 372, 424
Deissmann, A., 411
Demiurge, 42
Democracy, 201 f.
Demythologization, 380, 408, 465, 470, 474 ff.
Desan, Wilfrid, 397, 482
Descartes, R., *see* Cartesianism
Dialectical development, 406
Dialectical Idealism, 385 ff.
Dialectical Materialism, 389 f.
Diaspora, 3
Dibelius, Martin, 20, 410
Didachē, 28
Diderot, D., 328, 333
Diocletian, Emp., 19
Diognetus, Epistle to, 28
Dionysius, Bp. of Alexandria, 86
Dionysius, Bp. of Rome, 86
Dionysius the Areopagite, *see* Pseudo-Dionysius

Dioscorus of Alexandria, 99
Disciples of Christ, 360 f.
Disciplina arcani, 79
Dispersion of the Jews, *see* Diaspora
Divino Afflante Spiritu, papal encyclical, 442
Divorce, 400; *see also* Marriage *and* Sex
Docetism, 7, 32, 43
Dodd, C. H., 455
Dogmatic Epistle of Leo I, 99
Dominicans, 161, 185, 352, 412
Donation of Constantine, 80, 147, 201 f., 228 f.
Donatism, 77, 120
Dostoievsky, F. M., 458
Double standard, 48, 79, 145
Duchesne, L., 417
Dudden, F. H., 134
Dugmore, C. W., 222
Dusen, van H. P., 21, 487
Dynamic Monarchianism, 82 ff., 148; *see also* Adoptionism
Dyothelitism, 105 f.

Eastern Orthodoxy, 152 ff., 203, 443, 445, 457 ff.
East-West Schism, 152 ff., 203, 443
Ebionites, 12, 81, 82
Ecclesiasticus, 141
Eck, Johann, 236, 240, 248, 271
Eckhart, 131, 220, 229
Ecloge of Leo III, 108
Ecstasy, 45, 212 f., 219
Ecthesis of Sergius, 105
Ecumenical councils (ancient), 78, 87
Ecumenical councils (modern), 435 ff.
Ecumenical creeds, 78, 87 ff., 96 ff., 102 ff.
Ecumenism, 203, 367, 435 ff.
Eddy, Mary Baker, 364 f.
Education, 232, 328 ff., 340 ff., 365 f., 447
Edward VI, King, 261 f.
Edwards, Jonathan, 355
Edwards, Jonathan, Jr., 356
Eichhorn, J. G., 398, 406
Eissfeldt, O., 412
Elan vital, 419
Eleutherus, Pope, 50
Eliade, M., 477
Eliot, C. W., 365
Eliot, George, *see* Evans, Marian
Elizabeth I, Queen, 261

Elliott-Binns, L. E., 204
Ellis, J. T., 367
Emerson, R. W., 359
Emperor worship, 9
Empiricism, 291, 299 ff.
Encratites, 36
Enhypostasia, 97, 103, 106
Enlightenment, 304 ff., 328 ff., 356, 359, 381, 452
Enslin, M. S., 20
Ens Realissimum, 121
Ephesus, Council of (431), 98
Epiphanius, Bp. of Salamis, 18, 82, 111
Episcopacy, 26, 32, 44, 52, 62 f., 124, 165, 263, 265, 325, 426, 445
Episcopal Collegiality, 445
Erasmus, 221, 226, 230 ff., 238, 246 f., 251, 259, 278
Erigena, John Scotus, 131, 166 ff.
Eroticism, *see* Sex
Eschatology, 1 ff., 17, 27, 31, 44, 47, 71, 141 ff., 272, 363, 390, 458, 471, 474
Essences, 392; *see also* Existentialism *and* Universals
Essenes, 140 f.
Eternal generation (of the Son), 70, 89, 112; *see also* Logos
Ethical proof, 172, 376
Eucharist, 15, 28, 33, 56, 64, 79, 112, 134, 166 f., 206 f., 210, 213, 215 f., 237, 244, 248, 256, 261 f., 266, 273, 286, 339, 361, 418, 422, 444
Eugenius IV, Pope, 203, 216
Eusebius, Bp. of Caesarea, 12, 21
Eusebius, Bp. of Nicomedia, 88 ff., 94 f.
Eutychianism, 99 ff.
Evangelicalism, 326, 360, 424 f.; *see also* Methodism *and* Pietism
Evans, Marian, 379
Evil, 120 ff., 167, 169, 454
Evolutionism, 340 ff., 366, 379, 385 ff., 387, 403, 415, 418 ff., 446, 469, 480 ff.
Exarch, 146
Existentialism, 347, 390, 463, 468, 474 ff., 478 f.
Ex opere operato, 217
Exultate Deo, papal bull, 216

Faber, J., 247
Fabian, Pope, 85
Farag, F. R., 145
Farel, Guillaume, 250, 252

Farner, O., 257
Fascism, 441
Fasting, 28, 247, 426
Faulker, J. A., 64
Faustus of Riez, 128
Fénelon, François, 345
Ferdinand of Aragon, 226
Ferguson, J., 128
Feuerbach, L. A., 388
Fichte, J. G., 382
Fichter, J. H., 64
Field, J., 264
Fife, R. H., 245
Filioque, 152 ff.
Finegan, J., 413
Firmin, Thomas, 281
Flavian, Ptr. of Constantinople, 99
Flick, A., 233
Florence, Council of, 155, 203, 216 f.,
  227
Foakes-Jackson, F. J., 80
Fogazzaro, A., 415
Forged Decretals, 147, 149
Form criticism, 410
Fox, George, 275; *see also* Quakerism
Francis of Sales, 286
Francis I, King, 225, 239 f., 251 f.
Franciscans, 162, 193, 352
Francke, A. H., 316 ff.
Frankfurt, Synod of (794), 109 f.
Frankish monarchy, 79, 146; *see also*
  Holy Roman Empire
Franks, R. S., 106, 487
Frederick the Great, 330, 336
Frederick III, Elector of Saxony, 234,
  236, 238 f.
Frederick I Barbarossa, Emp., 198, 200
French Revolution, 332, 348 ff., 358
Freud, Sigmund, 388, 396, 464 f.
Friends, Society of, *see* Quakerism
Friends of God, *see* Gottesfreunde
Froben, John, 231
Froude, R. H., 426
Fuller, R. H., 413
Fundamentalism, 244; *see also* Bib-
  liolatry

Galileo, 294 f., 401
Gallican Articles, 343, 346, 349
Garrigou-Lagrange, R., 482
Gaunilo of Marmoutiers, 173
Gavin, F. S. B., 151
Geanakoplos, D. J., 156
Gelfand, M., 327

George, C. H., 268
George, K., 268
Gerhardt, Paul, 318
Germanus I, Ptr. of Constantinople,
  108
Gerrish, B. A., 245, 487
Gerson, Jean, 202
Gewrith, A., 204
Gibbon, Edward, 313
Gilson, E., 125, 178, 196, 394, 423
Glas, J., 361
Glossalalia, 143
Gnosticism, 6, 41 ff., 46, 51, 65, 118,
  143, 407
God-fearers, 4, 9
Goethe, 390, 424
Goguel, Maurice, 20, 411
Gollwitzer, H., 482
Goodspeed, E. J., 33, 40
Gore, Charles, 427
Goring, J., 281
Gospels, Canonical, 2, 51; *see also*
  Biblical criticism
Goths, 94, 119
Gottesfreunde, 221
Gottschalk of Soissons, 167
Grabmann, M., 196, 423
Graf, K. H., 403, 413
Grant, F. C., 449
Gray, E. D. M., 413
Great Awakening, 355
Gregory of Nazianzus, 91
Gregory of Nyssa, 91, 166
Gregory I (the Great), Pope, 131 ff.,
  165, 173
Gregory II, Pope, 108, 146
Gregory III, Pope, 146
Gregory VII, Pope, 150, 198 f.
Gregory IX, Pope, 160, 184
Gregory XI, Pope, 208
Gregory XII, Pope, 209
Gregory XV, Pope, 286
Grillmeier, A., 101
Groote, Geert de, 221
Grotius, Hugo, 277, 309
Gutenberg, Johannes, 228
Guyon, Madame, 345
Gwatkin, H. M., 95

Hadrian, Emp., 10, 12
Hadrian I, Pope, 109, 147
Hahn, H. F., 413
Handy, R. T., 367
Harbison, F. H., 245

Hardy, A. C., 482
Harnack, Adolf von, 145, 417, 430, 450 f., 471 f., 487
Harris, C. R. S., 196
Harrison, E., 327
Hartshorne, C., 481
Hartwell, H., 483
Harvard, John, 354
Healing, 364
Hegelianism, 167, 336, 382 ff., 390 f., 406, 415, 469
Heidegger, M., 394, 478
Hellenization of Christianity, 4 ff.
Heloise, 174
Helvetic Confession (1566), 256
Henōsis, 218 f.
Henry IV, Emp., 198
Henry V, Emp., 151, 198
Henry VI, Emp., 198
Henry VIII, King, 225, 259 ff.
Heraclius, Emp., 104
Herbert, Edward, 304 f., 308 ff., 329, 424
Herbert, George, 308
Heresy, 160
Hermas, 26 f.
Herod the Great, 9
Herrenvolk, 395, 442
Hexapla, 68
Hieria, Synod of, 109
Hilary of Poitiers, 138
Hildebrandt, F., 327
Hippolytus of Rome, 12, 84 f.
Historical proof, 173
Hitchcock, F. R. M., 56
Hobbes, Thomas, 299, 402
Hochstraten, J. von, 229, 235
Hoffman, Melchior, 272
Holbach, Baron von, 329
Holtzmann, H. J., 409
Holy Roman Empire, 79, 146 ff.
Holy Spirit, 15, 26, 40, 44 f., 70 f., 92 f., 143, 152, 154, 171 f., 271, 418
Homoeans, 91
Homoiousians, 91
Homoousios, 83, 86, 88 ff., 94 f., 171, 215
Honorius, Emp., 127
Honorius I, Pope, 105 f.
Honorius III, Pope, 161, 166
Hooker, Richard, 264 ff.
Hort, F. J. A., 399
Horton, W. M., 449
Hosius, Bp. of Cordova, 88, 90

Howard, W. F., 413
Hübmaier, B., 271
Hügel, Baron F. von, 415
Hugh of St. Victor, 179 ff., 216
Huguenots, 256, 343
Huizinga, J., 233
Humanae Vitae, papal encyclical, 447
Humanism, *see* Positivism *and* Renaissance
Humanistic religion, 380
Hume, David, 301 ff., 312 f., 335, 373
Hunter, A. M., 413
Huss, John, 204, 209 ff., 236
Husserl, E., 465
Hussey, Joan M., 156
Hutter, Jacob, 272
Huxley, Aldous L., 222, 459
Huxley, Julian, 479
Huxley, T. H., 402
Hyatt, J. P., 413
Hypatia, lynching of, 98
Hypostasis, 91 f., 97, 111, 122, 177

Iconoclasticism, 81, 108 ff., 146 f., 470
Idolatry, *see* Iconoclasticism
Ignatius, Ptr. of Constantinople, 153
Ignatius of Antioch, 29 ff.
Ignatius Loyola, *see* Jesuits
Image worship, *see* Iconoclasticism
Immaculate Conception, 174, 194; *see also* Mariology
Immanence and transcendence, 121, 304 ff., 332, 416, 476, 480 ff.
Immortalization, 5, 8, 15, 33, 54, 90 ff., 112, 124, 213 ff., 215, 218 f., 280, 408
Incarnation, 34, 38 f., 42, 53, 58 f., 70, 89 ff., 173, 178, 189, 213, 429 ff.; *see also* Logos *and* Mariology
Index, Congregation of the, 283, 447
Indulgences, 177, 192, 235; *see also* Penance
Infantilism, 464, 475 ff.
Infralapsarianism, 266
Inge, W. R., 433
Innocent I, Pope, 127
Innocent II, Pope, 175
Innocent III, Pope, 160, 179, 199, 204, 207
Innocent IV, Pope, 161
Innocent X, Pope, 346
Innocent XI, Pope, 285, 344
Inquisition, 160, 226, 283
Irenaeus, 50 ff., 89, 215
Irene, Regent, 109

Irresistible grace, 122, 127, 191, 346
Isabella of Castile, 226
Islam, 77, 104, 108, 146, 148, 182, 185, 203, 225

Jacob, Henry, 275
James, brother of Jesus, 11, 14
James, Epistle of, 29, 244, 456 f.; *see also* Legalism *and* Moralism
James VI, King, 266
James, William, 464, 482
Janelle, P., 287
Jansenism, 345 ff.
Jaspers, Karl, 393
Jauncey, E., 128
Jedin, H., 287
Jefferson, Thomas, 356
Jehovah's Witnesses, 363 f.
Jeremias II, Ptr. of Constantinople, 155
Jerome, 131, 399; *see also* Vulgate
Jesuits, 281, 283 ff., 330, 343, 346, 348 ff., 352
Jesus, teaching of, 1 ff., 338, 409, 431 ff., 456, 472, 475
Jewish Christianity, 12 f.
Joan of Arc, 204, 209
John, Gospel of, 2, 8, 32, 34, 44, 82, 84, 276, 399; *see also* Logos
John of the Cross, 286
John of Damascus, 110 ff., 182
John of Gaunt, 206
John of Leyden, 272
John the Baptist, 140
John XXII, Pope, 195, 201
John XXIII (1410–15), Pope, 203, 209, 441
John XXIII (1958–63), Pope, 441, 443, 447
Jonas, Hans, 20
Jones, R. M., 135, 222
Josephus, 11, 21
Judaism, 1 ff., 141; *see also* Anti-Semitism
Julian of Eclanum, 127
Julian the Apostate, 19
Jung, C. G., 476 f.
Justification by faith, 237, 242, 249, 265 f., 393, 468, 475, 479
Justinian, Emp., 102
Justin Martyr, 37 ff., 66, 306

Kant, Immanuel, 294, 320, 336, 371 ff., 390, 424

Kaufmann, W., 397
Keble, John, 425
Kelly, J. N. D., 33, 95, 151
Kempis, Thomas à, 221, 321
Kennedy, H. A. A., 411
Kenyon, F. G., 413
Kepler, Johann, 294
Kierkegaard, S. A., 347, 390 ff., 458, 468, 479
Kingdom of God, 1 ff., 431 ff.; *see also* Eschatology
Kingdon, R. M., 257
Klausner, Joseph, 411
Knowles, D., 163, 178
Knox, John, 257
Kristeller, P. O., 233
Kümmel, W. G., 20
Küng, H., 449
Kurtz, P. W., 367

Labadie, Jean de, 315
Laberthonnière, L., 415, 420
Labriolle, Pierre de, 49
Lachmann, Karl, 399, 409
Lacombe, Francois, 345
Lacroix, Jean, 342, 483
Lagrange, M. J., 412
Laity, 445; *see also* Church, nature of the
Lake, Kirsopp, 21, 411
Lamentabili, papal decree, 414, 422
Lanfranc, 170
Language, 460 ff.
Lateran Council (649), 131
Lateran Council (1215), 182, 199, 207
Latitudinarianism, 305; *see also* Liberalism
Latourette, K. S., 487
Latreia, 110
Latrocinium, 100
Laud, William, 266
Law, William, 312, 320 f.
Law of Moses, *see* Torah
Lawrence, D. H., 390, 479
Lay investiture, 170, 198; *see also* Conciliarism
League of Nations, 418
Leclercq, J., 222
Lefèvre, Jacques, 230, 251
Legalism, 29 ff., 39, 46, 55, 57, 132, 215, 253, 306, 313
Leibniz, G. W., 299, 336, 373 f., 381
Lenin, V. I., 458
Leo, Abp. of Bulgaria, 154

Leo III, Emp., 108, 146
Leo IV, Emp., 109
Leo I, Pope, 99
Leo III, Pope, 79, 148, 414
Leo IX, Pope, 154
Leo X, Pope, 229, 235, 259
Leo XIII, Pope, 262, 412, 423, 442
Leonardo da Vinci, 228, 291
Leontius of Byzantium, 97, 103, 106, 112
Le Roy, Edouard, 415, 420 ff., 462, 482
Lessing, G. E., 338, 339 ff., 379, 405 f.
Lex naturae, 265; *see also* Natural religion
Liberalism, 351, 357 ff., 365 f., 382, 414 ff., 428 ff., 451 f., 479 ff.
Lietzmann, H., 40, 80
Lindsey, Theophilus, 358
Littell, Franklin, 281
Little, V. A. Spence, 40
Liturgy, *see* Sacramentalism
Livingstone, David, 327
Locke, John, 268, 281, 295, 299 ff., 305 f., 317, 329, 374
Loetscher, L. A., 367
Löwith, K., 397
Logical positivism, 459 ff.
Logos, 34, 38, 40, 58, 67, 69, 82, 84 f., 88 ff., 92 f., 96 f., 111 f., 171, 421
Loisy, A. F., 415, 417, 438
Lollardry, 208, 259
Lombard, Peter, 179 ff., 216
Loofs, F., 86
Lord Herbert of Cherbury, *see* Herbert, Edward
Lord's Supper, *see* Eucharist
Lorenzo Valla, 228, 291, 305
Louis of Bavaria, 195, 201
Louis XIV, King, 343
Louis XV, King, 343
Loyola, Ignatius, *see* Jesuits
Luce, A. A., 106
Lucian of Antioch, 87 f.
Lutheranism, 195, 222, 225, 232, 234 ff., 246, 248 f., 253, 324, 393, 451, 456, 478 f.
Lyons, Council of (1274), 155, 197

Macarius of Antioch, 106
MacDonald, A. J. S., 222
MacIntyre, J., 178
Mackintosh, H. R., 106, 397
Macquarrie, J., 483
Maimonides, Moses, 183

Maintenon, Madame de, 343
Malebranche, N., 299
Manicheanism, 42, 110, 118, 122, 127, 144, 160
Manning, H. E., 425, 427
Manson, T. W., 455
Manuel, F. E., 342
Marburg, Articles of, 239
Marburg, Colloquy of, 248
Marcel, Gabriel, 394, 463
Marcionism, 41 ff., 51 f., 401
Marcus Aurelius, Emp., 38
Mariology, 10, 39, 53, 97 ff., 167, 174, 194, 280
Maritain, Jacques, 423, 450, 479
Mark, Gospel of, 2, 27, 409, 413
Marriage, 6, 17, 61, 123, 139, 141 ff., 149, 237, 274, 362, 400, 426, 447
Marshall, J. S., 268
Marsiglio (Marsilius) of Padua, 201 ff., 285
Martel, Charles, 104, 146, 226
Martin of Tours, 137
Martin I, Pope, 105
Martin V, Pope, 203
Martin, E. J., 113
Martineau, James, 365
Martyn, J. L., 20
Martyrdom, 32, 61; *see also* Apostasy
Marxism, 388 ff., 397, 441, 457 ff.
Mary Stuart, 263
Mary Tudor, 261
Mashiach, 3 ff.
Masoretes, 398
Mass, *see* Eucharist
Mass communication, 444
Mathys, Jan, 272
Matthews, W. R., 480
Maximillian I, Emp., 227
McCown, C. C., 413
McDonnell, K., 257
McGiffert, A. C., 86, 487
McNeill, J. T., 21, 257, 487
Medicine, *see* Healing
Meecham, H. G., 33
Melanchthon, Philipp, 230, 236, 239 f., 252, 261
Meland, B. E., 367
Melchiorites, 272
Melito, Bp. of Sardis, 37
Mendicant orders, 139, 161
Mennonites, 272
Mercier, D. J., 423
Mergers, ecclesiastical, 436 f.

Messiah, 2 ff., 456
Messianic secret, 409
Messianism, 390, 458; *see also* Eschatology
Metempsychosis, *see* Transmigration
Methodism, 321 ff., 424
Metzger, B. M., 413
Michael III ("the Tippler"), Emp., 153
Michael Cerularius, 154
Michelangelo, 228
Milan, Edict of, 19, 75
Mill, J. S., 379
Millenarianism, 27, 71, 363; *see also* Eschatology
Miller, Perry, 367
Milner, B. C., 258
Milton, John, 268, 281
Minette de Tillesse, G., 413
Minucius Felix, 37
Miracles, 302, 312, 408, 476
Missionary activity, 4 ff., 94, 132, 155, 161 ff., 208, 227, 241, 283 f., 317, 319, 321 ff., 345, 352 ff., 435 ff.
Modalist Monarchianism, 82, 84, 92, 172, 175
Moderate realism, 170, 177
Modernism, 351, 412, 414 ff.; *see also* Liberalism
Mohammedanism, *see* Islam
Molesme, Robert de, 159
Molinos, Miguel de, 344
Molumby, L. E., 449
Monarchianism, *see* Dynamic Monarchianism, Modalist Monarchianism, Monotheism, Antitrinitarianism, *and* Unitarianism
Monasticism, 49, 79, 89, 136 ff., 159 ff., 237, 242, 261, 445
Monk, R. C., 327
Monolatry, 9
Monophysitism, 99, 101, 102 ff., 108, 130
Monopsychism, 183 f.
Monotheism, 81 ff.
Monothelitism, 105, 131
Montanism, 44, 50, 84, 102, 407
Moody, E. A., 196
Moore, E. C., 397
Moralism, 29 ff., 39, 46, 53 ff., 59, 122, 132, 142, 177, 215, 249, 253, 280, 306, 313, 372, 476; *see also* Legalism
Moravianism, 211, 318 ff., 322
More, Thomas, 230 f.

Morgan, James, 64
Mormonism, 361 ff.
Mortal sin, 46, 48, 61, 63 f., 144; *see also* Penance
Mosaic Law, *see* Torah
Moscow, 155
Mott, J. R., 437
Münzer, Thomas, 238, 271
Murray, A. V., 178
Murray, John, 358
Mystēria, see Sacramentalism
Mystery religions, 5, 8, 213, 408
Mysticism, 69, 129 ff., 181, 193, 212 ff., 276, 286 f., 344 ff., 377, 381 f., 463 f., 465
Mythology, *see* Demythologization

Nantes, Edict of, 343
Napoleon Bonaparte, 148, 349
Nationalism, 203 f., 225
National Socialism, 441 f., 455, 475, 478
Natural religion, 303, 304 ff., 330 ff., 356, 372 ff., 386 ff., 390, 448, 466, 473, 479, 480 ff.
Nazarenes, 13, 81
Nazism, *see* National Socialism
Neill, S. C., 449, 483
Nelson, B. N., 258
Neo-orthodoxy (Protestant), 366 f., 451 ff.
Neoplatonism, 111, 118, 121, 129 ff., 144, 169, 183, 218, 469, 471, 480
Neo-Thomism, 193, 414, 423, 450 f., 479
Nero, Emp., 10
Nestorianism, 83, 96, 101, 103 f., 108, 127, 171
New, J. F. H., 268
New Israel, *see* Church, nature of the
Newman, J. H., 425 ff.
Newton, Isaac, 268, 281, 294, 298, 329, 373, 480
Nicea, Council of (325), 78
Nicea, Council of (787), 109
Nicene Creed, 87 ff., 90 f.
Niceno-Constantinopolitan Creed, 93 f., 286
Nicholas of Cusa, 221, 228 f., 293
Nicholas I, Pope, 153
Nicholas V, Pope, 228
Nichols, J. H., 487
Nicolaitanism, 149, 198; *see also* Marriage *and* Sex

Niebuhr, B. G., 408
Niebuhr, H. R., 367
Niebuhr, Reinhold, 367, 452 ff.
Nietzsche, F. W., 388, 394 ff., 458
Noetus, 84
Nominalism, 169, 171, 195, 205, 207
Nonconformity (English), 268
Nonjurors, 267
Novatianism, 48, 62, 77, 85
Nuclear war, 444
Numinousness, *see* Otto, Rudolf

Oberman, H. A., 211
Ockham, William of, 193 ff., 202, 205, 207, 234
Old Catholic churches, 351
Olga, Queen, 155
Ollard, S. L., 434
Olmstead, C. E., 367
Omnipresence, 121
Ontological proof, 172 f., 189, 296, 469
Optimism, 305, 454
Orange, Synod of (529), 128, 133, 138
Orange, William of, *see* William of Orange
Oratory of Divine Love, 282 f.
Organic Articles, 349
Origen, 67 ff., 89 f., 92, 110 f.
Original sin, 3, 6, 15, 38, 53 f., 58, 60, 63 f., 66, 120 ff., 126 f., 133, 139, 141, 165, 175, 192, 206, 214, 242, 254 f., 265 f., 280, 298, 304, 333, 358 f., 366, 453 f.
Osborn, E. F., 72
Other-worldliness, 16, 28 f., 141 ff., 160, 228, 231, 255
Otto, Rudolf, 222, 465 ff., 470
Oulton, J. E. L., 21
Ousia, 91 f., 111, 122, 177
Oxford Movement, 424 ff.

Pachomius, 137
Pacificism, 232, 271, 433, 444
Page, R. J., 483
Paley, William, 313
Pantheism, 167, 169, 183 f., 310, 385 ff., 478 ff.
Papacy, 63, 79, 132, 146 ff., 196 ff., 285, 350 ff., 445
Papal infallibility, 350, 414
Papal Schism, 206, 209
Papias, 27
Paradise, 17, 122, 139, 143, 333, 366; *see also* Eschatology

Parker, Matthew, 262
Parousia, 15; *see also* Eschatology
Pascal, Blaise, 285, 294, 330, 346, 347 ff., 380, 390, 479
Pascendi Gregis, papal encyclical, 414, 418, 422
Paschasius Radbertus, 167
Patripassianism, 58, 84 f.
Paul, Apostle, 4 ff., 14 ff., 81, 139, 143 f., 214, 219, 235, 241, 243, 411, 453
Paul of Samosata, 83 f., 96
Paul III, Pope, 240, 283 f.
Paul IV, Pope, 240, 282 f., 285
Paul VI, Pope, 443, 447
Payne, E. A., 268
Peacock, A., 483
Pelagianism, 122, 126 ff.
Penance, 26, 46, 47 f., 58, 61, 64, 84, 112, 133, 144, 166, 192, 243, 246, 261; *see also* Atonement
Penn, William, 276
Penzel, K., 287
Perry, R. B., 482
Persecution, 10 ff., 18 ff., 75 ff., 108 ff., 263
Persona, 91
Peter, Apostle, 13, 14, 197
Peter the Venerable, 175
Petrarch, Francesco, 227
Pfefferkorn, J., 229
Pfeiffer, R. H., 20
Pharisaism, 5, 214
Phenomenology, 465 ff.
Philip of Hesse, 239 f.
Philip II of Spain, 283
Phillips, C. S., 351
Philo, 66
Philp, H., 483
Photius, 152 f., 155
Pico della Mirandola, 227
Pietism, 315 ff., 321, 336, 372, 424 f.
Pilgrim fathers, 257, 264, 274 ff., 354
Pippin the Short, 146 f.
Pittenger, N., 483
Pius II, Pope, 210
Pius V, Pope, 192, 263
Pius VI, Pope, 349
Pius VII, Pope, 349
Pius IX, Pope, 194, 350, 414, 442 f.
Pius X, Pope, 414, 423, 442
Pius XI, Pope, 448
Pius XII, Pope, 394, 412, 440 f., 442, 448

Platonism, 164, 167, 169, 229, 389, 418
Pliny, the younger, 11
Plotinus, *see* Neoplatonism
Plumpe, J. C., 21
Pneumatomachoi, 93
Poincaré, Henri, 420
Polity, ecclesiastical, 63; *see also* Church, nature of the
Polycarp, 27
Polygamy, 362 f.; *see also* Marriage *and* Sex
Pontianus, Pope, 85
Positivism, 378 ff., 459 ff., 464, 469, 479 f.
Powicke, F. M., 268
Pragmatism, 377, 418 ff., 421 ff., 462, 464
Praxeas, 84
Predestinarianism, 15, 111 f., 120 ff., 126, 128, 133, 167, 191, 208, 238, 242 ff., 249, 254, 265 f., 276 f., 280, 346, 356, 389 f.
Pre-existence, 30; *see also* Logos *and* Transmigration
Presbyterianism, 257, 263, 266 f., 361
Price, George, 397
Price, H. H., 477
Price, Richard, 358
Prierias, Sylvester, 236
Priesthood of all believers, 240, 243, 266
Priestley, Joseph, 357 f.
Pringle-Pattison, A. S., 388
Probabilism, 285, 346
Process theology, 480 ff.
Proclus, 130
Progress, 366, 385 ff., 480 ff.
Proofs of God's existence, 172, 190 ff., 194, 195, 296, 303
Propaganda, Congregation of, 286
Proskunēsis, 110
Prosōpon, 84
Protestantism, 117; *see also* Reformation, Protestant
Pseudo-Dionysius, 129 ff., 166, 174 f., 181, 219
Psychoanalysis, *see* Freud, Sigmund
Pulcheria, Empress, 100
Punishments, *see* Rewards and punishments
Purgatory, 70, 123, 133, 166, 247
Puritanism, 263 ff., 266 ff., 353
Pusey, E. B., 426

Quadratus, 35
Quakerism, 275 ff., 353, 355, 455
Quartodecimanism, 27, 37, 50
Quasten, J., 21
Quesnel, Pasquier, 346
Quick, O. C., 222
Quietism, 271, 344 ff.
Quinque viae, 190 f.
Qumran, 140 f., 398

Racialism, 395, 442; *see also* Anti-Semitism
Racovian Catechism, 279 f.
Rahner, H., 72
Rahner, K., 483
Ramsey, P., 483
Ranchetti, M., 423
Randall, J. H., 233
Rashdall, Hastings, 178, 433
Rationalism, 295 ff., 328 ff., 371; *see also* Natural religion *and* Reason and revelation
Ratisbon (Regensburg), Colloquy of, 240, 282
Rauschenbusch, Walter, 452 f.
Raven, C. E., 101, 483
Realism, 169, 171, 207
Reardon, B. M. G., 434
Reason and revelation, 47, 176, 181, 183, 186, 220, 244, 279, 303, 304 ff., 330 ff., 337 ff., 356, 372 ff., 386 ff., 444, 448, 466, 479 f.
Recapitulation, 53
Rechabites, 140; *see also* Asceticism
Reformation, Protestant, 206, 234 ff., 246 ff., 259 ff., 270 ff.
Reginald of Piperno, 186
Regula veritatis, 51, 69
Reimarus, H. S., 338 ff., 405
Relton, H. M., 106 f.
Remonstrants, 277, 281; *see also* Arminianism
Renaissance, 225 ff.
Renan, J. E., 408, 417
Resurrection, 2, 17, 27, 34, 71; *see also* Immortalization
Retribution, *see* Legalism *and* Rewards and punishments
Reuchlin, Johannes, 228 f., 235
Revelation, *see* Reason and revelation
Reville, J., 434
Rewards and punishments, 30 ff., 60, 66, 123, 340 ff., 363 f., 376; *see also* Eschatology

Rilliet, J., 258
Rist, J. M., 72
Ritschl, Albrecht, 428 ff., 438, 468
Robber Synod, *see* Latrocinium
Robert de Molesme, *see* Molesme, Robert de
Roberts, D. E., 483
Roberts, R. E., 64
Robespierre, 336
Robinet, J.-B., 329
Robinson, John, 275
Rolt, C. E., 135
Romanticism, 212, 218, 320, 332 ff., 348, 378, 380 ff., 390, 408, 416, 418 ff., 424, 479
Roscellinus of Compiègne, 171, 174, 177
Ross, J. F., 487
Rouse, Ruth, 449
Rousseau, Jean-Jacques, 328 f., 332 ff., 340, 373
Rowley, H. H., 413, 455
Royce, Josiah, 388
Runciman, S., 156, 163
Rupp, E. G., 269, 281
Russell, Charles Taze, 363
Russell, E., 281
Rutherford, J. F. ("Judge"), 364
Ruysbroeck, J. van, 221
Ryan, J. K., 196

Sabatier, Auguste, 416, 438
Sabellianism, 84 f., 172
Sacramentalism, 32, 53, 56, 112, 120, 165, 181 f., 192, 212 ff., 243 f., 256, 276, 425 f.; *see also* Baptism *and* Eucharist
Sacramentum, 214
Sacrifice, 64, 393; *see also* Atonement *and* Eucharist
Saint-Cyran, Abbé de, 346
Sales, Francis of, 286 f.
Sanctification, 122 f., 192, 324; *see also* Holy Spirit, Mysticism, *and* Sacramentalism
Sandmel, S., 20
Sartre, Jean-Paul, 394, 397
Scandinavia, 241
Schaff, P., 21
Schelling, F. W. J. von, 382 f., 469
Schleiermacher, F. D. E., 320, 336, 380 ff., 406, 416, 424, 428, 466
Schmalkaldic Articles, 240
Schmemann, A., 483

Schneider, H. W., 367
Scholasticism, 164 ff., 179 ff., 231 f.
Schopenhauer, Arthur, 395, 418
Schwabach, Articles of, 239
Schwarz, C. F., 318
Schweitzer, Albert, 339, 410, 471 ff.
Science and religion, 291 ff., 304 ff., 328 ff., 343 ff., 371 ff., 401 ff., 414 ff., 428 ff., 450 ff.
Science and valuation, 429, 460, 468
Sciences, rise of, 291 ff.
Scopes, J. T., 402
Scott, C. A. A., 411
Scotus, John Duns, 193 f., 207, 217
Sectarianism, 435 f.
Selina, Countess of Huntingdon, 324
Sellers, R. V., 101
Semi-Pelagianism, 128, 138
Sens, Synod of (1141), 175
Septuagint, 10, 141, 399
Sergius of Constantinople, 105
Servetus, Michael (Miguel), 278, 291
Sex, 6, 8, 17, 42, 46, 61, 67, 122 f., 139, 141 ff., 149, 198, 237, 261, 362, 400, 447 f.; *see also* Celibacy, Marriage, *and* Monasticism
Short, C., 64
Short, H. L., 281
Sigismund, Emp., 203, 210
Simeon Stylites, 137
Simons, Menno, 272
Simony, 149, 198
Simpson, A., 269
Sixtus IV, Pope, 226
Slave mentality, 396
Smith, John E., 483
Smith, Joseph, 361
Smith, J. S. B., 314
Smith, S. H., 367
Smith, W. Robertson, 398
Smyth, John, 275
Sobornost, 457
Social gospel, 366, 427, 433, 452
Society for Promoting Christian Knowledge (S.P.C.K.), 321
Society for the Propagation of the Gospel in Foreign Parts (S.P.G.), 321
Socinianism, 273, 278 ff., 305, 358
Söderblom, Nathan, 438
Soissons, Synod of (1121), 174, 176 f.
Son of Man, 2 ff., 456; see also *Barnasha*
Sophronius of Jerusalem, 105

Sorbonne, 180
South India, Church of, 436 f.
Spencer, Herbert, 379, 387
Spencer, S., 222
Spener, P. J., 315 ff., 372
Spinka, M., 211, 488
Spinoza, Benedict de, 167, 299, 306, 310, 342, 381, 402
Spiritual marriage, *see* Mysticism
Stabilitas loci, 139, 161
Stace, W. T., 303, 397
Stacey, J., 211
States of the Church, 147
Stephen III, Pope, 147
Stevenson, J., 21, 80
Stewart, H. F., 351
Stewart, H. L., 434
Stirling, J. Hutchison, 388
Stoeffler, E., 327, 388
Stoicism, 58, 265; *see also* Immanence and transcendence *and* Pantheism
Storch, Nicholas, 271
Strauss, David Friedrich, 339, 407 f.
Stromberg, R. N., 314
Subordinationism, 70; *see also* Logos *and* Trinitarianism
Substantia, 91, 215
Suetonius, 10
Summae, 185
Supererogation, 192; *see also* Atonement, Penance, *and* Surplus merit
Surplus merit, 61, 134, 192; *see also* Atonement *and* Penance
Suso, Henry, 221
Swihart, A. K., 245
Syllabus Errorum, 350, 414, 440
Sylvester I, Pope, 80
Symbolo-fideism, 416, 422, 466
Synoptic Gospels, 2, 430 ff.; *see also* Biblical criticism

Taborites, 210
Tacitus, 10
Tarasius, Ptr. of Constantinople, 109
Targums, 399; *see also* Bible, translations of
Tatian, 36, 66
Tauler, Johannes, 221, 235, 321
Tawney, R. H., 258
Taylor, H. O., 178
Teaching of the Twelve Apostles, see *Didachē*
Teetotalism, 140; *see also* Asceticism

Teilhard de Chardin, P., 420, 480, 482; *see also* Evolutionism
Teleological proof, 60, 172, 190, 313, 330 f., 480
Temple, William, Abp. of Canterbury, 439, 480
Ten Commandments, 55; *see also* Moralism *and* Legalism
Tennant, F. R., 479
Tennyson, Alfred, Lord, 366
Teresa of Avila, 286
Tertullian, 45 f., 57 ff., 82, 84 ff., 92, 117
Tetzel, Johann, 235
Thackeray, H. St. John, 21
Theatines, 283
Theiōsis, *see* Deification
Thelēma, 105
Theodora, Regent, 109
Theodore of Mopsuestia, 97
Theodoret of Cyrrhus, 111
Theodosius I, Emp., 19, 76, 91, 93
Theodosius II, Emp., 98, 100, 102
Theodotus, 82
Theologia Germanica, 221, 235
Theological positivism, 429
Theophilus, 35
Theotokos, 97 ff.; *see also* Mariology
Thirty-nine Articles, *see* Anglicanism
Thomas, Roger, 281
Thomasius, Christian, 317
Thompson, R. J., 413
Three Chapters of Justinian, 103
Tillich, Paulus Johannes, 467 ff., 470
Tillotson, John, 307
Tindal, Matthew, 311 f., 337, 372
Tisserant, E., 113
Toland, John, 310 ff.
Toledo, Council of (589), 152
Toleration, 8, 75 ff., 80, 176, 263, 267 f., 277, 330, 335, 339, 354, 357, 446
Tome of Leo, 99
Torah, 13 ff., 38, 43, 55, 81
Torbet, R. G., 269
Torrance, T. F., 33
Totalitarianism, 446
Toulouse, Synod of (1229), 160
Tractarianism, 424 ff.
Traducianism, 59
Trajan, Emp., 11
Transcendence and immanence, *see* Immanence and transcendence
Transmigration, 110

Transubstantiation, 167, 207, 213, 216, 237, 244, 256, 286; *see also* Sacramentalism
Trent, Council of, 216 f., 285 ff., 426, 440
Trilling, Wolfgang, 442
Trinitarianism, 35 f., 58, 70, 78, 84 f., 87 ff., 91, 152, 154, 171 f., 175 f., 189, 276; *see also* Logos
Troeltsch, E., 488
Turbeville, A. S., 204
Turks, 155
Turmerlebnis, 234
Turner, H. E. W., 40
Tyndale, William, 261
Typos of Constans II, 105
Tyrrell, George, 415, 423

Übermensch, 395
Ulfila, 94
Ultramontanism, 349 ff., 414
Unam Sanctum, papal bull, 199
Underhill, Evelyn, 222
Uniats, 445
Unitarianism, 267 f., 278 ff., 357, 359, 365; *see also* Arianism, Dynamic Monarchianism, Modalist Monarchianism, *and* Monotheism
Unitas Fratrum, 211
Universalism, 71, 356, 358, 365; *see also* Unitarianism
Universals, 169 ff., 392
Universitas magistrorum, 179
Universitas scholari, 179
Universities, rise of, 179 ff.
Unmoved Mover, 188, 194; *see also* Cartesianism and *Quinque viae*
Urban I, Pope, 85
Urban II, Pope, 155
Urban IV, Pope, 184, 197
Urban VI, Pope, 202
Urban VIII, Pope, 346
Usury, 257
Utopianism, 455, 459; *see also* Millenarianism
Utraquists, 210

Valentinus, 51
Valla, Lorenzo, *see* Lorenzo Valla
Valuation, 460, 468, 473
Valuation and science, *see* Science and valuation
Vandals, 128

Vatican Council I (1869–70), 350, 414, 443
Vatican Council II (1962–65), 443 ff.
Vatican Library, 228
Vatke, W., 402
Vegetarianism, 13, 18; *see also* Asceticism *and* Eschatology
Verdun, Treaty of, 149
Verification principle, 460
Vicar of Christ, 199
Victor, Pope, 50
Vidler, A. R., 423
Vielhauer, Philipp, 413, 423, 456
Vienna Circle, 459
Vigilius, Pope, 103
Vincent of Lérins, 128
Virgin birth, 10; *see also* Mariology
Virtus sacramenti, 217
Visser't Hooft, W. A., 439 f.
Voltaire, 328 ff., 333, 357
Voluntarism, 193, 195
Vorgrimler, H., 449
Vulgate, 44, 131, 286, 399

Wace, H., 21
Wagner, R., 394
Walker, W., 488
Wallach, Luitpold, 151
Walsh, H. H., 367
Ward, James, 388
Ware, Henry, 359
Warens, Madame de, 332
Watkins, O. D., 222
Watts, Isaac, 320
Weatherhead, L. D., 483
Webb, C. C. J., 314, 351, 388, 397, 434
Weinberg, J. R., 178
Weingart, R. E., 178
Weinlick, J. R., 327
Weiss, Bernhard, 409
Weiss, Johannes, 471
Wellhausen, Julius, 403 ff., 410, 412, 451
Wendel, F., 258
Wenzel, King of Bohemia, 209 f.
Wesley, Charles, 321 ff.
Wesley, John, 319, 321 ff
Westcott, B. F., 399
Western Schism, 202
Westminster Confession, 266
Wette, W. de, 402
Whitby, Synod of (664), 132
Whitefield, George, 321 ff., 355

Whitehead, A. N., 303, 480 f.
Widengren, G., 125
Wieman, H. N., 303, 367, 397
Wigley, Thomas, 434
Wikenhauser, A., 20, 413
Wilberforce, S., 402
Wilberforce, William, 326
Wilbur, E. M., 281
Wilcox, T., 264
William of Auxerre, 216
William of Champeaux, 174, 177
William of Orange, 267
Williams, G. H., 281
Williams, Roger, 354
Williams, W. W., 163
Willoughby, H. R., 413
Winchester, Elhanan, 359
Wingren, G., 56
Winter, Paul, 20, 410
Wish-fulfillment, 388, 465
Wittgenstein, Ludwig, 460 ff.
Wolff, Christian, 336 f., 373
Wolfson, H. A., 107
Wolsey, Thomas, 260
Woodruff, Wilford, 362
Wordsworth, William, 212 f.
Worker-priests, 442

Workman, H. B., 163, 211
World Congress of Faiths, 483
World Council of Churches, aims of,
    439 f.
Worms, Concordat of, 151, 198
Worms, Diet of, 237, 239
Worship, 109 ff.
Wrede, Wilhelm, 409, 411
Wycliffe, John, 205 ff., 217, 250, 259
Wyttenback, Thomas, 246

Xavier, Francis, 284
Ximenes, Abp. of Toledo, 226, 282

Young, Brigham, 362

Zabriskie, A., 327
Zacharias, Pope, 146
Zahrnt, H., 483
Zealots, 3 ff., 210
Zenobia, Queen of Palmyra, 83
Zephyrinus, Pope, 47, 85
Zinzendorf, Count N. F. von, 318 ff.,
    323
Zosimus, Pope, 127
Zwingli, Huldreich, 239, 246 ff.,   253
Zybnek von Hasenburg, 209

THE EVOLUTION OF CHRISTIAN THOUGHT

Designed by R. E. Rosenbaum.
Composed by Vail-Ballou Press, Inc.,
in 11 point linotype Janson, 3 points leaded,
with display lines in monotype Janson.
Printed letterpress from type by Vail-Ballou Press
on Warren's 1854 text, 50 lb. basis,
with the Cornell University Press watermark.
Bound by Vail-Ballou Press
in Joanna Arrestox B book cloth
and stamped in All Purpose foils.